JUNG'S WANDERING ARCHETYPE

Is the Germanic god Wotan (Odin) really an archaic archetype of the Spirit? Was the Third Reich at first a collective individuation process? After Friedrich Nietzsche heralded the "death of God," might the divine have been reborn as a collective form of self-redemption on German soil and in the Germanic soul? In *Jung's Wandering Archetype* Carrie Dohe presents a study of Jung's writings on Germanic psychology from 1912 onwards, exploring the links between his views on religion and race and providing his perspective on the answers to these questions.

Dohe demonstrates how Jung's view of Wotan as an archetype of the collective Germanic psyche was created from a combination of an ancient discourse on the Germanic barbarian and modern theories of primitive religion, and how he further employed *völkisch* ideology and various colonialist discourses to contrast hypothesized Germanic, Jewish and 'primitive' psychologies. He saw Germanic psychology as dangerous yet vital, promising rebirth and rejuvenation, and compared Wotan to the Pentecostal Spirit, suggesting that the Germanic psyche contained the necessary tension to birth a new collective psycho-spiritual attitude. In racializing his religiously-inflected psychological theory, Jung combined religious and scientific discourses in a particularly seductive way, masterfully weaving together the objective language of science with the eternal language of myth. Dohe concludes the book by examining the use of these ideas in modern Germanic religion, in which members claim that religion is a matter of race.

This in-depth study of Jung's views on psychology, race and spirituality will be fascinating reading for all academics and students of Jungian and post-Jungian studies, religious studies and the history of religion.

Carrie B. Dohe was a guest researcher at the University of Marburg's Department of Religious Studies from 2010 to 2015, investigating how people use discourse about the divine to justify their social and political claims. Her current research looks at religiously-motivated environmentalist movements in Germany.

JUNG'S WANDERING ARCHETYPE

Race and religion in analytical psychology

Carrie B. Dohe

Routledge
Taylor & Francis Group
LONDON AND NEW YORK

First published 2016 by Routledge

2 Park Square, Milton Park, Abingdon, Oxfordshire OX14 4RN
711 Third Avenue, New York, NY 10017

Routledge is an imprint of the Taylor & Francis Group, an informa business

First issued in paperback 2017

British Library Cataloguing in Publication Data
A catalogue record for this book is available from the British Library

Library of Congress Cataloging in Publication Data
Names: Dohe, Carrie B., author.
Title: Jung's wandering archetype : race and religion in analytical psychology / Carrie B. Dohe.
Description: London ; New York : Routledge, 2016. | Includes bibliographical references and index.
Identifiers: LCCN 2016001167 | ISBN 9781138888401 (hardback)
Subjects: LCSH: Jung, C. G. (Carl Gustav), 1875-1961. | Archetype (Psychology) | Race. | Religion. | Jungian psychology. | Germany—Civilization—Psychological aspects.
Classification: LCC BF109.J8 D64 2016 | DDC 150.19/54092—dc23
LC record available at http://lccn.loc.gov/2016001167

ISBN: 978-1-138-88840-1 (hbk)
ISBN: 978-1-138-88839-5 (pbk)

Typeset in Times New Roman
by Swales and Willis Ltd, Exeter, Devon, UK

CONTENTS

FIGURES

ACKNOWLEDGMENTS

This work has been enriched by the feedback offered by other scholars and students from different countries at various workshops, conferences, and colloquia, and my own students in courses I taught at the University of Chicago and Philipps University in Marburg, Germany. In particular I wish to acknowledge the generosity, support, feedback, and criticism of Richard Noll and George Hogenson in the United States; Paul Bishop in Scotland; Nicolas Meylan in Switzerland; and Adelheid Hermann-Pfandt, Horst Junginger, and Jörg Lauster in Germany. Special thanks to Richard and Nico for their feedback on the final stages of the manuscript and to Richard for his continual support for the project. Thanks, too, to Florian Mildenberger and other participants at the "Master-Disciple Relationship in Interdisciplinary Discourse" Workshop at the Free University of Berlin (April 23–25, 2010), and the many conversations with insightful colleagues at the European Society for the Study of the Human Sciences Annual Conference in Würzburg in 2013.

Thanks to Michael Geyer and Paul Mendes-Flohr for feedback on an earlier version of the present work. A special thanks to Celia Brickman, whose rich commentary on earlier drafts improved the content and flow significantly. I am most indebted to Wendy Doniger, not only for her insightful comments on earlier drafts, but for her continued support and guidance through the process of seeking a book publisher. Thanks also to Bruce Lincoln and Stefanie von Schnurbein, in whose classes the seeds of this project were first planted at the University of Chicago.

Katja Triplett and especially Edith Franke deserve a special acknowledgment of gratitude for welcoming this wayward scholar into the Department of the Study of Religions at Philipps University of Marburg, providing me space to work there, as well as comments and encouragement along the way. The diversity of programming and resources, the good cheer of the colleagues, and the willingness of students and scholars alike to provide me with feedback on chapters and presentations has made the completion of this book possible.

In researching this project, I used several archives in Germany and Switzerland. I wish to thank the staff at the Literature Archive in Marbach am Neckar and at the ETH-Bibliothek in Zurich (Switzerland). A special thanks goes to archivist Antje Märke of the Federal Archive of Germany in Coblenz.

My editor Susannah Frearson deserves a big thank you for shepherding this book through the production phase.

Many thanks to Routledge and Princeton for granting permission to quote extensively from vols. 7 and 10 of Jung's *Collected Works*.

A hearty "herzlichen Dank!" to Christiane Strobach for her fine illustrations; to Stefanie Ullman for her wonderful help with editing; and to Barbara Gueldenring for her proofreading and comments. To dear friends who supported me during all phases of this project and especially during the strenuous *Endspurt: ganz herzlichen Dank*!

Any errors in the text are entirely my own. Every effort has been made to contact copyright holders of material used in this book, and any omissions brought to the attention of the Publisher will be corrected in future printings.

ABBREVIATIONS AND READERS' GUIDE

The abbreviations used in this work are as follows:

BA = Federal Archives of Germany, Coblenz (*Bundesarchiv*)

ETH = ETH-Bibliothek Zurich (Switzerland): ETH Zurich University Archives, C.G. Jung Papers Collection

CW = C. G. Jung, *Collected Works*

GW = C. G. Jung, *Gesammelte Werke*

EWD = *Etymologisches Wörterbuch des Deutschen*

INT = Internet site

In-text references follow different systems, as follows:

1 **Most sources, including Jung's private lectures:** I use the standard author-date citational system with page numbers provided, for example **(Gardell 2003, 149–151)**.
2 **Jung's *Collected Works* (CW) or *Gesammelte Werke* (GW):** Because all paragraphs in these works are numbered, I have followed the convention in Jungian studies to refer to volume and paragraph numbers, supplemented with the dates of the original publication and its final revision. For example, **(Jung GW 11 (1962 [1937]):2)**.
3 **Multi-volume works:** The volume number is given, followed by a colon and page number. For example, **(Jung 1988, 1:500)**.
4 ***Letters* of Jung and Sigmund Freud, and of Jung and Erich Neumann:** These use the convention of assigning a letter and number to each letter. Hence, **(29F)** refers to the twenty-ninth letter from Freud in the letter exchange between him and Jung.
5 **"Wotan":** When referring to the essay printed in CW 10, I refer to paragraph numbers; when referring to the original 1936 work, I use page numbers.
6 **German translations:** Unless otherwise indicated, all translations are my own. I have followed a convention in Germanic studies, which is to place the

original text right after the English translation. This allows a bilingual reader to read both texts immediately.

7 **Internet sites:** These are given in brackets and numbered in the order they appear in each chapter's bibliography; for example, **[INT2].** Due to the ephemeral nature of the Internet, I cannot guarantee that all of the websites will still be online once the present work is published. Hence, websites are listed with the date on which I last accessed them.

This work contains no footnotes because they are problematic in electronic books. There are also no footnotes for the following reasons: Routledge requires that I use official English translations of Jung's works wherever possible. However, my research uncovered several erasures, misleading editorial statements, and interpolations in the English CW that distort Jung's original meaning. Because I wanted to bring these textual changes to light, I decided against endnotes, and instead present these issues directly in the body of the text. Given my argument that Jung's CW are hardly transparent, I have striven to make my own text as transparent as possible.

My analysis of Jung's 1912 book is based on the original *Wandlungen und Symbole der Libido*, aided by Beatrice Hinkle's 1925 English translation. Hinkle moved Jung's main title into the subtitle and renamed the book *The Psychology of the Unconscious*. However, because various works of Jung are called *Psychology of the Unconscious*, I have retained his original title, in English translation, and refer to the book as *Transformations and Symbols of the Libido*, even though I cite Hinkle's 1925 translation.

Chapter 3 is a much-expanded version of "Analytical Psychology as Modern Revelation: C. G. Jung between Master and Scientist," published in 2015 in the conference proceedings for the 2010 workshop on *The Master-Disciple Relationship in Interdisciplinary Discourse* at the Free University of Berlin. It is republished here with permission of VDG Weimar. Chapter 6 is an expanded version of my paper, "'Wotan' and the 'archetypal Ergriffenheit': Mystical union, national spiritual rebirth and culture-creating capacity in CG Jung's 'Wotan' essay," *History of European Ideas* 37 (3):344–356 (2011).

1

"SOMETHING LIKE WOTAN"?

Introduction

If you were to stroll into a large American bookstore, one catering to the general public, and then make your way to the gender studies section, you would see several popular books on the mythopoetic men's movement, an all-male myth-and-ritual movement that gained widespread news coverage in the early 1990s. In the "metaphysics" section, you would discover books on Paganism, such as goddess-oriented Wicca and Germanic Ásatrú, as well as works on New Age Spirituality. These various movements have made headline news from time to time (Gardell 2003, 149–151, 282, 300) and works by some of their authors have spent months on the bestsellers list (e.g. Bly 1990; Kimmel 1995, 4). In the neighboring psychology section, you would find multiple titles by Swiss psychologist Carl Gustav Jung (1875–1961), founder of analytical psychology. One aspect that connects the aforementioned mythopoetic and new religious movements together is that they all utilize Jungian psychological concepts as doctrine and legitimation of their new spiritualities.

The popularity of Jungian ideas is not limited to Pagan practitioners and New Age Spirituality seekers; indeed, Jung seems to be a household name in the United States, at least among the white, professional or college-educated classes. While researching the present work, I encountered individuals with different occupations and from various walks of life who were acquainted with Jung's basic concepts: an actress who had had a theater class on archetypes; a life coach who uses Jung's core process with his clients; a member of Alcoholics Anonymous (AA), who has read the correspondence between Jung and AA co-founder Bill Wilson; and a Christian theologian, whose colleagues use Jungian psychology in their pastoral work. Furthermore, Jung seems to be quoted in just about every spiritually oriented book on self-help or unfolding your creativity published in the US, as well as in both scholarly and popular books dealing with new religious movements ranging from goddess spirituality to neo-shamanism to New Age. As the late sociologist of religion Martin Riesebrodt (1948–2014, *R.I.P.*) once said about the great man of German letters, Johann Wolfgang von Goethe (1749–1782): "No one ever reads him anymore, but everyone quotes him." Whether or not Martin's quip is applicable to Jung, the regular invocation of Jung's name indicates the stature Jung has achieved in the English-language world as a psychologist who understood the deeper mysteries of the human soul.

In contrast to the positive reception of Jungian ideas in Anglo-American culture, German responses have often been negative. When I told a cognitive therapist in my dance class in Berlin that I was writing on Jung, her immediate response was, "Wasn't he a fascist?" Furthermore, when I described the contents of Jung's "Wotan" essay to a language instructor from Germany, she recoiled; to her, the motif of a collective spiritual rebirth in "Wotan" smacked of National Socialist ideology. The striking disparity between American and German responses to Jung and his ideas may in part be explained by differences in cultural literacy: contemporary Germans learn about the horrors of their country's National Socialist past in school and therefore more easily recognize discourse that resembles that of Nazism. Like Jung, Nazi ideologies also used the language of holism and rebirth, although they coupled these ideas with those of racial supremacy and anti-Semitism.

What a careful reading of Jung's works shows is that his ideas are by no means free from racial thinking and a preoccupation with the Germanic. However, the redaction of Jung's works in English demonstrates a regular pattern of erasure and obfuscation of German-ideological ideas still often found in the German-language edition of Jung's *Collected Works*, as will be shown in the following pages. This claim might surprise many readers of Jung, because what appeals to them about his psychology is the more universalist perspective that Jung himself regularly articulated, as the following quote shows:

> Over this whole psychic realm there are motifs, that is, certain typical figures, which can be traced far back into history and even into prehistory, and may therefore be referred to as archetypes. They seem to me to be built into the very structure of man's unconscious, for in no other way can I explain why it is that they occur universally and in identical form.
>
> (Jung CW 16 (1951):254)

According to Jung, archetypes are the inherited, universal "primordial images" (*urtümliche Bilder* or *Urbilder*) of humanity that appear in religious symbolism and mythic motifs. Jung located the archetypes in the collective unconscious, an inherited and collective aspect of the psyche of all peoples. The chief archetype in Jungian psychology is the self, which is the center of the psyche and a psychological equivalent of the image of God. Archetypes perform an essential role in the individuation process, which is the psychic journey by which a person shifts the focus of his or her identity from the collectively formed and outwardly oriented ego to the inner center of the psyche to become psychologically whole. Inner psychological processes may correspond with outer events, representing the acausal connecting principle Jung called synchronicity. The concepts of archetypes, the collective unconscious, the individuation process and synchronicity are the chief Jungian terms found in books on and about New Age Spirituality (Tacey 2001),

Paganism (Crowley 1995), the mythopoetic men's movement (Moore and Gilette 1990), and related emerging spiritualities. These works, as well as many lexica on analytical psychology (e.g. Hark 1988, 25–29; Humbert 1992, 307–317; Samuels, Shorter and Plaut, 1986, 26–27) and introductions to Jungian thought (e.g. Meier 1977; Storr 1973), define archetypes as universal mythological motifs in accordance with the aforementioned quote. They regularly overlook the presence of the race-, nation-, or *Volk*-based archetype attested to in this quote from Jung's 1936 essay "Wotan":

> Wotan is a [primordial] Germanic datum of first importance, the truest expression and unsurpassed personification of a fundamental quality that is particularly characteristic of the Germans . . . Because the behaviour of a race takes on its specific character from its underlying images we can speak of an archetype "Wotan."
>
> (Jung CW 10 (1946 [1936]):389, 391)

The reason for the relative silence concerning Jung's theories of the racially delimited archetype Wotan and a collective Germanic unconscious becomes clear in light of the controversies these ideas engendered throughout the Nazi period and beyond. In 1946, Jung complained to his American patron Mary Conover Mellon (1904–1946) that he felt forced by his critics to republish his Nazi-era statements about Germany (Schoenl 1996, 53–54) in a small booklet called *Aufsätze zur Zeitgeschichte* (1946), translated into English in 1947 as *Essays on Contemporary Events*. Allen Dulles (1893–1969), the founding director of the CIA, had personally exonerated Jung after World War II of charges of having collaborated with the Nazis (Wasserstrom 1999, 153). Jung and his students then conducted a campaign to save Jung's reputation in the English-speaking world through articles such as Ernst Harms' 1946 article "Carl Gustav Jung – Defender of Freud and the Jews: A Chapter of European Psychiatric History under the Nazi Yoke," published in the *Psychiatric Quarterly*. This incurred the wrath of Albert D. Parelhoff, who had already started a letter campaign against Jung in 1945, in the *Herald Tribune* (Bair 2003, 515). However, controversy continued to dog Jung. In 1949, the Library of Congress Fellows in American Literature awarded the first annual Bollingen Prize in Poetry to the pro-fascist Ezra Pound (1885–1972), engendering a scandal into which Jung's name was dragged due to his connection to the Bollingen Foundation, publisher of his *Collected Works* (Bair 2003, 518; Corrigan 1967, 44).

These controversies were offset over the years by positive evaluations of Jung, such as that published by the U.S. weekly news magazine *Time*. On February 14, 1955, Jung appeared on the magazine's front cover, along with a banner that read, "Exploring the Soul: A Challenge to Freud." The magazine's medical section contained an article about Jung with a title that sounded less scientific than religious: "The Old Wise Man." The accompanying article portrayed Jung as a scientist who was able to see into the depths of the human soul and find there the solution to the malaise of modern society (Time 2012).

Given the decades-old controversy surrounding Jung and his "Wotan" essay, it is not surprising that scholars regularly consider this text mainly in conjunction with statements Jung made about Hitler and the "Aryan unconscious" throughout the Nazi era. Jung himself set the stage for this interpretation with the previously mentioned post-war publication, *Essays on Contemporary Events,* with a foreword and afterword written after the end of World War II. This book, republished in 1989, has had a significant influence on the way scholars tend to read the "Wotan" essay – as historically relevant to the Nazi era, but not reflective of Jung's thinking as a whole.

The foreword to the 2014 edition of *Essays on Contemporary Events* by the analytical psychologist Andrew Samuels follows a convention among some Jungians, who explain that Jung wrote his controversial wartime writings under the influence of his "shadow" (Samuels 2014; see also Neumann 1991, 288; Speicher 2002, 150). The *shadow* is a Jungian term indicating psychic contents that are incompatible with the ego and therefore repressed in the unconscious. This suggests that Jung could not have written these texts with clear conscious intent. Given this definition, one must wonder what Jung wished to imply when he explained World War II as Germany's struggle with its collective shadow. This was a post-war diagnosis that he made in his 1945 essay, "After the Catastrophe," and during his 1946 radio talk, "The Fight with the Shadow." Following these lines of interpretation, the German analytical psychologist Günther Langwieler extended the concept of the *shadow* to Germany's role in World War I, when he analyzed the so-called Germanic barbarian psyche in Jung's "The Role of the Unconscious" (1918). He also extended the idea of this barbarian psyche to "Wotan" (1936) to read both texts together as preoccupations with the shadow aspect of this collective psyche (Langwieler 2010, 31). This diagnosis differs radically from the much more hopeful one Jung himself made in "Wotan."

Besides describing Jung's wartime writings as influenced by his shadow, certain authors tend to write about Jung and his activities during the Nazi era in a passive voice, implying that Jung was not culpable of his words and actions because he had been "enthralled" by contemporary events (e.g. Buresch-Talley 2002, 51). At the same time, it has been argued that Jung got tangled in his own tendency to see himself as a "Wise Old Man" (e.g. Lewin 2009, 286) and was inflated with ideas similar to those touted by National Socialists (e.g. Ellwood 1999, 61). Finally, it has been argued that Jung's words could be easily distorted and "interpreted to mean just about anything" (Bair 2003, 521). This hardly seems a good defense; rather, it makes Jung seem like an incompetent writer.

Finally, some authors have dismissed the charges that Jung was an anti-Semite because he helped individual Jews during the war (e.g. Bair 2003, 460). Alternatively, they dismiss these charges as the complaints of Marxists and socialists or as trumped up by psychoanalysts loyal to Freud against the "apostate" Jung (e.g. Ellenberger 1970, 740, note 55). Once again, this claim may have partially originated with Jung. In 1936, Jung complained about a "Freudian propaganda campaign" against him in Holland (Bair 2003, 454) and in 1938, he claimed that a photo of himself, doctored to look stereotypically Jewish with a large nose and glasses, had been produced by Freudian Jews in Germany (Letter from Hauer to Jung, BA N1131/139, fol.13). In sum, these questionable claims have contributed to the incomplete analysis of Jung's interest in Wotan. What will be argued here is not that Jung was unequivocally pro-Germanic and anti-Semitic; rather, he believed that the group psyche that offered the best possibility for the emergence of a new collective orientation was the Germanic one. The signs of the times – the new religion of self-redemption, calls for collective national rebirth and a completion of the Reformation, and ancient Germanic myth – all told him this must be so.

Mention of a collective Germanic psyche points to a concept logically related to the Wotanic archetype and, like it, left unmentioned by many commentators on Jungian thought. This is Jung's theory of the racially and religiously differentiated collective or phylogenetic unconscious (but see Lewin 2009; Shamdasani 2003). Jung first discussed the idea in 1912, in *Transformations and Symbols of the Libido: Contributions to the History of the Development of Thought*, in conversation and competition with Sigmund Freud (1856–1939), who published his own theory of a phylogenetic unconscious at roughly the same time in his *Totem and Taboo* (1912–1913). In 1925, Jung illustrated his concept of a phylogenetic unconscious in a private seminar on analytical psychology that he gave in Zurich, calling it "the 'geology' of a personality" (Jung 1989, 133).

This idea was not marginal in Jung's thinking; rather, Jung was renowned for his "paleontology of the soul" (ETH Hs 1056:148) throughout the Weimar period. Furthermore, his disciple Jolande Jacobi discussed it in her 1940 book *Die Psychologie von C. G. Jung: Eine Einführung in das Gesamtwerk, mit einem Geleitwort von C. G. Jung*, a book that was translated into English two years later (1972, 49). Moreover, Jung discussed the stratified collective unconscious in two volumes that present his core process in full, *Psychological Types* (CW vol. 6) and *Two Essays on Analytical Psychology* (CW vol. 7), as well as in many minor essays. The concept of a racially and religiously differentiated phylogenetic unconscious underlies the basic premises of the "Wotan" essay and is the bridge that connects Jung's universalist and exclusivist definitions of archetypes previously quoted.

Jung had begun an intensive study of the literature from the science of religion in 1909, incorporating the anthropological theory of evolution into his work from 1912 onwards. This theory forms the basis of Jung's concept of the multilayered phylogenetic or collective unconscious. This has been discussed by the Jung historian Sonu Shamdasani (2003) and, following him, Nicholas Lewin (2009). Samuels (1992) previously called this idea "the psychology of nations." Jung theorized a primitive or archaic level of mind that was inherent in the brains of all people. However, other layers of this collective unconscious were specific to certain collectives, whether they be tribes, clans, nations, ethnicities or religious groups. Furthermore, only some people had individual consciousness. Those people Jung held to be primitive supposedly lived in a mental state mirroring that of the deepest layer of the collective unconscious.

As with Jung's controversial Germanic writings from the 1930s, some Jungian scholars have sought to understand Jung's writings on "primitives" as not only non-racist, but even anti-racist. For example, they reiterate Jung's evolutionary thinking, equating his own "encounter with the unconscious" with his encounter with contemporaries during his travels to East Africa in 1925 (e.g. Burleson 2005, 16), or even praise Jung's colonialist-era evolutionism as "post-colonial" and "eco-critical" (e.g. Rowland 2007, 661–662, 665). Jung's repeated references to "primitives" are said to be due to the lack of non-racist language in Jung's era (e.g. Lewin 2009, 131), which follows Samuels' argument (1993) that Jung failed to clearly articulate a non-dominant, non-Eurocentric perspective, because he was handicapped by the dominant language of race and racial science of his day (309–310). Finally, Jung's use of the word "primitive" as applied to people is separated from his thinking about the archaic level of mind (e.g. Bishop 2008, 502). This move is one Jung himself did not make; indeed, it seeks to obfuscate the fact that Jung regularly used the anthropological category as his evidence for the psychological one.

In contrast to these views, the post-colonial literature scholar Jo Collins (2009; 2008) analyzes Jung's dreams in Africa as revealing his beliefs in European supremacy. The Jungian analyst Roger Brooke describes Jung's binary oppositions between "primitive" Africans and "civilized" Europeans as a "colonialism of the psyche" (Brooke 2008, 38). This binary is based on Jung's reliance on the sociologist Lucien Lévy-Bruhl's theory of primitive mentality, as discussed by the historian of religions Robert Segal (2007). The psychotherapist Farhad Dalal demonstrates that Jung "*explicitly* equates: 1) The modern black with the prehistoric human; 2) The modern black conscious with the white unconscious; 3) The modern black adult with the white child" (Dalal 1988, 263). The psychologist Frantz Fanon (2008) delves deeper into Jung's binary, analyzing the way racism distorts the psyches of both whites and blacks. Finally, the historian Petteri Pietikäinen (1998) expands the scope of Jung's racializing by examining Jung's thoughts on "primitives" together with his theories of other collective mentalities.

Although these works offer worthy critiques of a highly troublesome aspect of Jungian thought, they overlook the fact that Jung extended the notion of *primitivity* to both Jews and people of Germanic stock. Hence, they miss the full range of connotations in Jung's use of the concept of the *primitive*, which are based on the ambivalence contained within the word itself. This term has always been like a coin with two sides: on the face, it suggests that which is virginal, natural, or original; on the reverse, what is savage, rough and raw (Kuper 2005, 34–35). Furthermore, the word contains both temporal and structural aspects: *primitive* means first, primary and original, but also simple and rudimentary (Brickman 2003, 15). When European scholars, missionaries and explorers applied the term to people, they had in mind both groups they considered innocent and uncorrupted, still living in a paradisiacal state before the fall, and those that were cannibalistic and uncivilized (18), desperately needing the fruits of civilization that the West offered – or imposed with force. In the works of Jung, the word *primitive* contains both meanings, regardless of whether Jung was talking about so-called primitive peoples or the primitive level of mind within the psyche of modern people. Jung's multi-faceted interpretation of the concept of *primitivity* is also central to his understanding of both Jewish psychology and the Germanic or "Aryan" unconscious.

Despite the aforementioned attempts to polish Jung's image from the tarnish of pro-German sympathies during the Nazi era, there is a relatively small but growing number of people in and beyond the English-speaking world who are not only familiar with Jung's theories of a Germanic-specific archetype and "Aryan" unconscious, but embrace them wholeheartedly. Members of the ethnic and racist branches of the Germanic religious movement known as Heathenism, Ásatrú, or Odinism often refer to Jung's writings on the Germanic psyche to justify their claim that religion is racially determined. They argue that, despite both the wane of belief in the ancient gods after the Germanic tribes converted to Christianity in the Middle Ages and the modern misuse of ancient Germanic symbols by the Nazis, the "religion of the North" is experiencing a rebirth because it is part of the genetic inheritance of people of northern European descent. Indeed, members of Ásatrú who believe that religion is a matter of race often use Jung's "Wotan" essay as their prooftext, where he wrote the following:

> An archetype is like an old watercourse along which the water of life has flowed for centuries, digging a deep channel for itself. The longer it has flowed in this channel the more likely it is that sooner or later the water will return to its old bed.
>
> (Jung CW 10 (1947 [1936]):395; as quoted in Gundarsson 1993, 2–3; Thorsson 1987, 172–173; ibid. 1998, 44)

Today, the "Wotan" essay can be found in book form along with discussions of Germanic rituals and oaths, information on the runes, and Old Norse poetic selections in a collection entitled *Temple of Wotan*, published by the "Aryan" supremacist Norse Pagan group, Wotansvolk (McVan 2000, 180–190). Various other groups that profess a mixture of Germanic revivalist and white nationalist beliefs have published the "Wotan" essay online [INT1]. Moreover, American Ásatrú leader Stephen McNallen, a resident of California, has utilized the "Wotan" essay in a polemical work against Mexican immigrants [INT2]. The ongoing deployment of the "Wotan" essay and its Germanic archetype shows that this work is hardly a mere historical curiosity, but is used to justify current claims about race, religion and national belonging. These larger issues appear in the ongoing uproar in the United States over the election and presidency of the first African-American president; an alarming spike in hate groups and white supremacist extremism in that country since 2000 (Southern Poverty Law Center 2011); and intense debates over immigration, religious affiliation and national identity raging on both sides of the Atlantic. Given these broader social issues, a thoroughgoing analysis of Jung's controversial work on "Wotan" and his belief in different national, racial and racial-religious psychologies is timely.

Argument of the book

My own interpretation of Jung's "Wotan" essay and his writings on a hypothesized Germanic psyche diverge sharply from the aforementioned ideas. The following pages show that "Wotan" is far from being merely a depth-psychological examination of National Socialism; rather, it portrays Jung's convictions of what constitutes the racial essence of the Germanic peoples (*Germanentum*). Furthermore, Jung did not formulate the ideas contained within the "Wotan" essay only in response to or under the influence of "contemporary events" (National Socialism) as he had claimed; rather, the themes of the work reflect key components of analytical psychology since its inception. The interpretation presented here repositions the "Wotan" essay within the context of Jung's entire oeuvre and his numerous writings in which Wotan appears.

Indeed, the "Wotan" essay was neither the first nor the last time Jung wrote about the ancient Germanic god. Jung first mentioned Wotan in his 1912 *Transformations and Symbols of the Libido*, and then again in 1928 in *The Relations between the Ego and the Unconscious*. Wotan was also regularly mentioned in Jung's private seminar in Zurich on Nietzsche's *Thus Spoke Zarathustra* that ran from 1934 to 1939. Post-"Wotan," Jung discussed Wotan in both private letters (to Erich Neumann in 1939 and Miguel Serrano in 1960) and in a public article (*Wotan und der Rattenfänger*, 1956). Wotan even appeared posthumously in Jung's purported autobiography, *Memories, Dreams, Reflections* (1965, 313). Hence, Jung's interest in Wotan spanned at least five decades. This probably derived from his childhood when, on stormy nights, he might have been told German folktales of the Wild Huntsman and his entourage charging through the forest or riding across the treetops (Blind 1986, 177–181).

The meaning of the Wotanic figure in Jung's works ranged from being a racially delimited to a universal archetypal form; from a symbol of psychological maturation to an archaic image of Spirit; from a psychological projection of the archetypal self to the shadow; and from an ancestral god of the Alemannic tribe to the force behind a universal spiritual awakening. Moreover, Jung compared Wotan to *ruah*, the spirit of God that hovered over the void before the first act of Creation (Genesis 1:2); to Christ, whom Jung considered to be the archetype of the self in its western manifestation; and *pneuma*, the Pentecostal Spirit that seized Christ's apostles and sent them to spread the good news of a new psychological orientation. Further comparisons include Dionysus, the Wandering Jew, and, after World War II, the Devil. These different appearances of Wotan in Jung's works, the significance of this mythological figure in Jungian psychology, and the impact of Germanic ideology on Jung's portrayal of Wotan are discussed in the following pages.

In order to form his image of the collective Germanic psyche in "Wotan," Jung relied on a 2,000-year-old discourse on the Germanic barbarian first formulated in ancient Rome. The Roman historian Publius Cornelius Tacitus (CE 56 – after 117) had not only attributed a few positive characteristics to the otherwise "barbaric" Germanic tribes, he also criticized his fellow Romans for having let the fruits of civilization soften and weaken them. When the writings of Tacitus were rediscovered in the fifteenth century, German humanists drew on the positive aspects of this picture to argue for inherent German virtues, over and against those of an outside, hostile power (See 1970, 9, 11). They thus laid the foundation for a valorization of the Germanic barbarian in the modern age.

By the late nineteenth century, the discourse on the Germanic barbarian had gone through several permutations. The disciplines of archaeology, anthropology, Germanic studies, and the comparative study of religions were coming into their own. At the same time, race became a pre-eminent scientific category that dominated all these fields of study, fed by the need to justify colonialist practices outside of Europe and establish and maintain national boundaries within Europe (Hobsbawm 1992, 108). Germanic studies scholars, philosophers, artists and founders of new religious movements in the larger German cultural domain incorporated the image of Rome as state-builder into the self-image of the Germans, while championing the wildness and youthfulness of the barbarian, claiming for themselves a profound sense for what was original and authentic. They then incorporated the negative portrayal of the Germanic barbarian as lazy, undisciplined and overemotional into the image of the "dark-skinned savage" of modern European colonial discourse. Furthermore, they expanded Tacitus's positive description of the Germanic tribes as youthful, unspoiled and free to include the traits of creativity and nobility, claiming these characteristics as unchanging racial attributes of themselves and their Germanic forebears. Moreover, Tacitus's image of Rome as over-civilized and degenerate may have found an echo in the view of Jews as both fossilized and corrosive. Finally, scholars in multiple disciplines secularized and legitimized these ideologically laden motifs through the scientific language of anthropology, psychology, medicine, racial science, and the science of religion.

As will be discussed in the following pages, both the Roman and modern portraits of the ancient Germanic peoples were utilized by Jung. He characterized the Germanic psychic essence as not only powerful and even dangerous, but also offering the possibility of individual and cultural rejuvenation. Moreover, Jung regularly portrayed "Jewish psychology" as simultaneously over-civilized and primitive, while describing "primitive" peoples outside of Europe as the living fossils of an earlier level of human psychic evolution. Finally, he relied on and contributed to the process of making these ideological motifs and dangerous stereotypes seem both timeless and natural by intertwining the eternal language of myth and the objective language of science in his psychological theory.

Jung's view of Wotan as Spirit was formed by his readings from what the German philologist and scholar of religion Max Müller (1823–1900) had named the "science of religion" (*Religionswissenschaft*). Like Jung, many early twentieth-century scholars of religion wrestled with the problem posed to religion by the

Enlightenment and its championing of reason. The promise of the Enlightenment was that science and reason would overcome all forms of irrationality. However, according to the German sociologist Max Weber (1864–1920), the outcome of this rationalizing process was the disenchantment of the world. While Weber and other scholars investigated religious ideas exclusively according to historical and cultural-genealogical perspectives, others, including the Protestant theologian Rudolf Otto (1869–1937), the archbishop of Uppsala Nathan Söderblom (1866–1931), the German Indologist Jakob Wilhelm Hauer (1881–1962), and the German historian of religions Joachim Wach (1898–1955), sought via science the revitalization of religion as a way to overcome the loss of ultimate meaning caused by the forces of modernization. Their preoccupations with themes such as law and redemption, messianism, mysticism, gnosis, and Nietzschean philosophical themes developed as a reaction to the disenchantment of society, representing what the sociologist of religion Volkhard Krech calls the "other side" of modernity (Krech 2002, 4). Many of these same themes resonated with Jung. His incorporation of key concepts from the science of religion into his psychological theory and his view of the "Germanic" collective psyche are themes that course their way through the following chapters.

The primary focus of research in the new field of religious scholarship was the origin and essence of religion, which led to a focus on "primitive religion" or on the "primitive" forms of "higher" religions and the monotheistic traditions. Scholars of religion often used a comparative approach based on the belief that similar mythical forms or motifs from different religions were derived from the same basic drives, ideologies, or structures. Through this approach, they sought to discover a presumed essence of religion or original proto-myth. This quest found support in a typical aspect of religions: as historian of religions Charles Long notes, religious myths and symbols express the imagined relationship between the human and suprahuman realms in terms that convey a sense of timelessness. Scholars on religion working at the turn of the last century misunderstood this atemporal aspect, common to all religions, as characterizing the whole of "primitive religion," which they then used as evidence for their different theories about the origin and essence of religion as such (Long 1986, 92). As the following discussion shows, Jung embraced this interpretation of "primitive religion" in formulating his view of the essentially timeless (Bishop 2008, 504) collective unconscious, which dreams in the eternal language of myth.

As historian of religions Robert Ellwood argues, however, myths as recorded and related are themselves always particular. Mythology, founded on the idea of a universal and all-encompassing meaning behind the individual phenomena, is a modern construct created through modern scholarly disciplines. The modern invention of mythology thus reveals a desire to discover a holistic view in the past that could be employed in the present to bridge the divisions between faith and reason, and between nature and society (Ellwood 1999, 21). Ellwood writes, "The return to the supposed world of mythology was a return really to the premodern world *as envisioned by the modern world*" (7; emphasis in original).

Jung relied heavily on scholarly works about "primitive religion" and comparative mythology to formulate both his theory of the archaic level of mind and his views of so-called primitive peoples, modern masses, Jewish psychology, and the Germanic unconscious. Jung argued that the psyche of all peoples everywhere contained the collective unconscious and the archetypes. The unconscious was "infantile" in both a literal and metaphorical sense, containing not only the basic instinctual drives, but also the primordial archetypes that could give birth to new insights and worldviews. However, so-called primitives lived perpetually in a mental state of collectivity, largely lacking individual consciousness. Jung therefore viewed "primitive mentality" as representing the psychological childhood of humanity, and "primitive man" as the living evidence of the archaic level of mind, which revealed itself to modern people through myth, in inspirational states, and via archetypal dreams. Jung often described Jews in a paradoxical fashion: as over-civilized and thus attracted to an instinctual-primitive psychological level; as having two cultures and yet also psychologically underdeveloped. In contrast, Jung believed that the psychological contents of people of Germanic descent showed signs of something embryonic – perhaps the reconciling symbol needed to reunite the fragments of modern society and create a renewed sense of greater meaning and life orientation.

The surge of interest in the "primitive" across the human sciences correlated with the spread of European imperialism around the globe. As the literary historian and post-colonial theorist Edward Said showed regarding the West's construction of the Orient, an imperial apparatus is by no means implemented only through brute force; rather, a wide range of disciplines, including the arts and humanities, have participated in the construction of Europe's "other." A constellation of ideas and images that had formed over centuries circumscribed how Western intellectuals could consider and understand the "other," while also creating the framework for their own production of the "other's" image (Said 1978, 3–5; see also Williams and Chrisman 1994, 8).

The interplay between power and knowledge as driven by colonialism has ancient roots. The fact of Roman invasion and domination of the lands north of Italy produced knowledge on several levels about the "barbarians," as Caesar's recognition of the *Germani* as a linguistic group separate from the Celts and Scythians illustrates (Lund 1986, 61; Wolfram 1997, 25); at the same time, the hierarchical framework through which that knowledge was produced in turn legitimized political and military domination of the people labeled barbarians. Centuries later, many of the same clichés that formed the stereotype of the northern barbarian were redeployed by Europeans against myriad peoples outside of Europe who were classified as primitive. Jung's own thinking about "primitive" mentality reflects these strictures of thought concerning the "other," while exemplifying how an intellectual not directly engaged in colonial administration still contributed to the legitimization of that institution through his work.

The discussion thus far raises the question: What does the primitive have to do with Wotan? The answer is: What could be more "primitive" – archaic, primordial, elemental – than the Spirit? Despite the various transformations of the mythical figure in Jung's oeuvre, Wotan by and large illustrates Jung's belief in the collective unconscious, which he once described as "an 'omnipresent' and 'omniscient' spirit." According to Jung, this spirit was responsible for producing a collective symbol that had created a sense of orientation on a society-wide level 2,000 years previously. Jung viewed the outbreak of new forms of religiosity in the Roman Empire as the collective unconscious searching for a collective psychological compensation to the brutality and uncontrolled sexuality of antiquity. He interpreted the story of the Pentecostal Miracle as if it were a psychic gale storm raging out of the collective psyche, with the archetype of the Spirit giving rise to Christianity, the religion that became the collective attitude in the West for the next two millennia.

In Jung's era, the belief in traditional Christianity was breaking down, engendering in its wake an explosion of new religious movements. Jung interpreted this phenomenon as a repetition of events from the Roman Empire 2,000 years previously. The collective orientation proffered by Christianity had lost its effectiveness; hence, Jung believed, the collective unconscious was once again on the move to produce a new reconciling symbol. The appearance of Wotan on the cultural horizon, which Jung described in 1936 in Romantic terms as the god of "storm and stress," appeared to him as the archetype of Spirit in its most primitive form as wind and storm, demonstrating a power mighty enough to usher in a new collective orientation. This occurrence differed radically from that of two millennia previously, however, because this time, the Spirit had not descended from above, but was issuing from "the blood" (Jung 1988, 1:500). Jung thus racialized the Judeo-Christian idea of spirit as the Germanic archetype Wotan, and in "Wotan" and his works on the Germanic unconscious, he suggested that this ethnic, racial, or *Volk*-based psyche contained the necessary tension to produce a new collective attitude. In essence, Jung's Germanic writings belong to the spectrum of the "Germanization of Christianity," as exemplified by Richard Wagner, Houston Stewart Chamberlain, and other now lesser-known authors.

Outline of the book

Chapter 2 surveys the genealogies of key terms that Jung used to develop his theory of a collective Germanic psyche. Along with *primitive* and *barbarian*, the terms discussed include *German*, *Germanic* and *Aryan*. These words and their changing meanings are discussed against the various cultural and historical backgrounds in which they first emerged and later developed. This brief overview of a 2,000 year-long development of overlapping and diverging discourses on a presumed Germanic essence, barbarianism and primitivity provides a historical and intellectual framework with which the reader may better understand the subsequent interpretation of Jung's ideas.

Chapter 3 explores how Jung intentionally positioned his psychological theory in a liminal space between and inclusive of science and spirituality, while he performed the roles of both doctor and spiritual master. Jung formulated his psychological theory as a solution to his era's social malaise, which many people believed stemmed from the rupture between faith and reason. This chapter positions Jung's work within the new educated bourgeois spirituality of self-redemption, which located the essence of religion within one's own inner being. Self-redemption promised to complete the German Reformation as an inward spiritual process.

Chapter 4 explores the concept of *primitivity* in Jung's psychology. It refers both to a universal archaic level of mind and to various peoples. Jung imported into his psychological theory a nineteenth-century anthropological, social-Darwinistic model of unilinear evolution. So-called primitives functioned in Jung's theory as the living evidence for the archaic collective unconscious and the archetypes. This archaic level of the psyche was also Jung's vehicle for his critique of modern society. Jung's model for the psyche as a house shows his theory was centrally concerned with a collective psyche that was of Germanic descent and of Protestant background.

Chapter 5 continues exploring the meaning of *primitivity* in Jung's work, focusing on the differences between *primitive* as infantile and *primitive* as signifying primordial and original, therefore promising rebirth. Jung applied the term *primitive* to both Jews and Germanic people, yet correlated these to two different definitions of the term. In the case of "Jewish psychology," Jung combined Freudian psychoanalytic theory and standard anti-Jewish stereotypes to describe Jews as infantile, materialistic, rootless, and effeminate. In contrast, Jung portrayed the "primitive" side of the Germanic peoples as the archaic source of psychic wholeness and renewal.

Chapter 6 analyzes Jung's 1936 "Wotan" essay in-depth to show that Jung saw National Socialism as a potential individuation process *en masse*. Employing the concept of *Ergriffenheit* (being deeply moved or gripped) that scholars of religion used to described an encounter with the Holy, Jung suggested that the Germans were capable of a collective spiritual rebirth. Because Jung believed that archetypes are the psychological counterparts to the biological instincts, this chapter further illustrates what he regarded as the particular Germanic instinct corresponding to the Wotanic archetype, and therefore what constituted the very essence of Germanism.

Chapter 7 examines the changes Jung made in his portrait of Wotan, Hitler and Germany post-"Wotan." Jung faced sharp reproaches for his writings and activities during the Nazi era, criticism that continues to this day. The chapter also examines the changing relationship between Jung and Nazi Indologist Jakob Wilhelm Hauer, who held a seminar on the role of race in religious evolution in the Psychological Club of Zurich in 1938. Finally, Jung's "Answer to Job" is examined, as his interpretation of the psychological evolution of God offers striking parallels to Jung's portrait of Wotan – parallels Jung refrained from mentioning.

Chapter 8 explores the reception of Jung's Germanic writings in the new religious movement known alternatively as Heathenism, Odinism or Ásatrú. Jung's status as a psychologist proves attractive to many founders of new religious movements who rely (often casually and unsystematically) on scholarly discourses to justify their new spiritualities. Jung's racialist writings appeal to the "ethnic" and racist branches of Heathenism, the members of which often claim that the current revival of Germanic religion is neither due to a revived interest in cultural heritage nor a reaction to globalization, but is rather caused by a genetically inherited Northern European "folk-soul."

Notes on methodology

The argument offered here brings together several key works. First, it seeks to extend the analysis of the scholar of psychology and religion Celia Brickman (2003) in her excellent study of the concept of the *primitive* in Sigmund Freud's works. Second, it positions Jung's Germanic writings within the highly commendable investigations of Germanic and Aryan ideology by the Scandinavian studies scholar Klaus von See (1970, 1994) and the historian of religions Stefan Arvidsson (2006). Third, it expands on the references to the reception of Jung in contemporary Heathenism made by the scholars of religion Jeffrey Kaplan (1997) and especially Mattias Gardell (2003) in their important studies of this new movement. Finally, the analysis of Jung's discourse draws on the works of other scholars who seek to illuminate the ideological claims embedded in discourses deemed politically neutral, either because, as myth, they are held to reveal eternal truths of a transcendental order or, as science, they are considered value-free and objective, and thus non-political. Jung's work regularly combines both kinds of discourses, thereby conveying the impression to many of his readers that they reveal a truth that is simultaneously scientifically valid and spiritually profound. Following the lead of the scholars whose theoretical works inform the present study, I employ here a hermeneutics of suspicion, which seeks to uncover the political interests embedded in a text that an author did not necessarily wish to reveal. By utilizing this method, I demonstrate that Jung was not an egalitarian thinker who, due to the discursive strictures of his day, failed to clearly articulate presumably non-judgmental insights about "the psychologies of nations." Instead, I show that Jung was personally invested in these discourses because he wished to formulate a psychological theory to validate and even valorize the self-identity of himself and the majority of his patients, one first unsettled by the disappointment in modernity and then deeply rattled by the catastrophe of World War I. These patients were modern, educated individuals, often of Germanic heritage and Protestant religious background, and were convinced of their own cultural and racial superiority.

To carry out a close reading of Jung's texts, I regularly used either the collected works of Jung in German (*Gesammelte Werke*, or GW), or his original publications. Much of the existing scholarly literature on Jung relies upon his English-language *Collected Works* (CW). Unlike the *Standard Edition* of his one-time friend and collaborator, Sigmund Freud, Jung's CW do not track his textual changes, many of which he made during and after World War II. Hence, the changes in his thought over time cannot be traced effectively through these volumes. Furthermore, the Jung historian Sonu Shamdasani has detailed the problems with the translations of Jung's works into English. Richard Hull (1913–1974), Jung's translator, was not well-versed in Jungian psychology and therefore sometimes misunderstood Jung's nuances. In other cases, the translation he made was simply false, in that he mistook one word for another and then translated the misunderstood word (Shamdasani 2005, 49–51; 51, fn. 136).

Still, a certain pattern of deletions, revisions, mistranslations and misleading editorial maneuvers leads me to suspect that Jung and his editors wished to salvage Jung's reputation after he had tarnished it by his writings during the Nazi era. These troubling textual issues are especially problematic for the analysis of the "Wotan" essay. Interpolations, later additions, and faulty translations could come to light only by recourse to Jung's original documents. For this book, I use the CW wherever possible, but where the GW or original document differs, I document the changes in the text. This basic research method will contribute significantly to our understanding of Jungian thought in the context in which it was formed – the broader German-cultural realm before World War II – and should therefore help rectify the distortion in our perception of Jung caused by the CW's lack of transparency.

Notes on terms

As the following discussion explains, terms such as *primitive* and *barbarian* are hardly neutral words objectively describing specific ethnic groups. This is also true of *Aryan*, *Germanic*, and *Jewish*. To indicate this ideological content, I have often set these words in quotation marks. When I relate the views of a given scholar, I refrain from using quotation marks. My purpose is to balance clarity of meaning and readability. When I refer to the word as a concept, I italicize it.

For my international readers: "black" as a designation for people of African descent is not pejorative within the United States. From W. E. B. DuBois' *Souls of Black Folks* to the Black Power movement of the 1960s and 1970s to today's protest slogan against police brutality, "Black lives matter!", "black" is not just a racial designation but a politicized identity marker. Like "black," "Indian" is the product of colonialism. Hence, many good-willed non-Indians argue it should be replaced by "Native American" and "First Nations." However, it is still used as a group identity marker in certain states, such as New Mexico, where the Pueblo dwellers still call themselves "Indians." "Jewish" is a seemingly objective term, describing members of the Jewish faith. However, early twentieth-century references to "the Jew" indicate not just a religious category, but also a racial one. I have sought to use non-pejorative group labels, while keeping in mind that all of these terms are political ones. Finally, "Aryan" as a racial term to denote Europeans is inaccurate and supremacist. Hence, it regularly appears in quotation marks.

Throughout these pages, I sometimes employ the "male generic," using *man*, *he*, *his*, etc. to designate the human as such. The male generic is by no means neutral; rather, it incorrectly assumes that men represent the whole of humanity, while women are somehow a subset of humanity, or an inferior or incomplete version of it. In writing about Jung's psychology, however, it has proved cumbersome and confusing to try to gender-neutralize his theory for several reasons. First, unlike modern English, German uses grammatical gender. Hence, the usual word for "human being," *der Mensch*, is grammatically masculine, as are all pronouns relating to it. Furthermore, Jung regularly wrote about categories of people in the singular: Man, Woman, the Jew, the Primitive. While these terms can be translated easily enough into English, *Germane* needs to be translated as an adjective plus noun, either "Germanic man" (reflecting the word's grammatical gender), or "Germanic person" (to be gender-neutral). Finally, like other male – and many female – authors writing before the feminist movement of the 1970s, Jung wrote in the male generic because his model of the human *was* male, and the metaphors, characteristics and values of his *Menschen* reflect Jung's middle-class, masculine assumptions. Despite the fact that he analyzed numerous female patients and trained many women to become practicing analytical psychologists, Jung's theory is largely a masculinist one. Hence, I have at times chosen to reflect Jung's masculinist bias by using the male generic.

Bibliography

Title

"something like Wotan": C. G. Jung, "The Relations between the Ego and the Unconscious" (1963 [1928]), *Collected Works* 7:218, ed. by Sir Herbert Read, Michael Fordham, and Gerhard Adler. New York: Pantheon Books; Princeton, NJ: Princeton University Press.

Sources

Arvidsson, Stefan. 2006. *Aryan Idols: Indo-European Mythology as Ideology and Science*. Chicago: University of Chicago Press.

Bair, Deirdre. 2003. *Jung. A Biography*. Boston: Little, Brown and Co.

Bishop, Paul. 2008. "The Timeliness and Timelessness of the 'Archaic': Analytical Psychology, 'Primordial' Thought, Synchronicity." *Journal of Analytical Psychology* 53(4):501–523.

Blind, Karl. 1986. "Wodan, the Wild Huntsman, and the Wandering Jew." In Galit Hasan-Rokem and Alan Dundes (eds), *The Wandering Jew: Essays in the Interpretation of a Christian Legend*. Bloomington: Indiana University Press, pp.169–189.

Bly, Robert. 1990. *Iron John: A Book about Men*. Reading, MA: Addison-Wesley.

Brickman, Celia. 2003. *Aboriginal Populations in the Mind: Race and Primitivity in Psychoanalysis*. New York: Columbia University Press.

Brooke, Roger. 2008. "Cultural Reflections on Jung's Concept of Individuation." *Psychological Perspectives* 51(1):36–53.

Buresch-Talley, Joan Dulles. 2002. "The C. G. Jung and Allen Dulles Correspondence." In Aryeh Maidenbaum (ed.), *Jung and the Shadow of Anti-Semitism*, Berwick, ME: Nicolas-Hays, pp.39–54.

Burleson, Blake W. 2005. *Jung in Africa*. New York: Continuum.

Collins, Jo. 2008. "The Ethnic Shadow: Jung, Dreams and the Colonial Other." *The Birmingham Journal of Literature and Language* 1(1): 22–30.

——. 2009. "Shadow Selves." *Interventions: The International Journal of Postcolonial Studies* 11(1):69–80.

Corrigan, Robert A. 1967. "Ezra Pound and the Bollingen Prize Controversy." *American Studies* 8(2):43–57.

Crowley, Vivianne. 1995. *Phoenix from the Flames: Pagan Spirituality in the Western World*. London: Thorsons.

Dalal, Farhad. 1988. "Jung: A Racist." *British Journal of Psychotherapy* 4(3):263–279.

Ellenberger, Henri. 1970. *The Discovery of the Unconscious: The History and Evolution of Dynamic Psychiatry*. New York: Basic Books.

Ellwood, Robert. 1999. *The Politics of Myth: A Study of C. G. Jung, Mircea Eliade, and Joseph Campbell*. Albany: State University of New York Press.

Fanon, Frantz. 2008. *Black Skin, White Masks*, trans. by Richard Philcox. New York: Grove Press.

Gardell, M. 2003. *Gods of the Blood: The Pagan Revival and White Separatism*. Durham: Duke University Press.

Grossman, Stanley. 1999. "C. G. Jung and National Socialism." In Paul Bishop (ed.), *Jung in Contexts: A Reader*. London: Routledge, pp.92–121.

Gundarsson, Kveldulf. 1993. *Teutonic Religion: Folk Beliefs and Practices of the Northern Tradition*. St. Paul: Llewellyn.

Hark, Helmut (ed.). 1988. *Lexikon Jungscher Grundbegriffe: Mit Originaltexten von C. G. Jung*. Olten: Walter.

Harms, Ernest. 1946. "Carl Gustav Jung – Defender of Freud and the Jews: A Chapter of European Psychiatric History under the Nazi Yoke." *Psychiatric Quarterly* 20(2):199–230.

Hobsbawm, Eric J. 1992. *Nations and Nationalism since 1780: Programme, Myth, Reality*. Second Edition. Cambridge, UK: Cambridge University Press.

Humbert, Elie. 1992. "Archetypes." In *Carl Jung: Critical Assessments*, ed. by Renos K. Papadopoulos, Routledge: London, pp.307–317.

Jacobi, Jolande. 1972. *Die Psychologie von C. G. Jung: Eine Einführung in das Gesamtwerk, mit einem Geleitwort von C. G. Jung*. Olten: Olten.

Jung, C. G. 1953–1991. *Collected Works*, ed. by Sir Herbert Read, Michael Fordham, and Gerhard Adler. New York: Pantheon Books; Princeton, NJ: Princeton University Press.

——. 1956. "Wotan und der Rattenfänger: Bemerkungen eines Tiefenpsychologen." *Der Monat: Eine internationale Zeitschrift* 9(97):75–76.

——. 1965. *Memories, Dreams, Reflections,* rec. and ed. by Aniela Jaffé, trans. by Richard and Clara Winston. New York: Vintage

——. 1988. *Nietzsche's Zarathustra: Notes of the Seminar Given in 1934–1939*, ed. by James L. Jarrett. Princeton, NJ: Princeton University Press.

——. 1989. *Analytical Psychology: Notes of the Seminar Given in 1925*, ed. by William McGuire. Princeton, NJ: Princeton University Press.

Kaplan, Jeffrey. 1997. *Radical Religion in America: Millenarian Movements from the Far Right to the Children of Noah*. Syracuse, NY: Syracuse University Press.

Kimmel, Michael S. (ed.). 1995. *The Politics of Manhood: Profeminist Men Respond to the Mythopoetic Men's Movement (and the Mythopoetic Leaders Answer).* Philadelphia: Temple University Press.

Krech, Volkhard. 2002. *Wissenschaft und Religion: Studien zur Geschichte der Religionsforschung in Deutschland 1871 bis 1933*. Tubingen: Mohr Siebeck.

Kuper, Adam. 2005. *The Reinvention of Primitive Society: Transformations of a Myth*. London: Routledge.

Langwieler, Günther. 2010. "'Wotan:' A Political Myth of the German Collective Unconscious: Three Debates of Shadow Aspects of the Collective Identities of Germans and Jews in the Germany of National-Socialism." In Murray Stein and Raya A. Jones (eds), *Cultures and Identities in Transition: Jungian Perspectives*, London: Routledge, pp.30–40.

Lewin, Nicholas Adam. 2009. *Jung on War, Politics and Nazi Germany: Exploring the Theory of Archetypes and the Collective Unconscious*. London: Karnac.

Long, Charles H. 1986. *Significations: Signs, Symbols, and Images in the Interpretation of Religion*. Philadelphia: Fortress Press.

Lund, Allan A. 1986. "Zum Germanenbegriff bei Tacitus." In Heinrich Beck (ed.), *Germanenprobleme in heutiger Sicht*, Komission für die Altertumskunde Mittel-und Nordeuropas. Second Edition. Berlin. Walter de Gruyter, pp.53–87.

McVan, Ron (ed.). 2000. *Temple of Wotan: Holy Book of the Aryan Tribes*. St. Maries, ID: 14 Word Press.

Meier, Carl A. 1977. *Jung's Analytical Psychology and Religion*. Carbondale, IL: Arcturus.

Moore, Robert and Douglas Gilette (ed.). 1990. *King, Warrior, Magician, Lover: Rediscovering the Archetypes of the Mature Masculine*. San Francisco: Harper SanFrancisco.

Neumann, Micha. 1991. "On the Relationship between Erich Neumann and C. G. Jung and the Question of Anti-Semitism." In Aryeh Maidenbaum and Stephen A. Martin (eds), *Lingering Shadows Jungians, Freudians, and anti-semitism*, Boston: Shambala, pp.273–289.

Pietikäinen, Petteri. 1998. "National Typologies, Races, and Mentalities in C. G. Jung's Psychology." *History of European Ideas* 24(6):359–73.

Post, Laurens van der. 1975. *Jung and the Story of our Time*. New York: Pantheon.

Rowland, Susan. 2007. "Response to Robert A. Segal's 'Jung and Lévy-Bruhl.'" *Journal of Analytical Psychology* 52:659–665.

Said, Edward. 1978. *Orientalism*. London: Routledge & Kegan Paul.

Samuels, Andrew. 1992. "National Psychology, National Socialism, and Analytical Psychology: Reflections on Jung and Anti-Semitism." *Journal of Analytical Psychology* (37):3–28.

Samuels, Andrew, Bani Shorter and Fred Plant (eds). 1986. *A Critical Dictionary of Jungian Analysis*. London: Routledge & Kegan Paul.

——. 1993. *The Political Psyche*. London: Routledge.

——. 2014. Foreword to C. G. Jung, *Essays on Contemporary Events: The Psychology of Nazism. With a New Forward by Andrew Samuels*. Princeton, NJ: Princeton University.

Schoenl, William. 1996. *Major Issues in the Life and Work of C. G. Jung*. Lanham, MD: University Press of America.

See, Klaus von. 1970. *Deutsche Germanen-Ideologie: Vom Humanismus bis zur Gegenwart*. Frankfurt am Main: Athenäum.

——. 1994. *Barbar Germane Arier: Die Suche nach der Identität der Deutschen*. Heidelberg: C. Winter.

Segal, Robert A. 2007. "Jung and Lévy-Bruhl." *Journal of Analytical Psychology* 52:635–658.

Shamdasani, Sonu. 2003. *Jung and the Making of Modern Psychology: The Dream of a Science.* Cambridge, UK: Cambridge University Press.

——. 2005. *Jung Stripped Bare by his Biographers, Even.* London: Karnac.

Speicher, Marga. 2002. "Jung, Anti-Semitism, and the Nazi Regime." In Aryeh Maidenbaum (ed.), *Jung and the Shadow of Anti-Semitism*, Boston: Shambala, pp.332–339.

Storr, Anthony. 1973. *C. G. Jung.* New York: Viking Press.

Tacey, David. 2001. *Jung and the New Age.* Philadelphia: Brunner-Routledge.

Thorsson, Edred. 1987. *Runelore: A Handbook of Esoteric Runology.* San Francisco: Weiser.

——. 1998. *Northern Magic: Rune Mysteries and Shamanism.* Saint Paul: Llewellyn.

Wasserstrom, Steven M. 1999. *Religion after Religion: Gerschom Scholem, Mircea Eliade, and Henry Corbin at Eranos.* Princeton, NJ: Princeton University Press.

Williams, Patrick and Laura Chrisman (eds). 1994. *Colonial Discourse and Post-Colonial Theory.* New York: Columbia University Press.

Wolfram, Herwig. 1997. *Die Germanen.* Munich: C. H. Beck.

Archived materials

Letter from Jakob Wilhelm Hauer to Carl Gustav Jung, March 26, 1938. Federal Archive of Germany (Coblenz): Cat. No. N1131/139, fol.13.

Letter from Oskar A. H. Schmitz to Carl Gustav Jung, December 4, 1926 (ETH-Bibliothek Zurich (Switzerland), ETH Zurich University Archives, Hs 1056:148).

Online news articles, surveys, and documents

Southern Poverty Law Center. 2011. "The Year in Hate and Extremism: Hate Groups Top 1000." *Intelligence Report* 141. http://www.splcenter.org/get-informed/intelligence-report/2011/spring (Accessed: May 1, 2011).

Time. 2012. "Carl Jung, Cover of Time Magazine in 1955." Available at: http://carljung depthpsychology.blogspot.de/2012/02/carl-jung-cover-of-time-magazine-in.html (Accessed: March 3, 2015).

Web pages

[INT1] Jung, C. 1946. *Wotan.* Available at: http://www.nazi.org.uk/jung-wotan.htm (Accessed: Oct. 10, 2009; no longer available as of Jul. 25, 2015).

[INT2] McNallen, Stephen. 2011. *Wotan vs. Tezcatlipoca: The Spiritual War for California and the Southwest.* Asatru Folk Assembly. Available at: http://www.runestone.org/about-asatru/articles-a-essays/150-wotan-vs-tezcatlipoca-the-spiritual-war-for-california-and-the-southwest.html (Accessed: May 1, 2011).

2

"BECAUSE WE GERMANIC PEOPLE STILL HAVE A GENUINE BARBARIAN IN US"

On ancient ethnographers, humanist thinkers, and modern theorists of primitive religion, or where Jung got his ideas

The problem

1918. This was the final year of the "Great War," a barbaric bloodbath that threatened to undo Europe's self-image as the civilized apex of human evolution. Europeans had raged against each other in a four-year-long battle that resulted in little more than carnage, demonstrating that they were more primitive than those non-Europeans they had colonized in the name of civilizing them. Carl Jung was one of many European intellectuals who struggled to understand a catastrophe that stretched the boundaries of comprehension itself. In 1917, he gave voice to his distress in *The Psychology of Unconscious Processes (Die Psychologie der Unbewußten Prozesse)*, stating that "[t]he present terrible disaster of the world war has greatly damaged the view of even the most optimistic believer in rational culture" (*Die gegenwärtige furchtbare Katastrophe des Weltkrieges hat auch dem optimistischsten Kulturrationalisten einen sehr dicken Strich durch die Rechnung gemacht*) (Jung 1917b, 68).

Jung had spent much of World War I developing and honing his theory of analytical psychology, in which he presented a model of the psyche divided into the personal unconscious, the collective unconscious, and individual consciousness. The personal unconscious is acquired during the course of one's lifetime. It contains psychological processes and events that have been either repressed or forgotten; perceptions that take place below the threshold of consciousness; and psychic contents that have not yet reached this threshold. Jung often used the term "personal unconscious" as a code for what he took to be the extent of the unconscious for Freud. To distinguish his own analytical psychology from Freudian psychoanalysis, he emphasized instead the collective unconscious. Jung believed that the collective unconscious was inherited and contained multiple layers of mind developed over the course of human history. It was thus profoundly old and incredibly powerful. In contrast, individual consciousness was in Jung's view a recent historical development. It was thus quite fragile, as evidenced, on an individual level by the widespread existence of neuroses, and collectively by World War I.

In the last months of the senseless war, Jung penned "The Role of the Unconscious," in which he claimed that the collective unconscious was the causative agent of the war just coming to a close. According to Jung, religious symbols had always channeled the instinctual and creative forces of the collective unconscious towards consciousness, helping to de-charge the unconscious, while making more psychic energy available for higher mental and cultural purposes. Since the age of reason and its disdain for religion, however, this important psychic channel has been blocked. Exemplifying his trend to psychologize historical, political and social events, Jung argued that the displacement of religion by reason led to the French Revolution, which he described as a "revolution of minds (*Geister*)," and "a colossal explosion of all the inflammable matter that had been piling up ever since the Age of Enlightenment" (Jung CW 10 (1918):22). This resulted in two very significant phenomena. First, the French Revolution had caught the attention of the collective Germanic soul, the deepest levels of which were pagan and primitive, and which still needed to be integrated with the civilized Christian portion to create a psychic whole. Second, the ashes remaining from the cataclysm of the French Revolution had been left smoldering in the collective psyche, finally to be fanned into the conflagration of World War I.

To elaborate on the meaning of the collective unconscious, Jung described the psychic dispositions of five categories of people: primitives and moderns, Jews and Christians, and people of Germanic stock. The primitive, according to Jung, lives in a world of psychological projections in a landscape populated by archetypal forms that appear as witches, demons, benevolent spirits and the like (para. 14, 44). Thus, primitives equate the chthonic and the spiritual, being incapable of differentiating inner subjective states from outer objects. Unlike primitives, "whose reflexes are purely animal" (para. 15), Jews are highly "domesticated," influenced by both ancient and modern cultures. Jews have a superficial relationship with the earth; they therefore implicitly lack connection with the spiritual power inherent in its chthonic depths. Hence, they are drawn to "primitive" sexual drives and power-plays (para. 18–19). In contrast to both the unconscious primitive and the cultured yet primitive-seeking Jew, Jung described the "Germanic barbarian" as having a split psyche, where the conscious, Christian and domesticated mind is cut off from the untamed, unconscious "blond beast" (para. 17). Jung then suggested that a Christian woman's dream revealed the way to reconcile the domesticated Christian and animalistic pagan portions (para. 30–31). A close reading of Jung's text shows that he equated the carrier of the inner "Germanic barbarian" with the modern Christian "Aryan European" (para. 18).

Before analyzing Jung's multi-faceted concept of *primitivity* regarding Germanic, Jewish, modern and primitive psychologies, this chapter provides a brief background sketch of the terms in question. It begins in the ancient world, as the words *Germanic* and *barbarian* do, and leads up to the modern era, when both *primitive* and *Aryan* found their place in European languages. In this latter epoch, Jews became Semites and Christianity was often Germanized or replaced by a Germanic faith. The following discussion sketches the historical background of these terms and concepts. This is to aid the reader in understanding the discussion that follows concerning Jung's diagnosis of the Germanic psyche and its Wotanic archetype.

The barbarian

According to Jung, the modern psyche contained an element not yet civilized, but still barbaric. The term *barbarian* is originally of Greek origin, and signified through its sound duplication babblers, non-Greeks deemed by Greeks to be inarticulate and therefore incapable of proper governance (Brickman 2003, 18; Städele 1991, 172). With this word, the Greeks created a strict division between what was considered civilized and what not (See 1994, 52). The terms *barbarian* and *civilized* thus form a semantic pair, the one unthinkable without the other (38).

The barbarian represented the uncivilized aspect of humanity, whose specter hovered on the edge of ordered society, constantly threatening to break in and wreak havoc (43). At the same time, those deemed uncivilized symbolized life free of the constraints of civilization, a positive state of being rooted in nature (Brickman 2003, 21). The *Bacchae* (405 BCE) of Euripides (ca. 480–406 BCE) portrays both sides of this coin. The god Dionysus entices the women of Thebes to take up residence in the hills surrounding the city, where they live in complete harmony with the wild animals there. The tables turn, and the enchanted women turn vicious, blindly destroying villages and ripping the king Pentheus to bits (Euripides 1925).

Despite the strict semantic division implied in the terms *barbarian* and *civilized*, the counter-image to the Greek was in fact not singular, but multiple (Kuper 2005, 21). While Greek ethnographers such as Herodotus (ca. 484–425 BCE) claimed to live in a democratic state, barbarians might be wild and free (Scythians), tyrants (Persians), or the oppressed in an absolutist state (Egyptians). Roman authors, too, created multiple images of the barbarian. For example, Julius Caesar (100–44 BCE) described the Celts as a highly organized society, with three distinct classes of priests, warriors and slaves, whereas the Germanic tribes were barely distinguishable from animals (Caesar, bk. 6, ch. 11–28).

The basic meaning of the word *barbarian* implies the ethnocentric attitude behind it, and ancient ethnographies about "barbarians" contained many ethnocentric and stereotypical elements (Städele 1991, 177). For example, Roman writers did not attempt to understand other people's social forms through native terms, but interpreted them through a Roman lens. They also generalized singular phenomena to entire groups, emphasized what they found unusual, and homogenized diverse peoples, presenting them as identical in appearance, manners and social organization (Lund 1986, 54). Moreover, ancient ethnographies often applied the same clichés to diverse peoples, such as describing barbarians as lacking self-discipline and self-control. This might mean they were irascible creatures, naturally prone to war and unable to be properly governed (See 1994, 51); or that they had slavelike natures and were prone to falling under the power of a tyrant (Kuper 2005, 22). However, they might be as innocent as animals, still living in a natural and pristine state (Brickman 2003, 21; Städele 1991, 177). Such stereotypes and clichés were often repeated by modern European anthropologists and scientists of religion whose works on "primitive religion" Jung read.

The Greeks explained the existence of barbarians with two different theories: either they were formed by climactic variations or they belonged to an earlier level of social development (See 1994, 38; Städele 1991, 172–173, 178). Both theories found resonance with intellectuals up to Jung's day. For example, the climate theory was used by Johann Gottfried von Herder (1744–1803) in his theory of a *Volksgeist* (spirit of a *Volk* [people]). In *Outline of a Philosophical History of Humanity,* he described how climate and geography influenced the development of a given people in body, mind, temperament and culture (e.g. Herder 1803, 247, 271, 364). By the late nineteenth century, the connection intellectuals such as Herder imagined between a territory and a *Volk* became both racialized and spiritualized in *völkisch* ideology.

Evolutionary theory was used by the Greek geographer Strabo (64/63 BCE–ca. 24 CE) to theorize three levels of development based on livelihood and locality, with human collectives beginning in forests, before developing into villages and cities. This evolutionary theory was then picked up by the Christian chronicler and Archdeacon of Brecon Giraldus Cambrensis (ca. 1146–ca. 1223) (See 1994, 40), and later, by thinkers in the Scottish Enlightenment. Like climactic theory, evolutionary theory became racialized by the late nineteenth century and was used widely in the comparative study of religions, anthropology and psychology. Both theories found a place in Jung's own analytical psychology, as subsequent chapters show.

Germanic, German, teutonic

When Jung wrote about an inner barbarian in 1918, he described a quality he believed belonged to a specific nation or *ethnos.* Given Germany's aggressor role in the war then just ended, Jung might have spoken of a German (*deutsch*) essence. Instead, he referred to the *Germanen.* The word *Germane* (pl. *Germanen,* "Germanic peoples") is of indeterminate etymology. It may be a Latin translation of one or another Germanic group term or a Celtic loan word (Wolfram 1997, 24–25). Similar to the term *Indian*, designating all peoples living in the Americas when Europeans first encountered them, *Germane* may be a non-indigenous group label that was later assumed by the various peoples to whom the term was applied (Lund 2009, 730–731). The Latin word *germanus* is attested in ancient descriptions of northern groups before Caesar began his war campaigns against Gaul, but usually in adjectival form. Caesar is considered the first to recognize that the peoples between the Rhine and the Weichsel Rivers comprised a linguistic or ethnic group separate from the Celts and the Scythians (ibid., 25; Neumann 1998, 79–83).

The word for German, *deutsch*, is not derived from an earlier tribal name, as are many European nations' names. Rather, the word derives from Middle High German *tiutsch, diut[i]sch*, Old High German *diutisc*, Anglo-Saxon *thiudisc*, Gothic *Þiuda,* to the reconstructed Germanic term **Þeuðō,* meaning "(a) people, tribe." The term *theodisca lingua* was an official designation of the Frankish-Germanic language in the early Middle Ages (fifth-tenth centuries CE). It was based on a west-Frankish adjective **Þiodisk,* in contrast to **walhisk*, meaning "Romance, Romanic." The word demonstrates the process of differentiation between the Old High German of the common people in the Frankish Empire's eastern half, and both the Old French of the Empire's western half and the Latin of the upper classes and the monasteries. Although both French and German were the languages of common people, French derived from the sacred language of Latin, while German descended from a "barbaric" language (See 1994, 157). These distinctions then developed into an opposition between continental German (including the Germanic dialects of the Low Lands) and the Romanized culture and language to the West (EWD 1989, A-G, 276; Siewert 2002, 35–36). By around 1090, the meaning of *diut[i]sch* had expanded to include the speakers of the language and the land where those speakers lived (Siewert 2002, 36).

Throughout the Middle Ages, the speakers of *tiutsch* were largely united in the Holy Roman Empire, which dissolved in 1806. After this date, the geographical designations *Germanien* (the Germanized spelling of the Latin *Germania*) and *Deutschland* took on two very different meanings, the former having been overladen with modern, nationalistic longings. For example, the word *Deutschland* in the Grimms' *Deutsches Wörterbuch* in the 1820s and 1830s simply designated "the land of the Germans." *Germanien*, on the other hand, conveyed a nostalgic glance back to the time when the ancient Germanic tribes had struggled to preserve their freedom against the colonizing Romans. This nostalgia reflected current German aspirations to preserve their culture and lands against Napoleonic domination and French hegemony (Reusch 2008, 104).

The term *Teuton* is not derived from *deutsch*, but from an ancient Germanic tribal name, the Teutons. In ancient times, the terror the Teutons spread during their migration from Scandinavia to Italy gave rise to the term *furor teutonicus*, used by Jung in his "Wotan" essay (Jung CW 10 (1947 [1936]):388). By the eleventh century, the Latinized *teutonicus* had replaced *theodiscus* (EWD 1989, A-G, 276). In the late nineteenth century, German nationalists and racial theorists such as the British-born Chamberlain used *Teuton* as a collective term, as in his highly popular book, *The Foundations of the Nineteenth Century* (1899) (Chamberlain 1977). With the terms *teutonic* and *germanisch*, German nationalists (whether native-born or nativized) expanded their claims about Germanic culture and supremacy well beyond the state-defined boundaries of the Wilhelminian Empire to include not only other lands but a heroic past as well. It is against this background that Jung wrote not of a German barbarian, but of a Germanic one.

The Germanic barbarian

Jung's reference to a Germanic barbarian drew on a 2,000-year-old discourse that he was probably first exposed to when learning Latin as a child. To this day, Caesar's *The Gallic Wars* (58–49 BCE) is used in first-year Latin classes. In this book, Caesar included short "ethnographies" about the Celts and the Germanic tribes (Bk. 6, ch. 13–20 and 21–29 respectively). He argued that the Celts were of a higher order of barbarianism and therefore ought to be brought under Roman rule. In contrast, he described the Germanic tribes as far too animalistic to be domesticated. They were dedicated solely to hunting and warfare, he wrote, uninterested in cultivating fields or making clothes (ch. 23), and without any true religious cult, worshipping only the sun, fire and the moon (ch. 21). Despite their ability to work fine silver as decoration for their drinking cups (ch. 28), Caesar claimed the Germanic barbarians ran around half-naked in animal skins (ch. 21), as if symbolizing their animalistic nature. Caesar's depictions are by no means objective: whereas the Gauls were conquerable, Caesar apparently realized that fighting the Germanic tribes on the other side of the Rhine River might result not in new resources but in defeat (Zeitler 1986, 50–51).

Caesar's chapter on the Germanic barbarians was followed by a full ethnography, *Germania,* written ca. 98 CE or later by the Roman historian Publius Cornelius Tacitus (AD 56–after 117). Like Caesar, Tacitus did not write out of mere scientific interest or to create an objective portrait of another ethnic group. Rather, he had colonialist ambitions. The Germanic tribes had remained unconquerable and represented an untapped source of tribute (Städele 1991, 183–184). Furthermore, much to the horror of the Romans, a Cheruscan chieftain, the Roman-trained Arminius (18 /17 BCE–21 CE), had turned traitor and defeated several Roman legions in a battle in the Teutoburg Forest. Tacitus cynically nicknamed him "Germania's liberator" (Tacitus 1964, 2:88). Hence, it was time again to rally the forces, put down the Germanic threat and create a lucrative new source of income.

Tacitus began his book by creating a homogenous picture of the Germanic tribes, filled with stereotypes of the barbarian. For example, he portrayed the ancient Germanic tribes as completely alike in appearance; in fact, they looked suspiciously like the "barbarians" of Ceylon (Städele 1991, 311). They were also highly militarized, uninterested in and indeed too lazy for agriculture (*Germania*, ch. 4, 13; See 1994, 36; Städele 1991, 312), because they were simple, ill-tempered, and lacking in discipline (Lund 1986, 60; Städele 1991, 313). Tacitus pictured the Germanic tribes as too animalistic to be ruled by a king – making them dangerous to their southern neighbors – but also free of domination (Städele 1991, 320–321; Lund 1986, 66–67). These negative depictions were partially balanced by positive ones, for Tacitus also described the Germanic tribes as unspoiled, with no desire for illicit sexuality, decadence or luxury (*Germania*, ch. 18). This praise probably reflected not admiration for the northern barbarians but rather a barb to his fellow Romans, whose sexual laxity Tacitus considered almost as debauched as that of "barbarians" (ibid., ch. 18–19; Städele 1991, 343).

Although these two works brim with clichés about barbarians, the Romans also had grounds to fear the peoples to the north. In 410, the Visigoths invaded Rome; this sacking of the city was followed by the invasion of the Vandals in 455. The weakened western half of the sprawling Roman Empire finally crumbled in 476 when the Germanic Odovecer declared himself the king of Italy. These historical events only strengthened the view of the barbarian as a horrific wild creature, symbolizing the elements in humanity that disrupt and destroy society.

In the Middle Ages, the term *barbarian* was transformed from an ethnic into a religious designation, to signify the unconverted heathen. Alternatively, the barbarian might already be a Christian, but one whose sins were so grave that he became a Wild Man (or less frequently, a Wild Woman), whose sinning nature had turned his once pale skin black (Gilman 1982, 12–13). In the Renaissance, the barbarian was remembered as the destroyer of classical civilization.

While the term *barbarian* tends to signify the terrifying side of the uncivilized, Europeans continued to harbor positive fantasies about a place outside the established order where one might be free of social constraints. In this positive image, humans lived in a state of natural goodness and morality. In the Middle Ages, some scribes imagined a "Land of the Blest." In the Renaissance, this image continued to find resonance, as certain authors imagined a paradise overseas (Brickmann 2003, 21).

The Germanic barbarian in the time of humanism

These two images began to converge in the time of German humanism, when Tacitus's *Germania* and *Annales* were rediscovered. German humanists and the Pope were locked in battle as the humanists struggled to wrest more autonomy from papal authority, and the works of Tacitus played an ideological role in this fight. In 1457–58, the future Pope Pius II, Enea Silvio Piccolomini (1405–1464) wrote a commentary on *Germania* called *De ritu, situ, moribus et conditione Germanie,* in which he contrasted the primitiveness of ancient Germanic life to the abundance and refinement the Germans now enjoyed due to the influence of Christianity. In response, German humanists such as Jacob Wimpheling (1450–1528), Ulrich von Hutton (1488–1523), and Konrad Celtis (1459–1508) argued that the ancient Germanic peoples also exercised virtues inherent to themselves, such as loyalty, chastity, fairness, generosity and honor. When Tacitus' *Annales* was rediscovered in 1515, Arminus was hailed as a freedom fighter for the fatherland (See 1994, 63). Centuries later, with the founding of the Wilhelminian Empire, a memorial to Arminius, Germanized as Hermann, was established in Detmold, Germany, where it still stands.

According to the Scandinavian studies scholar Klaus von See, the reception of Tacitus by the German humanists created a model of the *Germanen* that continued to find deployment for the next 500 years of German history. This model involved two processes. First, Tacitus had attributed some positive characteristics to the *Germanen,* ones he saw as belonging to a more "primitive" stage of development;

however, the German humanists interpreted these virtues as part of the essence of Germanism. Second, Tacitus had constructed his image of the *Germanen* as an antithesis to that of the Romans; the German humanists embraced this antithetical model, expanding it to all things "Roman." These two points became inextricably intertwined in the image of the *Germanen* as a young, uncorrupted, and vital nation over and against an over-civilized, degenerate, and formalistic one. Von See traces the deployment of this ideology from the German humanists to the struggle between the Reformers and papal Rome in the sixteenth century;

Figure 2.1 The Cheruscan leader Hermann and the reformer Martin Luther. An illustration from the satirical magazine *Kladderadatsch* (1875) commemorating the unveiling of the Hermann Memorial in Detmold, Germany. Hermann declares that he conquered; Luther, that he will. The common enemy, Rome, appears in the background.

to the rejection of the classical rules of French poetry by the *Sturm und Drang* movement; to the Franco-Prussian war and Chancellor Bismarck's unsuccessful Protestant *Kulturkampf* (cultural battle) against German Catholics; and to polemics against the Versailles Treaty in 1919 (See 1970, 10). By the late nineteenth century, this model had been modified in Germanic and Scandinavian studies to align the "Northern" and the "Germanic" against their alleged opposites (Engster 1986, 47). Under the influence of the new fields of philology and comparative mythology, the Germanic North was united with the Roman South in the "Aryan" or Indo-European family, and the "Semitic" took the place of the oppositional force (See 1970, 13). In Jung's "Role of the Unconscious," he contrasted the Germanic barbarian to "the Jew."

The "blonde beast"

According to Jung, the psychological aspect he called barbaric was comparable to a "blonde beast." Having studied Latin, Jung was probably familiar with the philosophy of Seneca (ca. 1–65 CE), who described the barbarian as a lion, a creature full of fury. However, Jung's source for this designation was more likely a modern philosopher: Friedrich Nietzsche (1844–1900), whose *On the Genealogy of Morals* (1887) celebrated the barbaric "blonde beast" as the creator of all higher cultures and the strong individual who could recreate his own life as a work of art (See 1994, 59; Arvidsson 2006, 150–152). Nietzsche flipped Seneca's negative image of barbarians on its head to claim they constituted the "ruling race" (*Herrenmenschen*) (See 1994, 59). The *blonde Bestie* symbolized the noble, heroic races and classes who cared little for security and comfort, exulting instead in victory and cruelty, and inspiring fear and resentment in those they ravaged.

Nietzsche argued that morality began as a class-race difference, with "good" originally signifying what was noble and fair, and "bad" denoting what was common and dark. These polar extremes found expression in opposing races, the blond, Aryan "master race" who had conquered the dark-haired pre-Aryan "slave race." The image of the blonde beast as a "barbarian" and "the evil enemy" was created by those who suffered from its predations (Nietzsche 1968, 6/2:288–291).

Yet it was not these enslaved dark-skinned Europeans who created the dreaded slave morality. Rather, the Jews committed spiritual revenge by radically reevaluating the masters' values and introducing slave morality, which elevates the poor, sick, and weak above the masters. They thereby domesticated their violent overlords. Nietzsche deplored the domesticators of the "blond beasts," but believed that, though seemingly tamed, the latter still bore a leonine instinct within their souls (ibid.; see Lincoln's critique, 1999, 118–119).

In Nietzsche's description of the "blond beast," he included Japanese and Arabian nobility (Nietzsche 1968, 6/2:289). However, he also mentioned "the fury of the blond Germanic beast" (*dem Wüthen der blonden germanischen Bestie*) (291), paving the way for the "blond beast" to be interpreted as an essential characteristic of a presumed Germanic essence by later German authors (Zernack 1996, 504).

For example, the art historian Wilhelm Worringer (1881–1965), in *Problems of the Gothic Form* (*Formprobleme der Gotik,* 1911), contrasted Latin classical and Germanic Gothic styles, characterizing the former as harmonious, balanced, and peaceful, and the latter as restless, passionate, and reaching for the transcendental. His work gave rise to the term *Gothic man*, soon followed by the fairly synonymous *Faustian man* of the historian Oswald Spengler (1880–1936). During World War I, the French hurled the term "barbarian" as a pejorative at their enemy Germany, sparking a note of protest from the important art critic Karl Scheffler (1869–1951) in *The Gothic Spirit* (*Geist der Gotik,* 1917). Here, Scheffler interpreted the barbarian as "a condition of originality and nearness to nature" (*Ursprünglichkeit und Naturnähe*). Scheffler further argued that some peoples were so constituted that they were destined to become civilized, while others were not; some peoples, presumably the Germans, remained essentially barbaric, containing in their soul "something dark, wild, and powerful" (*etwas Dunkles, Wildes und Gewaltsames*) (See 1994, 60).

As will be discussed in the following pages, the ancient, medieval and modern portraits of the ancient Germanic barbarian were incorporated by Jung into his theory of the Germanic unconscious. He characterized the Germanic barbarian psychic essence as unredeemed and undomesticated, as powerful and even dangerous. At the same time, it was the source for rejuvenation, creativity, youthfulness and rebirth.

Ancient Germanic mythology

Intellectuals in Jung's day often read ancient Roman texts about the Germanic barbarian together with medieval sources on Germanic mythology to create an image of what they believed represented the true German(ic) essence. Especially important in this quest were the main existing literary sources on Germanic mythology, the medieval Icelandic *Poetic Edda* and *Prose Edda*. The *Poetic Edda* was put on parchment by an anonymous author ca. 1270. The manuscript contains two groups of poems carefully differentiated from each other, the first relating tales of the gods and the second, the deeds of heroes. The *Prose Edda* was written by the Christian Icelandic chieftain Snorri Sturluson (1179–1241) in ca. 1220 as a book on skaldic poetry. Skaldic poetry is based on word plays known as *kennings*, which encapsulate whole mythic stories in cryptic phrases. To preserve the meanings of the kennings, Snorri created the figure of King Gylfi, who receives instruction in Germanic mythology by three gods disguised as kings. Many, but not all, of these mythic elements also appear the *Poetic Edda* (Faulkes 1987, xiii–xiv).

The *Eddas* describe a system of nine worlds surrounding a central world-tree, Yggdrasil. The chief divine pantheon, the Æsir, includes the head god Odin (in German, Wotan), his wife Frigg, their son Baldr, the god Thor (son of Odin's mistress Earth), and the war god Tyr, among others. These gods occupy an upper realm called Asgard, while humans live in a middle realm, Midgard. Below is the world of the ordinary dead overseen by the goddess Hel. An upper realm called Valhalla is reserved for warriors who die heroically in battle. There they prepare for *Ragnarök,* the final battle between the gods, their enemies the giants, and the forces of nature. A second pantheon of gods, the Vanir, includes Njord, his children Frey and Freyja, and Hoenir. Elves, dwarves, land spirits, giants and guardian spirits complete this mythological world. Functionally, the Æsir are related to law, sovereignty, magic, and war, whereas the Vanir are generally connected to the various expressions of fertility and the production of both human beings and nature (Lindow 2001; Turville-Petre 1964).

Contemporary scholars interpret these texts in accordance with other literary products of high medieval Christian culture (e.g. Clunies Ross, 1994 Lindow 1997). The works reflect not only the cultural conditions and social norms of Scandinavia in the Christian Middle Ages, but also the peculiarities of Icelandic culture, a kingless, kin-based, immigrant community that solved disputes through feud (Byock 1988; Miller 1990). Although the *Eddas* and sagas of Iceland contain information about ancient Germanic religion, they reflect more about medieval Iceland in the High Middle Ages than they do about the pre-Christian Germanic past (Zernack 1997, 145).

The interpretations of Old Norse literature that Jung would have been familiar with differed sharply from this contemporary view, because in the time of Romanticism, the *Eddas* came to signify "Germanic Mythology" (Zernack 1997, 145). Due to the relative dearth of literary evidence for the pre-Christian past on continental Germany, Romantic scholars embraced the Scandinavian literature as their own, appropriating it under the rubric of "Germanic-German" (*Germanisch-Deutsch*), or even conflating the pan-national word *germanisch* with the national *deutsch* (Hartwich 2000, 12). For example, Jacob Grimm (1785–1863) described the entirety of Germanic mythology as "German," as his title *Deutsche Mythologie* shows (1835).

Romantic scholars believed that the Eddic texts contained an authentic witness to the heathen past; a scholar simply had to dig down, metaphorically speaking, through stratified layers of text to reach earlier deposits of tradition (Zernack 1997, 146). Since the *Eddas* contain Nibelungen material belonging to continental Germany, this "archeological view" of the literature seemed reasonable. It found widespread appeal, especially among nationalists seeking an alternative antiquity for Germanic culture than the classical Greek and Roman world. They imagined Germanic mythology as a unifying cultural force behind Christianity that descended back into prehistory. They believed this mythology captured the collective memory of their ancestors in poetic form, encoding law, morality, and religion (Hartwich 2000, 11). These interpretative moves allowed Germans to embrace the *Poetic Edda* as their own. With the growth of Germanic Faith movements a century later, the *Edda* even came to be seen as a kind of Germanic Bible (Zernack 1997, 153–154).

The Germanic barbarian, Nietzsche's "blonde beast," and ancient Germanic mythology: these three discursive threads were woven together by a number of scholars in Jung's day, including the publisher Eugen Diederichs (1867–1930),

Old Norse scholar Andreas Heusler (1834–1921), and one-time Lutheran minister Arthur Bonus (1864–1941). Bonus initiated the publication of the *Thule Collection* (*Die Sammlung Thule*, 1911–1930), a multivolume German translation of the *Eddas* and sagas. He was aided by the Swiss Andreas Heusler, one of his era's most important Old Norse scholars and a great popularizer of this literature. Heusler and the series' editor Eugen Diederichs argued that the Icelandic materials conveyed an authentic image of the Germanic peoples, one reflected in Nietzsche's blonde beast (Zernack 1996, 504–505). These men considered northern Heathens to be proud, realistic, autonomous, and free-thinking. They believed the sagas conveyed the image of the Nietzschean master race, who combined a will to power with a warrior's ethic. In other words, they read into the Icelandic materials the contemporaneous longings for heroic individuals who could overcome the ills of modern society (Zernack 1996, 506–507; Engster 1986, 71–73).

The Germanization of Christianity

When Jung argued in "The Role of the Unconscious" that a Christian woman's dream contained the solution to the split Germanic psyche, there was a variety of interpretations of Christianity's relation to *Germanentum*. For example, many Germans denounced Catholicism and touted Protestantism as the form of Christianity most expressive of the German national spirit (Lächele 2001, 168; Smith 1995). An early and influential thinker in this regard was the Orientalist Paul de Lagarde (b. Paul Boettischer, 1827–1891). Considered a founding father of modern anti-Semitism, Lagarde advocated a Germanic Christianity shorn of Pauline teachings. Having come of age when the German nation was still but a dream, he argued that German unity was to be formed not through politics or economics, but rather through a spiritual connection based on a shared German "spiritual character" (in German, *Gemüt*). He believed that the original Christians' faith in Christ should prioritize an individual's inner religious experience and personal revelation of God over dogma. Dogma was Jewish, claimed Lagarde, derived from the Hebraic legalism of St. Paul (Mosse 1964, 33).

Continuing Lagarde's break with orthodoxy in favor of German Christianity, Bonus advocated a "Germanization of Christianity" (*Germanisierung des Christentums*) (Bonus 1896). He wanted a Christianity based on the principles of heroism and inner freedom, as found in the medieval Icelandic sagas. Like Lagarde, Bonus rejected church dogma in favor of a "personal experience of God" (Lächele 2001, 165). Bonus further emphasized a "natural nationhood" (*natürliches Volkstum*), a kind of self-identity that doubled as a national affirmation. Such a claim was typical of the Protestant milieu of the Wilhelminian Empire (ibid.). Bonus thus understood Christianity not as a universal but as a national religion, and reinterpreted Christ as a "German Jesus," representing German ideals. Finally, Bonus advocated the revamping of the national educational system to focus on German traditions instead of Latin and Greek classics (166).

From Germanic Protestantism to a free-Protestant-based Germanic faith

Two highly influential representatives of the Germanization of Christianity are the composer Richard Wagner (1813–1883) and the racial ideologue Houston Stewart Chamberlain (1855–1927). Both men also influenced Jung's thinking on Christianity and Germanism. Wagner's works reflected certain particularities of the educated classes of his day. The members of these classes were highly critical of the mass capitalist society Germany had become, and also feared that new classes and foreigners would only make matters worse. Their longed-for solution to their woes was a collective spiritual rebirth, not through a return to the Church, but through art (Châtellier 1996, 576; Field 1981, 162). Hence, Wagner dedicated himself to creating a new kind of sacred art, one imbued with Germanic and Christian motifs, and laced with racial theory. He helped formulate a kind of German Protestantism, arguing that Christianity "addresses a purely-human nature," while the Germans have a special aptitude to grasp that which is "purely human" (Wagner 1966, 4:155). He apparently believed the Jews lacked this ability, because he doubted whether Jesus was even descended from them and heavily criticized the "subjection" of Christ's first impoverished believers to "Jewish law" (6:233).

In an essay called "The Wibelungen" (1848) (the spelling here is correct), Wagner used Nibelungen material to create a Germanic-Christian myth that he considered to be of world-historical significance. His was less a tale of triumph than one of a fall; hence, the need for a redeemer (Hartwich 2000, 198–199). According to Wagner, the Germans constituted the oldest and most venerable royal lineage. It descended from a son of God, Siegfried, who was none other than Christ the Redeemer. Wagner wrote, "[I]n the German Folk survives the oldest lawful race of Kings in all the world: it issues from a son of God, called by his nearest kinsmen *Siegfried*, but *Christ* by the remaining nations of the earth" (Wagner 1966, 7:289; italics in original). Hence, Wagner suggested not just a special aptitude of the Germans for the "purely human" doctrine of Christianity, but an actual kin relationship to the world's redeemer.

Wagner's opera *Parsifal* (1882) was the artistic manifestation of his theoretical writings in which he wove into the legend of the Grail "Aryan" ideology, themes of natural and cosmic regeneration, and the motifs of Christian redemption and sacrifice (Field 1981, 162; Hartwich 2000, 195). The historian Geoffrey C. Field describes the opera as a "massive racial theodicy, laden with blood imagery and confused Christian symbolism," in which the chaste hero Parsifal redeems the Aryan race from the impurity of racial admixture (Field 1981, 162–163, quote on 162). Wagner based his opera loosely on the poem *Parzival* by the medieval poet Wolfram von Eschenbach (ca. 1160/80–ca. 1220), but more so on the poem's modern German commentaries. In particular, Wagner used translations by the Germanic studies scholars Karl Simrock (1802–1876) and Albert Schulz (San-Marte) (1802–1893), who read the legend of Parzifal together with Grimm's

Deutsche Mythologie in order to find traces of Germanic religion in the medieval tale (Hartwich 2000, 187–188). In Wagner's version of the legend, the story culminates on Good Friday, the day of Jesus' sacrifice. This sacrifice redeems humanity, as is traditionally understood in the Christian church. However, Wagner added a pagan element, in that Good Friday also renews nature. Hence, Christ's crucifixion ushers in the fertile season of springtime and brings forgiveness to sinners, creating both a higher level of ethics and culture and a union between the human and natural worlds (195–197).

Wagner's ideas were propagated far and wide by the racial ideologue Houston Stewart Chamberlain. British by birth, Chamberlain was captivated by German arts and culture and therefore immigrated to Germany (Field 1981, 3). He became a chief propagandist for Wagner and the Bayreuth Circle, even marrying Wagner's daughter Eva (1867–1942). Trained in science, Chamberlain was a great synthesizer of ideas; unfortunately, the ideas that predominated in his writings were Wagnerian philosophy, Wilhelminian-era racist and nationalist thought, and Germanic-Protestant ideology (4).

Chamberlain's *The Foundations of the Nineteenth Century* (1899) was addressed to the nationalist Protestant middle classes of Germany, expressing both their "buoyant spirit" and their "nagging fears of moral decline" (Field 1981, 2). According to Chamberlain, the foundations of his own era were the classical world, the teachings of Christ, and the Teutonic spirit. Jews were the enemy, both then and now. Chamberlain described Christianity as a religion of experience (Chamberlain 1977, 1:177). He interpreted Jesus not as a Jewish reformer or a revolutionary against Roman occupation, but as a warrior – most likely Aryan, Chamberlain believed – fighting against the sludge in the human soul. He came not to redeem the world, wrote Chamberlain, but to inaugurate a new human species, advocating a total change in inner experience to create the conditions of a spiritual and moral rebirth (1:193, 195) and a "new consciousness of self" (1:196). Against the supposedly subjective, egoistic and exclusive nature of Judaism (1:403–404), Christ's religion was mystical (1:413), bearing a message of inner fall and redemption that created a strong inner morality (1:196–197). Finally, having initiated a "transformation of the inner man" (2:50), Christ counted as the first true individual and his teachings bestowed a value on the whole human being, including one's inner self, that was previously unknown (1:7).

Chamberlain then detailed the accomplishments of Europe and attributed all of them to the Teutons. For him, the Teutons were the redeemers of the world; with their "pure blood and unbroken youthful vigor," they had, for example, rescued the West from the "bestial" racial chaos reigning in the Roman Empire (1:495). The Teutons again proved their heroism in the Protestant Reformation, which Chamberlain called a "revolt" [. . .] "of the Germanic soul against un-Germanic spiritual tyranny" represented by Roman Catholicism (1:512). When claiming that the Teutons loved freedom, Chamberlain interpreted the cliché of barbarian freedom anew to fit Wilhelminian middle-class values and European colonialist ideology. He argued that some races (blacks and Semites) clearly lacked the capacity for freedom; in contrast, Teutons strive after it, expressing it in art, the public square, and the state. The Teutons are not radical individualists, however; rather, by choosing his own master, the Teuton remains loyal to himself (1:547). Finally, the Teutons balance the individual and the collective better than the Romans and Greeks, making them the equals of those two ancient peoples (1:543).

Whereas Wagner and Chamberlain both articulated a Germanic Protestant ideology, Jakob Wilhelm Hauer (1881–1962) eschewed Christianity altogether in favor of a Germanic Faith. A Christian missionary as a young man, Hauer failed to find in the church the profound religious experience he had had as a child, when he felt deeply moved (*ergriffen*) by a higher power (Hauer 1923, 49–50). His quest for a religion that matched his own experience attracted him to the ancient Indian teachings he encountered during his missionary work. He turned his personal interest into a professional one by becoming a professor of Indology at the Karl Eberhard University of Tubingen in 1921.

Before assuming his professorship, in 1920 Hauer founded the *Bund* (Covenant) *der Köngener*, named after Köngen near Esslingen. The Covenant reflected the basic ideas of Free Protestantism, a nineteenth-century form of liberal theology both in and against the Protestant churches that sought to give people alienated by the church a religious orientation (Kubota 2003, 96). Through the Covenant, Hauer wanted to unite disparate groups in a non-institutionalized religious community that advocated spiritual renewal based on a joint ethical and national foundation (43–44; Baumann 2005, 14). The Covenant attracted members of Pietistic school-based Bible circles and the Free German Youth Movement, as well as young men whose experiences on the war front led to disillusionment in traditional church leadership (Baumann 2005, 27; Kubota 2003, 51). Unlike the male-dominated German Youth Movement, the Covenant also welcomed girls and women (Kubota 2003, 53). In fact, a prominent member until 1933 was Marianne Weber (1870–1954), a women's rights activist and the wife of the sociologist Max Weber (Baumann 2005, 27).

In 1933, Hauer founded the Consortium of the German Faith Movement (*Arbeitsgemeinschaft der Deutschen Glaubensbewegung*). Many prominent racial ideologues assumed leading roles, including the philosopher Ernst Bergmann (1881–1945), eugenicist Hans F. K. Günther (1891–1968), historian Herman Wirth (1885–1981), and artist Ludwig Fahrenkrog (1867–1952), to name a few. As with the Covenant, Hauer recognized that many Germans had lost their faith in Christianity, but longed for a spirituality connected to an organized community (Kubota 2003, 217). The German Faith Movement sought to unite a wide range of non-institutionalized religious groups, ranging from *völkisch* to German(ic)-religious to Free-Protestant groups, including Hauer's own Covenant, to create an alternative spirituality to the Christian church (ibid.; Baumann 2005, 13).

In the same year that Hauer co-founded the German Faith Movement (1933), he also wrote an open letter to the Lutheran Church opposing the Augsburg Confession and called for the creation of an imperial church (*Reichskirche*) that would place at the center of its faith the revelation of God "in the great forms of German history, German space, and German fate" (*in den großen Gestalten der deutschen Geschichte, im deutschen Raum und im deutschen Schicksal*) (Hauer 1933, 4). Hauer hoped to gain official recognition for the German Faith Movement as an officially-recognized religious body allowed to practice and school children. This would allow Germans to fulfill their "destiny" (*Schicksal*) and form a new Germanic-German faith based on the living divine power within themselves (Hauer 1934, 7). Many people heeded his call: in 1935, an estimated 18,000 people turned out to hear Hauer lecture on German Faith at the Sportpalast in Berlin (Baumann 2005, 79).

Hauer's belief in a living power deep in the soul is one he extended beyond the Germanic realm to ancient India, the purported birthplace of the "Aryans." In resonance with Jung's use of ancient Rome as a distant mirror for his own society, Hauer compared the current loss of faith in Christianity with a similar changing of the gods among the ancient Indo-Aryans. He believed that, in order to survive the collapse of the old religion, the ancient Indo-Aryans were forced to turn inward to their own souls. They thereby made the tremendous discovery of the self, an unshakeable aspect of one's innermost being (Hauer 1935, 36–38).

While Bonus, Wagner, and Chamberlain all claimed that the Germanic essence had a natural affinity for the message of Christ, others rejected Christianity and Christ altogether. Similar to Hauer, they reinterpreted German(ic) history as driven by a racial, national, or *Volk*-based spiritual essence. For example, Julius Langbehn (1851–1907), author of *Rembrandt as Educator* (*Rembrandt als Erzieher*, 1890), disavowed Christ as the bridge between God and humanity; instead, he saw the people (*Volk*), imagined as an organic unity, as the mediating force between the individual and the cosmos. He portrayed the Germans as the only genuine artists, whose natural landscape, the woods, had provided them with spiritual profundity. In contrast, the Jews had originated in the desert, a landscape that rendered them spiritually barren and rootless (Mosse 1978, 97).

Völkische ideology

What all of these authors shared in common was adherence to a diffuse *völkisch* ideology. The adjective *völkisch* is derived from the German noun *das Volk* (sing.), which means "the people." In antiquity and the early Middle Ages, *Volk* indicated not an organic unity of blood relatives, but a group of men from different linguistic groups gathered into an army (Wolfram 1997, 11). *Völkisch* (Anglo-Saxon *folcisc,* early modern High German *volckisch)* was fairly synonymous with Latin *popularis,* indicating that which belonged to or was characteristic of the common people or natives of a country. German humanists used the term *Volk* to indicate a political collective united through shared culture, language, and history. It was then given an emotional tone by the Romantics (*Duden* 2007, 902; Mosse 1978, 36–37). In the pre-Wilhelminian revolutionary era, German nationalists used the term *Volk* to unite the lower classes against upper-class domination. Because the Church supported the political elites, the word also took on an anti-Christian tone (Baumann 2005, 13).

Delays in the founding of the longed-for nation-state conditioned Germans to define nationalism in cultural terms (Mosse 1964, 149), which helped foster the understanding of *Volk* as an organic unity, whereby an individual was connected to the "people" in his innermost being (4).

The idea of the *Volk* was foundational to Herder's theory of the *Volksgeist*. Although this Christian theologian believed in the unity of humanity as created by God, he nevertheless proposed that each people (*Volk*) had its own unchanging, collective, and organically-developed spirit, shaped by a specific climate and geography and manifested in a shared language, mythology, and customs (Lincoln 1999, 53; Mosse 1978, 36–37). The idea of a *Volksgeist* then became intertwined with a normative ideology about origins and group membership, which defined a mythic collective with a common prehistory, ancestral territory, and shared language, customs, myths and values (Arvidsson 2006, 7; Ellwood 1999, 22; Lincoln 1999, 53). By the late nineteenth century, *völkisch* thinkers racialized the concept of the *Volksgeist,* imbuing the word with an alleged biologically-based national or racial essence. They thus defined the national community (in German, *Volksgemeinschaft*) and its territory in essentialist terms that excluded those deemed racially different, particularly Jews (Mosse 1964, 4).

Despite the former lower-class and even anti-aristocratic connotations of *Volk*, *völkisch* ideologues loaded the term with noble connotations, suggesting that the Germans were superior to other people (Mosse 1964, 151). *Völkisch* ideology therefore found favor with people from many walks of life in German culture, including politicians, students, veterans, and workers (Mosse 1964, ch. 8, 9, 12, and 14). Middle-class youth, both in the German Youth Movement (*Wandervögel*) and at the university, were drawn to the political right and embraced many aspects of *völkisch* ideology (173, 192–195). High-school textbooks emphasized the destiny of the German *Volk* and its special mission (154), and secondary schools and boarding schools were established with special *völkisch* curricula, sometimes set in the countryside (160–161). Still, *völkisch* ideology often justified a hierarchy within the *Volk*: some were called to gather in an exclusive association or covenant (*Bund*) centered around a charismatic leader who had the vision of a seer or a prophet (151).

Völkisch authors sought to overcome the social malaise of modern society by seeking spiritual solutions that met the needs of a purported *völkisch* essence (Pietikäinen 2000, 524). They claimed that the *Volk* had a deep inward spirituality, which fostered a religion of love and moral consciousness based on an inner compass, not adherence to laws and dogma (Field 1981, 163, 194). Their *Volk* was creative, authentic, and even "primitive" in the sense of being in touch with nature and the life force of the cosmos (Mosse 1964, 26). The members of the *Volk* strove towards the light of the sun, reflecting their intuition of the life force, their recognition of the cosmic astral order, and their grasp of the light of thought (Hauer 1937, 2; Baumann 2005, 81). Between 1870 and 1945, there were close to seventy religiously-oriented *völkisch* groups active in Germany (Schnurbein 1996, 172), ranging from Christian to German(ic) Faith groups.

Within this cultural milieu, the ambivalent and shifting connections Jung made between the Germanic and the Christian and discussed in the following pages appear as typical reflections of contemporaneous thought about Christianity in the heyday of German nationalism.

The *Volk* versus "the Jew"

In Jung's "Role of the Unconscious," he contrasted the beastly Germanic barbarian, who had a particularly deep and serious connection with the earth, to the Jew, who almost floated above the Germanic landscape, as if unable to set down roots in its fertile depths. These descriptions resonate with a key component of *völkisch* ideology. The term "rootedness" summed up the *völkisch* vision of the unity of the individual, the *Volk*, and the land. Like the German oak, the *Volk* was rooted in the native soil, yet striving towards spiritual heights. The land included not just the woods and mountains, but also the landscape filled with traditional villages and rural settlements. This national landscape represented an older social structure with stable classes, excluding those people and processes seen as not belonging: the new urban dwellers, foreigners, Jews, and modern society more generally (Mosse 1964, 16–17).

As the previous discussion shows, classical authors already argued that the natural environment determined a people's physical and mental characteristics. This idea began to be racialized in the Romantic era, so that a collective's basic racial characteristics were thought to be derived from its original homeland. Jews came originally from the desert; just as this landscape was arid, so presumably was the Jewish mentality, lacking in creativity and vitality (Poliakov 1996, 286). Furthermore, the lack of a Jewish homeland made Jews restless, condemned to wander eternally like the Wandering Jew of folklore (Gilman 1993, 12; Poliakov 1996, 285). The French neurologist Jean-Martin Charcot (1825–1893) compared the many Jews he treated for vagabondage at his famous Salpêtrière clinic to the Wandering Jew, implying that the need to wander was inherent in Jewish mentality (Meige 1986, 191).

Lacking both land and creativity, Jews were imagined as parasites, feeding hungrily on other people's goods, services, and cultural achievements (Gilman 1993, 26). Devoid of true spiritual depths, Jews were accused of being both materialistic and unscrupulous. They were seen as intellectual, legalistic, and interested mainly in trade and business (See 2006, 10). Once viewed by Christians as the stumbling blocks on the road to salvation, in a secularized age Jews became the great hindrance towards earthly happiness, and were blamed for everything from egoism and atheism to the soullessness of materialism, from the uprootedness of urban life to the agricultural crisis in the countryside, and from finance capitalism to bolshevism (Field 1981, 190; Mosse 1964, 130–131, 141; Mosse 1978, 135–136, 149). Medical doctors gave these views a scientific stamp of approval; for example, some claimed that Jews suffered from mental illnesses due to their drive for profit (Gilman 1993, 95).

By the late nineteenth century, these characteristics had been transformed from linguistic into racial ones. For example, Chamberlain, in *The Foundations of the Nineteenth Century,* cited the French Orientalist Ernest Renan (1823–1892), who had argued that the Semitic languages lacked the ability to express "the feeling of the Infinite" (Chamberlain 1977, 1:426). The Semites, Chamberlain declared, were instead bound to their law, making them an intolerant race (1:404).

Jung, too, was willing to blame Jews in such sweeping terms – long before his association with Freud. The notes of the lectures he delivered to his university fraternity Zofingia attest that, in his second lecture held in 1897, Jung praised the "noble" German physicist and astronomer Johann Karl Friedrich Zöllner (1834–1882), who had sought to prove the existence of a fourth dimension through the study of spiritualism. In contrast to this praise, Jung denounced the alleged "Judaization of science and society," which blocked Zöllner's work, leading the man to die "broken in body and spirit." Despite some scientific support for Zöllner's ideas, the "Berlin Jew came out on top" (Jung 1983, para. 108). This example suggests that Jung's anti-Semitic remarks cannot be dismissed as simply an expression of his grudge against Freud. Rather, before and after his association with Freud, Jung employed stock stereotypes about Jews, combined with *völkisch* ideology. After his break with Freud, however, he added Freudian analysis to his description of "Jewish psychology," as will be shown in Chapter 5.

Indo-European mythology and the Aryan myth

When Jung wrote on the Germanic barbarian in 1918, he used the term "Aryan European" to describe the possessors of this psychological aspect. In doing so, Jung was following the established scholarly discourse of his day. Germanic has been recognized as a branch of the Indo-European linguistic family since 1786, when the English philologist Sir William Jones (1746–1794) proposed a family relationship both in language and myth between Latin, Greek, Sanskrit, Gothic and Celtic (Arvidsson 2006, 17, 18). What was a rather straightforward scholarly observation, however, quickly became enmeshed in questions of collective identity, belonging and exclusion.

Shortly before Jones' recognition of the Indo-European language family, the French Orientalist Abraham Hyacinthe Anquetil-Duperron (1731–1805) introduced the word *Aryan* to Europe in 1771. Anquetil-Duperron connected the Greek name for the Medes, *Arioi*, to the Avestan self-designation *airyanəm vaejah-* and the name of Iran. His French translation of the *Avesta* (1771) and its subsequent translation into German introduced the term *Aryan* into these two European languages. In 1819, the German poet and scholar Friedrich Schlegel (1772–1829) connected the term with the German word for "honor" (*Ehre*), and saw it as a self-designation for a people who committed noble and honorable deeds (See 2006, 15).

Jones's discovery and Anquetil-Duperron's translations sparked a phase of Indomania in Europe from 1790 to 1820, which Arvidsson calls *Aryan*

Romanticism (Arvidsson 2006, 23, 17, 105–106). European scholars eagerly took up the study of ancient legal, mythic and poetic texts from India (and later, Iran), claiming that all higher culture originated there. This idea spread quickly as ancient India became the screen of projections for diverse wishes of European intellectuals. For example, Voltaire praised India to criticize Christianity; in contrast, Jones used his Indian studies to validate the biblical story of Noah. Furthermore, German scholars such as Schlegel, Friedrich Creuzer (1771–1858), and Joseph Görres (1776–1848) saw in ancient India a distant mirror for European medieval feudal society. Contained in this comparison of past societies was a critique of contemporary events: their longing for these other times and places expressed their resentment towards Napoleonic domination (Arvidsson 2006, 35, 40–41).

The embrace of India, the term *Aryan* and the Indo-European language family hypothesis reflect both the growing secularization of Europe and the influence of the discovery of new lands on European thought. For centuries, Europeans embraced the biblical story of creation as their own. They divided the known world into three parts, aligning them with Noah's sons Ham, Shem and Japheth as primordial ancestors. Although Japheth and Shem were claimed by various groups, Ham was seen as the ancestor of the Africans. These sons, or biblical figures, were often connected to characters from classical Troy and indigenous European gods. A case in point is the prologue to the *Prose Edda*, which begins with the story of Genesis and the Flood, then has Odin leaving Troy to head north to establish new kingships (Snorri 1987, 1–5).

The relatively stable biblical worldview received a shock during the Age of Discovery (Brickman 2003, 33). Europeans' growing awareness of previously unknown lands and peoples in the Americas and elsewhere dealt a heavy blow to biblical genealogies, but also to the belief that all humans descended from Adam and Eve. This view, known in scientific terminology as monogenesis, was challenged during the Enlightenment, as European intellectuals turned Noah's three sons into racial categories, with whites (usually) described as the Japhetic race, Shem becoming the basis of the word *Semitic* and *Hamitic* understood to mean black Africans (15–17). Enlightenment thinkers then speculated whether these different races had different points of origin, a theory called polygenesis (Poliakov 1996, 175).

As faith in the biblical creation myth faded, the interest in finding a new myth of origins grew – one that was solidly connected to Europe. Jones' discovery of the familial relationship of European languages fit the bill. In 1813, Thomas Young (1773–1829) invented the term *Indo-European*. Ten years later, in 1823, the Orientalist Julius von Klaproth (1783–1835) coined the word *indogermanisch* (Arvidsson 2006, 20). The latter term became popular in the broader German cultural realm due to growing German nationalism (ibid.).

Jones' discovery exercised a wide-ranging influence in European thought. First, his discovery of the Indo-European family of languages led to the theory that a single proto-language was the ancestor to the various Indo-European tongues. This in turn generated the theory of an original community of speakers of this hypothesized language (Lincoln 1999, 54–55). Second, the new Indo-European family trumped older antagonisms within European ideology, such as the Germanic-Roman opposition in Germany, and the theory of Two Races (Frankish and Gallo-Roman) in France. Henceforth, all of these groups were subsumed under the category of *Indo-European* or *Aryan* (See 2006, 16–17). Third, this new story of origins transformed the old Jewish-Christian opposition. As Europeans came to see themselves, first linguistically, then racially, as "Aryan," Jews were similarly transformed into "Semites." The foundation of the Germanic ideology developed by the Humanists was maintained to a degree, in that one's self-identity was formed over and against an antagonistic "other." This "other" was originally Rome, but as Italic was unified with Germanic in the Indo-European language family, Jews or Semitic took the place of the oppositional "other" (See 2006, 10; Lincoln 1999, 56). Stereotypes about ancient Romans as rational, intellectual, businesslike and law-bound were then transferred to Jews, while ancient Romans began to appear more Germanic (See 2006, 10).

Jones believed the original homeland for the Indo-Europeans lay in Asia, which supported his belief in the biblical narrative. However, some German scholars interpreted the idea of an ancestral homeland in Asia as evidence of a glorious past, arguing that their ancestors had conquered territory from India to Iceland. They found mythological support for this view in the *Prose Edda*, which portrays the Germanic high god Odin as migrating north from Troy, as well as in legends of the Germanic tribal migrations, known in German as the *Völkerwanderung* (Lincoln 1999, 55).

In the early nineteenth century, interest in the "Aryan" was more prominent in France than in Germany. French thinkers articulated an image of the "Aryan" as free, independent, dynamic and creative, with the "Semitic" acting as a counter-image. They theorized freedom as an essentially Indo-European trait: the Semite was bound to Judeo-Christian traditions, while the Aryan represented the modern, independent individual (See 2006, 20–21). A forerunner of this theory was the philosopher Voltaire (1694–1778) who had stereotyped Judaism as fossilized, law-bound and dogmatic (Mosse 1964, 129).

These ideas were further fostered by the linguistic research that gave rise to the distinction of language families in first place. Renan argued that the Indo-European languages were living and organic, while the Semitic language family was fossilized and inorganic (Field 1981, 203; Said 1978, 143). Monotheism had frozen the Semitic spirit, while the Aryan spirit had remained flexible. Ironically, although Christianity's roots lay in Judaism, Renan also believed that Aryans had an affinity for the message of Christ, arguing that "the view that Christianity is the most genuine form of the Aryan religion is to a great extent true" (as quoted in Poliakov 1996, 260).

By the late nineteenth century, the word *Aryan* found widespread resonance for several reasons. First, scholars considered it a native category unlike the scientific construct *Indo-European*. Second, it became part of the discourse of racial anthropology, paving the way for its transformation into a racist term denoting a superior and conquering race (Arvidsson 2006, 20–21; See 2006, 13). Third, the racial theorist Count Arthur de Gobineau (1816–1882) popularized the term in his book, *On the inequality of human races* (*Essai sur l'inégalité des races humaines*) (1853–1855) (See 2006, 21). Finally, similar to the linguistic slide between *germanisch* and *deutsch*, certain German scholars elided *arisch* (Aryan) and *deutsch* (See 1994, 222). For his part, Jung twice set *germanisch* and *arisch* together in opposition to *jüdisch:* in his 1918 "The Role of the Unconscious" and again in his 1934 essay, "The State of Psychotherapy Today" (see Chapter 5).

Over the course of the nineteenth century, the image of "the Aryan" became more masculinist, aggressive and white. A critic of British colonialism, the German Sanskritist Friedrich Max Müller (1823–1900) had imagined an Aryan wholeness, with an active expansive European half and a passive, introverted Asian counterpart (See 2006, 27). Later scholars rejected his view, instead seeing the Aryans as an active warrior race that conquered more passive races (Poliakov 1996, 253). Gobineau's book had helped stimulate this trend: although he admired the Jews, he depicted the Aryans as a conquering race (See 2006, 21). European thinkers then feminized those people they imagined their Aryan forefathers as conquering (Poliakov 1996, 205). For example, Gustav Klemm (1802–1867), argued in his history of civilization that humanity was comprised of active or male races and passive or female races. Klemm perversely imagined the former as "heroes" swarming down from mountains to rape and conquer the peaceful lowlanders (252–253). Finally, many scholars stripped the ancient Aryans of their Indian origin and affiliated them instead with the "Nordic" (See 2006, 30). In similar fashion to the Germanic hero of Bonus, Heusler, and Diederichs, the "Aryan" became the desired self-image of upper- or middle-class Western men, who saw in this self-fabricated distant mirror a justification for their domination of women, members of the working-class, and colonized peoples around the world (Poliakov 1996, 272).

Nature mythology

By the mid-nineteenth century, nature mythology had become the dominant paradigm in comparative religious studies. The leading figure in nature mythology was Müller, who spent most of his career in the United Kingdom. He translated the *Rig Veda*, and worked on the *Sacred Books of the East* series (1879–1910). He also wrote books such as *Introduction to the Science of Religion* (1873) and *Chips from a German Workshop,* in which he divided mythology into three groups: Aryan, Semitic and Turanian.

Müller came from a Lutheran background and was influenced by liberal theology. He rejected both orthodoxy and atheistic rationalism, while also downplaying the Bible as a source of historical truth. As a member of the Church of England, he rejected priestly authority. Still, he believed in the truth of a Christ-centered Christianity, and believed that the scientific comparison of myths and religions would validate the essence of Christian myth and symbolism (Arvidsson 2006, 74–75; Sharpe 1975, 42–45).

Müller believed that the origin of religion began in solar worship, as well as with early humans' speculations about the causative agents behind the finite things they perceived in their environment. Moreover, grammatical gender played an important if deceptive role. Grammatical gender led ancient peoples to personify natural entities, such as the sun. Müller referred to this process as the "disease of language." The heavens evoked in early humans the feelings of infinity (Sharpe 1986, 43), and through the personification of the sun, the belief in a beneficent father-god residing in an infinite heaven arose. Ironically, in Müller's mother tongue German, as in other Germanic languages, the sun is feminine. His argument is thus based more on a scientifizing of the traditional understanding of Christ as the light and the son of his heavenly father God.

Many nature mythologists following Müller focused specifically on Indo-European religions, arguing that they featured a beneficent deity of light. For some scholars, Indo-European religions validated basic Christian myth and symbolism, while others focused more on a pagan interpretation. For example, the British historian George W. Cox (1827–1902), in his book, *The Mythology of the Aryan Nations*, aligned Aryan mythology, the movement of the sun, and Christian self-sacrifice (Cox 1870, 1:168). Charles Morris, in *Aryan Sun Myths: The Origin of Religion* (1889) reinterpreted Christian themes and Indo-European myths through solar mythology: the sun was the savior, born of Father-Heaven and Mother-Earth or Night, and the twelve apostles were the zodiacal figures (Morris 1889, 29–30). Furthermore, Baldr was a sun-god; his mother, a virgin-goddess (74). Franz Josef Mone (1796–1871) focused on ancient Germanic religion. He put Odin (Wotan) in the position of the heavenly father-god, describing him a figure of sacred light (Arvidsson 2006, 65). Finally, Hans von Wolzogen (1848–1938), the editor of the Wagnerian *Bayreuther Blätter*, interpreted the *Poetic Edda* through a nature-mythological lens, with Odin's son Baldr as a Christ-like figure who dies and is reborn in the spring, introducing traditional Christian virtues such as peace, justice, and forgiveness of sins (Wolzogen 1875, 142–143). Jung was to incorporate these nature-mythological interpretations of mythology into his psychological theory and in particular in his diagnosis of Nazi Germany (see Chapter 6).

Evolutionary anthropology

Nature mythology was largely replaced by evolutionary anthropology (Krech 2002, 125). Like Indo-European studies, the anthropological theory of evolution provided Europe with a scientific myth of origins, this one legitimizing both the development of modernity within Europe and European colonialism abroad. The industrial revolution of the second half of the nineteenth century revolutionized many aspects of society. Medieval feudalism gave way to capitalist production, while religious belief declined as society became more rationalized, scientific and bureaucratic (Kuper 2005, 11). At the same time, European nations extended their colonialist reach between 1815 and 1914 to cover about 85 per cent of the entire globe (Said 1978, 41). The changes within European society and its growing power outside its borders led many intellectuals to ponder the brave new modern world that had emerged out of a traditional or primitive past (Kuper 2005, 11).

Evolutionary theory was first developed by thinkers of the French and Scottish Enlightenment, who classified peoples into stages according to whether they were hunters (savages), pastoralists (barbarians), or city-dwellers (civilized) (Brickman 2003, 34–35; Stocking 1968, 114; for a four-tiered model, see Kuper 2005, 30). Although not all peoples had reached the higher stages of evolution, all societies had begun at the primitive level. Scholars argued whether this common basis was economic, religious or psychological depending on their own field of research. Evolution was actually less linear than triangular or even pyramidal, with a dark-skinned majority located at the bottom of the pyramid, and white men positioned at its crown (Stocking 1968, 119).

Note the definition of the term *barbarian*. The barbarian no longer represented the lowest rung of the evolutionary ladder, but was replaced by the savage (from Latin, *silva*, forest) or "natural man" (*Naturmensch* in German). In Freud's terminology, this lowest rung was occupied by *die Wilden;* Jung, instead, wrote about *die Primitiven*.

Most scholars agreed that the most primitive human society no longer existed, but could be hypothesized, based on the main characteristics of contemporary "primitive" societies. Basically, they imagined an original human society as organized into clans or groups of families (*gentes*) that descended from one ancestor, either male or female. Each clan was represented by a totem, to which one pledged allegiance. Marriage was forbidden between women and men of the same clan. Some scholars argued for an original horde that practiced "primitive promiscuity." All property – including women – was communal. At some point, a tremendous revolutionary leap forward was made, resulting in the institutions of private property, monogamous marriage, the bourgeois family, and the territorial state (Kuper 2005, 5), all the hallmarks of modern society (11).

According to the anthropologist Adam Kuper, "None of this would be particularly remarkable if the notion of primitive society was substantially accurate. But it is not. The whole conception is fundamentally unsound" because "[t]here are no fossils of social organization" (5). No contemporary peoples are primitive, in the sense meant by many leading European intellectuals at the turn of the last century. Rather, fully modern human beings evolved in Africa (6). Furthermore, one cannot empirically study primordial societies. Human collectives of the Upper Paleolithic era in Europe were probably small-scale groups of hunters and gatherers; little more can be firmly ascertained (7). Contemporary hunters and gatherers cannot necessarily supply accurate information about groups long extinct, because today's foragers live in modern states and have adapted to the conditions thereof (9). What contemporary groups do generally indicate is that marriage and family are universal; exchange relationships are important; and only men hunt. These groups also tend to lack powerful leaders, as well as significant social differentiation except between men and women (9). But beyond these basic similarities, says Kuper, the differences among contemporary hunting and gathering societies are too extreme to justify the homogenized picture of "primitive" society painted by European scholars at the turn of the last century (9). In what almost reads like a fine Freudian twist, Kuper writes, "Not to put too fine a point upon it, the history of the theory of primitive society is the history of an illusion. It is our phlogiston, our aether" (10). It is an illusion on which Jung based his theory.

Even though leading anthropologists from the turn of the last century realized that the theory of primitive society was deeply problematic (10), evolutionary theory proved to be extremely fruitful, generating an enormous wealth of literature across academic disciplines (Stocking 1968, 112), as theorists searched for the origin and essence of culture, marriage, law, morality, ethics, and religion (Sharpe 1986, 174). In the field of religion, evolutionary anthropologists were generally interested in either the belief in supernatural beings or the feeling of the uncanny as the origin of religion (Krech 2002, 72). For example, the British anthropologist Edward Burnett Tylor (1832–1917) proposed the theory of animism derived from the belief in souls in his book *Primitive Culture* (1871) (Arvidsson 2006, 126). Following him, the folklorist Sir James Frazer (1854–1941) published *The Golden Bough,* proposing an evolutionary move from the magical manipulation of spirits to the religious propitiation of gods to the rational perspective of science. In contrast, the ethnologist R. R. Marett (1866–1943) theorized a pre-animistic stage of religious evolution based on irrational factors, such as fear, awe of natural phenomena, and the sense of a supernatural power, or *mana* (Arvidsson 2006, 126–127; Sharpe 1975, 66–70). Before him, Andrew Lang (1844–1912) proposed that religion originated in "an unanalysable *sensus numinis*" (as quoted in Sharpe 1975, 61). The scholars of religion Rudolph Otto and Nathan Söderblom both believed that the essence of religion lay in an encounter with the Holy, which Otto termed *the numinous*; they, along with Hauer, described this experience as one of being deeply moved or seized (*ergriffen*) in one's core. Chapter 4 will look more closely at some of the theories that strongly influenced Jung's view of the gripping nature of archetypes.

Arvidsson categorizes evolutionary anthropology together with the new field of folklore as *Aryan naturalism.* He argues that Aryan Naturalism represented a significant shift away from both Aryan Romanticism and nature mythology in several respects. First, Aryan Romanticism concentrated on "higher" cultural products created by elites, such as poetry and mythology, while philology was one of the main methods of research. Aryan naturalists, in contrast, focused their research on the "lower levels" of society and their material products in the fields of archeology, anthropology, and ethnology. For example, the German folklorist Wilhelm Mannhardt (1831–1880) theorized that the original Indo-European religion was based on the worship of fertility spirits, fawns, tree-spirits, and the like, with the belief in gods a secondary development (136). Second, nature mythology embodied the values of bourgeois idealism and liberal humanism (Arvidsson

2006, 124). Aryan naturalism instead was based on social Darwinism, evolutionary theory, and racial science. Aryan naturalists also exhibited a greater interest in nationalism, vitalism, and *völkisch* "authenticity" (125). The search for national foundations had begun already with the efforts of Jacob and Wilhelm Grimm (1786–1859), who sought to rediscover an authentic German culture by interpreting contemporary peasant beliefs and practices as "survivals" of ancient Germanic religiosity (132).

The Aryan barbarian

The rise of National Socialism to the status of a state power strongly influenced Germanic and Indo-European studies, in that scholars introduced a noticeably more optimistic and aggressive tone into their work. They scoured sources on the ancient "Aryan" and Germanic past for role models of warriors who were simultaneously rulers and state leaders (Engster 1986, 77) who led their people to new heights of glory and power. For example, the university instructor Karl Vietor (1892–1951) championed the *völkisch* powers that had been unleashed by the Third Reich. He believed a new chapter of German history had begun, as National Socialism marshalled the German people in the march forward towards new goals (Engster 1986, 77). Likewise Friedrich Neumann (1889–1978), the rector of Göttingen University during most of the Nazi era, wrote in 1936 that Germanic history formed the bedrock and inner unity of German history. He pushed this history back to the movement of Indo-Europeans out of a hypothesized original homeland in the third millennium BCE to substantiate his claim that wandering was an inherent characteristic of the Aryans. This movement was not that of the homeless and racially different Semitic nomads; rather, the wandering of the Indo-Europeans represented the movement of colonialists who conquered new territories when the old one had become too narrow (Engster 1986, 78–79).

Arvidsson refers to this increasingly aggressive portrayal of ancient "Aryans" and Germanic peoples as *Aryan Barbarism*, which dominated Indo-European studies from 1930 to 1945. Aryan Barbarism can be divided into an *ideology of order* and *barbarian ideology* (Arvidsson 2006, 179). Representative works indicate how different thinkers could pull together various theories of religion and Indo-European mythology to create a holistic image of Germanic or "Aryan" religion, while simultaneously reversing the ancient image of the Germanic barbarians: not the destroyers of (ancient) culture, the Germanic peoples were rather creators of civilization. The *ideology of order*, which focused on the nature-mythological theme of a cosmic battle between light and dark forces, is represented by the university instructor and Wagnerian devotee Leopold von Schröder (1851–1920). In his work, *Arische Religion* (1914–1916), Schröder combined evolutionary anthropology and Indo-European philology with the theory of a primordial monotheism, a Tylorian animism, and a veneration of life and movement contained in nature worship (160). The Aryans, he claimed, were the bearers of culture, now and always, and he declared that the mystery of "Aryan" religion had been fulfilled in Wagnerian Bayreuth (158). *Barbarian ideology*, which hypothesized male fellowships (*Männerbünde)* and ecstatic cults in ancient Indo-European society, found expression primarily in the Vienna school of Germanic philologist Rudolf Much (1862–1936). His student Lily Weiser (Weiser-Aall) (1898–1987) wrote *Ancient Germanic Male Initiations and Associations* (*Altgermanische Jünglingsweihen und Männerbünde*, 1927), which was followed by Otto Höfler's *Secret Cultic Associations of the Germanic Peoples (Kultische Geheimbünde der Germanen*, 1934). Höfler (1901–1987) portrayed ancient Germanic male warriors as bound together ecstatically in a cult of the dead, which granted them the power to cultivate the virtues of order and dedication and to found the state (Engster 1986, 84–85). Because only the ancient Germanic associations demonstrated a natural talent to create state societies (85), claimed Höfler, the Germanic peoples therefore had the world-historical mission to establish and rule states (91).

Given the political implications of these ideas, the new National Socialist government found these scholars quite useful for its propaganda machine. In particular, students from Schröder's school were recruited to work for Alfred Rosenberg (1893–1946), the chief ideologue of the National Socialist party (NSDAP), whereas Höfler conducted research for the Institute of Cultural Heritage (*Ahnenerbe*) of the *Reichsführer* Heinrich Himmler (1900–1945) (Arvidsson 2006, 180–181). These ideas in turn found further employment in arenas that many people assume are politically neutral and even hostile to Nazi ideology, such as Jung's psychological theory. As will be shown in Chapter 6, Jung incorporated certain themes of *Aryan barbarism* into his diagnosis of the Third Reich in "Wotan," including the goal-oriented wandering of an all-male association and the conflict between forces of dark and light.

Conclusion

This chapter provided a brief overview of some of the main terms under examination in this book. As this sketch shows, Jung derived his psychological profiles of different religious and racial groups in large measure from the literature he read, including the contemporaneous scholarship on religion. The following discussion highlights how Jung applied the ideas contained therein to his writings on "Germanic," "Jewish" and "primitive" psychology. The following discussion focuses on the multiple meanings the concept of *primitivity* in Jung's theory, showing how these meanings overlap and diverge with each other in his descriptions of different human collectives. But first, Chapter 3 situates Jungian thought against another background: the crisis of faith in traditional religion in his day and the cultural pessimism characteristic of the broader German cultural realm. Jung's ideas about *primitivity* were shaped by these factors as well, as was his theory more generally.

Bibliography

Title

"Because we Germanic people still have a genuine barbarian in us": C. G. Jung, "Über das Unbewusste" (1918), *Gesammelte Werke*.10:19. Olten: Walter, 1971. My translation.

Sources

Arvidsson, Stefan. 2006. *Aryan Idols: Indo-European Mythology as Ideology and Science*. Chicago: University of Chicago Press.

Baumann, Schaul. 2005. *Die Deutsche Glaubensbewegung und ihr Gründer Jakob Wilhelm Hauer (1821–1962)*. Religionswissenschaftliche Reihe 22. Marburg: Diagonal.

Bonus, Arthur. 1896. *Von Stoecker zu Naumann. Ein Wort zur Germanisierung des Christentums*. Heilbronn: Eugen Salzer.

Brickman, Celia. 2003. *Aboriginal Populations in the Mind: Race and Primitivity in Psychoanalysis*. New York: Columbia University Press.

Byock, Jesse L. 1988. *Medieval Iceland: Society, Sagas, and Power*. Berkeley: University of California Press.

Caesar, Julius. 1919. *The Gallic Wars*, trans. by H. J. Edwards. C. B. Loeb Classical Library. Cambridge, MA: Harvard University Press.

Chamberlain, Houston Stewart. 1977. *Foundations of the Nineteenth Century*, trans. by John Lees. Introduction by George L. Mosse. New York: Howard Fertig.

Châtellier, Hildegard. 1996. "Wagnerismus in der Kaiserzeit." In Uwe Puschner, Walter Schmitz und Justus H. Ulbricht (eds), *Handbuch zur 'Völkischen Bewegung' 1871 – 1918*, München: Saur, pp.575–612 .

Clunies Ross, Margaret. 1994. *Prolonged Echoes: Old Norse Myth in Medieval Northern Society*. Odense: Odense University Press.

Cox, George W. 1870. *The Mythology of the Aryan Nations*. 2 vols. London: Longmans, Green, and Co.

Duden. 2007. *Das Herkunftswörterbuch von Duden*. 4th ed. Mannheim: Dudenverlag.

Ellwood, Robert. 1999. *The Politics of Myth: A Study of C. G. Jung, Mircea Eliade, and Joseph Campbell*. Albany: State University of New York Press.

Engster, Hermann. 1986. *Germanisten und Germanen: Germanenideologie und Theoriebildung in der deutschen Germanistik und Nordistik von den Anfängen bis 1945 in exemplarischer Darstellung*. Volume Sixteen, Texte und Untersuchungen zur Germanistik und Skandinavistik, Frankfurt am Main: Peter Lang.

Etymologisches Wörterbuch des Deutschen (EWD). 1989. Vol. A–G. Berlin: Akademie Verlag.

Euripides. 1925. *The Bacchanals. In Four Volumes*, trans. by Arthur S. Way. London: William Heinemann; New York: G. P. Putnam's Sons.

Faulkes, Anthony. 1987. Introduction in Snorri Sturluson, *Edda*, trans. and ed. by Anthony Faulkes. London: Dent, pp. xi–xxiii.

Field, Geoffrey G. 1981. *Evangelist of Race: The Germanic Vision of Houston Stewart Chamberlain*. New York: Columbia University Press.

Gilman, Sander L. 1982. *On Blackness without Blacks: Essays on the Image of the Black in Germany*. Boston: G. K. Hall.

——. 1993. *Freud, Race, and Gender*. Princeton, NJ: Princeton University Press.

Hartwich, Wolf-Daniel. 2000. *"Deutsche Mythologie:" Die Erfindung einer nationalen Kunstreligion*. Berlin: Philo Verlag-Gesellschaft.

Hauer, Jakob Wilhelm. 1923. *Die Religionen: Ihr Werden, Ihr Sinn, Ihre Wahrheit*. Berlin: W. Kohlhammer.

——. 1933. *Verfassungsänderung oder Revolution der Kirche: Ein offener Brief an den Deutschen Evangelischen Kirchenausschuß und an die Reichsleitung der Glaubensbewegung "Deutsche Christen."* Stuttgart: C. L. Hirschfeld.

——. 1934. *Was will die Deutsche Glaubensbewegung? Flugschriften zum geistigen und religiösen Durchbruch der Deutschen Revolution*. Fifth Booklet. Stuttgart-S: C. L. Hirschfeld.

——. 1935. "Symbole und Erfahrung des Selbst in der indo-arischen Mystik." *Eranos Jahrbuch* 2:35–96.

——. 1937. *Glaubensgeschichte der Indogermanen*. Stuttgart: Kohlhammer.

Herder, Johann Gottfried Von. 1803. *Outlines of a Philosophy of the History of Man*, vol. 2, trans. by John Godfrey Herder by T. Churchill. London: Luke Hansard.

Jung, C. G. 1917. *Die Psychologie der Unbewußten Prozesse: Ein Ueberblick über die moderne Theorie und Methode der analytischen Psychologie*. Zurich: Rascher & Cie.

——. 1953–1991. *Collected Works*, ed. by Sir Herbert Read, Michael Fordham, and Gerhard Adler. New York: Pantheon Books; Princeton, NJ: Princeton University Press.

——. 1983. *The Zofingia Lectures: Supplementary Volume A of the Collected Works of C.G. Jung*. Princeton, NJ: Princeton University Press.

Krech, Volkhard. 2002. *Wissenschaft und Religion: Studien zur Geschichte der Religionsforschung in Deutschland 1871 bis 1933*. Tubingen: Mohr Siebeck.

Kubota, Hiroshi. 2005. *Religionswissenschaftliche Religiosität und Religionsgründung: Jakob Wilhelm Hauer im Kontext des freien Protestantismus*. Frankfurt am Main: Lang.

Kuper, Adam. 2005. *The Reinvention of Primitive Society: Transformations of a Myth*. London: Routledge.

Lächele, Rainer. 2001. "Germanisierung des Christentums." In Stefanie von Schnurbein and Justus H. Ulbricht (eds.), *Völkische Religion und Krisen der Moderne: Entwürfe 'arteigener' Glaubenssysteme seit der Jahrhundertwende*. Würzburg: Königshausen & Neumann, pp.165–183.

Lincoln, Bruce. 1999. *Theorizing Myth: Narrative, Ideology, and Scholarship*. Chicago: University of Chicago Press.

Lindow, John. 1997. *Murder and Vengeance among the Gods: Baldr in Scandinavian Mythology*. Helsinki: Suomalainen Tiedeakatemia.

——. 2001. *Norse Mythology: A Guide to the Gods, Heroes, Rituals, and Beliefs*. Oxford: Oxford University Press.

Lund, Allan A. 1986. "Zum Germanenbegriff bei Tacitus." In Heinrich Beck (ed.), *Germanenprobleme in heutiger Sicht*, Komission für die Altertumskunde Mittel-und Nordeuropas. Second Edition. Berlin. Walter de Gruyter, pp.53–87.

——. 2009. "Wie die Indianer und die Germanen zu ihrem Namen kamen: Ein Vergleich." In Wilhelm Heizmann, Klaus Böldl, and Heinrich Beck (eds), *Analecta Septentrionalis: Beiträge zur nordgermanischen Kultur- und Literaturgeschichte*. Berlin: Walter de Gruyter, pp.730–744.

Meige, Henry. 1986. "The Wandering Jew in the Clinic: A Study of Neurotic Pathology." In Hasan-Rokem and Dundes (eds), *The Wandering Jew: Essays in the Interpretation of a Christian Legend. Bloomington: Indiana University Press,* pp.190–194.

Miller, William Ian. 1990. *Bloodtaking and Peace-Making: Feud, Law and Society in Saga Iceland*. Chicago: University of Chicago Press.

Morris, Charles. 1889. *Aryan Sun-Myths: The Origins of Religion*. London: Trübner & Co.

Mosse, George L. 1964. *The Crisis of German Ideology: Intellectual Origins of the Third Reich*. New York: Grosset & Dunlap.

——. 1978. *Toward the Final Solution: A History of European Racism*. New York: Howard Fertig.

Neumann, G. 1998. "II. Sprache und Dichtung: Name und Namen." In Heinrich Beck (ed.), *Germanen, Germania, germanische Altertumskunde*, Second Completely Revised and Expanded Edition. Berlin: de Gruyter, pp.79–85.

Nietzsche, Friedrich. 1968. *Zur Genealogie der Moral*. In *Nietzsche Werke: Kritische Gesamtausgabe*. Ed. Giorgio Colli and Mazzino Montinari, 6/2. Berlin: Walter de Gruyter, 1968.

Pietikäinen, Petteri. 2000. "The 'Volk' and its Unconscious: Jung, Hauer and the 'German Revolution.'" In *Journal of Contemporary History* 35(4):523–39.

Poliakov, Leon. 1996. *The Aryan Myth: A History of Racist and Nationalist Ideas in Europe*. New York: Barnes & Noble Books.

Reusch, Johann J. K. 2008. "Germans as Noble Savages and Castaways: Alter Egos und Alterity in German Collective Consciousness during the Long Eighteenth Century." *Eighteenth-Century Studies* 42(1):93–129.

Said, Edward. 1978. *Orientalism*. London: Routledge & Kegan Paul.

Schnurbein, Stefanie von. 1996. "Die Suche nach einer 'arteigenen' Religion in 'germanisch-' und 'deutschgläubigen' Gruppen." In Uwe Puschner, Walter Schmitz und Justus H. Ulbricht (eds.), *Handbuch zur 'Völkischen Bewegung' 1871–1918*, Saur: Munich, pp.172–185.

See, Klaus von. 1970. *Deutsche Germanen-Ideologie: Vom Humanismus bis zur Gegenwart*. Frankfurt am Main: Athenäum.

——. 1994. *Barbar Germane Arier: Die Suche nach der Identität der Deutschen*. Heidelberg: C. Winter.

——. 2006. *Ideologie und Philologie: Aufsätze zur Kultur- und Wissenschaftsgeschichte*. Heidelberg: Universitätsverlag Winter.

Sharpe, Eric J. 1975. *Comparative Religion: A History*. Second Edition. La Salle, IL: Open Court.

Siewert, Sylvia. 2002. *Germanische Religion und neugermanisches Heidentum: Zur Rezeptionsgeschichte germanischer Religion und zum Problem der Kontinuitätsfrage aus religionswissenschaftlicher Sicht*. Frankfurt am Main: Lang.

Smith, Helmut Walser. 1995. *German Nationalism and Religious Conflict: Culture, Ideology, Politics, 1870–1914*. Princeton, NJ: Princeton University Press.

Stocking, George. 1968. *Race, Culture, and Evolution: Essays in the History of Anthropology*. New York: Free Press.

Städele, Alfons (ed.). 1991. *Agricola / Germania von Cornelius Tacitus: Lateinisch und Deutsch*, ed., trans. and commentary by Alfons Städele. Munich and Zurich: Artemis & Winkler.

Sturluson, Snorri. 1987. *Edda*, trans. and ed. by Anthony Faulkes. London: Dent.

Tacitus, Cornelius. 1964. *Annalen*, trans. by August Horneffer. Stuttgart: Alfred Kröner.

Turville-Petre, E. O. G. 1964. *Myth and Religion of the North: The Religion of Ancient Scandinavia*. London: Weidenfeld and Nicolson.

Wagner, Richard. 1966. *Prose Works*, trans. by William Ashton Ellis. 8 vols. New York: Broude Brothers.

Wolfram, Herwig. 1997. *Die Germanen*. Munich: C. H. Beck.

Wolzogen, Hans von. 1875. *Die Edda: Götterlieder und Heldenlieder; Aus dem Altnordischen*. Leipzig: Philipp Reclam.

Zernack, Julia. 1996. "Anschauungen vom Norden im deutschen Kaiserreich." In Uwe Puschner, Walter Schmitz und Justus H. Ulbricht (eds), *Handbuch zur 'Völkischen Bewegung' 1871–1918*. Saur: Munich, pp.482–511.

Zeitler, W. M. 1986. "Zum Germanenbegriff Caesars: Der Germanenexkurs im sechsten Buch von Caesars Bellum Gallicum." In Heinrich Beck (ed.), *Germanenprobleme in heutiger Sicht*, Komission für die Altertumskunde Mittel-und Nordeuropas. Second Edition. Berlin: Walter de Gruyter, pp.41–52.

3

A "FAR FINER AND MORE COMPREHENSIVE TASK FOR PSYCHOANALYSIS"

Science, religion, and self-redemption in analytical psychology

The solution

As the introduction to Chapter 2 shows, Jung explained his views on Germanic, Jewish and primitive psychologies when diagnosing the cause of World War I in his 1918 article, "The Role of the Unconscious." He also proposed a possible cure by describing a patient's dream: an elderly Christian woman found herself in church, singing hymns of praise. Yet out the window she espied a bull racing wildly out of control, leaping and then breaking its leg. Shocked and moved, the woman looked away, hoping someone would put the animal out of its misery (Jung CW 10 (1918):30). In contrast to the dreamer, Jung proposed looking more deeply at the bull. He did not relate the bull in the woman's dream to sexuality – a Freudian interpretation he staunchly rejected (para. 32). Rather, using his technique of amplification, Jung moved beyond the dream's Christian framework, tracing the bull back to the ancient Roman religion of Mithraism (para. 31). The bull, wrote Jung, represented the collective animal instincts Christianity had denied and which had now been unleashed in World War I. What was needed was not more denial and repression – which had proved to be futile anyway – but the (Christian) virtues of love, pity, and compassion. The crippling of the animal instincts was a necessary step to civilizing the psyche, but still, humanity's animal side needed to be acknowledged and integrated. It should also be trusted, for the crippling in this dream came not from Christianity but from instinct-bound nature itself (para. 31).

Jung suggested that once the Christian faith had been challenged, the human's animal side that Christianity had so long repressed could come to the fore. As his reference to Mithraism indicates, religious forms and symbolism deemed long extinct or foreign were apparently still alive in the depths of the collective psyche and were popping up through the cracks in the veneer of Christian civilization. Just one year before in his *Collected Papers on Analytical Psychology*, Jung had even proposed that the Christian era was over: "if the signs of the age are not deceptive," he wrote, "we are now in the great final settlement of the Christian epoch" (Jung 1917, 406).

The Europe of Jung's day was indeed experiencing a process of de-Christianization, as foreign faiths sprang up in place of the Church, and Jung mentioned religions such as ancient mystery cults, Buddhism (exemplified by Arthur Schopenhauer's philosophy), and Christian Science (which Jung described as a "higher evolutionary form of shamanism"). In contemplating what appeared in 1918 to be the end of the Christian era, Jung looked back in time to its beginning, as if gazing into a distant mirror, and wrote:

> This picture reminds us vividly of the first centuries of our era, when Rome began to find the old gods ridiculous and felt the need to import new ones on a large scale. As today, they imported pretty well everything that existed, from the lowest, most squalid superstition to the noblest flowerings of the human spirit. Our time is fatally reminiscent of that epoch, when again everything was not in order, and again the unconscious burst forth and brought back things immemorially buried. If anything, the chaos of minds was perhaps less pronounced then than it is today.
>
> (Jung CW 10 (1918):22)

While one may dispute Jung's collective psychological explanation for the death of the Christian god in his era and the subsequent emergence of other religions in Europe, Jung accurately observed that Christianity was losing ground, especially among Protestants in German-speaking countries. This crisis of faith generated a widespread search for a new source of spiritual stability, one that spoke to individuals through their own heart and lent them guidance through their dreams, yet one that they could also ground in scholarship on comparative mythology. What the new religious seekers wanted was a form of faith seemingly founded upon facts, a spirituality they could seam together with science, and an ideology that honored their individuality. What this quest led many people to was Jung's analytical psychology.

An overview of analytical psychology

Born in Switzerland in 1875, Jung studied medicine at the University of Basel from 1895 to 1900. He then worked at the Burghölzli Clinic in Zurich, treating schizophrenic patients from 1900 to 1909. During this time, Jung achieved renown for his work with word association experiments, based on quantitative methods (Jung, CW 2). In 1906, Jung became a strong proponent of Freud's psychoanalysis and a practicing psychoanalyst (Homans 1995, 47). Jung then broke with Freud in 1912 with the publication of *Transformations and Symbols of the Libido*, in which Jung first began to articulate what he later called the collective unconscious and archetypes. Beginning in 1913 and continuing intensively through World War I, Jung had what has been described as a psychotic episode (Shamdasani 2005, 86); a "creative illness" (Ellenberger 1970, 672–673; cf. Homans 1995, 33–34); an "identity crisis" (Homans 1995, 75ff.) and a "confrontation with the unconscious" (Jung 1965, Chapter. 6). During this psychological crisis, Jung experienced a series of gripping fantasies, which he later translated into scientific terms as the key concepts of his own analytical or complex psychology (ibid., 192). At the culmination of his crisis, Jung published his influential work, *Psychological Types* (1921), and assumed his new identity as the founder of analytical psychology, a critic of Freud and of modern society, and a reinterpreter of Christianity through his own school of psychology (Homans 1995, 79).

Some chief concepts in Jung's psychological theory include the collective unconscious and archetypes, the individuation process, psychological types, psychic compensation, the reconciliation of oppositions and the transcendent function. According to Jung, the collective unconscious is an inherited ancestral psychic deposit that is a dynamic source of instincts and archetypes. Jung defined archetypes as the psychological counterparts of the biological instincts, as well as possibilities for universal and mythological images that have been recurring since prehistory and that are of an original and creative character (CW 10 (1918):12–13; CW 7 (1960 [1943]):101–102). The archetypes play a key role in individuation.

Individuation is the process by which a person becomes differentiated from the collective. This process allows the basic personality characteristics one is born with to unfold and develop into their fullness, creating a sense of psychic wholeness or "indivisibility" (Jung CW 7 (1960 [1943]):186). The process of individuation begins with the dissolution of the persona, the collective social mask one presents to the world (para. 245–247). The psychic energy then moves inward to the contrasexual aspect of the psyche, either the anima in men or the animus in women (para. 296–340). Jung believed that the anima is related to a man's emotions, and the animus to a woman's intellect. When the archetype is constellated, that is, activated, Jung claimed in heteronormative fashion that a man becomes overly emotional, and a woman highly opinionated and bent on fixed ideas.

The anima or animus is also the gateway to the unconscious, where the mana personality may be encountered. The mana personality is a same-sex archetypal aspect and incorporates an idealized image, or imago, of the parent of the same sex as the individual (para. 374–379). In the mana stage, one may actually feel that one has merged with the deity; however, this stage does not represent the completion of the individuation process. Rather, release from this archetype makes way for the emergence of the self, the end goal of the individuation process and the true center of the psyche. The self is "the God within us" (Jung CW 7 (1963 [1928]):399) or the *imago Dei*, something at the heart of our psyche that remains mysterious, transcending human comprehension and rationalization (para. 400). Jung compared the release from the mana personality and the emergence of the self to the experience of initiation rituals and baptismal rites, through which a person emerges with a new identity as if reborn (para. 384, 393).

Extraversion and introversion refer to opposite orientations of psychic energy, the former towards the outer world of objects, and the latter toward the subjective inner world of the psyche. These terms refer to general psychological processes, yet also denote typical psychological types of people, the extravert and the introvert respectively. Each psychological type may also be distinguished by four basic psychological functions: thinking, feeling, sensation and intuition (Jung 1921, Chapter 10). Jung believed that one function may be predominantly conscious, and its opposite, unconscious.

Jung argued that psychic energy flows only due to the tension of opposites, which he believed to be foundational to the structure of the psyche. In his view, the oppositions of the ego and unconscious stand not in a conflictual, but rather in a compensatory relationship (CW 7 (1963 [1928]):274), because the psyche is a self-regulating system, constantly seeking balance between the oppositions within it (CW 7 (1960 [1943]):111). These oppositions may be reconciled through a middle way, or symbolically through a quaternity, as revealed in patients' dreams and fantasies and in religious symbolism (Bishop 1999, 9; see examples in Jung CW 9/I, images 1–24 and CW 9/I, images 1–54). The tension between the ego and the unconscious gives rise to the transcendent function, which produces a reconciling symbol that unifies the two halves of the psyche on a higher psychological level (Jung CW 6 (1921):825).

Jung interpreted psychological regression and dreams differently than Freud, who believed that unresolved childhood conflicts of a sexual nature were responsible for adult neuroses. Freud believed dreams to be (often disguised) wish fulfillments related to oedipal conflicts, with their manifest content a censored version of their real meaning, the latent content (Freud 1942, 126, 283ff.). In contrast, Jung argued that present-day difficulties, not unresolved childhood issues, often instigated a neurosis; incestuous fantasies may thus demonstrate that a patient's psychic energy has regressed to parental archetypes to find in the depths of the psyche a solution to a present-day problem (Grossman 1999, 105). Jung further proposed a theory of "psychosynthesis" (McGuire 1974, 138J), meaning that the unconscious has a prospective function. Through this function, the unconscious may produce dreams that anticipate a person's possible future psychological development (Jung CW 7 (1960 [1934]):197). These dreams may appear before the onset of an illness, portraying in symbolic form and with visionary clarity the coming events in life (Jung 1912, 55; Grossman 1999, 106).

Jung did not see the symbolism of dreams as masks or distortions of unconscious wishes incompatible with the ego, but accepted the symbols at face value. In contrast to Freud's technique of free association, by which a patient forms a chain of associations leading away from the manifest content to the disguised and censored latent content of a dream image (Ellenberger 1970, 498), Jung proposed amplification to elaborate the meaning of a dream symbol. He amplified a symbol by using associations both offered by the patient and culled from books on mythology to create a complex of interpretations which could reveal the potential trajectory of a patient's future psychological development (Jung CW 8 (1950 [1928]):309; Grossman1999, 107). Jung further suggested writing out, drawing or painting all fantasies and dreams to bring unconscious complexes and emotional disturbances into the light of consciousness (Jung CW 8:167–168).

The Jungian legend

Jung's theory earned him academic accolades throughout his life. These included honorary doctorates from Clark University in Worcester, Massachusetts (1909); Harvard (1936); Calcutta (1937); Oxford (1938); and Geneva (1945). He was also elected an honorary fellow at the Royal Society of Medicine in London (1939) (Ellenberger 1970, 674–677). Despite this scientific recognition, others objected to the seemingly esoteric aspects of Jung's theory (e.g. Jung 1973, 1:345–350). For example, the Austrian Jewish philosopher of religion Martin Buber (1878–1965) claimed in 1952 that Jung was a gnostic. Using a narrow definition of religion, Jung counter-argued that his theory did not rest on divine revelation. Hence, he preached no new religion; rather, he was a physician, attending to the sickness of the present day (Jung CW 18/1 (1952):1511). Faced with the repeated assertions that he was a philosopher, Jung answered that he was a scientist (Bair 2003, 475) who used the comparative method in his research on the human psyche (Jung CW 11 (1962 [1937]):2).

Jung had laid the blame for these charges of mysticism at Freud's feet after the two men broke off relations with each other in 1913 (Jung 1965, 167). However, Jung himself had compared psychoanalysis to religion three years previously. In a letter dated January 13, 1910, Freud had suggested to Jung that psychoanalysis might "affiliate with a larger group working for a practical ideal," such as "an International Fraternity for Ethics and Culture" (McGuire 1974, 174F). In his reply dated February 11, 1910, Jung dismissed Freud's suggestion, for he considered such groups puritanical and overly intellectual, lacking a necessary rootedness in the deeper instinctual streams offered by myth (178J). Jung did not believe that an ethical fraternity could deal with the "archaic-infantile driving force" that he claimed was the very power of life itself. In a rather ecstatic vein, Jung wrote:

> I imagine a far finer and more comprehensive task for psychoanalysis [. . .] I think we must give it time to infiltrate into people from many centers, to revivify among intellectuals a feeling for symbol and myth, ever so gently to transform Christ back into the soothsaying god of the vine, which he was, and in this way absorb those ecstatic instinctual forces of Christianity for the *one* purpose of making the cult and the sacred myth what they once were—a drunken feast of joy where man regained the ethos and holiness of an animal. [. . .] Yet what infinite rapture and wantonness lie dormant in our religion, waiting to be led back to their true destination! A genuine and proper ethical development cannot abandon Christianity but must grow up within it, must bring to fruition its hymn of love, the agony and ecstasy over the dying and resurgent god, the mystic power of the wine, the awesome anthropophagy of the Last Supper . . .
>
> (McGuire 1974, 178J)

One can imagine that the Jewish atheistic recipient of Jung's letter felt alarmed at the direction in which his "Aryan" crown prince was planning to take his kingdom of psychoanalysis. In fact, Freud responded rather sharply on February 13, 1910, that he did not wish to be considered the founder of a new religious movement, and that the need for religion "must be sublimated" (McGuire 1974, 179F). Two years later, in *Totem and Taboo*, Freud implicitly refuted Jung's interpretation of the Last Supper as an ecstatic religious celebration by arguing that the Eucharist confirmed his oedipal theory (see Chapter 5).

In contrast, Jung's letter reveals that he was already considering psychoanalysis as the means to overcome the crisis of faith in Christianity, not by dismissing this religion as either oedipal or illusionary (cf. Freud 1968), but by reinterpreting it through a psychological lens. According to Jung, Christianity arose as a collective psychological compensation to the instinct-driven brutality and Dionysianism that had ruled ancient society (Jung 1912, 389). However, Christianity itself had gone too far in a spiritual direction, suppressing the instinctual and corporeal sides of humanity. Hence, the collective adaptation offered by Christianity was breaking down and needed to be replaced by a collective orientation of the same significance and power, yet one inclusive of the entirety of the human being.

Even long after Jung broke with Freud and established his reputation as an analytical psychologist, the mystique surrounding him continued to grow. For example, the C. G. Jung Institute opened in Zurich in 1948 as a training and research institute. At the same time, Jung came to be known as the "Wise Old Man" of Küsnacht, who attracted visitors from around the world (Bishop 1999, 6–7). The figure of the Wise Old Man is one of the chief archetypes of Jungian theory, one particularly laden with power, wisdom, and charisma (Jung CW 7 (1963 [1928]):389–390). Furthermore, at a memorial service in New York held six months after Jung died, the analytical psychologist Edward F. Edinger (1922–1998) praised Jung as "the originator of a whole new era in man's understanding of himself" (as quoted in Bair 2003, 625). Finally, in an early biography, Jung's friend Laurens van der Post defended Jung's status as a scientist (Post 1989, 105–107); yet he also likened him to a knight with a special destiny (Post 1989, 100–106, 112), a redeemer even, "through whom the universe dreamt a dream, giving [Jung] the capacity and the courage to live it, and our desperate time the vision that could save it from itself" (275). The kind of image that Post developed of Jung is what the historian of psychology Sonu Shamdasani has dubbed "the Jungian Legend."

Shamdasani argues that the genealogy of modern depth psychology (that is, psychology that focuses on the unconscious) is usually and incorrectly traced back to Freud and Jung as the field's original ancestors. The origin story follows the theme of the "Great Men in History," in that their respective schools are viewed as the products of their own genius, rather than embedded in a network of ideas and associations spanning decades. Shamdasani draws on the work of the historian of dynamic psychiatry Henri Ellenberger to describe the "Freudian legend," according to which Freud, through self-analysis, discovered the unconscious and the psychological significance of dreams and sexuality. This legend has been dismantled in recent decades through historical research that has placed Freud's theories within the context of psychology and related fields at the turn of the last century. However, the "Jungian Legend" lingers on. According to this story, Jung was a disciple of Freud who "broke away" to make his own discoveries and found his own school based on them (Shamdasani 2003, 11–13). This legend ignores the work Jung achieved before his association with Freud, the other psychologists who played significant roles in Jung's development as a scientist, and the network of ideas that laid the foundation for Jung's psychological theory.

Shamdasani attributes the development of the "Jungian Legend" to Jung's followers and biographers, rather than to Jung himself (Shamdasani 2005, 4–5). For example, Shamdasani discusses the distortions in Jung's image created by his purported autobiography, *Memories, Dreams, Reflections,* which shows Jung heroically sacrificing his relationship with the neurotic Freud to risk the battle with the unconscious and create a new, more holistic psychology (Jung 1965, 167–168). Jung appears as the exemplar of individuation, who resisted the tide of rationalism and materialism represented by Freudian psychology and, through his own journey to the depths of the unconscious, discovered the god-image within. As Shamdasani points out, this portrait suggests that the two most important figures in Jung's life were Freud and God (Shamdasani 2005, 31).

Memories, Dreams, Reflections has significantly influenced Jung's image, as it has outsold all books written by Jung himself, and has often been read uncritically as an autobiography (Shamdasani 2003, 23). Early reviewers compared this work to the confessions of Saint Augustine and Rousseau, while biographers ranked Jung among the saints and spiritual masters, furthering the process of sanctifying him (Shamdasani 1999, 37). Moreover, the book damages Jung's self-portrait as a scientist, since it strips his ideas out of the network of scholarly associations in which anyone deserving this nomenclature is expected to be engaged.

Jung disavowed that *Memories, Dreams, Reflections* was his autobiography, claiming it was written by his secretary Aniela Jaffé (Jung 1972, 3: 293). Indeed, except for the first chapters on childhood memories, the rest of the book is a compilation of interviews conducted by Jaffé, which she then highly edited, cutting and pasting in sections from other interviews. She also deleted significant if rather unseemly aspects of Jung's life, such as his decades-long affair with Toni Wolff (1888–1953) and his associations with Nazi psychotherapists (see Chapter 5). She also left out his recollections of other scholars important in his development, including the Swiss psychiatrists Eugen Bleuler (1857–1939) and Théodore Flournoy (1854–1921), and the American psychologist and philosopher William James (1842–1910) (Shamdasani 2005, 29–31). Richard Hull, Jung's translator, even accused Jaffé of censorship (44).

At the same time, Jaffé had assumed the task of answering Jung's correspondence for him in his later years, reading her responses aloud to him for his approval. The fact that Jung empowered Jaffé to "write in his name" (Shamdasani 2005, 25) problematizes Shamdasani's general picture of *Memories, Dreams, Reflections* as a falsified portrait of Jung (35). Rather, Jaffé may have been working within a tradition in which assistants often wrote "nearly autobiographies," with significant input from their master or teacher (Florian Mildenberger, personal communication). In addition, the Jungian psychologist Barbara Hannah, who knew Jung personally, claimed that Jung had discussed with her much of what was later written in *Memories, Dreams, Reflections* (Hannah 1982, 7). Hannah's testimony suggests that the picture of Jung in his autobiography is one that was developed not just by Jung's close associates, but also by Jung himself. The Germanist Paul Bishop argues that the book portrays "what [Jung] wanted us to think about him," and he calls the book a "case-study of self-mythopoesis" (Bishop 1999, 14).

This dual image of Jung has led scholars to understand him in different, yet overlapping ways. For example, the scholar of Western esotericism Wouter Hanegraaff has described Jung as a German Romantic esotericist, who sought to bridge both religion and psychology with pre-occultist esotericism (Hanegraaff 1996, 501). Furthermore, the analytical psychologist Andrew Samuels has analyzed Jung's striving to be a leader (Samuels 1992). The clinical psychologist Richard Noll sees Jung as a leader of his own cult, a prophet of a new religion based around himself (Noll 1994). While these views have merit, the (self-) presentation of Jung in *Memories, Dreams, Reflections* also shares several affinities with the category of the master as defined by the historian of religions Joachim Wach (Wach 1988, 1–32). Wach was roughly Jung's contemporary and, like Jung, intellectually interested in the prophets and masters that appeared on the German cultural stage in the early twentieth century (Kippenberg 2010, 4, 19).

In his study, Wach contrasts the master to the teacher, explaining that teachers relate to their students through the intermediary of an object, whether that be a craft, skill, or body of knowledge. The individual person of both teacher and student is of secondary importance. Indeed, any particular teacher or student could be replaced by another, since their relationship is primarily mediated through the object of mutual interest. Students seek out teachers based on what and how well they teach, while students are expected to learn it well enough that they may someday become teachers themselves (Wach 1988, 1–2).

In contrast, the relationship between masters and disciples is immediate and personal. Neither master nor disciple is therefore truly replaceable. Furthermore, that which is conveyed from master to disciple comes from the master's personality; hence, a master must be fully him- or herself (in Jungian terms, individuated). Wach suggests that a mutual process of recognition is necessary for each party to occupy his or her role. Disciples are called to discipleship, yet someone becomes a master only through recognition by the disciple: "it is the disciple who ordains his master to mastership" (3). Hence, a master is never a master alone; to be a master, one needs disciples.

Wach differentiates the master not only from the teacher, but from the prophet as well. He describes the master as one who responds to a higher calling, agreeing to fulfill a mission or special task. This entails knowledge of the true nature of the world, its destiny and underlying essence, and the revelatory truth within the master's own being (11). This knowledge is not necessarily religious in a strict sense; rather, it entails "the objective knowledge of the structure of the world," as well as "something subjective . . . namely, the nature and function of one's own being in it" (11). The special nature of the master's knowledge differentiates the master from the prophet. Like the teacher in Wach's definition, the person of the prophet could be replaced by another. The person of the master, however, is irreplaceable, due to the truth within the master's own being (12).

Wach's strict division of the two concepts of master and teacher departs substantially from an earlier meaning of master in the West. In the Middle Ages, a master was the head of a guild and a well-trained craftsman who transmitted his skills and knowledge to his apprentices (Norton 2002, 223). In that context, the term "master" is loosely synonymous with Wach's definition of teacher. When Ellenberger referred to various psychologists as masters and their students as disciples (e.g. Ellenberger 1970, 669, 676), he may have been speaking within a tradition in which "master" indicated a person who possessed an exceptional level of knowledge or skills in a particular area. As someone known for his erudite, captivating conversation, his vast knowledge, and his outstanding psychotherapeutic skills (680), Jung certainly earned the nomenclature of master in this completely non-metaphysical sense, denoting a well-trained and highly competent teacher esteemed by his students.

Yet several aspects of Jung's portrait in *Memories, Dreams, Reflections* demonstrate strong parallels to Wach's more spiritually inflected definition of master, such as the special mission assigned to the master due to the indwelling knowledge of the true nature of the world (Wach 1988, 11). In the childhood section of Jung's autobiography – the section he wrote himself – Jung referred to a dream that he claimed he had when he was only three or four years old. In an underground cave, he saw a Dionysian-like phallus standing upright on a throne (Jung 1965, 11–13). Through this frightening yet majestic image, Jung implied that, long before he was old enough to understand theological disputes, he had already been inducted into the chthonic mysteries, which portrayed the "other face of God" (168) than that recognized by the church of his day. He also reported having had two personalities, a Number One, the "schoolboy of 1890," and a Number Two, who existed in mystical union with the Godhead (45). Various other episodes in Jung's childhood paint a portrait of someone who, early in life, had been called by the living god (Post 1975, 216), such as the teenage Jung's vision of a great turd tumbling out of heaven and smashing the roof of the Basel Cathedral, as if God himself were rejecting the empty formalism of church-based Christianity (Jung 1965, 39).

Wach's description of the master and Jung's recollections share other affinities as well. For example, Wach says a master is often tempted to keep his hard-earned knowledge to himself, because he fears others will either misunderstand him or that his truth could harm those incapable of understanding this higher knowledge (Wach 1988, 9). In *Memories, Dreams, Reflections,* Jung wrote he felt unable to share his visions with anyone, claiming to know no one throughout the first part of his life who understood and was open to such experiences (Jung 1965, 100). Not even Freud, Jung claimed, a man for whom Jung once professed having "boundless admiration" and even a "religious crush" (McGuire 1974, 49J) and whose teachings Jung once staunchly defended, was unable to accept the totality of the psyche. Jung accused Freud of suffering from a neurosis that made him cling to a "reasonable solution" (Jung 1965, 166), as if mirroring the rationalism of modern society itself. Ultimately, Jung had to sacrifice his relationship with Freud and face abandonment by all of his associates (167), a claim he had already made in his 1925 private seminar on analytical psychology (Jung 1989, 25). This was far from true: not only did many close associates continue their relationships with Jung (Jung 1989, 25, fn. 21; Noll 1994, 204); he also established an association in 1913 to further his own psychological theory (Bishop 1999, 5). Yet Jung's claim implies that his isolation was necessary to escape both the distractions of the world and the ruling materialism and rationalism of his day, in preparation for his encounter with the numinous, revelatory powers deep within the unconscious.

According to Wach, the master understands the essence of reality; hence, outward appearances and the concerns of the mundane world lose their attraction, and the master subsequently withdraws from them (Wach 1988, 17). Jung's self-presentation appears to contradict Wach's assertion when Jung wrote that it was absolutely necessary to keep a firm hold on reality, his family and work, to withstand the confrontation with the unconscious (Jung 1965, 189). However, Jung also states in the Preface to *Memories, Dreams, Reflections*, "In the end the only events in my life worth telling are those when the imperishable world irrupted into this transitory one [. . .] All other memories of travels, people and my surroundings have paled beside these interior happenings" (4–5).

This statement has recently found an echo in a new, posthumous work by Jung, published in 2009 as *The Red Book: Liber Novus*. It contains the illustrations of the dreams and fantasies Jung had during his "confrontation with the unconscious" from 1913 to 1919, which he circulated privately among close associates (Post 1975, 180–183). *The Red Book* in no way represents a diary; Jung continued to work on it until 1930, when his studies on alchemy diverted his attention (Hoerni 2009, viii). What is significant about *The Red Book* for the present discussion is that Jung claimed that it contained all the basic components of his later theory (Shamdasani 2003, 25). The red-covered book is a facsimile of an oversized manuscript over 200 pages long of richly detailed, painstakingly hand-painted images and calligraphy in Latin, Greek and German. Despite his insistence that he was a doctor, the book does not evoke comparisons with scientific treatises, such as an illustrated work on anatomy or botany, but rather to religious works – even the writer of the dustcover's text compares it to a devotional *Book of Hours*.

The very presentation of the book perpetuates the image of Jung as the sole originator of his school of psychology, rather than his theory developing within a web of scientific ideas and relationships. Although Shamdasani is critical of the "Great Men of History" interpretation of the founding of depth psychology, he is also, ironically, the editor of *The Red Book.* Emblazoned in gold on the back cover, at the top of the dust cover, and on an unpaginated page of its own opposite the table of contents is the following quote from Jung, dated 1957:

> The years, of which I have spoken to you, when I pursued the inner images, were the most important time of my life. Everything else is to be derived from this. It began at that time, and the later details hardly matter anymore. My entire life consisted in elaborating what had burst forth from the unconscious and flooded me like an enigmatic stream and threatened to break me. That was the stuff and material for more than only one life. Everything later was merely the outer classification, the scientific elaboration, and the integration into life. But the numinous beginning, which contained everything, was then.
>
> (Jung 2009)

In keeping with the mythical image of Jung developed in *Memories, Dreams, Reflections* – that he was focused on the inner world to the exclusion of those outer events which simply are of secondary importance anyway – the addressee and context of this quote are left unmentioned.

The quote above also indicates that Jung tried to render scientific and objective what was ultimately a subjective psychological experience. That is, Jung intentionally positioned his psychology in between and inclusive of the two poles of science and spirituality, in order to bridge the gap between them that not only Jung, but many of his contemporaries, believed to be the fundamental source of the malaise of modern society. By doing so, Jung thereby also positioned himself between the two poles of master and scientist, as will be explored below.

Jung's self-deification

Given the comparison of Jung to Wach's definition of the master, should Jung be considered a spiritual master or a gifted scientist? This dilemma becomes only more complex when considering a vision Jung had that was foundational to the formation of his psychological theory. This vision – Jung's deification – is absent from his autobiography. However, Jung reported the fantasy in his private seminar on analytical psychology held in Zurich in 1925. In December 1913, Jung had a vision in which he encountered two figures, the wise old man Elijah and the young, blind woman Salome. Jung later interpreted the former as the archetype of the mana personality and the latter as the anima. In his vision, the blind Salome called Jung the Christ and worshiped at his feet, while a serpent squeezed Jung in its coils. Jung believed the snake represented his psychic energy in an introverted state, that is, as moving inward towards the innermost part of the psyche. During this ordeal, Jung assumed the posture of the Crucifixion, and his face was transformed into that of a beast of prey, such as of a lion. Jung had become the god Aion, which means the "eternal being." The snake (a symbol for darkness, earth, and winter) and the lion (symbolizing heat, dryness, the sun, and summer) represented the oppositions, and Jung became, in effect, the (specifically masculine) reconciling symbol between them, "the creative womb of the man," comparable to the Holy Grail in Wagner's *Parsifal*. At the end of the ordeal, Salome arose, healed of her blindness (Jung 1989, 96–99, quote on 99).

Jung told his audience that most of the vision's symbolism was derived from the ancient cult of Mithras. Mithras (Persian, Mithra) was a god of obscure origins whose cult became widespread among soldiers of the ancient Roman Empire, who brought his cult north into Germanic lands. Mithras was regularly depicted slaying a bull. Noll explains that the lion in Jung's vision represented "participants," the first grade of full membership in the Mithraic cult, which Jung knew from his reading on mythology (Noll 1999, 68). Jung did not discuss his readings with his audience, however; rather, he described the fantasy as if he had actually experienced it. Jung told his audience, "These images have so much reality that they recommend themselves, and such extraordinary meaning that one is caught. They form part of the ancient mysteries; in fact it is such figures that made the mysteries" (Jung 1989, 97). In other works, Jung explained that the collective unconscious was limited by neither time nor space; thus, it gives rise to the sense of timeless expansiveness and immortality (Jung CW 9/1 (1954 [1939]):249). Noll argues that in Jung's vision, the collective unconscious acted like a psychic time machine, allowing Jung to participate directly in a Mithraic initiation rite. In fact, Jung called the vision both "an initiation" and a "deification" (Jung 1989, 98). How should one understand Jung's extraordinary vision and his interpretation of it?

The symbolism of Jung's vision is a mixture of Christian and pagan sources, which Noll describes as "Aryan," due to Mithras' possible origins in Persia. Noll therefore asserts that Jung's vision represents a racialized *imitatio Christi,* and that Jung believed himself to have been deified as the Aryan Christ. Due to the resulting psychic inflation (meaning that the ego identifies itself with the feeling of divinity), Noll argues that Jung believed himself to be a prophet and founder of a personal religion or "cult" (Noll 1994, 213–215, 223–224), a claim which Shamdasani refutes (Shamdasani 1998, 52–54; yet see Shamdasani's letter to Noll dated July 29, 1992, where he indicates he thought along similar lines, Noll 1997b). Shamdasani says Noll failed to prove that this incident, mentioned only one time in public, became the ruling motif of Jung's life (Shamdasani 1998, 50). Shamdasani's assertion is not entirely correct; Jung did not share this vision in public, but rather, in a private seminar, the notes of which were approved by him and circulated only among participants (De Angulo 1989, xx). These facts lend credence to Noll's claim that Jung had an esoteric, private doctrine alongside his exoteric, public one. This fantasy is, moreover, the culminating vision of the various dreams and visions that Jung shared with his audience over the course of the seminar. Given the significance of the vision of (self-) deification, what is truly striking about the seminar notes is the lack of discussion about it, either on the day it was shared or in subsequent sessions of the seminar. The silence is indeed pregnant.

Shamdasani further refutes Noll's interpretation of this vision as an *imitatio Christi* by comparing the vision to published statements Jung made about the imitation of Christ. In several works, Jung interpreted Christ as an exemplary model of a person who followed his own path fully and faithfully, willing to sacrifice himself to do so. Jung saw in the *imitatio Christi*, then, the path of individuation (Shamdasani 1998, 52–54; Jung 2009, 293). Following this line of thought, Jung's fantasy of being deified can therefore be interpreted as Jung's arrival at the archetype of the self, the *imago Dei* within, and thus evidence of Jung's successful completion of the journey to individuation.

Jung's interpretation of the *imitatio Christi* is completely unorthodox and has strong affinities with the Nietzschean-inspired religion of self-redemption (Ulbricht 2001, 26). The philosophy of Friedrich Nietzsche (1844–1900) refocused attention away from otherworldly concerns to the body, the will to power, and to the dynamic of life itself (23). His theory of the Superman (*Übermensch*) pointed the way to the creation of the "new man," a secularized version of the Christian "new Adam" (26). Many artists and intellectuals championed Nietzsche's works after 1900, considering him to be the prophet of a new aesthetic religion and interpreting *Thus Spoke Zarathustra* as scripture (18). Jung's theory shows affinities with self-redemption through blending Nietzschean and Christian elements. First, he based his theory of individuation on Nietzsche's notion of self-overcoming (Bishop 1995, 8); and second, he interpreted Christ as an exemplar of individuation, so that to imitate Christ means to follow one's own path, even if that means leaving the Christian fold (Jung 2009, 293). Jung's *imitatio Christi* does not mean identifying oneself with the historical Jesus or with the figure of a redeemer; rather, it indicates that a person has integrated the archetype of the self into consciousness and has therefore become individuated.

In Jung's discussion of his vision of Aion, he explained to his audience that rejecting the images of the collective unconscious spells a retreat into rationalism (as with Freud) (Jung 1965, 154–155), while identifying with them can cause mental illness, as Jung later asserted was the case with Nietzsche (Jung 1988, 2:903). Rather than having identified with the divine vision, Jung showed himself capable of understanding and naming the images, allowing him access to the creative power of the archetypes. He said:

> When the images come to you and are not understood, you are in the society of the gods or, if you will, the lunatic society; you are no longer in human society, for you cannot express yourself. Only when you can say, "This image is so and so," only then do you remain in human society. Anybody could be caught by these things and lost in them – some throw the experience away saying it is all nonsense, and thereby losing their best value, for these are the creative images. Another may identify himself with the images and become a crank or a fool.
>
> (Jung 1989, 99)

Jung thus suggested that he was able to bring consciousness to bear on the figures and to name them for what (he believed) they were: archetypal images from the collective unconscious. In doing so, he was able to expand his own consciousness through assimilating the archetypes, thereby achieving the elusive goal of psychological wholeness. Jung thus managed to avoid psychic inflation, unlike Nietzsche, and rationalism, unlike Freud. Rather, in imitation of Christ, he became an exemplar of individuation.

The revelatory potential of analytical psychology

Both in the quote from the *Red Book* and in Jung's description of his deification, Jung employed two religious concepts: the state of being caught or gripped (in German, *Ergriffenheit*) and the numinous. Jung derived the latter and possibly the former concept from Rudolph Otto's influential book, *The Idea of the Holy (Das Heilige,* 1917) (Hark 1988, 120). *The Idea of the Holy* was an immediate success and was quickly republished in various languages (Harvey, preface to Otto 1958, x). Otto had coined the term *numinous* in order to analyze the Holy as "the Wholly Other" (Otto 1958, 25ff.), that is, as something completely ineffable and qualitatively different from anything else existing. He wished to distinguish this "overplus of meaning" apart from its later rationalizations as the "good," "moral," and "ethical" (5, 6–7).

The various elements that pertain to an encounter with the numinous include *mysterium tremendum* and *fascinans*. The term *mysterium tremendum* indicates the feeling of being confronted by something majestic and overpowering, which induces a state of intoxication, ecstasy, daemonic dread, awe, or rapture (12–17, 19–3). The element *fascinans* suggests that, although the numinous evokes a completely unnatural terror in the person it grips, it also exercises a force of attraction so captivating that a person willingly surrenders to its power (31–32). Otto described the feeling evoked by the "Wholly Other" as a "creature-feeling" (10), qualitatively different from any "natural" feeling (9), and he considered an encounter with the numinous to be the primordial religious experience.

Jung first started using Otto's term regularly in 1934 (Chapman 1988, 88) and psychologized it as the *numinosum* in his 1937 Terry Lectures on "Psychology and Religion" at Yale University, where he described it as a power capable of changing consciousness in a special way (Jung CW 11 (1962 [1937]):6, 9). In another work, Jung further interpreted Otto's description of the qualitatively unique feeling that an encounter with the Holy engenders as "a peculiar feeling of numinosity" when one is deeply moved (German: *ergriffen*) by the archetypes (Jung CW/GW 18/1 (1961):547).

While Otto theorized a radical opposition between the Holy that grips someone and the individual who is so moved, Jung removed the space between the two, because the archetypes that grip a person with their numinous energy are found in the collective unconscious that is part of the brain structure itself. By appropriating Otto's concept of the numinous, Jung thus psychologized the transcendent. This embodied sacred power makes self-redemption possible, in the way it is understood in analytical psychology – as the process of individuation.

The embodied power of the Holy is that which Jung in effect claimed he experienced during his "encounter with the unconscious," which he then integrated into his consciousness. He then used his own experience to formulate a new theory of psychology, through which he transmitted what he believed to be the original religious experience to a scientifically minded modern world.

Even before his break with Freud, Jung had begun formulating his later theory that the numinous archetypes have both a revelatory and creative character (McGuire 1974, 243J). In his 1925 seminar on analytical psychology, Jung expressed his belief that such a revelation was necessary, as traditional Christian symbolism no longer moved modern people. Deploying the Romantic theory of the *Volksgeist*, Jung explained to his audience that Eastern religious ideas such as the ancient Indian Atman and the Chinese Tao were originally revelations that "grew out of" the peoples among whom they appeared. However, these ideas were foreign to European culture and had become mere concepts, having lost their revelatory power. He thus derided the Theosophists for trying to create a living religion out of them (Jung 1989, 79). What was needed, Jung argued, was a revelatory experience that "has an ancient character" while also "in and of our own being" (80). He said:

> So our way has to be one where the creative character is present, where there is a process of growth which has the quality of revelation. Analysis should release an experience that grips us or falls upon us as from above, an experience that has substance and body, such as those things [*sic*] occurred to the ancients. If I were to symbolize it, I would choose the Annunciation.
>
> (Jung 1989, 80)

With these words, Jung invoked the Christian legend of the Archangel Gabriel's proclamation to Mary that she would be inseminated by the Holy Spirit and give birth to the future redeemer of humanity. Jung thus advocated nothing less than the manifestation of a redeemer; yet following the lines of his psychological theory, this redemptive entity was an instinctive religious factor to be discovered in the depths of one's own soul. The proclamation was not to be a message from God delivered by an angel, but, rather, an archetypal image arising from the collective unconscious in a dream or vision of an individual person. The redeemer was not a figure outside of oneself to whom one owed allegiance, but would instead be one's own redemptive power born out of the womb of one's unconscious.

To effect the desired revelation, Jung strove to awaken such experiences in his patients, as he explained in a letter to his student Oskar A. H. Schmitz (1873–1931), dated May 26, 1923. In this text, Jung considered the problem of the split Germanic psyche, which he believed to be comprised of a primitive and a civilized aspect. He proposed that the means for closing the fissure would arise from a conflict between the two portions of the psyche. Such a conflict would recapitulate the original encounter with God to which the early texts of Christianity bore witness. "We need some new foundations," he wrote, which would be "a new experience of God" (Jung 1973, 1:40). Jung explained to Schmitz that such an encounter would be both difficult and painful, and he considered it his duty to his students and patients to prepare them for just such an experience (ibid.).

This letter indicates that Jung believed that deep in the most primitive level of the mind lay a power that could create a new spiritual orientation. In line with Christian claims, this power appears to be universal. Yet, Jung's letter also indicates that this power could bring forth something tremendous specifically in the Germanic psyche. Through his psychotherapeutic practice, what Jung hoped to create in his patients of Germanic descent was nothing less than a reiteration of the original religious experience that gave birth to Christianity – and to analytical psychology.

Doctor or master? Four case studies

Jung's letter to Schmitz suggests that Jung might have considered his role as a doctor to include that of a spiritual director of sorts. Hence, the discussion now returns to Wach's theory on the master-disciple relationship to see how it might help us understand Jung's patients. Wach explains that the esoteric knowledge the master conveys to the disciple is dependent upon *kairos*, a Greek philosophical term that means the right or opportune time; for Wach, it signifies that the disciple "is awake in the decisive hour" (Wach 1988, 6). In a biblical sense, *kairos* indicates that the moment at hand is one divinely ordained (Mark 1:15). Thus, Wach's use of the term implies that a divine power plays a determining role in the interaction between masters and disciples (Wach 1988, 5–6).

The meaning of *kairos* as defined by Wach has affinities with Jung's explanation that the curative powers of the unconscious function only when the patient is ready to be healed – the doctor simply helps prepare the ground so that the unconscious may produce the reconciling symbol of an indwelling transcendent power that can resolve a neurotic conflict. In fact, the term *kairos* had been used by existential therapists to describe this very process (Ellenberger 1970, 21).

Jung's case studies also exemplify this process of *kairos*. For example, Jung once had a patient who could not separate herself psychologically from her father and thus failed to find a suitable mate. During the transference process, she projected her longings for both father and lover onto the doctor, Jung. In Jungian terminology, projection indicates the alienation and transference of one's own psychic content onto a person or object outside of oneself (Jung 1921, 657). In this case, the patient's dreams indicated to Jung that the projected contents were of a very curious nature. After the therapy had reached a stalemate, Jung decided to take a "wait and see" attitude, trusting that the patient's unconscious would find a solution. She then dreamt of a wind sweeping over a field, while a godlike father-figure rocked the child-patient in his arms. A Freudian-trained psychoanalyst might have focused on the father-figure, and interpreted the psychological complex as involving an unresolved infantile-sexual fixation on the father (as in the case of Fräulein von R; Lear 2005, 66–67). What caught Jung's attention, however, was the wind, an impersonal and pervasive force. Jung named this wind "Wotan" (Jung CW 7 (1943 [1928]):218).

Jung argued that the divine image in the dream symbolized an archaic image of God as wind and spirit, hence revealing a "longing for a god" and "a *passion* welling up from our darkest, instinctual nature" (Jung CW 7 (1963 [1928]):214; emphasis in original) that had somehow been cast into the collective unconscious in the fifteenth century. (Jung failed to explain how this was done.) This refers to the Renaissance and the resurgence of interest in ancient Greek and Roman literature, which Jung elsewhere claimed led to the "great schism" in Christianity known as the Protestant Reformation (Jung 1936, 171). Because the collective image of the divine had been made unconscious, wrote Jung, the longing for an impersonal divinity got shifted onto the personal, human realm. In the psychic life of the patient in question, her unconscious "religious attitude" expressed itself through the inflated images of esteemed persons in her personal life.

Jung suggested that this patient's unconscious spiritual love had become intertwined with her love for her father and with her sexuality. This condition led her to inflate her father and undervalue potential male partners. The presence of what was for Jung an underlying archetypal image – that is, Spirit – indicated to him that the patient's psychic energy was searching for a solution to her psychological problem that could not be met with means at the disposal of her conscious mind. As the images of an impersonal primordial divine force became more dominant in the woman's dreams, her psyche was able to disentangle her loves; the archaic divine image provided her the outlet she needed for her spiritual love, ending her father complex and opening the way for her to find a suitable mate.

In this published example, Jung presented himself as a humble doctor witnessing the autonomous power of the unconscious, which is the active agent that produces the healing moment of *kairos*. Yet private statements indicate that Jung understood his own role to be much more active and co-creative with the unconscious. For example, Tina Keller, the wife of the pastor Adolf Keller, began therapy with Jung in 1915. Jung encouraged Keller to "go your own way," to follow her own path to individuation. With her therapist's support, Keller moved beyond her heretofore roles of pastor's wife and mother by studying medicine and becoming an analyst (Bair 2003, 735, n. 33). At the same time, Jung also presented the process of individuation to Keller in ways that bears strong similarities to his explanation of analysis-as-Annunciation in his 1925 private seminar. Jung described Keller's transference process as if she were in love, not with the doctor per se, but with an archetypal image that he represented. If she were to recognize this same force within herself, she could release her attachment to Jung. He in his turn – in Keller's words – "owed me some spiritual value that would fertilize my psyche and my 'individuation' would be a 'spiritual child'" (as quoted in Noll 1997a, 179–180). Hence, in private treatment, Jung was not only a doctor providing feedback and support to a patient, but also a spiritual master, metaphorically inseminating at least his female patients, so that they could give birth to their own psychic redemption.

Jung's reinterpretation of the Christian myth as psychotherapeutic practice is even more pronounced in the notebooks of Jung's American patient, Fanny Bowditch Katz (1874–1967), a cousin of the American neurologist James Jackson Putnam (1846–1918) of Harvard Medical School. Putnam sent Bowditch Katz to Switzerland for treatment after she began having suicidal thoughts following her father's death (Noll 1997a, 167). She had treatment with Jung from 1912 to 1913, during which time Jung broke with Freud and had his vision of deification. Her notebooks reflect a switch in emphasis in the seminars offered by Jung's Society for Psychological Endeavors from lectures in 1912 on psycho-analysis, with examples drawn from word association tests and case studies, to discussions of alchemy in 1913, which Jung believed to contain the secret of rebirth (171).

Bowditch Katz seems to have understood analytical psychology as the path to a spiritually grounded self-autonomy. In a notebook entry from July 1, 1916, she wrote that one must learn to live by Christ's example. Following the Jungian interpretation of the Nietzschean-inspired *imitatio Christi* previously described, she wrote that, like Christ, one must live according to one's own inner guidance; by doing so, one becomes in effect equivalent to Christ (Noll 1997a, 186; Shamdasani 1998, 58). Bowditch Katz further reported a fantasy of Christ as the mediating element between the human and the divine, combining both in one person. Like Jung's "encounter with the unconscious" that revealed his personal myth, which he then illustrated (i.e. the *Red Book*), this fantasy became the foundation of her own Bible and personal religion (Shamdasani 1998, 62). These statements of Bowditch Katz reflect the Nietzschean-inspired form of self-redemption promised by analytical psychology.

Not all students of Jung experienced their analysis as a form of personal spirituality, and a statement by Jung's patient Harold Fowler McCormick (1872–1941) demonstrates the possible range of interpretations available to someone in treatment, based on her or his individual needs. Harold Fowler McCormick was the head of the company International Harvester and the husband to Edith Rockefeller McCormick (1872–1932), daughter of John D. Rockefeller (1839–1937). Edith was active in Chicago's upper-class social world until the death of one of her children. Her health suffered both mentally and physically from this personal loss, and on the advice of Harold's cousin, she sought treatment from Jung in Zurich beginning in 1913, with the family more or less in tow (Noll 1997a, 202–204, 207). Although Harold appeared to have been relatively mentally well-adjusted, he and two of the children also began therapy with Jung. The outbreak of World War I kept the family in Zurich and in treatment for several more years. The length of the stay, as well as the new ideas being expressed in their letters to the Baptist John D. Rockefeller, alarmed the older man. Harold attempted to allay his relative's fears by explaining what analytical psychology was in a letter dated October 31, 1915. His explanation indicates a tension between science and religion in Jung's psychology. He wrote:

> I have a simple little thought that "analysis" is good for everyone but necessary (in the sense of *helpful*) in proportion as one is not at one with himself. This last is mostly emphasized among those who are very *neurotic.* For a businessman it is *good*; for the poor tired soul, worn out by mental struggle with the world or himself, it is more needed.
>
> To me [analytical psychology] has two general aspects, one a scientific aspect: that is the knowledge and observance of certain laws of life, of human nature, etc.; and the other is metaphysical or spiritual . . . In the case of the tired soul the "religious attitude" – entirely different in precept from "religion" but of the same character, would appeal the more strongly . . . The whole work itself is the development of an *attitude* towards life and things, and this attitude when *found* directs one's daily life in almost everything . . .
>
> (as quoted in Noll 1997a, 219–220; emphasis in original)

One could speculate that the businessman Harold found analysis "good," in contrast to the agoraphobic Edith and the suicidal Bowditch Katz, both of whom had difficulties coping with their grief after the death of beloved ones. In their cases, the development of a "religious attitude" may have been necessary for them to regain basic functionality in their lives.

Yet another "patient" of Jung in dire need of a new "religious attitude" was modernity itself, and when discussing this case, Jung used the word *kairos*. For example, in *The Undiscovered Self* (*Gegenwart und Zukunft*, 1957), Jung brought together his roles of doctor, social critic, and spiritual master to analyze modern society as a patient, undergoing psychic dissolution. Jung described the twentieth century as a "'shape-shifting of the gods'" and interpreted modern art as a "symptom and symbol of a mood of universal destruction and renewal" (Jung CW 10 (1958 [1957]):585). Would this crisis lead to mass psychosis or to collective psycho-spiritual rebirth? As will be seen in Chapter 6, Jung's belief in his own prophetic powers to see the "true nature of reality" behind historical appearances led Jung to announce Nazi Germany as yet another moment of *kairos*, in both the tragic and biblical sense of the word.

The crisis of modernity and the need for a new revelation

By turning our gaze away from the person of Jung and towards the historical context in which he lived and worked, we see that other scientists of his time tried to restore a sense of wholeness and ultimate meaning to a world that many contemporaries experienced as fragmented and senseless. These thinkers were also sometimes portrayed as masters, whose works pointed beyond the disenchantment of society to a reenchantment of the world. This context opens up a much broader arena of research, which is the liminal (in-between) space between science and spirituality that not only Jung but other scientists and scholars of his day intentionally occupied. In this expanded view, Jung becomes less an exemplar and more of an example of a wide-ranging phenomenon in the broader German cultural realm in the decades before and after 1900, when masters and their disciples dominated several fields of human endeavor, from art, music and literature, to religion and spirituality, to psychology and science.

The era in which Jung came of age was marked by widespread cultural pessimism caused by the forces of modernity, including industrialization, urbanization, and the formation of mass society (Krech 2002, 49). Many European and specifically German intellectuals and artists reacted to the rapid social changes as if to a trauma. The rise of modern capitalism stimulated an insatiable hunger for new goods, while the norms of the rising middle class led to a stultifying conventionality. Industrial work was geared toward material production, stifling creativity, the instinctual drives, and aesthetic impulses. Max Weber expressed the anguish felt by many of his contemporaries when he wrote that the capitalist system "determine[s] the lives of all the individuals who are born into this mechanism, not only those directly concerned with economic acquisition, with irresistible force." In his view, modern capitalist society had become an "iron cage" (Weber 1992, 181). Jung added his voice to the general lament against modern, urbanized society in *New Paths in Psychology* (1912), in which he stated that modern people had lost their sense of meaning in work, their joy in procreation, and their faith in religion. Rather than directing his complaint towards the exploitation of workers, however, Jung demonstrated his romantic, anti-modern, and somewhat *völkisch* orientation by valorizing the presumed natural mode of production of male peasants, whom Jung imagined as happy lords of their world, living and working in harmony with nature, and celebrating the bountiful fertility of their wives (Jung CW 7 (1912):281–282).

The widespread feeling of crisis in European culture was exacerbated by the growth of natural science, which had undermined belief in traditional Christian faith (Ulbricht 2001, 10) without replacing the lost sense of transcendental meaning with a new one. Instead, science proffered a welter of bewildering and competing truth claims. During the late nineteenth century, the vogue in science was positivism, the belief in the supremacy of knowledge through the sense perceptions and a disregard for religious faith and subjective experience. By the time Jung began working at the Burghölzli Clinic, however, the reductionistic and mechanistic perspectives in science had come under attack from several quarters by people who instead advocated a holistic orientation (Harrington 1996, xvi). They denounced the one-sided emphasis on reason for its tendency to split human experience in two, while draining life of its aesthetic and emotional values (e.g. Bovet 1907, 3, 5). Science had been championed as both the means and the end of progress; but people started questioning the results of such "progress" that had fragmented society and that, with its competing truth claims, had undermined the greater meaning and sense of orientation once provided by religion (Ulbricht 2001, 15). The "hunger for wholeness" (*Hunger nach Ganzheit*) experienced by many contemporaries in a fragmented modern world increased during the Weimar era, with its class conflicts, political crises, and a humiliated Germany, the denizens of which clamored for a collective renewal (14; Harrington 1996, xx).

Modern science was not the only factor stimulating a crisis in traditional religious faith. Since the time of the Reformation, the educated German classes had been trained in a style of education heavily influenced by Christianity and classical Greek and Roman ideas. Under the ongoing processes of modernization, the religious impulse of the Protestant educated middle classes shifted out of the church to arenas originally considered mundane, including the nation, the family, work, and culture. Art, music and literature became arenas for religious expression, as did daily life and even the inner world of subjective emotions and experiences (Krech 2002, 12–13).

Jung remarked on these new religious phenomena in "Yoga and the West" (1936), in which he noted that the inward focus of Protestantism had undermined the belief in the Church as the source of salvation, which left individuals to find redemption elsewhere. Since the late 1800s, there had been a blossoming of new religious movements in Europe, most of the members of which were originally Protestant. Hence, wrote Jung, these various movements were, in effect, "Protestant sects" (Jung 1936, 172).

This new "bourgeois religiosity" (L. Hölscher, in Krech 2002, 11) revealed a split between objective religion (i.e. dogma, ritual, creed, and clerical authority) and its subjective experience. This split reflected the move away from institutionalized religion and towards the individualization of religious experience (Krech 2002, 9–13). Many theologians and intellectuals, both within and outside the church, began to articulate what the historian Thomas Nipperdey called a "religious mood" (*Gestimmtheit*), or a "'wandering' religiosity" (*'vagierende' Religiosität*), which expressed a religious impulse based on the feeling of an inner need, one that could no longer be satisfied by traditional religious forms (Nipperdey 2003, 143). The German philosopher and sociologist George Simmel (1858–1918) described this phenomenon as a "religious need or impulse" (*religiöses Bedürfnis*), in which one's own life-energy became a source of religiosity (Krech 2002, 51). Weber analyzed this new religiosity as the religion of intellectuals, who seek redemption not from material want that less-privileged social classes suffer from, but from an inner need generated by the disenchantment of the world caused by the intellectuals' rationalization of it (Weber 2001, 273). Jung psychologized the new religious impulse of the intellectuals and their veneration of their own life force as psychic energy that appears in mystical symbolism as the inner sun (Jung 1912, 86–87).

Thus, "salvation" and "redemption" became inner-worldly affairs, in which the religious gaze was turned from an imagined transcendent afterworld and refocused on earthly and corporeal existence (Krech 2002, 50). Stripped of the need for God's grace, humans – at least the educated bourgeoisie – came to be their own redeemers (Ulbricht 2001, 27). For example, Diederichs, who published many of the mythological and spiritual works Jung read, declared in 1892 that self-redemption was the new religion (23). Almost twenty years later, people were still forging paths to self-redemption, such as Fahrenkrog, who declared, "I proclaim to you self-redemption" (*Ich künde Euch die Selbsterlösung*) (27).

This new culture of spiritual seekers gave rise to a host of new movements, both international and national in scope. Movements with a more international reach included the monistic religion of the zoologist Ernst Haeckel (1834–1919) from the 1860s; Theosophy, founded by Helena Blavatsky (1831–1891) in 1875; Anthroposophy, by Rudolph Steiner (1861–1925) in 1912; and the life reform movement, characterized by nudism, vegetarianism, natural medicine, and rural communes, geared towards a general spiritual and cultural renewal (Schnurbein 1992, 239–42; Nipperdey 2003, 144–146). This inward-oriented, subjective form of spirituality was by no means limited to the German-language realm; indeed, British middle-class society between the wars developed what the scholar of religion Steven Sutcliffe refers to as "quest culture" (Sutcliffe 2007, 51ff.).

One group that attracted international attention was the Society for Free Philosophy (*Gesellschaft für freie Philosophie*), founded in Darmstadt, Germany in 1919 by Hermann Keyserling (1880–1946), a Russian-German aristocrat with family connections to Chancellor Bismarck. With the financial support of Ernst Ludwig (1868–1937), the Grand Duke of Darmstadt, Keyserling established the School of Wisdom *(Schule der Weisheit)* the following year, with a newsletter called *The Way to Completion* (*Der Weg zur Vollendung*). The School of Wisdom attracted many significant thinkers to its yearly week-long conferences, including the novelist Thomas Mann (1875–1955), philosopher Leopold Ziegler (1881–1958), cultural historian Oswald Spengler (1880–1936), Indian poet Rabindranath Tagore (1861–1941), and rabbi Leo Baeck (1873–1956), as well as hundreds of spiritual seekers, hungry for guidance as to how they might find within themselves their own individual "path to completion." The School aimed to create spiritually elite individuals who would forge new intellectual and moral values for the rest of society (Stephenson 1981; Landau 1964, 16–24). Keyserling believed that Jung's psychology could contribute significantly to the School's goals, and in a letter to Jung dated January 19, 1923, Keyserling's associate Oskar A.H. Schmitz explained that Jung's *Psychological Types* was used as a standard work at the School of Wisdom (ETH Hs 1056:64).

German-specific new religious groups included Fahrenkrog's League for the Culture of Personality (*Bund für Persönlichkeitskultur*) in 1908; Hauer's German Faith Movement, which lasted from 1933 to 1936; and a host of other *völkisch* and German Faith movements. Self-redemption was also interpreted as a specifically Germanic form of spirituality. For example, Fahrenkrog expanded his call for self-redemption through the Germanic-German Religious Community (*Germanische-deutsche Religionsgemeinschaft*), which he founded in 1912 (and later renamed the Germanic Faith Community, or *Germanische Glaubensgemeinschaft*). The goal of this association was to "lead the Germanic peoples to themselves" (*den Germanen zu sich selbst zu führen*) (Schnurbein 1996, 179).

As the example of Fahrenkrog shows, the notion of self-redemption became intertwined with Germanic and "Aryan" ideology in a time of deepening cultural pessimism, German nationalism, and growing anti-Semitism. According to this ideology, the "Aryans," Germanic peoples and, in particular, the Germans had a special religious sensibility. Believers in the Aryan Christ, adherents of the Erotic, worshippers of Wotan, and ecstatic seekers of the state of *Ergriffenheit* suggested that the deep, inward religiosity of the Germanic (Teutonic or Aryan) peoples proved that they had a divine mission in the world: to overcome themselves again and again in order to achieve ever higher spiritual states, justifying their aspirations to cultural and political world domination. This central idea was proclaimed by authors as seemingly disparate as the popular Wagnerian propagandist and racist theorist Houston Stewart Chamberlain writing on a Protestant-oriented Germanic spirituality (Chamberlain 1977, 1:512), the vitalist philosopher and Cosmic Circle member Ludwig Klages on the ancient Greek Eros (Klages 1981, 64, 67), the classical philologist Martin Ninck on *Wodan* (Wotan) (Ninck 1935, 190–191, 307), and Hauer on Indo-Germanic mystics (Hauer 1934, 181–182) and Vedic Indians (Hauer 1937, 29). The distance between their particular fields of endeavor and the religions involved indicate how widespread the belief in the basic claim of the Germanic-"Aryan" religious sensibility was in the decades before and after 1900. These four authors also appear in Jung's "Wotan" essay (see Chapter 6), suggesting that the underlying myth of that work is that of Germanic-"Aryan" spirituality, and that, conversely, the Germanic-"Aryan" myth has significant affinities with the Nietzschean-inspired spirituality of self-redemption.

These various religious and life-reform movements reflected the widespread cultural pessimism in Germany (Krech 2002, 49) and their members called for a collective spiritual rebirth due to their fear that European culture was dying (Ulbricht 2001, 15–16). Many people imagined Europe standing tensely on a threshold between one epoch passing away and another still waiting to be born (31). This tension gave birth to the Helvetica Society in 1907, which began publishing the journal *Knowledge and Life* (*Wissen und Leben;* later, *Die Neue Schweizer Rundschau*), for which Jung was later to pen his "Wotan" essay. In the inaugural issue, the editor Emil Bovet described the feeling among many of his associates that a kind of fermentation was in process, which was building up to a crisis and would create a new form of culture. The mood of the era indicated a "*general expectation of a great transformation*" (*allgemeine Erwartung einer grossen Wandlung*) (Bovet 1907, 2; emphasis in original). This feeling evoked both the longing for and fear of another explosive movement on par with the French Revolution (1). Reflecting the contemporaneous culture of personality (Krech 2002, 49), the journal's goal was to help locate and develop "personalities" (*Individualitäten*) who could stand above the masses and lead the way to a new age (Bovet 1907, 1).

To create "personalities" above the nameless masses of modern society, many people gathered around individuals they viewed as having already achieved this sought-after state. Indeed, masters and their disciples covered the cultural landscape from the late nineteenth to the early twentieth centuries. Poets, artists, writers and philosophers in particular were viewed as filled with charisma and having the deep spiritual vision of a prophet (Ulbricht 1997, 168; Mosse 1964, 209). For example, the operatic composer Richard Wagner claimed that the great spiritual insight of the artist-musician enabled him to speak for the *Volk* and initiate a collective renewal (Châtellier 1996, 588). The German poet Stefan George (1868–1933) developed a small elite all-male group based on aristocratic principles that stood against the mass society it despised and whose destruction it advocated (Norton 2002, x, 494). The realm of science, too, had its masters of both intellectual and spiritual profundity: although the colleagues of the Swiss neuroanatomist Constantin von Monakow (1853–1930) considered him a brilliant scientist, the writer Marie Waser portrayed him in *Encounter in the Evening: A Legacy* as a prophet proclaiming the divinity that he found in each cell of the human body (Harrington 1996, 72).

The desire for a master who could bring about the longed-for cultural renewal only increased after Germany's defeat in World War I. Jung psychologized this longing in a lecture he held at the Society for Psychical Research in 1919, called "The Psychological Foundations of Belief in Spirits." Reiterating the view he espoused a year earlier in "The Role of the Unconscious," Jung explained to his audience that what so-called primitives call "spirits" are collective complexes, which may "seek to replace the inadequate attitude of a whole people by a new one." These contents may be either "pathological fantasies or new but as yet unknown ideas" (Jung CW 8 (1965 [1919]):597). These collective complexes can influence whole populations when the collective psychological attitude no longer functions and a new one is needed. As this shift takes place, individuals may feel disoriented and the group as a whole may appear to be in a state of collective psychosis. This may be followed by the appearance of a healing presence, such as a strongly intuitive individual who is capable of articulating the new psychological attitude in such a way that it takes hold and spreads quickly throughout the population (para. 594–595). Jung illustrated his theory through a religious example: the story of the Pentecostal Miracle. Christ's apostles had been gripped by the Holy Spirit, and their strange behavior led outsiders to claim they were drunk. Despite their skepticism, Christ's message spread quickly, becoming the new collective psychological orientation of the West (para. 596). Holding this lecture in the shadow of World War I, Jung expressed a longing shared by many of his contemporaries for a leader who would initiate a collective spiritual renewal they believed the Germans desperately needed after their crushing defeat. Jung was to repeat these ideas seventeen years later in "Wotan."

The bridge between science and religion

The longing for wholeness led many artists and scholars to attempt to bridge science and knowledge with religion and "life" in a larger spiritual sense. For example, the Austrian writer and playwright Hermann Bahr (1863–1934) asserted in his 1890 manifesto *Modernity* (*Die Moderne*) that the way to renew society was to reconnect science with art and religion, for they were three aspects of one whole (Ulbricht 2001, 13). Avant-garde artists found their own way to unify all three spheres, combining new discoveries such as the x-ray with the Romantic and occult belief that artists were capable of peering beyond surfaces to an inner reality (Bauduin 2012). Jung's student Oskar Schmitz celebrated Goethe as the exemplar of the total man, combining science, art and spirituality in his work and life. He further advocated Jung's theory of psychological types and the individuation process as the path to creating a Goethe-like "complete person" (*Vollmensch*) (Schmitz 1928/29, 21–22).

Although some prominent scholars, such as Weber, rejected the idea that science could provide a kind of *Weltanschauung* (Weber 2004, 282–283), other scientists, especially in biology and psychology, clamored to overcome what the historian Anne Harrington calls "Machine society" (Harrington 1996, xv–xvi, Pietikäinen 2008, 605), where efficiency and technology were key, but which rendered human life meaningless (see quote by Wolfgang Köhler, Harrington 1996, 103). These scientists hoped to restore a sense of higher purpose and meaning to life, secured by the authority of science. For example, Monakow developed the concept of the *horme*, by which the organism was said to regulate and balance itself through compensation, and which contained an inherited memory. This theory posited a purposeful connection between the individual being and the whole of nature (88–91; Shamdasani 2003, 269). In the field of psychology, Felix Krueger (1874–1948), head of the Leipzig school of wholeness psychology (*Ganzheitspsychologie*), theorized an unconscious "structure" (a technical term of his psychology) that was teleologically oriented towards the production of wholeness and meaning (Pietikäinen 2007, 117–118). Max Wertheimer (1880–1943) developed the theory of *Gestalt,* an ordering principle working towards wholeness (Harrington 1996, 117).

Similar themes of wholeness are a hallmark of Jungian psychology. Indeed, Jung believed psychology – at least his version of it – was the arena of human endeavor most suitable for bridging both the split between science and religion and the fragmentation of the sciences (Shamdasani 2003, 2, 18, 22). Furthermore, Jung's concept of the archetypes shares affinities with the theories of *Gestalt* and *Ganzheitspsychologie*, in that archetypes ideally structure and guide the flow of psychic energy towards psychological wholeness (Jung CW 7 (1960 [1943]):186; Pietikäinen 2007, 118). In contrast, Jung denounced Freud's psychology as a product of Enlightenment rationalism and late nineteenth-century materialism, which rejected religion and the irrational side of life (Grossman 1999, 103). Jung's own anti-materialism and vitalism (Pietikäinen 2007, 103–104) are evident in his statement to his students in his 1925 analytical psychology seminar: "We seek life, not efficiency," he told them, "and this seeking of ours is directly against the collective ideals of our times" (Jung 1989, 68; cf. Shamdasani 2003, 222, 249). For his efforts, Jung was awarded the literature prize of Zurich in 1932 in recognition of his struggle against a "'psychology without a soul'" and the "one-sided" views of Freudian psychoanalysis (Ellenberger 1970, 674–675). (Ironically, this same year Freud was awarded the Goethe prize of Frankfurt for his contribution to psychology and German literary culture, 456.)

The picture of wholeness as imagined by many artists and intellectuals in Jung's era was hardly seamless, but was rife with the fissures of racial and religious exclusivism. Race had become a dominant category of thought in the nineteenth century: it was used to explain everything from the psychology of nations, to historical movements, to individual mores, and to spiritual evolution. Both science and spirituality were permeated by racial discourse around the turn of the last century, resulting in racial science on the one hand, and racial mysticism on the other (Mosse 1978, Chapters 6 and 7). In science, a subjective aesthetic judgment based on ancient Greek ideals and Tacitus' blonde-haired, blue-eyed Germanic stereotype became the spurious evidence many scientists used to argue that white people's physical appearance reflected an inner predisposition towards work, honesty, self-reliance, and freedom – that is, towards typically middle-class values (Mosse 1978, 48, 86). In contrast, the skin color and skull shape of blacks – often highly distorted in illustrations – allegedly proved that these people were lazy and animalistic, predestined to be slaves (68, 82), while the stereotyped large nose of the "Jew" betrayed the crookedness of his thoughts and mores (29, 30).

Scientific theories of race were often embraced by founders of new religious movements, such as by Blavatsky, the founder of Theosophy. Blavatsky's holistic thinking is evident in the title of her book, *The Secret Doctrine: The Synthesis of Science, Religion, and Philosophy* (1888). She emphasized the unity, love and beauty of all people, and called for brotherhood among all nations as part of a cosmic plan of evolution (Schnurbein 1992, 84). She also believed all religions revealed at least some of the "Divine Wisdom" (Santucci 2005, 1114). Combining ancient occult and modern Darwinistic thought, Blavatsky also claimed that souls evolve via reincarnation from the level of the ape through a racially stratified humanity to a suprahuman level. She theorized five different "root races," with the "Aryan" as the top race. This theory made room for speculation among followers about belonging to a racially defined "chosen people" (Schnurbein 1992, 84). This race was the one at the other end of the hierarchical ladder than those colonized non-Europeans Blavatsky referred to as "the lower races of men, now represented on earth by a few miserable dying-out tribes and the huge anthropoid apes" (Blavatsky 2011, 2:375).

Theosophical thought was extremely popular in the early twentieth century, especially in the German-speaking countries. Aspects of its teachings were combined with occult speculations and *völkisch* ideology in the mystical visions of "Aryan"-supremacist Guido von List (1848–1919). Embracing theosophy's pantheism but rejecting its universal brotherhood, List instead proposed that all great cultures of the "Aryans" descended from the *Germanen* (Schnurbein 1992, 140). In 1902, List suffered a period of temporary blindness, during which he developed an esoteric interpretation of the runes based on what he called "inherited memories" (*Erberinnerungen*). Even the racial mystic List paid tribute to science: a year later, he attempted to publish his ideas with the Imperial Academy of Sciences in Vienna (and his esoteric work was duly rejected) (88).

The marriage of science and religion in Jung's analytical psychology

Given this cultural backdrop, the seemingly vague contours of Jung's position in between science and spirituality take on sharper outlines. It was precisely because Jung was able to find a way to bridge science and spirituality through self-redemption that he came to be respected and even revered by so many of his contemporaries. Jung articulated in an extremely learned and evocative way the longings of many people of his era for a new source of ultimate meaning, appealing especially to those people who considered themselves rational and agnostic, yet who felt a lack of higher purpose and needed a "religious attitude" to lend meaning to their lives (Jung CW 11 (1948 [1932]):509).

Intellectuals such as Jung who sought to bridge science and religion found a model in the works of contemporaneous scholars in the academic study of religion (*Religionswissenschaft*), who sought to validate religion as such through what they considered to be a scientific method. Many early twentieth-century scholars defined "religion" based on the Enlightenment belief in a universal religion and the Romantic claim that humans had a natural aptitude for religion. In Germany, these views were further shaped by liberal theology and cultural Protestantism (Kubota 2005, 10–12). The historians of religions Hiroshi Kubota and Horst Junginger have argued that scholars such as Otto, Wach, Söderblom and Hauer sought to demonstrate the possibility of a new scientifically based dimension of religion – "religion" as already understood and informed by science. Kubota calls this a *religionswissenschaftliche Religiosität,* which he defines as a "religiously marked intellectuality" (*religiös geprägte Geistigkeit*) and a "religious-minded attitude" (*religiös-geistige Haltung*) that resulted from the "'scientific' [. . .] reflection on religion" (*'wissenschaftlichen' [. . .] Reflexion über Religion*) informed by Enlightenment, Romantic, and liberal Protestant ideas (10–14, quote on 14). This "theological study of religions," as Junginger calls it, was criticized both by the Church and by other scholars: the former saw it as not Christian enough; the latter, insufficiently scientific (Junginger 2008, 9). Jung's understanding of religion was not only shaped by two of these scholars, Otto and Söderblom; he also shared their "religious-minded attitude" and the Western and Protestant cultural assumptions that underlay their definition of religion as such. Moreover, Hauer was one of the first scholars in Germany to use Jungian theory after Jung's split with Freud. A specialist in ancient Indian religions, Hauer found Jung's theory comparable with Indian yogic practices (Dierks 1986, 83).

Jung converted many of the religious terms and concepts he found in his readings on comparative religion into psychological ones, in order to make them acceptable to a rationally minded society. In 1917, Jung explained that religious symbols were, in effect, projected forms of the archetypes, objectified or concretized as divine figures. Religious symbolism performed the essential psychological role of channeling psychic energy from the unconscious to consciousness, turning it into a valuable resource for creative purposes. In the modern rational age, this process was blocked, because people had rejected traditional religion and its symbol systems. However, these powerful forms of psychological adaptation could be made accessible to modern people by explaining them in scientific terms that met the needs and expectations of a rationalized society. Jung wrote:

> If . . . we apprehend the images of the unconscious as collective unconscious dominants, therefore as collective-psychological phenomena or functions, this hypothesis is in no way opposed to our intellect and conscience. This solution is rationally acceptable.
>
> (Jung 1917, 436)

In other words, Jung translated religious concepts and experiences into the terminology of psychological discourse, including his own self-described encounter with the numinous power of the archetypes. He thereby answered the need of and became the spokesman for multitudes of people in the modern West who longed to find a way to bridge the gap between science and religion in order to create a new holism out of the splinters of modern society.

Jung's patients were predominantly Protestant (with a minority being either Jewish or Catholic) and in the second half of their life. Furthermore, they considered themselves to be both intellectual and indifferent to the traditional religions in which they had been raised (Jung CW 7 (1963 [1928]):206, 218; Jung CW 11 (1962 [1937]):51; Jung CW 11 (1928):509). Yet the products of their unconscious often revealed to Jung an unconscious religious attitude, which Jung interpreted as an inherent part of the psyche, and which proved to be a necessary component of their healing process (Jung CW 7 (1963 [1928]):214; Jung CW 11 (1928):509). It was to these people that Jung oriented his message, which was conveyed by students such as Cary F. Baynes (1883–1977). In her preface to Jung's *Modern Man in Search of a Soul* (1934), Baynes explained that many people in the present era believed the world to be standing on the verge of a spiritual rebirth, but were unsure whether the best path to it was to be found through a return to the church or a full embrace of Enlightenment principles. As a solution to this false dilemma, Baynes offered Jung's theory, which represented a middle way between these two extremes. Jung's analytical psychology was thus the right path for those who have "outgrown the Church," but who also believed that "a religious attitude to life is as essential to them as a belief in the authenticity of science" (Baynes 2001 [1933], vii–viii).

Conclusion

Although Jung would have rejected the label of master, this analysis of his (self-) representation by way of Wach's theory of the master-disciple relationship demonstrates a number of close affinities. Jung presented his psychological theory as originating from his own personal encounter with the numinous character of the archetypal powers of the collective unconscious, rather than through systematizing in a new way the knowledge that had been taught to him by his instructors. He portrayed himself as having successfully negotiated the difficult and dangerous path of individuation to discover the god-image embedded within his own psyche, leading to an expanded consciousness and an individuality that distinguished him from the masses of modern society. Jung then translated his experience into psychological terms, in order to universalize it and render it rationally credible.

Wach's theory demands that our gaze be expanded beyond the person of Jung, however, for a master is never master alone, but must be recognized as such by disciples. Jung was able to articulate the longings of modern society for a reintegration of science and spirituality to such a degree that he became widely recognized as the masterly "Wise Old Man of Küsnacht." His insistence that he was a scientist and uninterested in founding his own school in no way counteracted the tendency of his disciples to sanctify him, but rather appears to have furthered it (Samuels 1993, 322–323), as he sought to validate spirituality in a secularized age, and to reenchant life and the human soul in the face of the disenchantment wrought by rationalism. Jung thus became an exemplar of one who traversed the narrow path between science and religion, experiencing within himself their reunification and pointing the way for others to follow.

Jung's psychological theory reflects its era in which many people sought spiritual solutions to the social malaise of modern society and the political catastrophe of World War I, not by returning to traditional forms of Christianity, but by turning inward to the depths of their own souls. Furthermore, his psychology mirrors the notion that spiritual renewal after a downfall was not only possible, but that a Nietzschean "going-under" might actually be an important step towards psychological wholeness. His theory promised individual self-redemption and psycho-spiritual integrity, yet on a higher level of psychic development than that manifested in the average person. Hence, Jung's school of thought also reflects the elitism of the time, in which many people sought out masters and their circles of the elected in the hope that they would lead society out of its stagnation and carry it to new spiritual heights.

The themes outlined here – Jung's role as both master and doctor, and individuation as a form of self-redemption – will be revisited in Chapter 6, in which Jung's "Wotan" essay is analyzed in full. That analysis will demonstrate that Jung played not only the role of doctor to his "patient," Germany, diagnosing the Third Reich as an individuation process *en masse*, but also performed the part of the spiritual master, pronouncing the time to be *kairos*, when the disciple awakens at the fate-ordained moment. The moment of awakening was to be an act of self-redemption on a mass scale – the long-desired spiritual rebirth of the entire German nation. As the aforementioned letter from Jung to Schmitz indicates, Jung took a special interest in the plight of the so-called Germanic psyche long before the rise of the Third Reich. Hence, Jung not only sought to bridge science and religion, but more specifically, racial science and racial mysticism, themes that will be explored in the following chapters.

Bibliography

Title

The phrase, a "far finer and more comprehensive task for psychoanalysis" is from the letter from Carl Gustav Jung to Sigmund Freud, Feb. 11, 1910, in *The Freud/Jung Letters: The Correspondence between Sigmund Freud and C. G. Jung*, ed. by William McGuire (Princeton, NJ: Princeton University Press, 1974), 178J.

Sources

Bair, Deirdre. 2003. *Jung. A Biography*. Boston: Little, Brown and Co.

Bauduin, Tessel M. 2012. "Science, Occultism, and the Art of the Avant-Garde in the Early Twentieth Century." *Journal of Religion in Europe* 5(1):23–55.

Baynes, Cary F. 2001 [1933]. Translator's Preface to *Modern Man in Search of a Soul,* by C. G. Jung, trans. by Cary F. Baynes. Abingdon: Routledge Classics [London: Kegan, Paul, Trench, Trübner & Co.], pp. vii–ix.

Bishop, Paul. 1995. *The Dionysian Self: C. G. Jung's Reception of Friedrich Nietzsche*. Monographien und Texte zur Nietzsche-Forschung 30. Berlin: de Gruyter.

— (ed.). 1999. *Jung in Contexts: A Reader*. London: Routledge.

Blavatsky, Helene. 2011. *The Secret Doctrine: The Synthesis of Science, Religion and Philosophy*. Two Volumes. Cambridge: Cambridge University Press.

Bovet, Emil. 1907. "Unser Ziel". *Wissen und Leben* 1(1):1–7.

Chamberlain, Houston Stewart. 2006. *Foundations of the Nineteenth Century,* trans. by John Lees. Introduction by George L. Mosse. New York: Howard Fertig.

Chapman, J. Harley. 1988. *Jung's Three Theories of Religious Experience*. Lewiston, NY: Edwin Mellen.

Châtellier, Hildegard. 1996. "Wagnerismus in der Kaiserzeit." In Uwe Puschner, Walter Schmitz und Justus H. Ulbricht (eds), *Handbuch zur 'Völkischen Bewegung' 1871–1918*, München: Saur, pp.575–612 .

De Angulo, Cary F. 1989. "Foreword." In Carl Jung, *Analytical Psychology: Notes of the Seminar Given in 1925*, ed. by William McGuire. Princeton, NJ: Princeton University Press.

Dierks, Margarete. 1986. *Jakob Wilhelm Hauer, 1881–1962: Leben, Werk, Wirkung; Mit einer Personalbibliographie*. Heidelberg: L. Schneider.

Ellenberger, Henri. 1970. *The Discovery of the Unconscious: The History and Evolution of Dynamic Psychiatry*. New York: Basic Books.

Freud, Sigmund. 1942. *Die Traumdeutung*. Volume Two/Three, *Gesammelte Werke*, chronologisch geordnet. London: Imago Publishing.

——. 1968. *Future of an Illusion*. Volume 21, The Standard Edition of the Complete Psychological Works of Sigmund Freud. London: Hogarth Press and the Institute of Psycho-analysis.

Grossman, Stanley. 1999. "C. G. Jung and National Socialism." In Paul Bishop (ed.), *Jung in Contexts: A Reader*. London: Routledge, pp.92–121.

Hanegraaff, Wouter. 1996. *New Age Religion and Western Culture: Esotericism in the Mirror of Secular Thought*. Leiden: Brill.

Hannah, Barbara. 1982. *C. G. Jung, sein Leben und Werk: biographische Aufzeichnungen*. Fellbach-Oeffingen: Bonz.

Hark, Helmut (ed.). 1988. *Lexikon Jungscher Grundbegriffe: Mit Originaltexten von C. G. Jung*. Olten: Walter.

Harrington, Anne. 1996. *Reenchanted Science: Holism in German Culture from Wilhelm II to Hitler*. Princeton, NJ: Princeton University Press.

Hauer, Jakob Wilhelm. 1934. *Deutsche Gottschau*. Stuttgart: Gutbrod.

——.1937. *Glaubensgeschichte der Indogermanen*. Stuttgart. Kohlhammer.

Hoerni, Ulrich. 2009. "Preface". In Carl Jung *The Red Book: Liber Novus*, ed. by Sonu Shamdasani, trans. by Mark Kyburz, John Peck, and Sonu Shamdasani. New York: W.W. Norton & Co, pp.viii–ix.

Homans, P. 1995. *Jung in Context: Modernity and the Making of a Psychology*. Second Edition. Chicago: University of Chicago Press.

Jung, C. G. 1912. *Wandlungen und Symbole der Libido: Beiträge zur Entwicklungsgeschichte des Denkens*. Leipzig: Franz Deuticke.

——. 1917. *Collected Papers on Analytical Psychology*, ed. by Constance E. Long. London: Baillière, Tindall and Cox.

——. 1921. *Psychologische Typen*. Zurich: Rascher & Cie.

——. 1936. "Yoga and the West." In *Prabuddha Bharata, or Awakened India*. Sri Ramakrishna Centenary Number, pp.170–177. ETH-Bibliothek Zurich (Switzerland): ETH Zurich University Archives, C. G. Jung Papers Collection Cat. No.: Hs 1379:185.

——. 1953–1991. *Collected Works*, ed. by Sir Herbert Read, Michael Fordham, and Gerhard Adler. New York: Pantheon Books; Princeton, NJ: Princeton University Press.

——. 1965. *Memories, Dreams, Reflections*, rec. and ed. by Aniela Jaffé, trans. by Richard and Clara Winston. New York: Vintage.

——. 1971. *Gesammelte Werke*. Olten: Walter.

——. 1972. *Briefe*, ed. by Aniela Jaffé with Gerhard Adler. Three Volumes. Olten: Walter.

——. 1973. *Letters*, sel. and ed. by Gerhard Adler, with Aniela Jaffé, trans. by R. F. C. Hull. Two Volumes. Princeton, NJ: Princeton University Press.

——. 1988. *Nietzsche's Zarathustra: Notes of the Seminar Given in 1934–1939*, ed. by James L. Jarrett. Princeton, NJ: Princeton University Press.

——. 1989. *Analytical Psychology: Notes of the Seminar Given in 1925*, ed. by William McGuire. Princeton, NJ: Princeton University Press.

——. 2009. *The Red Book*, ed. by Sonu Shamdasani, trans. by Mark Kyburz, John Peck, and Sonu Shamdasani. New York: W.W. Norton & Co.

Junginger, Horst. 2008. Introduction to *The Study of Religion under the Impact of Fascism*, ed. by Horst Junginger. Leiden: Brill.

Kippenberg, Hans. 2010. "Joachim Wach between the George Circle and Weber's Typology of Religious Communities." In Christian Wedemeyer and Wendy Doniger (eds), *Hermeneutics, Politics, and the History of Religions: The Contested Legacies of Joachim Wach and Mircea Eliade*, Oxford: Oxford University Press, pp.327–328.

Klages, Ludwig. 1981. *Vom kosmogonischen Eros*. Bonn: Bouvier.

Krech, Volkhard. 2002. *Wissenschaft und Religion: Studien zur Geschichte der Religionsforschung in Deutschland 1871 bis 1933*. Tubingen: Mohr Siebeck.

Kubota, Hiroshi. 2005. *Religionswissenschaftliche Religiosität und Religionsgründung: Jakob Wilhelm Hauer im Kontext des freien Protestantismus*. Frankfurt am Main: Lang.

Landau, Rom. 1964. *God is My Adventure*. London: Unwin Books.

Lear, Jonathan. 2005. *Freud*. Abingdon, Oxon: Routledge.

McGuire, William (ed.). 1974. *The Freud/Jung Letters: The Correspondence between Sigmund Freud and C. G. Jung*. Princeton, NJ: Princeton University Press.

Mosse, George L. 1964. *The Crisis of German Ideology: Intellectual Origins of the Third Reich.* New York: Grosset & Dunlap.

——. 1978. *Toward the Final Solution: A History of European Racism.* New York: Howard Fertig.

Ninck, Martin. 1935. *Wodan und Germanischer Schicksalsglaube.* Jena: Eugen Diederichs.

Nipperdey, Thomas. 2003. *Religion im Umbruch: Deutschland 1870–1918.* Munich: C.H. Beck.

Noll, Richard. 1994. *The Jung Cult: Origins of a Charismatic Movement.* Princeton, NJ: Princeton University Press.

——. 1997a. *The Aryan Christ: The Secret Life of Carl Jung.* New York: Random House.

——. 1999. "Jung the Leontocephalus." In Paul Bishop (ed.), *Jung in Contexts: A Reader.* London: Routledge, pp.51–91.

Norton, Robert. 2002. *Secret Germany: Stefan George and His Circle.* Ithaca, NY: Cornell University Press.

Otto, Rudolph. 1958. *The Idea of the Holy: An Inquiry into the Non-Rational Factor in the Idea of the Divine and its Relation to the Rational*, trans. by John W. Harvey. London: Oxford University Press.

Pietikäinen, Petteri. 2007. *Alchemists of Human Nature: Psychological Utopianism in Gross, Jung, Reich and Fromm.* London: Pickering & Chatto.

Post, Laurens van der. 1975. *Jung and the Story of our Time.* New York: Pantheon.

Samuels, Andrew. 1992. "National Psychology, National Socialism, and Analytical Psychology: Reflections on Jung and Anti-Semitism." *Journal of Analytical Psychology* (37):3–28.

——. 1993. *The Political Psyche.* London: Routledge.

Santucci, James A. 2005. "Theosophical Society." In Wouter J. Hanegraaf and Jean-Pierre Brach (eds), *Dictionary of Gnosis and Western Esotericism*, Leiden: Brill, pp.1114–1123.

Schmitz, Oskar A. H. 1928/29. "Die Psychologie C. G. Jungs." *Der Lesezirkel* 16(2):21–23.

Schnurbein, Stefanie von. 1992. *Religion als Kulturkritik: Neugermanisches Heidentum im 20. Jahrhundert.* Heidelberg: Winter.

——. 1996. "Die Suche nach einer 'arteigenen' Religion in 'germanisch-' und 'deutschgläubigen' Gruppen." In Uwe Puschner, Walter Schmitz und Justus H. Ulbricht (eds), *Handbuch zur 'Völkischen Bewegung' 1871–1918*, Saur: Munich, pp.172–185.

Shamdasani, Sonu. 1998. *Cult Fictions: Jung and the Founding of Analytical Psychology.* London: Routledge.

——. 1999. "Memories, Dreams, Omissions." In Paul Bishop (ed.), *Jung in Contexts: A Reader.* London: Routledge, pp.33–49.

——. 2003. *Jung and the Making of Modern Psychology: The Dream of a Science.* Cambridge, UK: Cambridge University Press.

——. 2005. *Jung Stripped Bare by his Biographers, Even.* London: Karnac.

Stephenson, Gunther. 1981. "Das Lebenswerk Graf Keyserlings aus heutiger Sicht." *Zeitschrift für Religions- und Geistesgeschichte* 33:32–41.

Sutcliffe, Steven. 2007. "The Origins of 'New Age' Religion between the Two World Wars." In Daren Kemp and James R. Lewis (eds), *Handbook of New Age*, Leiden: Brill, pp.51–75.

Ulbricht, Justus H. 1997. "'Veni creator spiritus,' oder 'Wann kehrt Baldur heim? Deutsche Wiedergeburt als völkisch-religiöses Projekt." In Richard Faber (ed.),

Politische Religion - religiöse Politik: *Hubert Cancik zum 60. Geburtstag*. Würzburg: Königshausen & Neumann, pp.161–172.

——. 2001. "' . . . in einer gottfremden, prophetenlosen Zeit . . . :' Aspekte einer Problemgeschichte 'arteigener' Religion um 1900." In Stefanie Schnurbein and Justus H. Ulbricht (eds), *Völkische Religion und Krisen der Moderne*: *Entwürfe 'arteigener' Glaubenssysteme seit der Jahrhundertwende*. Würzburg: Könighsausen & Neumann, pp.9–39.

Wach, Joachim. 1988. "Master and Disciple: Two Religio-Sociological Studies." In Joseph M. Kitagawa and Gregory D. Alles (eds), *Essays in the History of Religions*. New York: MacMillan, pp.1–32.

Weber, Max. 1992. *The Protestant Ethic and the Spirit of Capitalism*, trans. by Talcott Parsons. London: Routledge.

——. 2001. *Wirtschaft und Gesellschaft: Die Wirtschaft und die gesellschaftlichen Ordnungen und Mächte; Nachlaß*, ed. by Hans G. Kippenberg. Tubingen: J.C.B. Mohr (Paul Siebeck).

——. 2004. "The Vocation of Science." In Sam Whimster (ed.), *The Essential Weber*, London: Routledge, pp.270–287.

Archived Materials

Oskar A. H. Schmitz to C. G. Jung, January 19, 1923 (ETH-Bibliothek Zurich (Switzerland), ETH Zurich University Archives, Hs 1056:64).

Oskar A. H. Schmitz to C. G. Jung, December 4, 1926 (ETH-Bibliothek Zurich (Switzerland), ETH Zurich University Archives, Hs 1056:148).

Other Materials

Noll, Richard. 1997b. File name "Shamdasani - Kerr - Princeton University Press correspondence 1992 to 199412042014_0000.pdf." These documents were provided by Noll via email, Dec. 4, 2014, and have since been delivered to the Drs Nicholas and Dorothy Cummings Center for the History of Psychology in Akron, Ohio, where they remain unprocessed. Letter from Sonu Shamdasani to Richard Noll, July 29, 1992. PDF: "Correspondence related to the research and publication of the *The Jung Cult* (1994) and *The Aryan Christ*."

4

THE "PALEONTOLOGY OF THE SOUL"

The concept of primitivity and Jung's theory of the stratified phylogenetic unconscious

The conditionality of the psyche by the earth

On November 19, 1925, Keyserling wrote to Emma Jung about a future conference at his School of Wisdom. He wanted her to persuade her husband to deliver a lecture on "what interests him the most at the time, namely, the geology of the soul, the mneme" (*was ihn zur Zeit am meisten interessiert, nämlich die Geologie der Seele, die Mneme*). Keyserling had borrowed the term *mneme* from the German zoologist Richard Wolfgang Semon (1859–1918), who had theorized that the sensory impressions received by a single organism could create a memory imprint in the nerves, which in turn became inheritable (Shamdasani 2003, 190). More specifically, what Keyserling meant by this word was "the continuation of history in the unconscious" (*das Fortleben der Geschichte im Unbewußten*), that is, Jung's theory of an inherited, multi-layered collective unconscious (ETH Hs 1056:122).

A year later, Keyserling's close associate Oskar A. H. Schmitz, who had begun corresponding with Jung in 1921 (ETH Hs 1056:50), sent Jung a follow-up letter about the upcoming conference in 1927. Schmitz wrote in his letter dated December 4, 1926, that the participants most wanted to hear about what he called Jung's discovery: the phylogenetic unconscious or, in his words, the "paleontology of the soul" (*Paläontologie der Seele*) (ETH Hs 1056:148). Schmitz had heard Jung discuss the concept in 1925 when he attended Jung's private seminar on analytical psychology in Zurich. Although other psychologists had already theorized along similar lines since the turn of the century (see Chapter 5), Jung had claimed to have dreamt of a multi-layered phylogenetic unconscious during his trip to Clark University in 1909 (Jung 1989, 22–23).

Schmitz described Jung's model of the psyche as composed of a vertical axis, which could be explored in analysis, and a horizontal one, evidenced in non-European peoples whom Jung visited in 1925 and who occupied lower rungs of the evolutionary ladder than modern Europeans. The view that non-European peoples represented a lower level of evolutionary development that modern Europeans had transcended reflects the hierarchical and racist colonial discourse used widely in contemporaneous anthropology and the comparative study of religions. The ethnocentric and ideological content of this perspective was apparently lost on Schmitz, however, for he asserted that Jung's model had removed the collective unconscious from the realm of metaphysics by showing it to be a "reality of natural science" (*eine naturwissenschaftliche Wirklichkeit*) (ETH Hs 1056:148).

Keyserling and Schmitz finally had their wish fulfilled when Jung agreed to hold a lecture at the School of Wisdom conference on "Man and Earth" (*Mensch und Erde*), held April 24–30, 1927, in Darmstadt. In his lecture on "The Conditionality of the Psyche by the Earth" (*Die Erdbedingtheit der Psyche*), Jung portrayed the multi-layered psyche as a house with several floors: an upper floor decorated in a nineteenth-century European style; a main floor from the sixteenth century, with masonry taken from an eleventh-century residence tower; a cellar

Figure 4.1 Jung's 1927 model of the phylogenetic unconscious as a multi-storied house. This represents the house as Jung described it in his 1927 lecture "The Earth Conditionality of the Psyche" to the School of Wisdom's "Man and Earth" Conference in Darmstadt, Germany. Illustration by Christiane Strobach,

with a foundational wall from the Roman era; and finally, a cave with an upper chamber containing stone tools and a lower level holding ice-age faunal remains (Jung 1927, 108–109). Modern western children and contemporary adult primitives occupy the spaces below ground; they have virtually no conscious mind and thus a very limited worldview. The perspective of modern adults is broader, because they occupy the upper floor; however, modern people appear to be completely unaware of the totality of the psyche, being split off from the unconscious (109). This split is, according to Jung, characteristic of the modern Westerner, and is a decisive element differentiating this psyche from those of other peoples.

The metaphor of the house demonstrates that the concept of *primitivity* has two different yet related meanings in Jung's psychology (more will be explained in the following chapter). It refers both to a universal archaic level of mind and to various peoples. *Primitive* in both cases represents the earliest and lowest level in Jung's evolutionary model of the psyche. From this initial observation follows several others. First, despite Schmitz's stated belief that Jung "discovered" the "paleontology of the soul," Jung imported into his psychological theory a nineteenth-century anthropological, social-Darwinistic model of unilinear evolution. In Jung's psychologized version of this model, peoples he held to be primitive functioned as the living evidence for the archaic collective unconscious and the archetypes. Second, the archaic level of the psyche acted as a vehicle for Jung's critique of modern society and of scientific rationalism, as well as his desire to re-legitimize spirituality in an age marked by a crisis of faith in Christianity. Finally, the psyche as a whole in Jung's theory is not universal but is racially and religiously differentiated. Indeed, the house suggests that Jung's psychological theory was centrally concerned with a very specific collective psyche – one that was of Germanic descent and of Protestant background.

The archaic level of mind

In his lecture at the "Mensch und Erde" conference in Darmstadt, Jung elaborated on what he meant by the archaic level of mind and its relationship to contemporary "primitives." He compared the collective unconscious to a "primitive spirit . . . of venerable antiquity" (*einem primitiven Geiste . . . von ehrwürdigem Altertum*), which thinks in analogies, but is incapable of abstract thought (Jung 1927, 91). The collective unconscious belongs to all humans and even animals; it also houses the archetypes, which are themselves not images, but rather "possibilities of images" (*Vorstellungsmöglichkeiten*) (97–98). The archetypes give rise to mythology, which is a projection of the collective unconscious (99).

Jung explained how the archetypes were originally created: in the childhood of humanity, the affects produced by the repetition of typical processes became inscribed upon the human psyche. These affect-producing processes were both human and natural, including, for instance, the relationship between parents and children, rites of passage and the dawn. To illustrate, Jung described how solar hero myths were created by the feeling of redemption that primitive people have when the night and its terrors pass and a new dawn breaks (100–101, 104ff.). As Jung's explanation shows, he considered contemporary "primitive" and prehistoric humans to be interchangeable.

Jung further described the archetypes as "systems of readiness" (*Bereitschaftssysteme*) that are "simultaneously image and emotion" (*zugleich Bild und Emotion*) (108). They are found in the collective unconscious, which is the "source of instincts" (*Instinktequelle*) (106). He compared the unconscious to nature itself, "deeply conservative" (*ungeheuer konservativ*), and yet "transcending its own historical conditions in its acts of creation" (*in ihren Schöpfungsakten ihre eigene historische Bedingtheit wieder aufhebt*) (ibid.). Jung connected the instincts to the archetypes and said that, like nature, they are both strongly conservative and highly capable of adaptation. Jung further described the archetypes as the channel between the human psyche and nature, calling them the roots (*Wurzeln*) and the "chthonic aspect of the soul" (*der chthonische Anteil der Seele*) (108). Hence, Jung argued, archetypes are both instinctually strongly conservative and the source of creativity and renewal. They connect the human being to nature in a double sense, both to one's own and to that of the wider world.

Anthropological and religious-historical concepts of the primitive

Although Jung presented his psychological theory in universal terms, his model reveals racialized differences in his view of the psyche as a whole. Modern Europeans have, psychologically speaking, risen above the archaic level of mind, although their psyches have deep roots in its soil. In contrast, "primitives" live below the earth, that is, they mentally dwell in the collective unconscious (Jung 1927, 108–109). This primitive-civilized distinction would have made sense to the Darmstadt audience to whom Jung delivered his lecture in 1927. The members of this audience were well-educated, and thus already acquainted with contemporaneous theories of unilinear evolution proposed by anthropologists and scholars of the comparative study of religion. Like Jung's psychological "paleontology of the soul," the anthropological model of unilinear evolution had two axes, a vertical and a horizontal one. The vertical axis demonstrated the progress of Europeans from a presumed state of savagery, upwards through a barbarian level, and finally to the state of civilization. The implicit horizontal axis (or rather axes) of this theory represented the various non-white, non-western and non-modern peoples who were viewed as the historical evidence for Europeans' long march forward (Pietikäinen 1998, 362; Stocking 1968, 114, 131–132). The western theorists of social-Darwinist evolution filled in any lacunae in the historical evidence with ethnological data on contemporaneous non-western peoples, basing this questionable logical move on morphological similarities (Sharpe 1975, 55; Stocking 1968, 114).

Evolutionary theory revealed the admixture of a diffusionist model, because time was reckoned not only temporally, but also spatially. The modern West represented to itself the most highly achieved state of culture, and thus signified both "here" and "now," whereas people living contemporaneous to modern Europeans but far away from the presumed center of culture were said to be far away in time, that is, they were both "there" and "then" (Fabian 1983, 27, esp. figure 1.2). Indeed, "primitive" people were considered "living fossils," providing evidence of Europe's own past (Sharpe, 1975, 49; Thomas 2000, 50). The term *primitive* therefore signified not only the prehistory of all peoples, but also the current state of many present-day peoples, such as the Aborigines of Australia, whom Jung and others labeled a "stone age" culture (Jung CW 8 (1965 [1919]):570; Sharpe 1975, 49). The same held true for the barbaric stage, where certain ancient societies were compared to living ones: Jung, for example, compared the ancient Romans and the contemporary Pueblo Indians of New Mexico (Jung CW 10 (1933 [1931]):125). Finally, this same pattern of hierarchical ranking was applied to European classes and religions that western intellectuals considered atavistic, including not only the traditional European peasantry and Catholicism, but also the thoroughly modern working class and Christian Science (Brantlinger 1985, 182; Jung CW 10 (1918):22; Meyer 1883, 1:213; Sharpe 1975, 49, 62).

Western social scientists and scientists of religion in the late nineteenth and early twentieth centuries justified the evolutionary model by recourse to a presumed psychic unity of humanity. They argued that the human mind everywhere operated according to the same laws; hence, similar social or technological forms indicated similar mental levels (Krech 2002, 160; Sharpe 1975, 172). They also believed that the same essence of religion lay behind myriad religious phenomena (Krech 2002, 160). Underlying the claim of psychic unity is that of monogenesis, the belief in a common ancestry of all of humanity, which in turn was derived in part from the biblical story of creation, but by Jung's era, also based on secular grounds.

Beginning with the Enlightenment and the rejection of biblical genealogy, a range of European thinkers created a new model of separate ancestries known as polygenesis, which was incorporated into the otherwise monogenetic theory of unilinear evolution of the nineteenth century. According to this view, people at comparable stages of social development have similar mental levels, which are different from those of people who occupy other stages of development. Only the Semitic and the Aryan races, it was claimed, had been able to progress to the level of civilization, by increasing their mental capacities with each new discovery. Mirroring the ethnocentrism of ancient Roman authors, modern European intellectuals not surprisingly positioned their own society on the top rung of the evolutionary ladder. Their argument was based on circular logic, in that they failed to define the original mechanism for growth; however, the outcome was the claim that "primitives" were inherently limited in their capacity and hence biologically incapable of developing beyond their current level (Brantlinger, 182; Stocking, 120, 122; Thomas 2000, 51). Similar to Tacitus's homogenizing of the Germanic tribes, modern European (and American) scholars reduced extremely diverse groups of people to the male singular, inventing the figure of the dark-skinned "primitive man" who lived in a state of nature, mentally occupying a level approximating that of children at best, and animals at worst.

The evolutionary model was further supported by the recapitulation theory of the zoologist Ernst Haeckel (1834–1919), the dominant figure in German evolutionary biology at the turn of the last century. In 1866, Haeckel proposed that "ontogeny recapitulates phylogeny," meaning that an individual human fetus reiterated the evolutionary development of its species in the course of its own growth from embryo to infant. This evolutionary model was appropriated by anthropologists, who imagined that the evolution of the human species (phylogeny) followed the same development as the European individual (ontogeny). They claimed that "primitive" people outside of Europe were arrested developmentally at the level of childhood or adolescence, while only white, western men had reached full adulthood and civilization (Sharpe 1975, 57; Stocking 1968, 120).

The idea of recapitulation was employed in many theories on the origin and essence of religion (Krech 2002, 70) that Jung read. It was also used by several psychologists, including Freud, who employed it in *Totem and Taboo* (*Totem und Tabu,* 1913) to create a myth of origins for his Oedipal theory. The American psychologist Stanley Hall (1844–1924) also believed that the evolution of the human race was recapitulated in the development of modern children (Shamdasani 2003, 187–188).

Jung, too, incorporated anthropological views of "primitive man" via Haeckelian recapitulation theory into his psychological theory as early as his 1912 *Transformations and Symbols of the Libido.* Jung began this book with a discussion of two types of thinking, which he called "thinking with directed attention," and "dream or fantasy thinking." Fantasy thinking is associative; it is comprised of strings of images and a multitude of feelings. In contrast, directed thinking is logical, successional, and related to reality; as such, it forms the foundation of modern science and technology. According to Jung, directed thinking is not inherent in the minds of all peoples; rather, it resulted through the evolution and movement of psychic energy from basic instinctual drives to higher symbolic and cognitive psychological realms. Reality-oriented thinking was both adult and modern, whereas fantasy thinking was infantile and prehistoric, characteristic of both ancient mythological thought and the thinking of children and "lower races, like the negros" (Jung 1925, 13–26, quote on 26).

As this example and Jung's model of the house indicate, Jung essentialized so-called primitives as not only different from, but also inferior to, the modern adult Westerner. Jung imagined such people as living psychologically in a condition hardly removed from the instinctual state of animals, that is, living in a state of collective unconsciousness. Because of the lack of differentiation between inner and outer in the primitive mind, asserted Jung, primitives do not actively think; rather, thoughts come to them as if from outside. Furthermore, they project all their internal psychic events out onto the concrete world, populating the landscape with gods, demons, and other spirits (Jung CW 10 (1933

[1931]):128–130). Although Jung admired the peoples he labeled primitive for their "wholeness" and "vitality," he also considered them childlike, emotional, unconscious, and lacking rationality (Brooke 2008, 42). He equated their mentality with that of modern European children; unlike Western children, however, primitives were unable to evolve.

As with the anthropological model of evolution, Jung's theory rests on the theory of the psychic unity of humanity. However, Jung's portrayal of "primitives" as stuck on the lowest rung of the evolutionary ladder indicates the presence of polygenetic theory in an otherwise monogenetic model. Moreover, he theorized ethnic and national differences, further revealing polygenetic thinking in Jung's psychology. To wit, in his 1925 private seminar on analytical psychology, Jung described the phylogenetic unconscious not only through the metaphor of the house, but also via a diagram he called "the 'geology' of a personality" (Schmitz's "the paleontology of the soul"). In this illustration, he portrayed the unconscious like a mountain range: strata that pertain only to the individual and family are represented by the peaks; clan and nation levels are shared by some other mountains; and a whole range comprises the "Large Group" layer (here: "European man"). Underneath are three layers which must logically be found in the unconscious of all people, since they are *pre-human*: "Primate Ancestors," "Animal Ancestors in General," and "Central Fire," the last symbolized by the earth's molten core (Jung 1989, 133). Note that no layer appears that specifically connects all human beings with each other, a stratum that should have been entitled "humanity." This model suggests that Jung was more concerned with theorizing a bridge between modern Europeans and an original wellspring of psychic life than a common ground for humankind.

"Primitives" as the living evidence of Jungian psychological concepts

Many cultural theorists before Jung had attempted to legitimize their claims about modern institutions and ideas by seeking their origins in a primitive state free of the contingencies of the modern age. Like them, Jung sought evidence for his theory of the archetypes and the collective unconscious in the modern psyche by recourse to "primitive man." He employed the works of scholars of religion, such as Tylor, Frazer, and Meyer (see Chapter 2), psychologizing aspects of their theories on "primitive religion." For example, Tylor had proposed *animism* as the origin of religion. He considered primordial humans to be rational individuals who, having pondered the difference between living and dead beings, as well as apparitions in dreams and visions, thereby developed the belief in souls. From there, they imagined spirits, including great deities. For Tylor, this process involved thinking, not emotional states. Jung ignored the rationalism of Tylor's theory to interpret his ideas psychologically via the theory of feeling-toned complexes: the belief in souls is derived from complexes relating to the ego, whereas the belief in spirits comes from the archetypes and the collective unconscious (Jung CW 8 (1965 [1919]: 570–600).

In addition, Tylor had developed the theory of survivals, defining them as customs, opinions, and so on that, through habit, live on from generation to generation, even when they have outgrown their usefulness (Tylor 1873, 1:16; Sharpe 1975, 54). Tylor saw survivals as evidence of earlier stages of human cultural evolution. The theory of survivals shows up in Jung's definition of "archaism" (*Archaismus*), which refers to all psychic contents that have an "archaic" (*altertümlich*) character, and which could be designated as "relics" (*Relikte*). These "relicts" correspond to the characteristics of "primitive mentality" (Jung CW 6 (1950 [1921]):754). Jung considered the modern-day religion Christian Science a survival, comparing this spirit-based system of healing to shamanism (Jung CW 10 (1918):22; Jung CW 10 (1930):977). While Christian Science may have seemed atavistic to Jung, other "archaic" psychic contents – the archetypes – still performed an essential psychological function and conveyed potent psychic energy.

Jung also read Frazer's *The Golden Bough,* which presents a tripartite evolutionary schema leading from primitive magic to religion to science. The dismissal of religion in this theory surely was rejected by Jung; still, he found other ideas of Frazer useful. For example, Jung interpreted the dying and rising gods discussed by Frazer as symbols of the libido. Furthermore, Jung borrowed Frazer's concept of the "perils of the soul" to refer to the process by which a part of the psyche becomes unconscious, thereby slipping outside of conscious control (Jung 1966, 19).

In addition, Jung used *Indo-European Myths* (*Indogermanische Mythen*) by Elard Hugo Meyer in his own *Transformations and Symbols of the Libido.* Following Tylor, Meyer divided religious and mythical development into three evolutionary stages. The earliest stage, found in hunting and gathering societies, was characterized religiously by the belief in the soul (Meyer 1883, 211–212). The belief in souls was transformed into a belief in spirits in the evolutionary move to pastoralism, at which point people began imagining dark nature spirits, especially in the wind; like spirits, the wind is invisible, yet perceptible, forceful and restless (214). With the development of agriculture, state societies, and a priestly caste, the older wind and weather gods developed light-based characteristics and were sometimes transformed into gods, often taking on a national character (215–217). Meyer's influence can be detected in Jung's interpretation of the unnamed patient's dream described in Chapter 3, in which the impersonal wind took symbolic precedence over the figure of the father-god, leading Jung to claim that his patient's unconscious had manifested an archetypal image of the Spirit.

The ideas just discussed are rationalist theories of the origin of religion; these thinkers imagined religion to have emerged out of the thought processes of "primitive man." Jung, however, was more interested in theories of a foundational irrational religious force, such as those developed by the historians of religion Rudolf Otto (described in Chapter 3) and Nathan Söderblom. In *The Evolution of the Belief in God* (*Das Werden des Gottesglaubens,* 1916), Söderblom investigated three categories in "primitive" religions that he believed form the foundation for the belief in the divine: animism, the creator (*Urheber*), and power (*Macht*), the third category being the one that Jung incorporated into his psychological theory. The idea of power, wrote Söderblom, found expression in many primitive societies, through words such as *mana* (Melanesian and Polynesian), *wakanda* (Dakota and Sioux), *orenda* (Iroquois), and *hamingja* (Old Norse). These terms expressed the power of an impersonal supernatural force. This force was invisible, pervasive, indivisible and diffuse, yet localizable in bodies and objects. It was ethically neutral, but could be wielded and manipulated by humans for either good or ill purposes (34, 38, 54, 60, 62). But what this power really is, claimed Söderblom, was none other than the Holy, as recognized in "higher" religions (33). Söderblom rejected Frazer's categorical distinction between magic and religion, because magical rites often evoke an experience central to Söderblom's definition of religion as "submission and obedience to that which is mysterious and incomprehensible" (*Unterwerfung und Gehorsam dem Geheimnisvollen, Unfaßbaren gegenüber*) (202). He further claimed that the common denominator in religion from the most primitive rites to the emergence of monotheism was the experience of "being gripped" (*Ergriffenheit*) by the power of the divine (204, 321).

Jung incorporated Söderblom's explanation of *mana* into both his concept of the mana personality and his theory of psychic energy. Söderblom had claimed that whatever contains *mana* is both sacred and taboo. These characteristics are then embodied by remarkable humans in primitive societies, such as medicine men, and by the figures in creator-myths (182). Jung used these ideas to develop his own notion of the archetypal mana personality, which appears historically as the medicine man, the magician, the friend of God, the hero, and the saint (Jung CW 7 (1963 [1928]):375–377). As discussed in Chapter 3, the archetypal mana personality is an important way-station, as it were, on the path to individuation.

Moreover, in his 1928 article "On Psychic Energy," Jung contrasted his concept of libido as psychic energy to Freud's definition of libido as sexual drive. He theorized his own perspective as an energetic standpoint in contrast to the (presumably Freudian) mechanistic standpoint, supporting his theory by drawing on the concept of *mana* as developed by Söderblom and other scholars (Jung CW 8 (1971 [1928]):26–33). Jung also cited the historian of ideas Arthur O. Lovejoy (1873–1962), who grouped *mana* and other similar concepts not under the categories of "the holy" or "the sacred," but under the rubric of "primitive energetics," which Lovejoy believed to be the most elementary form of religion, preceding even the belief in souls (ibid., para. 114–130). Hence, the concept of psychic energy as theorized by Jung rests on the notion of the Holy as such, which becomes particularly constellated or intensified immediately before one's psyche manifests the self as its true center.

Along with rationalist theories, Jung was generally uninterested in sociological explanations for the origin and essence of religion, such as that provided by Emile Durkheim (1858–1917), who considered religion something eminently social (Durkheim 1965). Still, Jung was drawn to the works of several members of Durkheim's school, including Lucien Lévy-Bruhl (1857–1939), Henri Hubert (1872–1927) and Marcel Mauss (1872–1950). This is because Jung reinterpreted the sociological category of collective representations as a psychological-biological one – specifically, as the archetypes of the collective unconscious (Hubert and Mauss 1909, in Jung CW 7: 220; 8: 52, fn. 42).

Jung relied most heavily on the theory of primitive mentality developed by the French philosopher and sociologist Lucien Lévy-Bruhl. In his 1910 work, *How Natives Think (Les fonctions mentales dans les sociétés inférieures)*, Lévy-Bruhl speculated about what he believed to be the two basic mindsets of humanity, "primitive" and "modern." Primitive mentality can be characterized by mystical participation (*participation mystique*) and pre-logical thought. Primitives believe all things have a mystical connection to one another. They further hold that all objects (including people) can be fully both one thing and another simultaneously, an idea that defies the law of contradiction (Lévy-Bruhl 1985, 76–78, 361; Segal 2007, 636). Primitives have little individual consciousness due to the preponderance of collective representations, and therefore they think largely collectively. Lévy-Bruhl claimed that primitive mentality was not just a simpler, more elementary form of modern, western logic, but was actually a different way of perceiving and thinking altogether (Lévy-Bruhl 1985, 44; Littleton 1985, x; Segal 2007, 635–636). In effect, Lévy-Bruhl's argument implicitly problematizes the idea of psychic unity.

Lévy-Bruhl claimed that primitive thinking is dominated by collective representations and thus highly undifferentiated (Lévy-Bruhl 1985, 36). Jung interpreted this to mean that primitives are still identified with the collective psyche and therefore lack individual psychology (Jung 1927, 117). In addition, Lévy-Bruhl argued that the collective representations are impressed upon a member of primitive society through painful initiation rituals and strenuous tests, which create an intense emotional charge that in turn lend the objects involved a "mystic" quality (Lévy-Bruhl 1985, 36–37, 40, 42). Jung understood this to mean that the archetypes are emotionally charged responses to typical human experiences that have been repeated since time immemorial (Jung 1927, 104). Moreover, Jung used Lévy-Bruhl's concept of *participation mystique* to claim along with Söderblom that primitives do not differentiate between the subjective-psychic and the objective-natural, relating to the latter as if it were imbued with the magical power of *mana* (Jung CW 10 (1933 [1931]):128; Söderblom 1916, 86). Lévy-Bruhl sought to defend "primitives" against the charge of racial or biological inferiority by arguing that the logic we use is not universal, but is shaped by our cultural, technological and environmental conditions (Littleton 1985, vi, viii; Segal 2007, 636). Jung, on the other hand, psychologized Lévy-Bruhl's theory, seeing it as representing both the unconscious as such and the earliest psychological state of humanity (Segal 2007, 636).

Perhaps Jung's misunderstanding of Lévy-Bruhl's ideas has to do with the vagueness of the sociologist's basic categories. He did not clearly define the criteria he used to order societies into "primitive" and "not primitive." For instance, he gives China as an example of a society dominated by primitive mentality (Lévy-Bruhl 1985, 42). Yet China had a vast empire long before western Europeans did, including the advanced technology and state apparatuses needed to maintain it. The reader is left with the assumption that the working premise is "the West and the rest." Hence, Lévy-Bruhl's book is a prime example of both the vagueness of the term *primitive* as a category for other cultures, and the term's inextricable coupling to another term signifying its opposite, in this case, modern.

Jung in Taos

As Schmitz pointed out in his letter from December 4, 1926, Jung had sought confirmation of his theory of the archaic level of mind by visiting people he believed to be primitive. In January 1925, Jung journeyed to Taos Pueblo in the United States, and from October to January 1926, conducted the Bugishu Psychological Expedition in East Africa, to research primitive mentality. Five years later in 1930, Jung lectured on "Archaic Man" (*Der archaische Mensch*) (Jung CW (1930):104–147) to the well-educated audience of the *Lesezirkel Hottingen,* a literary fraternity in Hottingen near Zurich, where he discussed his encounters in both Taos and East Africa.

Jung reported a conversation he had had in Taos with the Hopi elder and chief Ochwiay Biano, known as Mountain Lake. His Spanish name was Antonio Mirabel (c. 1890–1975). Jung had attempted to explain the western view that the eye, not the sun, creates light. This led to an impassioned outcry from Mountain Lake, who insisted that light came from the sun, which was in fact the Father. Life was impossible without the assistance of the celestial divinity (para. 138).

This conversation supported Jung's interpretation of libido as psychic energy, which he had first discussed in his 1912 *Transformations and Symbols of the Libido* (Jung 1925, 142). According to Jung, libido often manifests in myths as the sun, light, and solar heroes. The libido is an inner, quasi-divine power and source of life, and the worship of God represents a projection of this enlivening power (96). Like the ancient Germanic peoples, who (according to Caesar) worshipped the sun (as well as the moon and fire), the Pueblo Indians (in Jungian theory) projected their collective psychic energy onto the sun.

Jung spent only a scant two days at Taos Pueblo, yet claimed to know "the mother-nations of North America pretty well" (Jung CW 10 (1930):961). Were that true, would he have stayed at a hotel named Columbus (Barton 2014, 4)? Indeed, Jung seemed to know rather little about his main Indian contact Mirabel, who was not a chief, tribal elder or holder of a tribal office, as Jung reported, but rather, a skilled impresario (ibid.). The native religious sentiments he conveyed to Jung were generalities already accessible to the public (Bair 2003, 336). Rather than a traditional spiritual leader, Mirabel was a shrewd political force for Indian rights, who refused a meeting with President Herbert Hoover, yet advised President Franklin Roosevelt on Indian affairs (Barton 2014, 5). Moreover, Mirabel was a regular guest at the house of his close friends, Tony Luhan and Mabel Luhan Dodge (1879–1962), the latter being a highly significant arts patron. The community of artists and intellectuals that had sprung up in Taos was one dedicated to merging European and Native American cultures to create a new sensibility (ibid.). Whatever Jung may have experienced in Taos, it was not an "authentic" primitive culture, but one very much in flux and in interaction with modern Western society.

The Bugishu psychological expedition

In October 1925, Jung traveled to East Africa with three companions: George Beckwith, a wealthy American and once Jung's analysand, who paid for the entire trip (Burleson 1973, 22; Bair 2003, 342); Peter Baynes, a British psychotherapist, Jung's first assistant in Zurich and Beckwith's analyst, who became the trip's organizer (Burleson 1973, 23); and Ruth Bailey, a nurse whom the men met on the ship en route to Africa and who was escorting her younger sister to her settler husband (38). Baynes took care of the process of acquiring the permission of the British Colonial Office to engage in field research among the peoples of Uganda, and the government even supplied a small stipend (23). Like most anthropological work undertaken under the aegis of European colonial power (Asad 1973, 17), Jung's Bugishu Psychological Expedition took place with official approval from a colonial office; in East Africa, that meant the British government and its district commissioners (DCs) (Burleson 1973, 104), because all the people Jung wished to study were living under the yoke of British colonialism.

Although Jung's entire trip lasted five months, the actual Bugishu Psychological Expedition took place within three weeks, and not among the Bugishu, because the DC forbade Jung from conducting his research with these people (109). Instead, he visited the Kôôny (pronounced "Cone"), a people who belong to a larger group known as Sâbâwōōt (pronounced Saa-boat), part of the Nilotic groups (the Kalenjin) in the Great Rift Valley. The Kôôny were known to outsiders in Jung's day as the Elgonyi (as is given in Jung's CW/GW). Elgonyi is an anglicized form of *Ilgoon*, a Masai name for the people who lived in caves on Mt. Elgon, located on the border between Kenya and Uganda. Unlike other groups in the region who had assumed a Bantu language as their own, the Kôôny people kept their own language and culture. In 1925, there were about 5,000 of them. The British colonial government had denied their claims to their ancestral lands by labeling them a "dying tribe." Their former caves were designated a "forest reserve," not a "native reserve," and many tribal members were forced by the government to move to Uganda (127–130). Hence, rather than living in a state of unchanged primitivity from time immemorial, the people who were informants for Jung's psychological research were living in a state of extreme distress due to British colonization.

According to the analysis of the Jungian and African studies scholar Blake Burleson, Jung misunderstood a good portion of what he saw and heard. Jung had assumed that his scant four weeks of studying Swahili on the boat to Africa would be adequate preparation to research the dreams of Africans (30). However, most rural Africans did not even speak Swahili (106); hence, Jung's first informants were his own hired porters (143). Jung's chief assistant and translator, a devout Sufi Somali named Ibrahim, considered himself far superior to the "uncivilized" Kôôny (103), and he did not speak their language. However, he did speak the language of the white colonialists. According to Fanon's analysis of how white colonialism affects black psychology, this placed Ibrahim a step closer to the white world, "lightening" him over and against the blacks he held to be more "primitive" (Fanon 2008, 21). Thus, conversations took place through three languages (Burleson 1973, 132) and were interpreted by two men who considered the Kôôny their inferiors. When Ibrahim misunderstood his Kôôny informants and assured Jung that the people had no collective name (133), Jung believed him, repeating this misunderstanding as evidence to support his claim that he had gathered psychological evidence from a people occupying probably the lowest rung of the evolutionary ladder (Jung CW 10 (1934 [1933]):280).

Jung went to Africa in order to conduct research on the archaic level of mind. He was a psychologist, not a colonial administrator. Hence, it is all the more astounding to read how much he acted in accordance with colonialist practices throughout his trip: he arrived at his destination under official British approval, with armed guards supplied by the DC, and held "palavers," or assemblies, announcing at the beginning of each session the *shauri* (Swahili for "agenda"). The word *shauri* was used for the complaint process in tribunals held by the DCs to adjudicate local disputes. By assuming this colonialist discursive practice, Burleson says, Jung practically guaranteed that he would achieve the very scanty results that he did (Burleson 1973, 143–144). In his public presentations of his Bugishu Psychological Expedition, however, Jung avoided critically examining his own role in this failure, instead blaming the "primitives" for their imputed inability to sit still and engage in the intellectual task of thinking (144). He also assumed the role of the paternalistic British colonialist when referring to his East African assistants with the mixed German-English designation, "meine Boys" (the English CW gives "our boys") (Jung CW/GW 10 (1969 [1931]):126). Finally, Jung also denied the history of those who have been colonized by effacing or even destroying evidence of that history (Childs and Williams 1999, 8, 26). For example, while gazing at an African warrior (or hunter, he thought), Jung described him as being exactly the same as a hunter 5,000 years before (Jung 1965, 254).

What Jung failed to understand is that the people he had imagined and wanted to study could be said to no longer exist. According to Fanon, the trauma of colonization profoundly affects the colonized culture (Fanon 2008, 164), splitting the personalities of the colonized between identification with their home culture and longing to belong to the culture of the colonizer (128, 132). The analytical psychologist Anthony Stevens described the "hunter" Jung saw from a train as the "two-million-year-old man within us all" and the "unactualized" Self (as quoted in Burleson 2005, 61). Burleson, who suggests the man was probably not a hunter, but a Masai warrior (59), compares him to the murderer of Jung's "heroic ideal" in his dream in 1913 (61). Such claims simply reiterate colonialist discourse about blacks as representing the psychological childhood of humanity.

These essentializing views of Jung and his followers ignore the violence of colonialist practice in Africa and elsewhere. Finally, they overlook how European domination has helped internalize a negative image of the colonized in the psyches of both the colonizers and the colonized (Fanon 2008, 165–168).

In a story that became the foundation for Jung's myth for the modern world, Jung imagined East African peoples as not only unevolved; he rendered them part of the non-human natural landscape. While Jung was surveying the Athi Plains and their grazing herds, he realized that the world must be recognized as such by human beings for it to have objective existence: "There I was now, the first human being to recognize that this was the world, but who did not know that in this moment he had first really created it" (Jung 1965, 255). This passage reveals that Jung assumed that all the people who lived in the vicinity of the Athi Plains were incapable of recognizing the world, due to a lack of individual consciousness. He continued:

> [I] had been looking about without hope for a myth of our own. Now I knew what it was, and knew even more: that man is indispensable for the completion of creation; that, in fact, he himself is the second creator of the world, who alone has given to the world its objective existence – without which, unheard, unseen, silently eating, giving birth, dying, heads nodding through hundreds of millions of years, it would have gone on in the profoundest night of non-being down to its unknown end. Human consciousness created objective existence and meaning, and man found his indispensable place in the great process of being.
>
> (Jung 1965, 256)

Jung had already said as much, and much more concisely, in his 1912 *Transformations and Symbols of the Libido*: "The world emerges when man discovers it" (*Die Welt entsteht, wenn der Mensch sie entdeckt*) (Jung 1912, 392). Still, this episode is known as the myth that Jung offered to modern readers to lend their lives a sense of ultimate meaning in a secularized age (Jung 1965, 255–256).

A reader of Jung might assume he had been inspired by his earlier trip to Taos Pueblo, where he learned from his Taos interlocutor Mountain Lake that the Taos people consider it their life's purpose to help their Father Sun across the sky every day. Although Jung wrote that he envied this myth that gave the Taos Pueblo Indians a sense of ultimate meaning (256), according to Jung's theory, the Taos Indians had projected their own psychic energy and the archetype of the life-force outwards onto the heavens as Father Sun. They therefore had not achieved a fully mature, modern level of consciousness. Jung believed that the ability to co-create with God was present only in those humans who were the most conscious (Jung CW 9/1 (1954 [1939]):177), those capable not only of projection, but also of the recognition of oppositions (ibid., 178). Given Jung's argument about the development of directed thinking, it appears that, for Jung, only racially specific humans could become co-creators with God, able to complete the act of creation put into motion by the supreme power of the universe. These humans were psychologically evolved Europeans like Jung himself. In contrast, those people Jung defined as "primitive" were, in his view, either evolutionarily lesser developed –or not human beings at all: at least in the case of East Africans, they were no more than the grazing herds on the Athi Plains, existing unconsciously in an ongoing cycle of birth, life, and death.

Jung's modern myth is, in effect, the myth of individuation, in which a European person becomes "whole, indivisible," and separated from the collective. The analytical psychologist Roger Brooke argues that Jung's theory of individuation contains a "colonialism of the psyche" (Brooke 2008, 38), which reflects the norms and values of modern Westerners, and effectively excludes non-white, non-western people. Brooke lists the exclusive binary oppositions that run throughout Jung's work (42):

White European / Black African
light / dark
civilized / primitive
conscious / unconscious
rational / emotional
disembodied / embodied
scientific / superstitious
repressed neurotic / paranoid psychotic
adultlike / childlike
personal / impersonal
individual / collective
separation / participation mystique
moral / amoral

These categories reiterate the stereotypes about Europe and its colonized "others" Jung found throughout works on "primitive religion" on which he based his theory of the archaic level of mind.

Burleson considers Jung's trip to Africa through the Jungian lens of the *puer aeternus* figure. He suggests this trip, like other European men's journeys to Africa, was a form of escape from the confines of modernity. He writes that the stereotype of Africa as the "dark continent" "offered the perfect objective correspondent to the collective shadow of the so-called 'civilized' Western world" (Burleson 2005, 12-13, quote on 13). Burleson's *puer aeternus* thesis certainly has merit, but it should be emphasized that Africa as Europe's "shadow" is the historical product of highly exploitative power relations between the two continents.

Furthermore, Jung's "discovery" of the light of his own consciousness while visiting black Africa may be understood within the context of stories about British explorers and missionaries who saw themselves as beacons of light in the dark of Africa (Brantlinger 1985, 176–178). Jung was familiar with at least some of these stories, such as the popular novel, *She* (1886–1887) by Rider Haggard

(1856–1925). This is the story of Ayesha, whom the Victorian studies scholar Patrick Brantlinger describes as "a beautiful white demigoddess ruling over a brown-skinned race" in the African interior (Brantlinger 1985, 198). For Jung, she was a literary representation of the anima (Jung 1989, 137). According to Brantlinger, stories such as *She* portrayed white men moving into the depths of the "dark continent," only to find another white man (or woman) deep in its interior. These literary figures were "heroic and saintly self-images" that reflected back to both author and audience their wishes to be sanitized of their guilt over the horrors of colonialism, while projecting their repressed desires and monstrous behavior onto the "natives" (Brantlinger 1985, 198).

Jung's journey to Africa also reflects what the anthropologist Johannes Fabian describes as a modern, secular view of travel developed in the Enlightenment, according to which a western man no longer went on a pilgrimage to experience God, but to complete his knowledge of "man" through new knowledge of non-western peoples, thereby achieving self-realization (Fabian 1983, 6–8). In Jung's own version of this genre, he traveled to Africa to find what he considered to be living representatives of the most primitive level of humanity, in order to learn about his own inner primitive side and thereby complete his knowledge of the human psyche. Jung did not portray himself as the colonizing and missionizing bringer of light and right religion to the "savage" Africans; rather, he claimed to discover within himself the source of light – consciousness – against the black backdrop of unconsciousness, understood in racial terms through Jung's theory of the evolution of thought.

Going "shenzi": blackness as mental illness

Jung apparently believed that the "Negro" – whether in Africa or in the United States – was primitive and thus impervious to change, an impression borne out by his 1930 article on American psychology, published in *Forum* magazine under the title, "Your Indian and Negroid Behavior" (Jung 1930, 193–199). This provocative title was probably chosen by the magazine itself, as none of the four existing manuscripts in the Jung archive at the Swiss Federal Institute of Technology in Zurich carry it. So, too, were the accompanying illustrations – gross caricatures of grinning, loose-jointed, big-lipped black men and hip-swinging black women (194, 198, 195, 199, 197). Yet the content is Jung's, conveying his own crass stereotypes of Americans, black, white, and native, that he initially formed during a visit to Buffalo, New York in 1909 (193) and published in his *Collected Works* as "Complications in American Psychology" (Jung CW 10 (1930):946–980). In this essay, Jung argued that the mannerisms of "Americans" – meaning people of western European descent – have been reshaped under the influence of blacks. White Americans' raucous laughter, their gossip and chattering, their nonchalant body movements and swinging gait, their intense sociability, emotionality, and sexual promiscuity, as well as the general hustle and bustle of everyday life, can all be traced to one source: "The Negro" (Jung 1930, 194–195, quote on

195). Although Burleson argues that the "blackening of the white soul in America was not necessarily something negative from Jung's perspective" (2005, 73), this positive assertion is problematized by Jung's own words: "Now what is more contagious than to live side by side with a rather primitive people?" (Jung 1930, 196). White and specifically Germanic-Americans are psychologically civilized, yet this civilized mentality covers a much deeper and older primitive psyche that becomes reactivated when Europeans and their descendants make contact with the "inferior man" (196). Only because African-Americans constitute a minority did Jung feel that they posed no serious risk of racial "contagion," as was presumably the case in Africa. These statements demonstrate Jung's general view towards blacks wherever they may live: they constitute the eternal primitive, incapable of psychological advancement, and always inferior and dangerous to people of European descent.

When Jung wrote of the influence of African-Americans on European-Americans in the United States, he did not use the language of cultural transmission, contact, diffusion, or assimilation. He also overlooked the fact of racial mixing that had already begun in the colonial era, when white male slave owners regularly raped and impregnated their black female slaves (Roediger 2008, 28–29). Instead, Jung used the language of disease. The alleged primitivity of black people was a contagion, said Jung, which "infects" whites psychologically. And when whites receive a high enough dose of blackness, they go mad.

Although it has been suggested that Jung's feeling for "the rhythms and values" of peasant life in Europe helped create in Jung an anti-colonial stance towards blacks (Burleson 2005, 160), Jung did not theorize psychic infection from peasants to moderns. Modern evolutionary theorists did, like Jung, position both European peasants and peoples of African descent lower on the evolutionary ladder than themselves. Moreover, in the Middle Ages, the European lower classes were imagined as black, as attested by the thirteen-century Eddic poem "The List of Rig" (*Rigthula*). In this poem, the god Heimdall visits three different houses and sleeps with the woman in each one. Each house represents a different class in medieval society, those of thralls, farmers and lords. A kind of evolutionary theory is hinted at in the ranking of these three houses according to age: the thrall, known as Great-Grandmother, is the oldest; then comes Grandmother, the farmer; last is Mother, the noblewoman. While the noble Mother has a snow-white neck and gives birth to a blonde-haired boy, Great-Grandmother bears an ugly, dark-skinned thrall (see Larrington 1996, 246–252 for the poem).

Furthermore, as mentioned in Chapter 2, the medieval Wild Man or Wild Woman had black skin. The color was not related to race, however, but rather to madness or immorality (Gilman 1982, 12–13). Blood purity is originally an aristocratic concern that was not connected to race, but to descent. The idea of racial infection may be traced back to sixteenth-century Spain, where Moriscos (Moors forced to convert to Catholicism under the new Spanish Catholic state), were seen as an infectious threat to Spanish identity articulated in terms of the purity of blood. By the eighteenth century, the idea of racial infection, shorn of religious connotations, had spread throughout the Spanish and Portuguese colonies. Finally, by the latter half of the nineteenth century, when European nations dominated most of the rest of the world, the theme of blood purity became enmeshed with biology and the concept of race. People of mixed race were viewed as a threat to the collective health of Europeans, for the "other" blood that flowed in a European's veins might cause an individual to betray European interests in favor of the colony (Stoler 1995, 51–52).

These various genealogies were brought together in Jung's era in the expression "going black." Blackness was akin to madness; "going black" was a mental illness in whites brought on by the racial contagion of blackness (Burleson 2005, 200). The condition indicated a mental regression, as attested in the words of analytical psychologist H. G. Baynes, Jung's travel companion to Africa. Baynes described the phenomenon of "going black" in explicitly evolutionary terms, as a "retrogressive movement" that "rejects the evolutionary principle of reciprocity and relatedness." He further described the phenomenon with the metaphor of disease, calling the colonialist who "'goes native'" . . . "the cancer-cell in the social body" (as quoted in ibid.).

The expression "going black" was also known as "going *shenzi*." According to Burleson, *shenzi* is Swahili for "uncivilized" (Burleson 2005, 93, note 5). In *Through the Brazilian Wilderness* (1914), Theodore Roosevelt described the term *shenzi* as a designation given by the Swahili people to the "wild bush natives" (Roosevelt 1914, 65). The term was picked up by European colonizers and coupled with the verb "going" to mean "going black, going primitive, going native" – that is, "going insane" – to denounce unseemly behavior on the part of other whites (Burleson 2005, 187–188). In this new context, the phrases "going *shenzi*" and "going black" came to signify a betrayal of the values of civilization, the very values the European settlers were supposed to bring to the presumably savage Africans (Brantlinger 1985, 193–194).

On his trip to East Africa, Jung witnessed certain individuals who had apparently suffered this fate, such as Mrs. Stricks, the hotel manager in Masindi, whom Jung described in a private seminar. Mrs. Stricks wore a lace robe and carried a lace sun umbrella, as if ready for a Sunday stroll in an English garden. Yet not all was right with Mrs. Stricks. As Jung explained to his audience, "The first time I saw her, she was jumping over hedges, waving her parasol at an escaping turkey, swearing like a nigger and then getting into a terrible fit of rage, foaming at the mouth and talking like a mad woman; she was indeed mad" (as quoted in Burleson 2005, 188). In Jung's diagnosis, the behavior of the European Mrs. Stricks was symptomatic of mental illness; the same actions in the case of a "nigger" would be, to Jung, *natural*. Thus, the mentality of blacks, according to Jung, is by nature similar to a state of psychosis, whereas the same behavior among whites in Africa who have "gone *shenzi*" constitutes a feral condition.

The Martinique poet and politician Aimé Césaire (1913–2008) suggests a radically different cause of what Jung called "going black." He argues that colonization, although often portrayed as a civilizing benefit bestowed on poor savages, is in fact about the expropriation of a people and their resources. Hence, colonization turns colonizers into savages, because colonization encourages the basest instincts in humans – greed and aggression. The colonizers then project their own brutality and savagery onto those they colonize. Not only those directly involved in colonization but those good bourgeois people back home are degraded by colonization, as they buy into the lie that the brutality wrought is for the good of the "savages" elsewhere. Furthermore, this brutality practiced abroad made possible the viciousness of Nazism in Europe (Césaire 2013, 173). Finally, once a people have been colonized, their training in the new regime convinces them to adjust to their subservient position. In this way, the myth of the primitive becomes reality (178). One would have hoped that Jung, with his years of psychotherapeutic experience, might have perceived these psychological processes. Yet he was too invested in his belief in essentialized racial psychologies and the theory of evolution, ideas foundational to his theory of the archaic level of mind.

The "inner primitive" of the modern western psyche

Jung believed that the modern western psyche could be characterized as fragmented, with consciousness being severed from the collective unconscious due to the loss of religious faith. Previously, religious symbolism drained off the collective unconscious, so to speak, transmitting its energy away from basic instinctual drives towards higher-level psychological functions. Since the beginning of the Age of Reason, however, religious symbolism was no longer able to perform this essential function; hence, the forces of the collective unconscious sought outlet in pathological expressions: neurosis among individuals, and on a collective level, world war. Jung even argued that the blocked instincts of "civilized" people were more destructive than those of "primitives," because the latter found more modest ways of exorcising them regularly (Jung 1921, 199).

In *The Psychology of Unconscious Processes*, Jung discussed an unresolved case of an anonymous woman patient struggling to overcome a psychological block related to a close female friend. Her dreams revealed a complex, that is, an unconscious assemblage of feeling-toned thought associations of high psychic intensity (Jung CW 3 (1907):79–82), buried deep in her unconscious that prohibited her therapy from progressing. During the transference process, she projected her unconscious complex onto Jung through the image of a demon. Jung explained that the demonic image may represent the archetype of the shadow, those aspects of one's personality that are disowned and repressed due to their incompatibility with the ego, and "the most dangerous aspect of the dark half of the person that has not yet been acknowledged" (Jung CW 7 (1960 [1943]):152). However, it could also represent the archetype of the "magical dämon," which Jung found expressed in literary form in Gustav Meyrinck's Golem, Nietzsche's Zarathustra, and Goethe's Faust. He described this archetype (à la Meyer again), as "the lowest and most elementary concept of God," which often appears as "*dark-skinned* and of *Mongoloid type*, when it represents a negative and perhaps dangerous aspect," similar to a tribal medicine man or sorcerer (para. 154, emphasis in original). Jung's emphatic remarks show that he found this archetypal image deeply troubling, especially when a person projected it onto other people, making them appear magical and even demonic. Jung therefore admonished his readers to realize the real source of this magical image, which was their own unconscious material. Once a person recognizes the demonic figure as an aspect of his or her own psyche, the projection ends. But this initial step towards resolution of the psychological disturbance needs to be followed by the equally difficult task of integrating the archetypal figure into consciousness. In order to synthesize the primordial psychological aspect into the more highly developed level of consciousness, religious symbolism must be employed, as it "speaks" the language of the archaic level of mind (ibid.). Jung wrote:

> Upon one side we should have the differentiated modern ego, whilst upon the other a kind of uncivilized negro representative of a thoroughly primitive state. That would mean we should have what really does exist, a crust of civilization over a dark-skinned brute; the cleavage would be distinct and demonstrable before our very eyes. But such a dissociation requires immediate synthesis and cultivation of what is undeveloped. There must be a union of these two aspects.
>
> (Jung CW 7 (1960 [1943]):154)

In this quote, the archaic layer of the white, civilized European psyche is portrayed as its alleged opposite: black, uncivilized, and even subhuman. This is a centuries-old motif in European culture, by which the lowest classes of society or social outsiders were color-coded black and described as animalistic or diseased. However, these motifs became racialized in the modern world, and Jung's theory reflects this shift. In keeping with Jung's views that people of African descent are unwaveringly "primitive," Jung equated blackness with *primitive*, even when discussing an aspect of the European psyche. He thus maintained the status of Europeans as civilized by displacing the primitive side of the modern European psyche onto what amounts to an inner Negro. He further naturalized colonial relations between Europe and Africa by placing these relations within the psyche of the modern Westerner.

This observation is underscored by Jung's account of a dream he had while in East Africa. He dreamt that an African-American barber he had gotten to know in Tennessee attempted to apply a hot iron to his head and thereby kink his hair. Jung interpreted this barber as his inner primitive aspect. It had become activated by the preponderance of black Africans surrounding Jung, and the European found himself on the verge of "going black" (Jung 1965, 272). Once again, the hypothesized inner primitivity of whites was imagined by Jung to be symbolically black, reflecting his statements on blacks that indicate he believed people of African descent to be inherently primitive, no matter where they lived, what their occupations were, and what languages they spoke.

The work that discussed the female patient and her projected demon contains an impassioned preface, in which Jung expressed his distress over the disaster of World War I. In this passage, Jung spoke not of an inner black savage brute, but of an inner barbarian. According to Jung, the war demonstrated:

> the problem of the chaotic unconscious which slumbers uneasily beneath the ordered world of consciousness. This war has pitilessly revealed to civilized man that he is still a barbarian, and has at the same time shown what an iron scourge lies in store for him if ever again he should be tempted to make his neighbor responsible for his own evil qualities.
>
> (Jung CW 7 (1960 [1943]):4)

Although Jung's reference of the "inner barbarian" may simply be a metaphorical flourish, the predominance of evolutionary thinking in his psychological theory indicates otherwise. What is not clear is in what sense he meant his readers to understand this reference to the "barbarian." Was this another reference to the shadowy "dark-skinned brute" that Jung described in the aforementioned case? Or was this "barbarian" the dangerous psychological one-sidedness that resulted from the evolutionary move out of the wholeness of the undifferentiated collective unconscious to individual consciousness (Jung 1921, 293)? Perhaps Jung had in mind the animalistic Germanic barbarians as portrayed by Caesar and Tacitus, irascible creatures ever ready to rush wildly into battle? While Jung regularly engaged in the colonial discourse of his own day to describe non-western peoples, he apparently at times employed the colonial discourse of another era to describe the frightening aspects of his own ethnic group's collective psyche. The concept of the *primitive* is often color-coded black in Jung's works, but perhaps not always so. Possibly the negative aspect of the *primitive* or *barbarian* may have been either black or white to Jung; the *civilized*, in contrast, Jung color-coded white.

Unlike the anguish he expressed over World War I, Jung's writings on modern society often convey an attitude of disdain. For example, in *The Undiscovered Self* (1957), Jung denounced modern society, both east and west of Switzerland, describing their populations as masses representing a "sort of collective possession" (Jung CW 10 (1958 [1957]):490). Like the European in Africa, the individual who gets caught up in this collectivized state of mind is vulnerable to being psychically infected by the "affective judgements and wish-fantasies" of the masses (ibid.; also para. 493). Jung criticized not just the homogenization of the population in communist countries, but modern western constitutional states as well, due to their obsession with scientific rationalism and population measurements that reduced individuals down to mere statistics of means and averages (para. 493–494, 501, 544). Both forms of society repress the drive towards individuation that Jung believed to be the product of a long and difficult process of evolution. These modern states, then, revert back in Jung's view to the earliest form of human society, which he considered primitive, collective and politically oppressive. "Thus the constitutional state drifts into the situation of a primitive form of society," wrote Jung, namely, into "the communism of a primitive tribe where everybody is subject to the autocratic rule of a chief or an oligarchy" (para. 504). Not even the Church escaped his critique, for he believed institutionalized religion contributed to the problem of social collectivization and the loss of individuality (para. 529, 536). In general, Jung viewed the modern masses as living in a state of a primitive collective unconscious horde, incapable of developing the inner drive towards self-realization (Jung CW 7 (1963 [1928]):291).

Jung warned that the archaic level of mind was a potential powder keg of dangerous instinctual forces, as well as a powerful vacuum pulling the individual back into an undifferentiated mass of collective thinking, feeling, and action. However, Jung also believed that the oldest and deepest part of the psyche was the wellspring of intuition and the repository of the archetypes, which give rise to new religions, worldviews and scientific insights (Jung CW 10 (1918):13; Jung CW 8 (1950 [1928]):342). As an example, Jung mentioned a patient he once had at the Bürghölzli Clinic in Zurich, who claimed the world was his picture book. He would demonstrate this by simply turning around, which he interpreted as turning a page in his book (Jung CW 7 (1943 [1928]):141). Jung thought this idea was a primitive one, similar to Schopenhauer's world as will and representation. The difference between the poor schizophrenic and his rudimentary, personal image and the broad vision of the philosopher Schopenhauer is that the former's conscious mind had been overwhelmed by the power of the collective unconscious, whereas the philosopher was able to connect his conscious mind with the power of the collective images and abstract them, thereby being able to present such collective ideas in universally valid language (141). Furthermore, in "On Psychic Energy" (1928), Jung argued that the primitive idea of *mana* was based on an archetypal form for energy. This same archetype underlay the law of the conservation of energy, first formulated by the German doctor and physicist Julius Robert von Mayer (1814–1878). Like "primitive man," wrote Jung, Mayer did not derive his concept by way of directed thinking, but while in a state of inspiration; however, unlike "primitive man," Mayer was able to engage this archetype with the conscious portion of his mind in order to articulate the archetypal pattern in scientific and objective terminology (Jung CW 7 (1960 [1943]):106–109). Through the example of Mayer, Jung in effect implied that his model of psychic energy was also derived from this same archetype, perceived concretely by "primitives" as the Polynesian *mana,* the Algonquian *Manitou*, the Iroquois *orenda,* and the Bantu *mulungu*, yet abstracted and universalized as psychic energy by the "civilized" Jung (para. 106–109).

As these examples illustrate, Jung interpreted the concept of the *primitive* as an elementary and evolutionarily anterior psychological aspect of the Westerner's psyche. Furthermore, his view of it is double-edged, mirroring the ambivalence encoded in the concept itself, from the ancient work of Tacitus, who both praised and condemned the ancient Germanic tribes, to the modern western view of non-western peoples as either "noble savages" or "dark-skinned brutes." This ambivalence extended to Jung's description of modern people as exemplified by the model of the psyche as a house discussed at the beginning of this chapter. Modern people can think logically, according to Jung, but are also cut off from the creative wellspring of the collective unconscious. However, according to Jung's logic, it is ultimately not civilization per se and its creators that have gone astray, but the primitive or barbarian aspect of the European psyche and its animal instincts. Jung proposed his solution for integrating the inner barbarian or primitive in language mirroring the ancient cliché of the barbarian as animal and the medieval Church's view of the barbarian as unbeliever: the inner barbarian, he wrote, was both "undomesticated" (*nicht domestiziert*) and "unredeemed" (*unerlöst*) (Jung 1921, 375). Moreover, it is when the archaic level of mind is separated from that of consciousness that disaster results, as the powerful instinctual forces residing there have no healthy outlet.

One could speculate that Jung viewed the distance between the primitive and the civilized not as a straight line but as a loop. As will be discussed in the next chapter, Jung believed that those people with a well-developed individual consciousness could delve into the collective unconscious to rest, gather strength, and find inspiration. Moreover, in his disdain for both scientific rationalism and communism, Jung criticized neither the primitive, nor the civilized per se, but rather, an *over*-civilized state that had degenerated into a state of primitivity. By invoking the concept of the *primitive*, however, Jung obscured the fact that both scientific rationalism and communism are the products of *civilization*. Jung described so-called primitive peoples as inherently inferior; he displaced the supposedly inferior side of the psyche onto the image of "primitive man;" and he articulated a vision in which the fruits of the archaic level of mind can be harvested only by the "civilized" aspect of the psyche. Through these three maneuvers, Jung ultimately salvaged the concept of *civilization*, and the identity of those he claimed could embody it – European men like himself.

The house as a model of the Germanic-Protestant psyche

Returning once more to Schmitz's letter from December 4, 1926, Schmitz claimed that Jung's "paleontology of the soul" had two axes, a horizontal and a vertical one. The discussion up to now has investigated the horizontal axis. What follows is an examination of the vertical axis in Jung's "paleontology of the soul." Jung found an apt illustration for such a theory through the image of his multi-storied house, the floors of which represent different eras. Jung may have borrowed the latter idea from the German historian Karl Lamprecht (1856–1915), who argued that each epoch was shaped by a given dominant, or a particular feeling that dominated and governed all other feelings, perceptions, and attitudes (Shamdasani 2003, 282–283). If so, then Jung in his typical fashion psychologized a historical model. Unfortunately, Jung did not explain in his

Darmstadt lecture why he assigned the eras he did to the different floors of the house. Hence, the significance of these centuries for Jung's theory will be investigated by reference to other works.

In his lecture on "The Conditionality of the Psyche by the Earth," Jung began his explanation of his model with the top floor of the house, which he said was decorated in a nineteenth-century style, not in a mode belonging to the era in which Jung actually delivered his lecture. The late nineteenth century witnessed the acceleration of the modernization process in Germany and greater functional differentiation of the structures of society, which in turn generated a sense of social fragmentation among the general public (Krech 2002, 3). Jung projected this modern perception of fragmentation back in time onto the Roman era, and it appears as the split between consciousness and the unconscious in Jung's model of the house. The significance of the split placed in the Roman era will be discussed below.

Below the top floor, said Jung, was a floor decorated in a sixteenth-century style. To his German audience of 1927, this century would bring to mind events specifically related to Christianity in the Germanic world. The sixteenth century most probably refers to the Reformation. The Reformation was interpreted by many people in Jung's day as an achievement of the Germanic spirit (Lächele 2001, 167), and they believed the cure for modern society's ills would be a new German Reformation, one that would occur within the soul of each individual (Ulbricht 2001, 29–30). Various authors proposed different ideas about how this would happen. The *völkisch* Protestant theologian Friedrich Anderson (1860–1940) believed that the Reformation would be completed by a "Germanizing of Christianity within ourselves" (*Verdeutschung des Christentums in uns selbst*), whereas the *völkisch* publicist Ernst Hunkel (1885–1936) interpreted the coming Reformation as a revival of ancient Germanic religiosity. For Eugen Diederichs, the new Reformation would be an aesthetic, mystic-tinged religion focused on this world and shorn of "Jewish-transcendental speculation" (*jüdisch-transzendenten Spekulationen*) about an afterworld (30).

Jung had his own views on the Reformation. In his "Wotan" essay, he claimed that Germany was a "land of spiritual catastrophes," and after World War II, he specifically named the Reformation as an example of just such a spiritual disaster. Jung further interpreted the Reformation as an event that had shattered the unity of the Catholic Church. This event reflected on a deeper level the loss of the heretofore reigning collective orientation (Jung 1936, 171–172). The liberation of the forces of the collective unconscious after the Reformation manifested centuries later, in Jung's era, in the outbreak of new religious movements and especially the resurgence of Gnosticism, as if the collective unconscious were searching for a new collective adaptation (Jung 1917, 406). Like the aforementioned authors, Jung also believed that any kind of new Reformation or revolution should best take place in one's innermost being.

To return to Jung's lecture: the sixteenth-century floor of Jung's house, he said, was supported by masonry taken from an eleventh-century tower. The eleventh century had witnessed both the Crusades and the final conversion of the Scandinavians to Christianity. Both events came to preoccupy Jung in the final years of World War I and were incorporated into his writings, both private and public. In 1916, Jung penned "The Seven Sermons to the Dead" (*Septem Sermones ad Mortuos*), an esoteric work on self-redemption which he circulated privately among his closest associates. (These Sermons were printed in the German but only described in the English version of *Memories, Dreams, Reflections*). Speaking in the voice of the ancient Gnostic Basilides (who taught 117–138 CE), Jung described Alexandria, Basilides' center of teaching, as the center of the world and the midpoint between east and west (Jung 1962, 389). A group of crusaders have returned from Jerusalem, not having found what they had sought there: redemption. Basilides then informs them that the god they seek cannot be found outside of themselves, but is to be sought within their own souls. The divine would appear as an inner sun (397–398). Although Jung wrote this text in fictional form and dressed it in ancient Gnostic garb, he had already discussed the inner sun as a symbol of psychic energy in his 1912 *Transformations and Symbols of the Libido*, and he would come to use it as a metaphor for the self twelve years later in *The Relations between the Ego and the Unconscious* (Jung CW 7 (1963 [1928]):400).

According to Jung, the eleventh century was also when Christian thinkers began occupying themselves with the Anti-Christ. This interest corresponded in time with the completion of the conversion of the Germanic heathens around 1000 CE. As Jung knew, the Medieval Christian Church had transformed Wotan into a devil. This Christian interpretation might be reflected in Jung's 1918 "The Role of the Unconscious," where he wrote that Christianity had split the Germanic barbarian psyche in two, and a new reconciling symbol was needed to bridge the gap between the light and dark portions of this collective ethnic psyche (Jung CW 10 (1918):17). Given the preponderance of references to the inner sun in Jung's works, one may speculate that the form this reconciling symbol was to take would be of a solar nature.

One story of the multi-layered house in Jung's lecture remains to be explained. In three different versions of the psyche as a multi-storied house, Jung described this dwelling as having a cellar from the Roman era, that is, below the threshold of consciousness. Jung explained this Roman cellar in his lecture in Darmstadt by saying,

> [W]hen a system of adaptation begins to fail, a general restlessness arises, and an attempt is made to find new, appropriate forms to deal with the unconscious. A shining example of this is the Roman Empire.
>
> [W]enn ein solches Anpassungssystem anfängt zu versagen, so entsteht allgemeine Beunruhigung, und es setzen Versuche ein, neue passende Formen für den Umgang mit dem Unbewußten zu finden. Ein glänzendes Beispiel hiefür ist die römische Kaiserzeit.
>
> (Jung 1927, 107)

In this quote, Jung once again referred to the multiple new religious movements dotting the cultural landscape of the Roman world 2,000 years previously and, implicitly, the German-speaking world of his own day. In fact, Jung regularly interpreted whole epochs or cultures through the lens of his analytical psychology, as if the psyche of the individual corresponded to the collective psyche of a people or time period. Jung's description of the Roman Empire is a case in point. During his *Zarathustra* seminar on June 24, 1936, Jung described the Roman era as a clash between psychic oppositions, as if an entire epoch were experiencing either a neurosis or an individuation process *en masse.* He described two very different forms of mentalities he believed existed in Roman society, "the world of the slaves and the world of the highly differentiated mind" (Jung 1988, 2:1030), the latter presumably belonging to the slave-holding class of philosophers, historians and politicians. Jung implicitly applied his theory of the emergence of the transcendent function due to the tension of the outer and inner portions of the individual psyche to society at large, viewing different groups as representing the psyche's two poles. He thereby also naturalized hierarchical class relations. In this picture, the slaves of antiquity are equivalent to contemporary "primitives," who in turn represent the primordial collective unconscious. The Roman slave-holding class is effectively aligned with modern Western man, and represents individual consciousness. In Jung's view of ancient Rome, the tension between the two class-based extremes finally produced a powerful force that Jung termed the *Ergreifer*, which was none other than "the manifestation of the spirit in its most original form," as witnessed in the Pentecostal Miracle (ibid.).

However, the collective adaptation provided by Christianity had broken down, so Jung believed, and a new orientation was being sought, apparently to be produced through the tension between the *primitive* and the *civilized*, however understood. In Jung's discussion of the collective of Rome, the tension created was between classes; in the case of the female patient who projected her inner demon onto Jung, this tension was between the black primitive and the civilized white components of her own psyche. And in the collective case of the Germanic psyche? This tension spanned the dark primitive and light civilized portions fragmented by the conversion to Christianity, which Jung had already explained in "The Role of the Unconscious."

What the reconciliation of the two halves of the psyche could produce might be as significant as the force – Christianity – that had caused the original split. Jung said as much in his private letter to Schmitz, dated May 26, 1923. Here, Jung referred to a rather pale-skinned primitive, the Germanic barbarian of ancient lore. He described the collective psychological malaise among contemporary people of Germanic descent, the original source of which was the fragmentation of the barbarian Germanic psyche by the imposition of the foreign and more highly developed Christianity, which crippled the German's natural evolutionary process. In implicit reference to the legend of St. Boniface (ca. 672/675–754) felling Donar's (Thor's) sacred oak to convert Germanic heathens to Christianity (Leinweber 1983, 18), Jung interpreted the oak as having belonged instead to Wotan, and wrote, "Like Wotan's oaks, the gods were felled and a wholly incongruous Christianity, born of monotheism on a much higher cultural level, was grafted upon the stumps. The Germanic man is still suffering from this mutilation" (Jung 1973, 1:40). The tension of psychic extremes that helped give birth to a new collective orientation 2,000 years previously was now to be found within the collective psyche of a single people. "In part we need new foundations," Jung wrote to Schmitz. "We must dig down to the primitive in us, for only out of the conflict between civilized man and the Germanic barbarian (in German: *dem germanischen Primitiven*) will there come what we need: a new experience of God" (Jung 1972, 1:62; 1973, 1:40; ibid.). Jung's proposed solution entailed a necessary, if also painful, conflict between the civilized and primitive portions of the Germanic psyche, which would recapitulate the original encounter with God to which the early Christian texts bore witness (ibid.). Jung presumably meant the Pentecostal Miracle. Jung advocated not a return to the Christian Church, but to the "primitive" roots within the Germanic soul, to generate an experience on par with that which occurred 2,000 years previously, one that created the world-transforming religion of Christianity.

The path to rejuvenation and the prayer to the light

During his trip to East Africa, Jung witnessed a ritual of the Kôôny that he described both in his lecture on "The Conditionality of the Psyche by the Earth" (Jung 1927, 101; Jung CW 10 (1933 [1931]):144) and three years later in "Archaic Man." Jung reported that the Kôôny people leave their huts at sunrise, spit or blow vigorously into their hands, and then hold their palms up towards the sun. Jung asked the Kôôny why they did this, but they were unable to provide an answer. Jung emphasized the alleged ignorance of the Kôôny regarding the significance of their ritual: "It was impossible to get an explanation, and it became clear to me that they knew only what they did and not why they did it" (Jung CW 10 (1933 [1931]):144). Jung explained that the Swahili word *athista* means both "sun" and "god", while breath and spittle are substances of the soul. Hence, this ritual symbolizes the offering of one's soul to the Supreme Being in gratitude that the terrors of the night have been dissolved with the coming of dawn, bringing with it a feeling of redemption (Jung 1927, 101).

Despite Jung's presentation of himself as a scientist undertaking ethnopsychological research, his explanation is neither innocent nor objective. Rather, Jung once again performed the role of colonialist, claiming to possess knowledge about the "others" that the "others" lacked about themselves. While seeking to understand the "other," Jung exercised the power to define, explain, and even produce the "other" as subject, and for his own purposes (Brantlinger 1985, 166; Said 1978, 12). This claim to knowledge is exemplified by the statement by Burleson that Jung misunderstood this ritual, practiced throughout western Kenya and eastern Uganda. The word *asista* (not *athista* or *adhi'sta*, as Jung wrote), means both "god" and "sun," but this does not mean the two are equivalent. *Asista* is the name for the supreme being, the creator god, who gifted humans with the sun in order to produce food. East Africans see the light of day as distinct from the sun (Burleson 2005, 163–165). According to Burleson, Jung ignored the metaphysics of the Kôôny people by which they themselves explain their ritual, focusing instead on the emotions imputed to them by Jung (164). Jung was thus able to appropriate this ritual to support his theory of archetypes as automatic, affective responses to regularly recurring events, such as the sunrise. Given that Jung claimed that so-called primitives are largely driven by instincts rather than rational thought and regularly project their inner psychic contents out onto the world, one can surmise that Jung interpreted the morning ritual of the Kôôny as concrete evidence of an innate religious function in the psyche, specifically, the sun-like archetype of the self, projected outward onto the physical sun in the sky.

There are several images that would probably have come to the minds of Jung's audience members in both Darmstadt and Hottingen as they heard him describe this Kôôny ritual. The first is the painting known as *The Prayer to the Light* (*Das Lichtgebet)* by the German artist Fidus (see the cover of Arvidsson 2006). Born Hugo Höppner (1868–1948), Fidus developed an artistic style that mixed symbolism and *Jugendstil* with Romantic, Germanic, and life-reform themes, especially nudism and naturalism. His work reflected the desires of the petite bourgeoisie, portraying *völkisch,* utopian images of the past (Schuster 1996, 634–635). Fidus believed himself to be a "man of revelation" (*Offenbarungsmensch*), whose art would contribute to the revitalization of society (639), especially through the temples he designed to consecrate a new Germanic culture and art. He promoted his ideas by holding slide shows throughout Germany and Switzerland (640).

Between 1890 and 1938, Fidus created eleven versions of *The Prayer to the Light* in which an androgynous young man stands naked on top of a cliff, his long blond hair waving in the breeze. The sharp rocks call to mind the fjords of Scandinavia that Fidus had once visited, suggesting a "Nordic" setting. The young man stands with his legs together and his arms upraised in salutation to the sun, creating the Y-shaped form of *algiz,* the z-rune (ᛉ). Called the life-rune by Guido von List, this symbol further emphasizes a "Nordic" theme. The painting was popular among members of Fidus' milieu who wanted to replace Christianity with a Nordic-Germanic religion that they believed corresponded to their racial soul (German Historical Museum, n.d.). In 1913, Fidus published *The Prayer to the Light* as a postcard for the Free German Youth Day (*Freideutscher Jugendtag*), which took place in October on the Hohe Meißner Mountain in Hesse, Germany. The postcard was eagerly snatched up by the participants, who later displayed it on their walls at home. This image also became the dominant symbol of the life-reform movement (Schuster 1996, 641–642).

In 1908, Fidus joined fellow artist Ludwig Fahrenkrog's Germanic Faith Community (638), a group that combined Germanic religion with the spirituality of self-redemption. Fahrenkrog's paintings reflected these themes. For example, he painted his own version of *The Prayer to the Light,* called *The Holy Hour (Die heilige Stunde)* in 1918. The sun rises to the left; the observer must therefore be north of the unfolding scene. This includes a naked young man, his legs together and his hands raised, so that his body forms the life rune as he greets the dawning sun. A group of people, some naked, others clothed in ancient classical garb, stand behind him, entranced by the morning light (Wolfschlag 2006, 39–40, 82).

An image that bears striking similarities to the paintings of solar worship by Fidus and Fahrenkrog was published in 1923 in *Recreating the Individual: A Study of Psychological Types and Their Relation to Psychoanalysis*, written by the analytical psychologist Beatrice M. Hinkle. Drawn by a female patient, the image portrays a naked woman viewed from behind, her legs together and her arms raised overhead in greeting to the dawning sun, which is just beginning to appear above a hill in front of the woman (reproduced in Noll 1997, n.p.). Hinkle insisted that this and other images shown in the book were the product of the collective unconscious and had an "archaic" quality to them. Instead, writes Noll, the impulse was probably Fidus' *Lichtgebet* (Noll 1997, 265). To this observation one could add Fahrenkrog's *Die Heilige Stunde*. Finally, Hinkle was intimately familiar with the solar themes of Jung's *Transformations and Symbols of the Libido,* of which she was the translator. These images, found in both English- and German-speaking countries, indicate their widespread popularity among the various life-reform, self-redemption, and other spiritual "quest" movements during the world wars (Sutcliffe 2007; Landau 1964).

Arms raised in Y-formation, legs together, in supplication to a Higher Power – these are the basic elements of a much older and much more widespread image: the Crucifixion. In the "Earth-Conditionality of the Psyche," Jung drew no explicit parallels between the ritual of the Kôôny and similar European phenomena. However, in "Archaic Man," Jung offered a thought experiment to his European audience members that would have called to mind the symbol of the cross. Jung enters Zurich as a foreigner, wishing to examine the customs there. He speaks with a Mr. Müller and a Mr. Meyer (equivalents of "the man on the street"). Both men no longer attend church and insist they know nothing of religious rituals. Oddly enough, Mr. Müller is observed hiding colored eggs in his garden at Easter. Like the Kôôny, Mr. Müller is confused by the questions about his actions, insisting he is doing what has always been done. At the end of the thought experiment, Jung concluded, "Archaic man everywhere does what he does, and civilized man knows what he does" (Jung CW 10 (1933 [1931]):145).

Jung's audience members, which included such illustrious names as Rainer Maria Rilke (1875–1926), Hugo von Hofmannsthal (1874–1929), Hermann Hesse (1877–1962), Thomas Mann (1875–1955), and Albert Schweitzer (1875–1965) (Bishop 2008, 502), might have been tempted to see Mr. Müller – and themselves – as the civilized opposites of the African primitives. Yet it is significant that Jung insisted Mr. Müller did not understand his Eastertime actions. According to Jung, many modern people live their lives in a relatively unconscious and collective state; only "higher types" develop a neurotic conflict that can generate the drive towards self-realization. Rather than aligning himself with Mr. Müller, Jung contrasted himself both to the unconscious primitive who cannot individuate, and the unconscious modern man, who has the potential to do so. Jung demonstrated his own presumed civilized status by being able to explain the meaning of the rituals of both: the Kôôny offer their souls by way of the breath or spittle in their palms to God, symbolized by the sun, whereas the archetypal meaning of Easter relates to the (here, unnamed) crucified Christ, hanging on the cross in a position replicating the life-rune, offering his spirit to the Father. Jung ended his talk by quoting Luke 23:46: "Lord, into your hands I command my spirit." Elsewhere, Jung described Christ as a chief symbol of the archetype of the self, who, as the second Adam, brings the human being full circle from his original primordial state of unconscious wholeness to a restoration of that wholeness on the level of consciousness. Christ was also, according to Jung, the exemplar of individuation and the symbolic equivalent of the sun (Jung CW 9/2 (1951):70; Jung 2009, 293; Jung CW 10 (1958 [1957]):529, 536; Jung CW 10 (1959 [1958]):808). In his lecture on "Archaic Man," then, the allegedly instinct-driven, childlike and predominantly unconscious primitives bear living witness to the truth of the Crucifixion, understood as the preeminent symbol of self-redemption.

Conclusion

Jung claimed to have garnered empirical evidence for primitive mentality during his travels among peoples he believed to be psychologically living in a time historically prior to that of modern Western Europe. Yet the strong affinities between his descriptions of the so-called primitive people he encountered and those found in western ethnographic literature from the ancient Greco-Roman world suggest that Jung carried with him into the field long-standing and deeply ingrained stereotypes about the barbarian or primitive "other." Indeed, Jung tended to overlook obvious religious, cultural, linguistic and even geographical changes among populations in order to characterize some people by an unchanging primitive essence. Closer examination of the role that the character "primitive man" plays in Jung's work demonstrates that "he" functions as the living proof for Jung's theory of the archaic level of mind, which is both the curse and the cure of the modern Westerner.

The double meaning of the term *primitive* in Jung's theory reflects the ambivalence in his image of the so-called civilized individual due to Jung's critique of modern materialism and his anguish over World War I, a torment that was shared by Keyserling, Schmitz, and many of their contemporaries. Jung reinterpreted the image of the "noble savage" as an inner source of renewal and restored wholeness, slumbering in the depths of the modern western psyche. He reworked the "ignoble savage" as the instincts escaping civilized man's self-regulation, which has gained civilized man a place at the top of the international power hierarchy while costing him the joy of experiencing the body and nature as they are. Jung could be sharp in his criticism of "Aryans," calling them tyrants who ruined the world in their attempts to rule it (Jung CW 10 (1933):185). In Jung's effort to articulate the source of both the malaise of modern society and its cure, he stripped off the persona of the so-called civilized person to reveal a deeper level of mind he called "primitive." Yet he reinstated civilization as an exclusively European characteristic by arguing that consciousness was the product of an evolutionary process that so-called primitives had yet to experience – and indeed, were psychologically incapable of doing so. He displaced the problems and catastrophes of modern society onto the "primitive" aspects of modern man and society, while affirming that only so-called civilized people have the individual consciousness necessary to harness the beneficiary powers of the primitive. More specifically, Jung created a metaphor of the psyche by way of the multi-storied house that implicitly limited full psychological development and hence the capability for individual autonomy to Christians and Europeans, and especially to Protestants and people of Germanic descent. In sum, Jung sought to secure his own identity and more generally that of the white, modern, western man of Protestant background, in the face of the crises wrought by the forces of modernity. He did so through his theory of individuation, to which both the "primitive" and "modern man" of mass society act as foils.

Bibliography

Title

"paleontology of the soul": Oskar A. H. Schmitz to C. G. Jung, December 4, 1926 (ETH-Bibliothek Zurich (Switzerland), ETH Zurich University Archives, Hs 1056:148). My translation.

Sources

Asad, Talal (ed.). 1973. *Anthropology and the Colonial Encounter.* London: Ithaca.

Bair, Deirdre. 2003. *Jung. A Biography.* Boston: Little, Brown and Co.

Barton, David. 2014. "C.G. Jung in Taos: A Creative Mis-Encounter." Talk given at the *International Association for Jungian Studies* 2014 meeting. Available at: http://www.academia.edu/7517105/C.G._Jung_in_Taos_A_Creative_Mis-Encounter (Accessed: July 25, 2015).

Bishop, Paul. 2008. "The Timeliness and Timelessness of the 'Archaic': Analytical Psychology, 'Primordial' Thought, Synchronicity." *Journal of Analytical Psychology* 53(4):501–523.

Brantlinger, Patrick. 1985. "Victorians and Africans: The Genealogy of the Myth of the Dark Continent." *Critical Inquiry* 12(1):166–203.

Brooke, Roger. 2008. "Cultural Reflections on Jung's Concept of Individuation." *Psychological Perspectives* 51(1):36–53.

Burleson, Blake W. 2005. *Jung in Africa.* New York: Continuum.

Césaire, Aimé. 2013. "Discourse on Colonialism." In Patrick Williams and Laura Chrisman (ed.), *Colonial Discourse and Post-Colonial Theory: A Reader.* Abingdon, Oxon: Routledge, pp. 172–180.

Childs, Peter and R. J. Patrick Williams. 1999. *Introduction to Post-Colonial Theory*. London: Prentice Hall.

Durkheim, Emile. 1965. *The Elementary Forms of the Religious Life*. New York: Free Press.

Fabian, Johannes. 1983. *Time and the Other: How Anthropology Makes its Object*. New York: Columbia University Press.

Fanon, Frantz. 2008. *Black Skin, White Masks*, trans. by Richard Philcox. New York: Grove Press.

Gilman, Sander L. 1982. *On Blackness without Blacks: Essays on the Image of the Black in Germany*. Boston: G. K. Hall.

Jung, C. G. 1912. *Wandlungen und Symbole der Libido: Beiträge zur Entwicklungs-geschichte des Denkens*. Leipzig: Franz Deuticke.

——. 1917. *Collected Papers on Analytical Psychology*, ed. by Constance E. Long. London: Baillière, Tindall and Cox.

——. 1921. *Psychologische Typen*. Zurich: Rascher & Cie.

——. 1925. *Psychology of the Unconscious: A Study of the Transformations and Symbolisms of the Libido; A Contribution to the History of the Evolution of Thought*, trans. by Beatrice M. Hinkle. New York: Dodd, Mead.

——. 1927. "Die Erdbedingtheit der Psyche." *Der Leuchter* 8:83–137.

——. 1953–1991. *Collected Works*, ed. by Sir Herbert Read, Michael Fordham, and Gerhard Adler. New York: Pantheon Books; Princeton, NJ: Princeton University Press.

——. 1962. *Erinnerungen, Träume, Gedanken*, rec. and ed. by Aniela Jaffé. Zurich: Rascher.

——. 1965. *Memories, Dreams, Reflections*, rec. and ed. by Aniela Jaffé, trans. by Richard and Clara Winston. New York: Vintage.

——. 1966. *Psychology and Religion*. The Terry Lectures. New Haven: Yale University Press.

——. 1972. *Briefe*, ed. by Aniela Jaffé with Gerhard Adler. Three Volumes. Olten: Walter.

——. 1973. *Letters*, sel. and ed. by Gerhard Adler, with Aniela Jaffé, trans. by R. F. C. Hull. Two Volumes. Princeton, NJ: Princeton University Press.

——. 1988. *Nietzsche's Zarathustra: Notes of the Seminar Given in 1934–1939*, ed. by James L. Jarrett. Princeton, NJ: Princeton University Press.

——. 1989. *Analytical Psychology: Notes of the Seminar Given in 1925*, ed. by William McGuire. Princeton, NJ: Princeton University Press.

——. 2009. *The Red Book*, ed. by Sonu Shamdasani, trans. by Mark Kyburz, John Peck, and Sonu Shamdasani. New York: W.W. Norton & Co.

Krech, Volkhard. 2002. *Wissenschaft und Religion: Studien zur Geschichte der Religionsforschung in Deutschland 1871 bis 1933*. Tubingen: Mohr Siebeck.

Lächele, Rainer. 2001. "Germanisierung des Christentums." In Stefanie von Schnurbein and Justus H. Ulbricht (eds), *Völkische Religion und Krisen der Moderne: Entwürfe 'arteigener' Glaubenssysteme seit der Jahrhundertwende*. Würzburg: Königshausen & Neumann, pp.165–183.

Landau, Rom. 1964. *God is My Adventure*. London: Unwin Books.

Larrington, Carolyne. 1996. *The Poetic Edda*. Oxford: Oxford University Press.

Leinweber, Josef. 1983. *St. Bonifatius: Leben und Wirken*. Fulda: Bistum Fulda.

Lévy-Bruhl, Lucien. 1985. *How Natives Think,* intro. by C. Scott Littleton, trans. by Lilian A. Clare. Princeton, NJ: Princeton University Press.

Littleton, C. Scott. 1985. "Introduction." In Lucien Lévy-Bruhl, *How Natives Think,* trans. by Lilian A. Clare. Princeton, NJ: Princeton University Press, pp.i–viii.

Meyer, Elard Hugo. 1883. *Indogermanische Mythen.* First Volume. Gandharven. Berlin: Ferd. Dümmlers Verlangsbuchhandlung.

Noll, Richard. 1997. *The Aryan Christ: The Secret Life of Carl Jung.* New York: Random House.

Pietikäinen, Petteri. 1998. "National Typologies, Races, and Mentalities in C. G. Jung's Psychology." *History of European Ideas* 24(6):359–373.

Roediger, David R. 2008. *How Race Survived U.S. History: From Settlement and Slavery to the Obama Phenomenon.* London: Verso.

Roosevelt, Theodore. 1914. *Through the Brazilian Wilderness.* New York: Charles Scribner's Sons.

Said, Edward. 1978. *Orientalism.* London: Routledge & Kegan Paul.

Schnurbein, Stefanie von. 1992. *Religion als Kulturkritik: Neugermanisches Heidentum im 20. Jahrhundert.* Heidelberg: Winter.

Schuster, Marina. 1996. "Fidus: Ein Gesinnungskünstler der völkischen Kulturbewegung." In Uwe Puschner, Walter Schmitz und Justus H. Ulbricht (eds), *Handbuch zur 'Völkischen Bewegung' 1871–1918.* Saur: Munich, pp.634–650.

Segal, Robert A. 2007. "Jung and Lévy-Bruhl." *Journal of Analytical Psychology* 52:635–658.

Shamdasani, Sonu. 2003. *Jung and the Making of Modern Psychology: The Dream of a Science.* Cambridge, UK: Cambridge University Press.

Sharpe, Eric J. 1975. *Comparative Religion: A History.* Second Edition. La Salle, IL: Open Court.

Söderblom, Nathan. 1916. *Das Werden des Gottesglaubens.* Leipzig: J. C. Hinrichs'sche Buchhandlung.

Stocking, George. 1968. *Race, Culture, and Evolution: Essays in the History of Anthropology.* New York: Free Press.

Stoler, Ann Laura. 1995. *Race and the Education of Desire: Foucault's History of Sexuality and the Colonial Order of Things.* Durham: Duke University Press.

Sutcliffe, Steven. 2007. "The Origins of 'New Age' Religion between the Two World Wars." In Daren Kemp and James R. Lewis (eds), *Handbook of New Age*, Leiden: Brill, pp.51–75.

Thomas, David Hurst. 2000. *Skull Wars: Kennewick Man, Archaeology, and the Battle for Native American Identity.* New York: Basic Books.

Tylor, Edward B. 1873. *Primitive Culture: Researches into the Development of Mythology, Philosophy, Religion, Language, Art and Custom.* Second Edition. Two Volumes. London: John Murray.

Ulbricht, Justus H. 2001. "'. . . in einer *gottfremden*, prophetenlosen Zeit . . . :' Aspekte einer Problemgeschichte 'arteigener' Religion um 1900." In Stefanie Schnurbein and Justus H. Ulbricht (eds), *Völkische Religion und Krisen der Moderne: Entwürfe 'arteigener' Glaubenssysteme seit der Jahrhundertwende.* Würzburg: Könighsausen & Neumann, pp.9–39.

Wolfschlag, Claus. 2006. *Ludwig Fahrenkrog: Das goldene Tor; Ein deutscher Maler zwischen Jugendstil und Germanenglaube.* Dresden: Zeitenwende.

Materials from the ETH-Bibliothek Zurich (Switzerland): ETH Zurich University Archives, C.G. Jung Papers Collection

Letters

Oskar A. H. Schmitz to Carl Gustav Jung, December 4, 1926. Hs 1056:148.
Carl Gustav Jung to Oskar A. H. Schmitz, March 15, 1921. Hs 1056:50.
Hermann von Keyserling to Emma Jung, November 19, 1925. Hs 1056:122.

Articles

Jung, C. G. 1930. "Your Negroid and Indian Behavior." *Forum: The Magazine of Controversy* 83(4):193–199. Hs 1379:112.
Jung, C. G. 1936. "Yoga and the West." In *Prabuddha Bharata, or Awakened India.* Sri Ramakrishna Centenary Number, pp.170–177. Hs 1379:185.

5

"BALDR COMES HOME"

From the paleontology of the soul to the invention of a Germanic mythology

Introduction

When Schmitz requested a lecture on the "paleontology of the soul" to the School of Wisdom (see Chapter 4), he attributed the discovery of a purported phylogenetic unconscious to Jung. Perhaps Schmitz came to his conclusion when he heard Jung explain this theory in his 1925 private seminar on analytical psychology, describing it metaphorically as a multi-storied house. Jung claimed not to have consciously developed the model; rather, he had *dreamt* of the house, implying that he had received an archetypal message from the collective unconscious concerning its very structure. Jung further said that this dream, which he had had in 1909, had laid the foundations for *Transformations and Symbols of the Libido*, that is, for the new view of psychological processes developed therein, which differed substantially from the perspective offered by Freudian psychoanalysis (Jung 1989, 22–23; Jung 1965, 158).

The dream represents significant divergences between Freudian and Jungian theory, not only in respect to dream analysis, but also regarding the nature of the archaic collective unconscious and the concept of *primitivity*. The last chapter already considered several meanings of *primitivity* in Jung's work. First, it examined the concept as related to the most archaic level of mind, the collective unconscious and the archetypes. Second, it discussed how Jung considered so-called primitive peoples as living fossils, providing evidence for this aspect of the psyche. Finally, Jung used the concept to critique modern mass society, which he often described as a primitive horde. This chapter explores two more meanings of the concept of *primitivity* in Jung's work, which are based on the differences between *primitive* as *infantile* (such as in the presumed psychology of "primitive" people, still enmeshed in the biological instincts) and *primitive* as signifying *primordial* and *original*, therefore promising rebirth. Jung applied the term *primitive* to both Jews and Germanic people, yet with very different meanings, correlated to these two basic definitions of the term. In the case of "Jewish psychology," Jung described Jews as infantile, materialistic, rootless, and effeminate. These ideas were based on age-old anti-Jewish stereotypes first promulgated by Christians as part of their axe to grind against the people they held to be Christ's murderers, yet secularized and made the stuff of racial science beginning in the eighteenth century. However, Jung portrayed the "primitive" side of Germanic peoples (*Germanen*) as the archaic source of psychic wholeness and renewal. The changing definition of the *primitive* or the *archaic* along racial and religious lines is evident in Jung's work as early as 1912, and in numerous writings throughout the Weimar and Nazi eras. It also played a determining role in his unique interpretation of the Wandering Jew and its significance for the Germanic Christian psyche. Finally, it shaped the narrative of the posthumous *Memories, Dreams, Reflections,* specifically the representations of Freud and Jung's dream of the house.

A dream of a new science: Jung's night-time excavations in the psyche as a house

There are at least three published versions of Jung's metaphor of the house, the best-known being the one in *Memories, Dreams, Reflections.* Jung's image of the house was not consistent; in all three versions, the floors above ground were assigned to different eras without explanation. In 1925, Jung said he dreamt of a very complicated house from the Middle Ages, with multiple stairs, rooms, and hallways. From the street were stairs leading down to a vaulted Gothic room, and then into a cellar. In the dream in *Memories, Dreams, Reflections,* gone are the floors from the nineteenth and sixteenth centuries that Jung had described in his 1927 lecture at Keyserling's School of Wisdom conference. Instead, the upper level has a salon with rococo-style furnishings (possibly evoking the rationalism of the Enlightenment), and the ground floor appears to be from either the fifteenth or sixteenth century, although furnished in an unspecified medieval style. The underground portion of the house always contains a cellar from the Roman era, as well as an underground space – either another cellar or a cave – with pottery shards and bones, which became two skulls in *Memories, Dreams, Reflections*. Freud is shown in this book attempting to interpret the two skulls as a death wish Jung harbored against others. Jung, however, wrote that he had already realized that the dream represented a model for the structure of the psyche (Jung 1965, 158–160).

A couple of remarks are in order about these dreams. First, that a denizen of Zurich should dream of Roman ruins is hardly surprising; Zurich is built on the ruins of a Gallo-Roman town called Turicum. Roman ruins are still to be seen to this day, including a remnant of a wall on the Lindenhof. This is the site of a castle from Roman times where, in 1798, the citizens of Zurich swore an oath on the constitution of the Helvetic Republic. Second, what is presented in *Memories, Dreams, Reflections* depicts stories that Jung told throughout his life, which he changed according to context. This observation takes into account both Shamdasani's critique of Jaffé's editorial maneuvers (see Chapter 3) and the difference in the dream's details, which will be noted in reference to Jung's letters to Freud and the notes from his 1925 private seminar. Finally, these differences in detail indicate that the dreams discussed here were not reported as they were actually dreamed. Time and again authors retell Jung's childhood dreams uncritically, as if the octogenarian had remembered his dreams exactly as he had dreamt them at the age of sixteen or three. Indeed, as the previous comparison shows, the three published accounts of Jung's dream of the psyche as a house are not the same. Surely Jung could have checked the accuracy of his own narrative, had that been important. Given the discrepancies, I assume that the dreams reported in *Memories, Dreams, Reflections* are narrated with specific detail and in a given sequence in order to perform important rhetorical strategies. A case in point: rather than following a Freudian analysis of his phallic dream at age three as representing castration anxiety or an incipient case of the Oedipal complex, Jung portrayed it archetypally, as an archaic image of the libido in the Jungian sense of the term (see below). This interpretation, often repeated by Jung's commentators, thereby supports the dual image of Jung as both a psychologist and a spiritual master.

Returning to the dream of the house, it appears in Jung's autobiography in the chapter on Sigmund Freud. Although the events in question may be historically accurate, the presentation of them acts as a vehicle for Jung's critique of the founder of psychoanalysis. Jung dated the dream to the two doctors' trip back from Clark University in Worcester, Massachusetts (Jung 1989, 22), where both he and Freud received honorary doctorates and delivered lectures at the invitation of the psychologist Stanley Hall. Jung and Freud spent a good deal of time together during the seven weeks of the trip, analyzing each other's dreams (Jung 1965, 156–158; ibid. 1989, 22). Jung recounted that he was unable to fully analyze one dream by Freud, however; the older man refused to reveal private information pertinent to the analysis, because it might have revealed the source of his neurosis, stating, "I cannot risk my authority!"(158) Freud's placing of authority above truth, wrote Jung, highly damaged Jung's respect for his once-esteemed colleague; indeed, the incident became a turning point in their relationship, foreshadowing its end. This episode comes only a few pages after it is related that Jung, early in his career, overcame the temptation to publish a paper on his experimental findings without mentioning Freud. He feared the opprobrium that would befall him should he link himself in any way with the controversial psychoanalyst, but Jung made the decision to be honest. "You cannot build your life upon a lie," he thought to himself (148). The proximity of these events within the text, one portraying Jung as bravely choosing to be honest at the risk of social censure, and Freud suppressing the truth to protect his authority, creates a portrait of Jung as virtuous and courageous, and Freud as unscrupulous and even neurotic.

Furthermore, the dream of the house acted as Jung's evidence for his theory that dream symbolism is not just personal and wish-fulfilling, as Freud believed, but can also be archetypal in nature. Moreover, the dream seemed to prove the theory of the phylogenetic unconscious as imagined by Jung – the house was itself an archetypal expression of the stratified collective unconscious, with its various layers relating to the family, the clan, the nation, and different ethnic groups (Jung 1989, 133). However, the idea of a phylogenetic unconscious was not new, nor was the model of the psyche as a house. The French philosopher and psychologist Théodule Ribot (1839–1916) had as early as 1896 developed the notion of an ancestral unconscious, which he differentiated from the personal unconscious (as did Jung). Furthermore, in Freud's *Studies in Hysteria* (1893), the Viennese doctor Josef Breuer (1842–1925) had described the psyche through the model of a house, without it being a phylogenetic model (Myers 2009, 516–520). In this same work, Freud described his case studies as excavations into various strata of the psyche. In 1908, the Swiss psychologist Édouard Claparède (1873–1940) discussed the model of the psyche as a house and the idea that the psyche contained ancestral remnants in "Quelques mots sur la définition de l'hystérie" (1908), published in *Archives de Psychologie* (519–520). Freud alluded to Claparède's work in his letter to Jung dated December 8, 1907 (McGuire 1974, 55F), and Jung did so himself in "Abstracts of the Psychological Works of Swiss Authors" in the same year. Moreover, Stanley Hall, with whom both Jung and Freud stayed during their trip to Clark University, believed in a psychologized version of Haeckelian recapitulation theory, in that the individual psyche contains within itself the entire history of the evolution of the human race (Shamdasani 2003, 188). Jung's dating his dream of the house to 1909 may very well point to Hall's influence (234); moreover, this was Jung's first opportunity to observe different racial communities in interaction, which may have influenced the development of his "'geology' of a personality" with its separate mountain ranges indicating different large collectives of people. Finally, in the years between their visit to Clark University and the publication of their 1912 works, Freud's *Totem and Taboo* and Jung's *Transformations and Symbols of the Libido*, Freud and Jung discussed the idea of a phylogenetic unconscious at considerable length in their correspondence. In *Memories, Dreams, Reflections*, however, none of these possible sources for Jung's ideas of a phylogenetic unconscious are mentioned. Instead, extending back at least to his private lectures of 1925, Jung regularly portrayed his theory as having manifested as an archetypal dream, the symbolism of which he was then able to translate into scientific terms.

The customs officer and the crusader

In Jung's autobiography, the description of the psyche through the model of a house immediately follows two reports of Freud's fainting spells, as if they pertained to the fundamental differences in the men's theories as exemplified by their dream theories. Earlier in the book, Jung reported that he had suffered fainting spells as a child, which he overcame through willpower and strength of character (Jung 1965, 31–32). In contrast, the older Freud still suffered from such spells (156–157); in the context of this narrative, these were symptomatic of his unresolved neurosis. The first spell occurred in 1909 in Bremen, before the men departed on their trip to the United States. Jung had been eagerly discussing a report he had read about ancient corpses preserved in peat bogs in Germany. Freud, however, found his interest morbid, and accused

Jung of harboring a death-wish against him (156). The second fainting spell took place four years later, at the Psychoanalytic Congress in Munich, during a debate between Jung and unnamed devotees of Freudian psychoanalysis. The psychoanalysts claimed that the ancient Egyptian pharaoh Amenophis IV (Ikhnaton) had erased his father's name from cartouches as an expression of his unresolved father complex; Jung instead defended the pharaoh's actions as a religious innovation relating to his founding of monotheism (157; Jung 1925, 106). During the discussion in which Jung again mentioned the peat-bog corpses, Freud fainted, and Jung picked him up and carried him to a sofa. Upon regaining consciousness, the older man looked at Jung "as if I were his father." Jung then emphasized that "the fantasy of father-murder was common to both cases" (Jung 1965, 157). In other words, Jung used "Jewish" psychology – Freud's theory of the Oedipal complex – to analyze the Jewish Freud.

The relationship between the two men was in reality quite different than its presentation in *Memories, Dreams, Reflections*. Freud had addressed the issue of both fainting spells in his letter to Jung dated Nov. 29, 1912, where he attributed their cause to migraines. He further admitted that his migraine-induced fainting spells might also have had a psychosomatic origin (McGuire 1974, 329F). In this line, Freud may have been referring to his unresolved and self-diagnosed "neurosis," which was sexual in nature. Perhaps it was related to his affair with his sister-in-law Minna Bernays (Bair 2003, 164), which smacked of incest. Or perhaps it had to do with his homosexual desires (Boyarin 1997, 206). As the Jewish studies scholar Daniel Boyarin notes, fainting constituted a "performance of femaleness" in fin-de-siècle culture and Freud assumed male-desiring men were similar to women in that both were presumably passive in their sexual aims (213). In either case, Freud's sexual issues would have underscored stereotypes about Jewish men as incestuous and effeminate, stereotypes Jung used in his writings on "Jewish" psychology (see below).

Furthermore, Freud had accused Jung in this letter of having an unresolved father complex, which may have been nearer to the mark. After all, despite Freud's inability to interpret all of Jung's dreams, Jung admitted in 1925 he had wanted to continue dream analysis with Freud during their trip to Clark University, because "I felt myself to be his son" (Jung 1989, 22). However, the narrative of *Memories, Dreams, Reflections* neatly inverts the father-son roles played and discussed by Freud and Jung throughout their relationship; not Jung but Freud was a neurotic suffering from an unresolved Oedipal complex. Furthermore, Jung linked himself in kin fashion to the psychologist Théodore Flournoy, who shared Jung's interests in mediumistic phenomena. He even referred to Flournoy as his "revered and fatherly friend" (Jung 1965, 162), perhaps finding in the esteemed scholar a replacement for the troubled relationship he had with his own father, who had failed to provide his young son with adequate answers to his questions (53).

The dream of the psyche as a house and the fainting spells recounted in *Memories, Dreams, Reflections* create a portrait of Freud as authoritative, neurotic, deceptive and effeminate. He appears as completely fixated on his own theories of wish-fulfilling dreams and the Oedipal complex, rejecting any evidence for other possible interpretations of dreams. In contrast, Jung appears as younger, stronger, and more virile in both body and will. While these portrayals may have partly reflected the two men's actual personalities and their age difference, the descriptions of these episodes are also laced with racial stereotypes: the Jew as fossilized, law-bound, effeminate and dogmatic; the Aryan as virile, moral and strong in will (see Chapter 2).

Almost twenty years Jung's senior, Freud witnessed the conversion of religious stereotypes into secular, biological terms, with the subsequent claim that Jews constituted an alien race (Gilman 1993, 12, 16–17). Jung was born at a time when the identity of Jews as a presumed race was little questioned, and anti-Jewish stereotypes had become part and parcel of the medical theories in which both men were trained (12). These stereotypes were also promulgated by Western Jews who often exhibited the split consciousness of the colonized, so aptly described by Fanon in *Black Skin, White Masks*. According to Fanon, people who occupy an oppressed cultural position often both resist and identify themselves with the values of the majority, while despising members of their own minority group (Fanon 2008, 20). Several scholars have suggested that Freud, too, as a westernized Jew often displaced anti-Jewish stereotypes onto Eastern Jews (Gilman 1993, 13; Brickman 2002, 69).

Furthermore, Jewish and non-Jewish scientists often viewed Jewish males as feminized (Gilman 1993, 42), a kind of "third sex" in between male and female, similar to the stereotype of the male homosexual that developed around the turn of the last century (165; Boyarin 1997, 229). Many medical theorists considered Jews to be particularly prone to supposedly more feminine mental illnesses such as hysteria, a claim that remained an article of medical science for decades (Gilman 1993, 117, 119). For example, this idea was used by Charcot whose work on hysteria influenced Freud. Although the younger Freud had admired Charcot, he ultimately rejected the theory that hysteria was due to heredity, in large measure due to the theory's anti-Semitic connotations (94–95; Boyarin 1997, 209). Still, psychoanalysis came to be seen by some doctors as a "Jewish pseudoscience" and a form of "mass hysteria" within the medical profession (Gilman 1993, 115).

After Jung declared his allegiance to Freud's theory, the latter made him his "crown prince" and heir. Jung's charisma, intelligence, and expressed devotion to Freud certainly helped in the selection process. So did his racial status. Freud and his circle of associates that comprised the "Vienna school" of psychoanalysis were Jewish, whereas Jung counted as "Aryan," and Freud wished to bequeath his intellectual legacy to an heir whose racial heritage would prove that psychoanalysis was not purely a "Jewish national affair" (Abraham and Freud 1965, 38; Gilman 1993, 31, 33).

The stereotypes common in Jung's era of Jews and Germanic peoples – the former being fossilized, law-bound and rootless, the latter creative, wisdom-seeking and dynamic – were condensed into symbolic form in a dream Jung had of a customs officer and a crusader, which he reported both in his 1925 seminar and in his autobiography. In the version of the dream from *Memories, Dreams, Reflections*, the customs officer is a peevish, shadowy Imperial Austrian bureaucrat, "one of those who still couldn't die properly." Jung interpreted this figure as Freud, due to his censorious attitude to the living unconscious (Jung 1965, 163). Condensed into Jung's dream-image of Freud as a fossilized customs officer is the stereotype of the soulless, materialistic "Wandering Jew" who cannot die, rendered lifeless through his fixation on the law.

In contrast, Jung's description of the crusader portrays the Romantic-*völkisch* ideal of the Germanic seeker of wisdom and power. In Jung's dream, a crusader walks through a noonday rush hour crowd in what was both an Italian city and Basel. In sharp contrast to the fossilized customs officer, the knight was "full of life and completely real," with a "numinous" quality, suggesting to Jung an archetypal figure and ongoing living presence in the unconscious, about whom "everyone knows" – except, of course, for the rationalist Freud and his ilk (164–165). The knight refers back to the age of alchemy and the quest for the Grail, and represents the epitome of the seeker of hidden wisdom – that is, Jung himself: "My whole being was seeking for something still unknown which might confer meaning upon the banality of life," he wrote (165).

In Jung's 1925 discussion of the dream, both figures could not die properly. Jung told his audience that the knight represents an archetypal Christian figure from the twelfth century, the era of Meister Eckhart (1260–1328) and knighthood. The ideas symbolized by the archetypal figure were born in that epoch, and had since died. Yet they were being revived in Jung's own era (Jung 1989, 38–39). Without actually having designated himself the knight, Jung led the reader of his autobiography to see him, in contrast to the living corpse of Freud, as the crusader full of life, seeking the Grail. Yet to his audience in 1925, Jung claimed through his vision of being deified that he *himself* was the Grail, the "reconciling symbol between [oppositions]" (98).

The image of the Grail points to its immediate cultural source in Wagner's paean to Germanic Christianity, *Parsifal* (1882) (see Chapter 2). Jung interpreted the Grail and Wagner's *Parsifal* in his 1921 *Psychological Types*, where he described both the vessel and the opera through the lens of pagan mythological motifs and Gnostic ideas. He argued that the Grail was a feminine symbol that pointed beyond the Christian Mother Mary to the pagan Great Mother and the Gnostic Sophia. The medieval Grail legend arose not from Christian canonical sources, Jung argued, but rather either from a Gnostic tradition that survived the persecution of the heresies, or from the (presumably collective European) unconscious as a compensatory reaction to official Christian doctrine. Jung further argued that the sexual motifs found in Grail symbolism derived from libidinal energy that was channeled away from expression in corporeal sexuality to the unconscious, where it manifested as an erotically tinged religious symbol. Hence, the Grail symbolized the spiritualization of sexuality (Jung 1921, 330–331). As an archetypal image, it was also religious in character (311).

Jung read Wagner's *Parsifal* as portraying the psychic conflict of oppositions and the problem of the libido when bound to the instincts and to nature. In an indirect rebuttal to Freudian sexual theory, Jung wrote that the sexual point of view was adequate for infantile – and hence pathological (*krankhaften*) – aspects of the psyche, but failed to represent the psyche as a whole (310). Rather, the problem portrayed in *Parsifal* was that of the orientation (*Einstellung*) of sexuality. Kundry represents its undomesticated state, whereas the union of oppositions through the reconciling symbol of Parsifal as the redeemer channels the libido to a higher level of psychic development (308–311).

Four years later, Jung again mentioned the Grail in his 1925 private seminar. Here, Jung did not elucidate the meaning of the Grail symbolism in his deification vision beyond calling it "the creative womb of the man" (Jung 1989, 99). In this vision, Jung took the place of Parsifal, the redeemer in Wagner's opera. Jung thus symbolically overcame Freud's sexual theory by drawing on the Wagnerian idea of spiritualizing nature to create a higher level of consciousness. Given the backdrop of Wagnerian racial and religious ideology, and the Mithraic and Christian symbolism of Jung's vision, one must question whether Jung's critique of Freud was in part driven by his beliefs about racial differences. Like Wagner, Jung may have believed that the German (Aryan, European) and the Christian were most capable of discerning the inner truth of things and understanding that which is "purely human." This interpretation diverges from Noll's claim that Jung fancied himself to be the "Aryan Christ;" still, Jung's own writings on the Grail point to a kind of Aryan-Christian ideology at the heart of both his own theory and his critique of Freud. In fact, it appears in his first work on the collective unconscious, his 1912 *Transformations and Symbols of the Libido*.

Two versions of the phylogenetic or collective unconscious

Soon after returning from Clark University, Jung plunged into the study of archaeology and mythology, describing in a letter dated October 14, 1909, to Freud his state of fascination when dealing with the material (McGuire 1974, 157J). Freud had already expressed an interest in mythology to Jung in 1908 (Myers 2009, 522), and he therefore encouraged Jung in his pursuits (McGuire 1974, 158F, 160F), apparently never imagining the very different conclusions Jung was formulating. Freud had come to believe that the Oedipal complex was the basis of "religious feeling" (270F), which he then modified to include infantile helplessness (171F). Jung at first agreed with Freud's sexual interpretation of myth (162J), but as he continued to study, his ideas about the original meaning of myth and the incest taboo changed course. He came to see that the incest taboo was regressively reactivated by free-floating anxiety (315J); that is, a present feeling could send a person back into an infantile state. This observation would have profound effects for his theory of the phylogenetic unconscious.

Jung's readings led him to a very different understanding of the meaning of incest in both fantasy and mythology, which he explained in his 1912 *Transformations and Symbols of the Libido*. This book originally appeared in two parts in the *Yearbook for Psychoanalytical and Psycho-Pathological Research* (*Jahrbuch für psychoanalytische und psychopathologische Forschungen*) in 1911 and 1912. In this work, Jung analyzed the fantasies of an American woman called Frank Miller (an unusual name for a woman) as an incipient case of schizophrenia. Using the technique of amplification, Jung strove to illuminate the deeper psychological significance of her fantasies and dreams by expanding their symbolism using mythology, legends, poetry and more, ranging from ancient Vedic texts, to the legends of the Wandering Jew and the Islamic figure Al-Kadhir, to the poems of Friedrich Hölderlin (1770–1843). Following the model he found in works on comparative religion, Jung combined philological speculation with comparative mythology, at times overloading the text with so many examples that the thread of his argument threatened to snap. Jung's book was simultaneously a theory of psychological maturation, a mythologizing of the bourgeois individual, a refutation of Freudian psychoanalysis, and a defense of the Christian myth by way of its psychological reinterpretation.

The title refers both to Jung's theory that the libido is capable of shifting from one psychological realm to another and to his redefinition of the term "libido" itself. As a doctor who had specialized in the treatment of Dementia praecox, or schizophrenia, Jung believed that a theory of mental illness predicated on the sexual drive could not sufficiently explain the causes and conditions of a mental disease characterized by the inability to adapt to reality (Jung 1925, 142–143). Nor did the sexual theory adequately explain the wealth of fantasies produced by Jung's patients, which Jung believed bore close similarities to mythological motifs and symbolism (155). Hence, he rejected Freud's definition of libido as "sexual drive," replacing it with "psychic energy" (142), by which he meant a force similar to Schopenhauer's will (135–136, 146) and the more general idea of longing (102, 137). Based on his new interpretation, Jung therefore asserted that the libido often appears mythologically as the sun, light, and fire, as solar heroes, and as the phallus, the latter representing a divine creative power, not the masculine sex drive and organ of insemination (524, fn. 76, 130). This redefinition of libido as psychic energy, longing, and a source of creativity also enabled Jung to revalorize religion as such against Freud's reduction of religion to an infantile sexual conflict.

As validation of this new theory, Jung described the hallucination of a particular Burghölzli patient (unnamed by Jung, the man was Emile Schwyzer, who lived 1862–1931). The schizophrenic patient hallucinated that he saw the sun with a phallus hanging down from it; when the man moved his head, the phallus unleashed a wind. Jung compared this image to one found in an ancient Mithraic liturgy found in a book by Albrecht Dietrich *(Eine Mithrasliturgie*, Leipzig 1903*)* and translated by G.R.S. Mead (*A Mithraic Ritual* (London, 1907). In 1912, Jung wrote that his student Johann Jakob Honegger (1885–1911) was the doctor who reported the hallucination (Jung 1912, 94), yet in subsequent works, Jung portrayed himself as the attending physician with whom the patient shared his vision (e.g. Jung CW 8:318; see also Bair 2003, 848–849). This misrepresentation may have to do with the significance of the man's fantasy for Jung's theory. Like the unconscious Kôôny (Elgonyi), whose morning sun salutation Jung interpreted as evidence of the archetype of the self (see Chapter 4), the schizophrenic patient provided evidence of the correctness of Jung's interpretation of the libido as psychic energy as opposed to Freud's reduction of this energy to the sexual drive. To a Freudian psychoanalyst, a sun with a phallus would obviously have been susceptible to a completely different reading.

In the context of *Transformations and Symbols of the Libido*, the hallucination of the sun with a phallus that produces the wind brings together several significant theories of the origin of religion. William Jones and Richard Payne Knight (1751–1824) had speculated in the eighteenth century that religion began with the worship of the powers of generation, both phallic and solar. By Jung's day, this theory had made great inroads into esoteric and theosophical thought (Bogdan 2009, 84). Moreover, Max Müller had claimed religion began through solar worship, whereas Elard Hugo Meyer argued for an earlier phase symbolized through the wind (see Chapters 2 and 3). Jung, in his turn, interpreted the sun and the phallus (not as a sexual organ but as a creative principle) as symbols of the libido as psychic energy. Furthermore, as Jung knew from his childhood education at his father's side, the Spirit of God played a determining role in the creation of the cosmos (Gen. 1:2) and the origin and spread of Christianity (John 3:8; Acts 2:2). Hence, the poor schizophrenic, who, Jung insisted, had no chance of reading such theories himself, hallucinated an image that combined all of these symbols, as if he were seeing the most archaic and holistic archetype of the divine.

These elemental symbols of the religious experience were not the only aspects of mythology that led Jung to reject Freudian psychology. Jung believed that not only the father but also the mother occupied a significant position in ancient myths. The mother and her heroic son became chief figures in Jung's creation of his own overarching mythic motif, a kind of *Übermythos*. Symbolically, the mother has two meanings in Jung's 1912 book: she represents the desire of an individual to remain in an underdeveloped, immature role, and she also symbolizes the unconscious itself. She therefore also represents the possibility for a dual birth: a mortal one and a spiritual rebirth. Jung argued that a patient's apparent incestuous desires actually expressed the wish to return to the womb – not the physical womb, but the symbolic womb of the unconscious. Jung rejected Freud's literal interpretation of the incest prohibition as only a taboo against sexual relations between family members; instead, Jung considered the prohibition symbolically, as a psychic means to rechannel the libido away from its childish attachment to the parents and towards symbols of rebirth that allow the adult personality to emerge. Through this movement, the libido becomes spiritualized and available for higher cultural purposes. Hence, religious symbolism played an essential role in the civilizing process, and was, to Jung, also fully natural, representing a necessary psychological truth.

According to Jung, the solar hero symbolizes both the libido and the individual, or more specifically, the individual who seeks to free himself from his parents to achieve his own redemption and fulfill his own destiny (Jung 1925, 429, 434). In a psychologized version of the Protestant work ethic understood as self-redemption, Jung asserted that the infantile hero must be sacrificed "through a complete devotion to life" (453), meaning very specifically "regular work" (455). Furthermore, the hero has two aspects, a mortal and an immortal one, corresponding to the dual mother. The overcoming of the infantile personality through the renunciation of childhood is symbolized by the death of the hero, who sacrifices himself so that he may be reborn, that is, so that the adult personality can develop. According to Jung, the maternal unconscious may be harnessd only through someone dedicating himself to dealing with reality, which then allows him access to the unconscious as a source of renewal. He who shirks the obligations of life, however, will sink again into unconscious oblivion (428). The symbolic transformation that the libido undergoes in this process shifts desire from the physical mother to the real source of life – one's own libido, which is, in effect, an inner quasi-divine power, symbolized by an inner sun or fire. God is thus a projection of the living force within the human being: "If God, the sun or fire is worshipped, then one reveres one's own vital force (German: *Trieb*), the libido," Jung wrote (Jung 1912, 82; Jung 1925, 96). In effect, Jung expressed in psychological terminology a basic tenet of the new spirituality of self-redemption, in which the divine is to be sought within one's own being. Finally, the "willed introversion of a creative mind," which Jung espied in Faust, is not a sign of infantile regression; rather, it indicates a symbolic return to the mother for a short respite, so that an individual may gather more strength to continue along the path of his adult life (Jung 1925, 336). (This step back to prepare to leap forward is the final motif of the "Wotan" essay, discussed in Chapter 6.)

While Jung was writing this book, Freud was working on his own version of a phylogenetic unconscious, which he published in *Totem and Taboo: Some Points of Agreement between the Mental Lives of Savages and Neurotics*. It was originally published as four essays in the periodical *Imago* (Vienna), the first two appearing in 1912 and the last two in 1913. In this work, Freud developed a phylogenetic myth for the Oedipal complex, in which he imagined à la Darwin that the original human society was a primal horde ruled over by a supreme patriarch. The patriarch's violent overthrow by his sons led to the establishment of religion, the super-ego, bourgeois morality and a law-bound civil society ruled by a collective of men (Freud 2001, 140–146; Brickman 2003, 52).

These two theories of a phylogenetic unconscious rest on the notion of the *primitive*, which is both a psychological and an anthropological category. Psychologically, it indicates an infantile and less-differentiated level of universal human psychological development. Anthropologically, it denotes non-western, darker-skinned peoples, whose cultures were deemed rudimentary and thus evolutionarily prior to that of modern Westerners. These two meanings of *primitive* were inextricably bound together, because the theory of the collective unconscious was based on the image of "primitive man" found in contemporary anthropological literature (on Freud, Brickman 2003, 4–5). Freud and Jung utilized Lamarckian theory, which stated that acquired characteristics may be inherited, and the Haeckelian recapitulation theory to connect these two definitions of *primitivity* together, in order to equate the psychology of modern European children with that of adult "primitives" (66–67). Furthermore, both psychologists believed that what constituted primitive psychology in adult Westerners belonged to their unconscious, reappearing in their dreams and in the symptoms of the mentally ill (80).

However, there are also important differences in how the two men imagined the primitive level of mind. The scholar of psychology and religion Celia Brickman shows that Freud's view of the primitive unconscious is characterized by "lack," especially of rationality and restraint, a sense of reality and time, and the ability to perform logical functions (81). Jung would have agreed, but for him, the "archaic unconscious" also suggests fullness, as he believed it contains both the wisdom of humanity and the archetypes laden with the power of numinosity.

Freud argued that the primitive levels of psychological development did not disappear with maturation, but remained in a latent state within the psyche (or in a manifest state in the case of neurosis). Hence, Brickman argues, Freud's understanding of the concept of *primitivity* defied the self-identity of many modern Europeans who believed they had risen above both "primitives" and their own primitive past (80). At the same time, Freud failed to disengage his concept of primitivity from its colonialist and racist associations. Therefore, he maintained the racist view of "primitives" as inferior by describing the primitive level of mind as infantile. Furthermore, although he gave the *primitive* a place within the European psyche, he also reasserted European claims to supremacy by maintaining that only Europeans were capable of psychological maturation and civilized mental development (5). As the discussion in Chapter 4 shows, Jung's view of European psychology shares affinities with those of Freud. However, in many works Jung also defined *European* differently than Freud; while Freud implicitly included both Jews and "Aryans" within this category, Jung separated them, and did so by means of his multivalent view of *primitivity*.

Indeed, Freud's and Jung's notions of *primitivity* differ significantly in ways integrally connected to their divergent views of religion. Freud's model of psychological development implies a trajectory from an infantile primitive state to the civilized, adult and rational mind (Brickman 2003, 65–74). Within this range, Freud positioned religion at the end of primitive infantile psychology. He mapped his theory of psychological maturation onto the evolutionary anthropological models of Tylor and Frazer, arguing that the lowest stage of animism and magic was based on the omnipotence of thoughts, characteristic of infantile narcissism. He then aligned the next stage of religion with the object love of children for their parents. Finally, he interpreted the final evolutionary move to science as the post-religious level of mind of the adult who has adjusted himself to reality (Freud 2001, 90). In this model, neurotic symptoms often reveal a regression to an earlier psychological level that is simultaneously primitive and infantile (Brickman 2003, 83–84).

Jung agreed that the primitive unconscious contains infantile, instinctual and sexual matter, but he believed that it cannot be restricted to these contents. The primitive unconscious is also infantile in the sense of being embryonic and creative, promising new life and rejuvenation. To illustrate this point, Jung mentioned the Orphic myth of Phanes, the androgynous Greek god of light, who burst forth from a primordial wholeness before the beginning of both time and sexual differentiation (Jung 1925, 147). Jung's model of psychological development therefore contains a potentially fruitful circular movement, in that regression may indicate the flow of libido to the level of the collective unconscious and the archetypes, the creative energies of which may be marshaled for the purposes of rejuvenation and innovation when consciously integrated. Hence, in his theory of *primitivity*, the archaic level of mind is a necessary component of psychic wholeness on a higher, conscious, adult level of psychological development.

These general differences in the interpretation of the significance of religious symbolism between Freud and Jung extend to two central figures in Jung's narrative: Mithras and Christ. Jung theorized that the birth of the Mithraic and Christian religions were psychological compensatory movements to the uncontrolled libido's domination of the ancient Roman world, where people lived under the compulsion of their unconscious incestuous wishes and emotions (454–455). Christianity offered the clear advantage for the evolutionary development of the human mind. Most depictions of the god Mithras show him slaying a bull, which Jung interpreted as the symbolic renunciation of the individual's animal nature or sexuality (473–474). This symbolic sacrifice initiated the domestication of "man's" animal nature, but the images of Mithras show that he – and presumably those ancients whose psyches Mithras symbolized – did not make this sacrifice with complete willingness (473, 475). Whether Christ's sacrifice was fully voluntary is unclear from Jung's text; however, the Crucifixion differed from the deed of Mithras in that it involved Christ's entire person. Hence, it symbolized more truly the complete renunciation of the infantile personality, which made possible the development of the autonomous adult individual (475–477). Jung wrote:

> The comparison of the Mithraic and the Christian sacrifice plainly shows wherein lies the superiority of the Christian symbol; it is the frank admission that not only are the lower wishes to be sacrificed, but the whole personality. The Christian symbol demands complete devotion; it compels a veritable self-sacrifice to a higher purpose.
>
> (Jung 1925, 478)

Jung then implicitly suggested that Christ's sacrifice made him a preeminent symbol of the libido, comparable to the king-like sun, which "voluntarily breaks its sceptre, the fructifying rays," knowing it will be resurrected (449). In these lines, Jung read the traditional comparison of Christ to the sun through a depth-psychological lens.

Although Jung interpreted Christ's crucifixion to symbolize the process of adult maturation that is valid for the whole of humanity (295), he described the symbol in ways that limited its effectiveness to the modern Germanic West. First, Jung described the Last Supper in ways that resonated with the new religion of self-redemption. According to Galatians 3:28, both the Jewish and Gentile members of the church community are "all one in Christ." Yet, Jung wrote that the wine and the bread of the Eucharist represent "the food of the immortals," who "are brothers with Christ." The prepositional change indicates the incipient development of Jung's *interpretatio Christi*, in which Christ is a model of individuation. Christ is transformed in this passage from the redeemer of humanity into a symbol of a psychological state theoretically capable of being achieved only by the modern individual who is willing to sacrifice his own infantile personality, making possible both psychological maturation and the discovery of a divine source within his own being (Jung 1925, 372, 411).

Second, Jung suggested that the psycho-spiritual power of Christian symbolism had been actualized only in the West, resulting in real power and innovation. "It is superfluous to speak of the effect of this symbol [the Crucifixion] upon the unconscious of Occidental humanity," wrote Jung. "A glance over history shows what creative forces were released in this symbol" (Jung 1925, 478).

Finally, the only figure Jung believed truly equal to Christ was Wotan, whose self-sacrifice Jung compared to the Crucifixion (Jung 1912, 408, fn. 1; Jung 1925, 559, n. 54). According to the Eddic poem, "The Sayings of the High One" (*Hávamál*), Odin hangs himself on the World-Tree Yggdrasil, stabbing himself with a spear. This self-sacrifice grants him access to the runes (Larrington 1996, 34), a word that means both "script" and "mystery." Thus, Wotan sacrificed himself to gain practical and esoteric wisdom.

Jung did in one instance apply Freud's theory of infantile sexuality – when he briefly turned his attention to "the Jew." In stark contrast to Christian symbolism, which Jung interpreted as capable of releasing dynamic forces necessary for psychological maturation, the Jewish deity, he wrote, arose from an unconscious infantile compulsion. Jung retold the story of the Pharisee Nicodemus in John 3:1–10, who could only understand Jesus's teaching that "one must be reborn" by literally returning to the womb of one's mother. Jesus, however, explained that a person must separate himself from his family and be born anew from the Spirit. Jung interpreted this New Testament story psychologically as a symbolic expression of the development of the autonomous adult individual. The "Jew," however, was excluded from the process of psycho-spiritual rebirth, due to his incestuous feelings and "extraordinary fixation to the family" (Jung 1925, 454).

Jung's assertion reflected a widespread medical opinion that Jews were prone to mental illness due to their endogamous marriage practice. Christian commentators considered this form of marriage a transgression of the incest taboo, a breach that "primitives" also made (Gilman 1993, 94, 100-101, 106). Freud for his part argued that "primitives" clung to the incest taboo, for this claim bolstered his own primordial myth of the Oedipal Complex (Freud 2001, 1ff.). Freud also later claimed (in *Group Analysis*) that "primitives" via religion and patriarchal family relations are enthralled to authority, both subjected to yet desiring it (Brickman 2002, 63). The westernized Freud seems to have tried distancing himself from negative stereotypes about traditional Eastern "Oriental" Judaism by suggesting in the 1920s that Judaism more generally was "primitive."

Whereas Freud lumped all religions together under the rubric of *primitive*, Jung instead created a sharp divide between Christian symbolism, which leads to psychological maturation, and the Jewish religion, which he described in ways similar to Freud's views on "primitives."

In lines stricken from the revised version of Jung's 1912 book (cf. CW 5:644), Jung wrote:

> Both tendencies serve the same goal – the liberation of man; the Jew from his extraordinary fixation to the family, which does not imply higher development, but greater weakness and more uncontrolled incestuous feeling, [and which] produced the compensation of the compulsory ceremonial of the cult and the religious fear of the incomprehensible [*sic*] (*unzurechnungsfähigen*: irrational and unreliable) Jehovah.
>
> (Jung 1925, 454)

> [Beide Tendenzen dienen demselben Ziele, nämlich den Menschen zu befreien, einerseits [*sic*] den Juden aus seiner außerordentlichen Bindung an die Familie, die nicht höherer Einsicht, sondern größerer Weichheit und Unbeherrschbarkeit des inzestuösen Gefühles entspricht, daher die Kompensation dafür das Zwangszeremoniell des Kultus und die religiöse Angst vor dem unzurechnungsfähigen Jahwe ist.]
>
> (Jung 1912, 388–389)

The word *unzurechnungsfähig* is a legal term indicating that a person is incompetent because he or she is of unsound mind. This term therefore seems incongruent when applied to a divinity other than, say, a trickster god (although trickster gods are not necessarily either crazy or incompetent). Hinkle translated *unzurechnungsfähig* into English as "incomprehensible," which is misleading. The Christian God is also traditionally understood as incomprehensible, in the sense of ineffable or mysterious, but not in the sense of being a reckless, babbling fool. According to the Protestant theologian Jörg Lauster (personal communication), the word *unzurechnungsfähig* is not a theological concept at all; hence, Jung's word choice is provocative. In the given context, the word should best be understood to mean that a human cannot rely on the god in question, because the god's actions appear irrational or incompetent. What Jung suggested here is what he would later write in *Psychological Types*, that the infantile parts of the psyche were also pathological; however, in his earlier work, he also racialized this view.

The implied comparison between Jews and "primitives" in Jung's lines disappeared in Jung's contrast of Jews with the ancients. Unlike the Jews, who, Jung indicated, were compelled by the laws and prophets of the Yahweh cult to control their libido, the ancients allowed their libido free reign. This led them (like "primitives") to a "level of ungovernableness and subjection to the emotions." Only with the coming of Christ, the "Redeemer and Physician of that time" did humanity learn "the sublimation of the incestuous libido" through regular work (Jung 1925, 454–455) and the "values of personhood" (255).

Freud's publication of *Totem and Taboo* followed Jung's *Transformations and Symbols of the Libido*, and in certain respects reads as if it were a refutation of that chronologically earlier work. This is particularly illustrated by Freud's handling of the figures of Mithras and Christ. In line with his *Urmythos* of the Oedipal complex, Freud argued that the slaughter of a bull by Mithras symbolized one brother willingly acting alone to kill the father, sparing his brothers guilt (Freud 2001, 153). Furthermore, the Crucifixion proved that the original crime was patricide, because only murder demands the sacrifice of one's own life as expiation (154). Finally, the Eucharist represents the triumph of the son over the father by assuming his place. Following the scholar of religions W. Robertson Smith's argument about the meaning of communion (*Lectures on the Religion of the Semites*, 1889), Freud argued that those at a communal feast devour and thus identify themselves with the being which is eaten. In the case of the Eucharist, it is not the father who is ingested, but the blood and body of the brother who committed patricide. Hence, the rite liberated the sons from the father and elevated his murderer to the status of a god (154). Freud's refutation of Jung's Christ-centered psychological innovations and his reduction of Christian symbolism to an Oedipal conflict could only have confirmed in Jung's mind his stereotype of Jewish psychology as infantile and trapped in childhood family relations.

In Freud's phylogenetic myth of the origins of the Oedipal complex, the actors are racially and religiously homogeneous. Jung instead correlated the emergence of the autonomous individual out of the web of family and social relations with Christian and Germanic symbolism. In fact, along with the passages just cited, Jung drew these connections in the very first chapter of his book. He argued that the evolution of thinking from fantasy-based to directed thinking occurred during the era of medieval scholasticism, when the subject of thought was still fantasy-based (that is, speculative, as shown in the question about how many angels could fit on the head of a pin), but the process of thinking had shifted to a logical, analytical mode (Jung 1912, 20; Jung 1925, 23). As support for his theory, Jung cited Nietzsche's *Beyond Good and Evil,* in which the philosopher wrote that the millennia-long struggle against Christianity had produced "a magnificent tension of spirit in Europe" (Nietzsche 2002, 4). Jung transformed Nietzsche's anti-Christian and European-wide statement into a reference to a Germanic, and implicitly, Christian biological essence, writing that "Nietzsche had guessed [. . .] at the biological background of this phenomenon when he spoke of the 'beautiful tension' of the Germanic mind which the Middle Ages created" (Jung 1925, 23).

According to Jung, therefore, directed thinking was the product of an evolutionary process that took place in the West under the impact of a Germanic racial essence and the Christian religion, which together produced the powerful currents and tensions that gave birth to both modern science and individual consciousness.

Moreover, Jung's psychological interpretation of the Christian myth is accompanied at every juncture by a reading from *Faust*. Jung cited the claim by the Swiss historian Jacob Burckhardt (1818–1897) that Faust was a "great primitive conception" (in German, *ein großes urtümliches Bild*, Jung 1912, 35, fn.1) that constituted an essential element of the collective German spirit (Jung 1925, 490, n. 42). The term *urtümliches Bild* was first applied to Faust by the German doctor and Romantic artist Carl Gustav Carus (1789–1869) to describe the scene in Goethe's tragedy in which the protagonist descends to the mysterious realm of "the mothers" (*Faust*, Part II, Act I, Scene 5). In *Transformations and Symbols of the Libido*, Jung interpreted this scene as evidence of the movement the libido makes to the unconscious in order to rejuvenate itself. By implication, then, Faust was for Jung a specifically Germanic archetype, which instinctively led those people in whose psyches it resided to go under (introvert) to the unconscious and grasp what Jung claimed was to be found there: wisdom, power, and renewal.

The significance of the Freud-Jung debate extends well beyond the two men in question and connects with larger political and social issues of exclusion and belonging. The ideas of both men were born out of and, indeed, indebted to the contemporaneous rise of German nationalism and growing anti-Semitism. Freud's own racial and religious status as Jewish influenced the formation of his theory, in that he strove to develop a universal theory of psychological development to combat the growing anti-Semitism of his day (Brickman 2003, 13). Jews were regularly "primitivized" as the "negroes" of Europe, a darker-skinned, mongrel race crossed with Africans (Gilman 1993, 20–21, 108). In his psychological theory of infantile sexual development, Freud displaced stereotypes about Jewish men onto "primitives," in this case meaning non-white, non-western people who constituted Europe's colonized "other" (23, 98; Brickman 2003, 58). In contrast to primitives, Freud spoke of modern Europeans – Jews and Christians, "Aryans" and "Semites" – without differentiation, thereby implicitly uniting the *Aryan* and the *Semitic* under the single rubric of *civilization*.

Jung, on the other hand, formed a psychological theory based on his own racial and religious identities, with ramifications that extended to his notion of the primitive. A significant portion of people sharing Jung's Germanic racial affiliation and Protestant religious background were experiencing a crisis of meaning and loss of orientation at the turn of the last century. To be sure, many Jews found themselves in a similar crisis, both newly arrived immigrants from Eastern Europe and modern western Jews who advocated assimilation to the dominant European culture. As with his Christian patients who considered themselves to be intellectual and without need of religious faith until the onset of a psychological crisis, Jung encouraged his Jewish patients to rediscover a source of faith within themselves, yet one specifically Jewish. However, the overwhelming majority of Jung's patients reflected his own identity of Germanic and Protestant, and he derived the terms by which he formulated his psychological theory from this particular racial and religious matrix.

Jung argued that Freud's theory was not universally valid: its overwhelming focus on sex was both offensive and reductionistic, devaluing the importance of the religious factor in psychology (Bair 2003, 167). This element became essential in Jung's theory, for he believed that the affective responses generated by presumably universal and archaic religious symbolism could lift the modern individual out of his isolation to identify with the whole of humanity (Jung CW 7 (1963 [1928]):21; Shamdasani 2003, 302) – or at least with a significant portion of it. For both Freud and Jung, religion was related to the concept of *primitivity*, but in ways that only partly overlap. As in Freudian psychoanalysis, the concept of the *primitive* in analytical psychology designates the West's racial "other," that is, those peoples who constituted the objects of Europe's and America's colonizing efforts. Like Freud, Jung used the term to disparage colonized people as living in a state of undifferentiated collective unconsciousness; unlike Freud, however, Jung also sometimes described them positively as still being connected with all of life. Furthermore, Jung connected the term *primitive* to two other so-called races: *Semiten* (meaning Jews) and *Germanen* (people of Germanic descent). In Jung's view, Jewish psychology was primitive in the sense of being infantile, driven by the will to power and the sexual instinct, as well as collectively determined. Yet when Jung spoke of the Germanic psyche, the term often denoted the kind of positive psychic tension that Jung believed produced directed thinking in the West – creative, forceful, and vital.

Differing primitivities of the "Germanic barbarian" and "Jewish psychology"

Jung first discussed the Germanic barbarian in "The Role of the Unconscious" (1918). Although he wished to address the psychological causes of a war in which Switzerland was not an aggressor, he described those responsible in terms that included himself. "[. . .] We Germanic people still have a genuine barbarian in ourselves," he declared ([. . .] *wir Germanen haben noch einen echten Barbaren in uns*) (Jung GW 10 (1918):19). In the same line in the English CW, the term "Germanic people" has been deleted, leading an unsuspecting reader to assume Jung was diagnosing a universal psyche. He was not. Nor did he use the term *deutsch*, a national designation to which he, as a German Swiss, was related but did not belong. Instead, he used a broader linguistic and ethnic term, *Germanen*, which in Jung's day invoked a utopian collective image and a presupposition of an unchanging group essence. It was to this unchanging *Volk* essence that Jung believed he belonged.

Jung described this buried Germanic barbarian as a "blond beast," an image which he borrowed directly from Nietzsche's *On the Genealogy of Morals,* as shown by the marked passage in the copy Jung owned (Bishop 1995, 129). Jung did not share Nietzsche's unconditional valorization of the *blonde Bestie*, most probably due to the catastrophe of the world war that separated him from the philosopher. Nor did he correlate the pairs of oppositions that Nietzsche proposed (between noble-common, light-dark, and good-bad) with different races or classes; rather, for Jung, these pairs of oppositions were united in the original wholeness of the primordial unconscious, and were broken apart through the development of individual consciousness. However, Jung did agree with Nietzsche that an outside force acted as the domesticating agent, though Jung's evaluation of it was more ambivalent than that of Nietzsche. As he would claim years later in conversation with Miguel Serrano (Serrano 1966, 52), Jung wrote that the foreign religion Christianity had split the Germanic barbarian psyche in two, cultivating the lighter (perhaps the spiritual?) portion for civilization while repressing the darker (the chthonic?) side, thereby crippling the instincts of the Germanic man (Jung CW 10 (1918):17, 26). Jung described the undomesticated portion as a lion roaming in its cage, an autonomous psychic power that could seize the civilized portion of the Germanic man's mind, resulting in either a psychological or social revolution (para. 17). Although Jung described this gripping power as "the evil essence" (*Das böse Wesen*) (para. 19), his stance towards this unincorporated psychic aspect was by no means purely negative: this repressed content may be dangerous, he wrote, but it also offered the possibility of regeneration, rejuvenation and even rebirth (para. 20).

In line with the model set up by Tacitus and reiterated by the German humanists (see Chapter 2), Jung contrasted the Germanic barbarians with their alleged opposites. In Jung's day, these were the Jews. "The Jew" (in singular) had two cultures, wrote Jung, that of the classical world (*die antike Kultur*) and the host country (*Wirtsvolk*) (para. 18). The word *Wirtsvolk* is a term from the field of biology, meaning the organism to which a parasite attaches itself. In the late nineteenth century and through the Nazi era, racial ideologues (including Adolph Hitler) used the term to designate Europeans or more specifically Germans, whom they believed were being fed upon by the parasitical Jews (Benz 2004, 86).

One might be tempted to think that Jung believed the Jews belonged to the culture of antiquity. However, as Chamberlain had already claimed, Jews did not belong to the classical world (which was "Aryan"), but were its enemy, an ancient antagonism that was still current in central Europe. Furthermore, although the Hebrew Bible (Old Testament) provided evidence of a rich ancient Hebraic culture, in "The Role of the Unconscious," Jung did not refer to the culture of the Old Testament. Hence, Jung implied in this passage a claim he would restate later in "The State of Psychotherapy Today," which is that Jews lacked the ability to create their own cultural forms. By using the word *Wirtsvolk*, Jung also demonstrated his adherence to *völkisch* ideology and its vicious dehumanizing of Jews as parasites.

Due to their lack of culture, Jews also had little contact with the earth and were therefore not burdened with the dangerous earnestness characteristic of the *Germanen*. Jews were domesticated to a much greater degree than the barbaric

Germanic man, thought Jung; that meant that they lacked the ability to draw nourishment from the earth. As Jung would explain in 1927 at the School of Wisdom "Man and Earth" conference, the earth was symbolically the equivalent to the collective unconscious. Hence, Jung implied in "The Role of the Unconscious" that Jews were unable to access the inspirational, creative powers of the collective psyche. Instead, their overcivilized state led them to seek compensation through recourse to that which Jung considered primitive (Jung CW 10 (1918):18). As examples of the Jew's affinity for that which is primitive, Jung pointed to the work of the two Jewish psychologists Freud and Alfred Adler (1870–1937). According to Jung, both men's theories were materialistic, the former focused on primitive sexuality, the latter on primitive power-plays (para. 19).

In this brief sketch of "the Jew," Jung reiterated reigning stereotypes of Jews as rootless and materialistic. Yet what about the presumed Jewish predilection for the primitive aspects of the psyche? Was Jung here influenced by the stereotype of the Jew as the "white negro" of Europe (Gilman 1993, 20–21, 108; fig. 5.1)? If so, Jewish primitivity differed markedly from that of black primitivity: as Jung's article "Complications of American Psychology" shows, he believed that blacks remained primitive, no matter where they lived, what languages they spoke or what occupations they held. Unlike the primitive "natural man," the Jews had culture – in fact, two of them, but neither they created themselves. How could they? According to *völkisch* ideology, the earth Jews carried in their collective psyches was the dry desert, which was responsible for the Semites' alleged lack of creativity. Jung implied that Jews

Figure 5.1 Eduard Schwechten, 1896, *Das Lied von Levi*, p. 13, illustrations by Siegried Horn. This illustration shows that Jung's portrayals of Jews, blacks and Native Americans as essentially primitive in an infantile sense were hardly his own invention, but were common stereotypes in his day.

were blocked from drawing sustenance from lands to which they did not belong. Perhaps this explains why Jung claimed that the Jew compensated for his overly cultured state through recourse to only one kind of primitive mentality – instincts and power drives – and not to the deeper, more primordial mentality, which housed the archetypes and their creative numinosity. Furthermore, Jung combined the stock stereotype of primitives as instinct-driven and materialistic with Tacitus's critique of Rome as a degenerate civilization. The result was a portrait of the "Jew" as the *Germanen's* "other" who was simultaneously primitive and overcivilized, bound by instinct yet alienated from nature.

Jung's description of Jewish psychology as primitive found further deployment in his 1928 book, *The Relations between the Ego and the Unconscious*. Despite Freud's and Adler's claims that their theories were universal, Jung dismissed them as Jewish and therefore not universally valid. Indeed, he argued, the very claim of universalism was demonstrative of collective mentality and therefore primitive. Jung thus implied that Jewish mentality in general was collective, lacking true individuality. Furthermore, as Jung explained in a footnote, Jewish psychology was not shaped by certain religious presuppositions; rather, it emerged as an expression of a qualitatively distinct racial essence. Jung wrote:

> Thus it is a quite unpardonable mistake to accept the conclusions of a Jewish psychology as generally valid [. . .] No doubt, on an earlier and deeper level of psychic development, where it is still impossible to distinguish between an Aryan, Semitic, Hamitic and Mongolian mentality, all human races have a common collective psyche. But with the beginning of racial differentiation essential differences are developed in the collective psyche as well.
>
> (Jung CW 7 (1963):240, fn.8; orig. Jung 1928, 54, fn. 1)

In this passage, Jung mixed philological and anthropological models together with biblical genealogy: *Aryan* and *Semitic* referred to language families; in Max Müller's tripartite classification, the third term, *Turanian*, included *Mongolian* (Arvidsson 2006, 77). Moreover, *Semitic* and *Hamitic* were both derived from Noah's three sons, Ham, Shem, and Japhet (31). In line with his era's thinkers, Jung then read all of these categories through a racialized anthropological lens.

Despite the confusion of categories, this quote demonstrates the influence of polygenetic thought in Jung's otherwise monogenetic theory. In the passage, Jung stated emphatically that there is a collective psyche, built into the brain structure of all peoples everywhere. (Ironically, Jung condemned universalist claims when made by Jewish psychologists, but found it unproblematic when he made his own.) Yet he then suggested that racial differentiation was about as old as humanity itself. If it were not, then a "Jewish" psychology should be able to make quite fundamental, universally valid claims. As discussed previously, however, Jung's image of the collective psyche – his "'geology' of the personality" –contained no layer specific to all humans. The quote further indicates that Jung believed race to be essential to a person's psychology and fairly impervious to change, despite transformed social conditions, migration, and cultural exchange. (But see Chapter 8 for a significant exception).

In this same work, Jung described a patient's father complex that was preventing her from finding a suitable mate and the compensatory movement in her unconscious that produced a paternal dream figure connected to the wind (see Chapter 3). Jung interpreted the wind as an archaic image of the divine, a primordial nature-demon, "something like Wotan" (Jung CW 7 (1963 [1928]):218). For Jung's understanding of Wotan as Spirit, Jung may very well have had in mind not only Meyer's work but also Jacob Grimm's description of Wotan as an "*all-pervading creative and formative power*" (Grimm 1880, 133; emphasis in original). However, Jung did not mention these works on Indo-European and Germanic myth. Instead, he turned to biblical and Semitic sources and placed Wotan within a network of associations that seemed to bridge the gap between "Aryans" and "Semites:" this primitive image of God was expressed in the Greek word *pneuma*, the Hebrew *ruah*, and the Arabic *ruh*, all terms for breath and spirit (218). The archaic image of God as Spirit seemed therefore to be universal, appearing in both Aryan and Semitic psyches, because it arose from the most collective level of the unconscious: "Here is an historical image of world-wide distribution

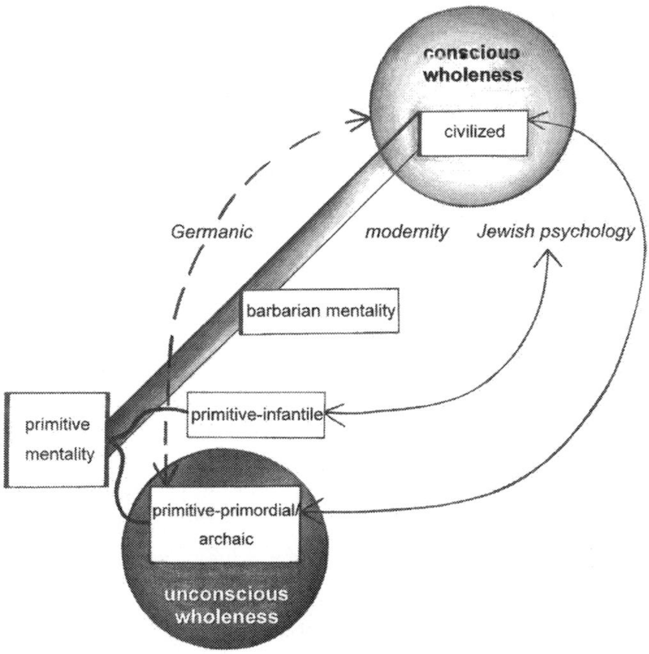

Figure 5.2 Jung's concept of primitivity in relation to modern mass society, Jews, and people of Germanic stock. Illustration by Christiane Strobach, ©2015. All rights reserved.

that has come into existence again through a natural psychic function," wrote Jung. "This is not so very surprising, since my patient was born into the world with a human brain." Yet Jung's universalist assertion is particularized to the Germanic peoples in Jung's original text, which has been preserved in the German-language *Gesammelte Werke*. Directly following the words "a human brain," the English version of this text reads, "which presumably still functions today much as it did of old" (Jung CW 7 (1963 [1928]):219). In German, the line continues thus: "which presumably still functions today the same way as among the ancient Germanic peoples" (*das heute vermutlich noch in derselben Weise funktioniert wie bei den alten Germanen*) (Jung GW 7 (1963 [1928]):219).

Jung seemed to suggest that Semitic peoples also carried the archetype of the Spirit in their mental makeup, since *ruah* is Hebrew and *ruh* is Arabic. However, Jung's rant against Jewish psychology in the same text implied that Jews were cut off from the level of the archaic and were stuck at the level of the primitive, meaning underdeveloped, collective, and enmeshed in the instincts. In contrast, his apparently Germanic patient had access to the primordial source of the divine which Jung specifically named Wotan, a full five years before the inception of the National Socialist state in Germany and eight years before Jung penned "Wotan."

A "psychotherapy of German descent"

Jung's writings on the presumed psychological differences between Jews and their opposite, whether Germanic, Aryan, or Christian, continued into the 1930s in the *Journal for Psychotherapy and Related Fields Including Medical Psychology and Psychic Hygiene (Zentralblatt für Psychotherapie und ihre Grenzgebiete einschliesslich der medizinischen Psychologie und psychischen Hygiene,* hereafter *Zentralblatt)*. This was the main organ for the General Medical Society for Psychotherapy (*Allgemeine Ärztliche Gesellschaft für Psychotherapie*). After Hitler became the *Führer* of Germany, the Society was forced to conform (*gleichschalten*) to Nazi ideology. Dr. Ernst Kretschmer, the then-current president of the Society, resigned in protest on April 6, 1933. The Board of the Society then offered Kretschmer's position to Jung, who until then had been vice-president. Jung became president of the Society on June 21, 1933 (Cimbal 1933, 141–142), and editor of its journal as well. He held these posts until 1940 (Samuels 1993, 300).

By late 1933, the suggestion had been made that the Society as a whole should be restructured as a supranational organization with different national groups, and individuals who could not participate in their country's national group were welcome to apply as individuals (Jung CW 10 (1934b):1035; Jung 1972, 1:177–178). Jung had sought the aid of the Jewish lawyer Vladimir Rosenbaum to rewrite the statutes to allow Jewish practitioners, disenfranchised in Germany, to remain members (Bair 2003, 448–449). Jung saw this action as providing evidence that he was no anti-Semite (453). In fact, however, Jews were still allowed to join the new German Society until 1938 (Cocks 1985, 134). One wonders therefore if this was simply a tactical move on Jung's part to quell international criticism against him, especially in light of his extremely callous refusal to help Rosenbaum in 1937 after the man had been released from jail following his aid to anti-Franco forces (Bair 2003, 450).

In the December 1933 issue of the *Zentralblatt*, the first since its temporary suspension, Jung wrote an editorial addressing the changes in the Society. He also brought to the scholarly table the alleged differences between Germanic and Jewish psychology. Jung began by arguing that "one-sided and mutually exclusive methods of observation" had gained significant influence, not only among scholars, but among educated lay people, creating undue confusion concerning the "basic facts (in German, *Grundtatsachen*) of the human psyche." Jung believed this confusion had to do with fundamental differences, using the word *Verschiedenheiten*, a German word that points to something much more essential than the English translation "differences" suggests. He wrote:

> It will therefore be the primary task of the *Zentralblatt* to give impartial appreciation to all objective contributions, and to promote an over-all view which will do greater justice to the basic facts of the human psyche than has been the case up till now. The [fundamental] differences [*Verschiedenheiten*] which actually do exist between Germanic and Jewish psychology and which have long been known to every intelligent person are no longer to be glossed over, and this can only be beneficial to science.
>
> (Jung CW 10 (1933):1014–1015; Jung 1933, 139)

Jung argued that the "personal equation" plays a particularly significant role in psychology, and could falsify practices and theories (Jung 1933, 139). He asserted that this implied no devaluation of Semitic psychology, just as discussing the particularities of East Asian psychology suggested no devaluation of the Chinese (140). In Jung's terminology, the "personal equation" indicates the largely unconscious subjective factors that partly determine how a person views the world (Shamdasani 2003, 55; Lewin 2009, 30). Jung was certainly justified in his view that psychotherapists must be aware of how their personal perspectives and life-experiences influence their theories. Indeed, Jung may be commended for having introduced training analysis into the psychoanalytic movement, so that analysts could become conscious of their own biases and perspectives and therefore form a more objective view of their patients (Shamdasani 2003, 54–55). However, various factors can influence the "personal equation," such as a person's gender, class standing, and educational level. Yet in his very first editorial of the Nazi-conformed *Zentralblatt*, Jung introduced a discussion of the "personal equation" only as defined by the alleged difference between Jewish and Germanic psychology (Jung 1933, 139). He could hardly expect his colleagues to believe his claim that he had done this simply for the sake of science and not out of political or personal motives.

This same issue contained a statement from the psychotherapist Dr. Matthias Göring (1897–1945), a cousin of Reichsmarschall Hermann Göring (1893–1946). In numerous writings, Jung referred to Göring's note as a "manifesto" (*Manifest*) (Jung CW 10 (1934a):1021; Jung 1972, 1:190) and "pledge of allegiance" (*Treuegelöbnis*) (Jung 1972, 1:175, fn. 6); and the editors of his *Briefe* hint at ill intent against Jung with its publication behind Jung's back (ibid.). Yet the writing in question was in fact a news item, listed under "current news" (*Aktuelles*) and directly following Jung's editorial. Carrying the title, "Communication from the Reichsführer of the 'German General Medical Society for Psychotherapy,'" this news item announced that a new German General Medical Society for Psychotherapy (*Deutsche allgemeine ärztliche Gesellschaft für Psychotherapie*) had been formed on September 15, 1933, as an organization for those German doctors who believed that it was their task to treat the "entirety of the personality" (*das Ganze der Persönlichkeit*) of their patients, but especially for those doctors who "are willing to train and practice an art of healing in terms of the national-socialist worldview" (*die willig sind, im Sinne der nationalsozialistischen Weltanschauung eine seelenärztliche Heilkunst auszubilden und auszuüben*). Göring in effect announced that German psychotherapists were to become tools of Nazi propaganda, preaching to their patients Nazi ideology robed in the scientific dress of psychological discourse. Göring wrote:

> The Society assumes that all of its members who publish and hold lectures have studied Adolf Hitler's book *Mein Kampf* with all scientific seriousness and recognize it as foundational. The Society will participate in the work of the people's Chancellor to inculcate in the German people a heroic, self-sacrificing spirit.
>
> [Die Gesellschaft setzt von allen ihren schriftstellerisch und rednerisch tätigen Mitgliedern voraus, daß sie Adolf Hitlers grundlegendes Buch „Mein Kampf" mit allem wissenschaftlichen Ernst durchgearbeitet haben und als Grundlage anerkennen. Sie will mitarbeiten an dem Werke des Volkskanzlers, das deutsche Volk zu einer heroischen, opferwilligen Gesinnung zu erziehen.]
>
> (Göring 1933, 140–141)

Göring's German Society would double as the national group for Germany inside the new International Society for Psychotherapy. Hence, two Societies with the name *Allgemeine ärztliche Gesellschaft für Psychotherapie* would henceforth exist, the one preceded by "Supranational" (*Überstaatliche*) to be headed by Jung, and the other, preceded by the word "German" (*Deutsche*) to be led by Göring (Cimbal 1933, 142–143; Jung 1972, 1:175, fn. 3).

Göring's news article and Jung's editorial unleashed a wave of criticism directed at Jung, including a scathing condemnation published by the psychologist Gustav Bally (1893–1966) on February 27, 1934, in the *Neue Zürcher Zeitung*.

In an article entitled "Psychotherapy of German Descent" (*Deutschstämmige Psychotherapie*), Bally denounced Jung's assumption of the presidency of the *gleichgeschaltete* General Medical Society for Psychotherapy. All members not adhering to a *völkisch*-nationalistic orientation (*völkisch-national gesinnnten*) and all Jewish members had been excluded, which "decimated" (*dezimiert*) the Society's membership. Bally challenged Jung on his orientation to the new Nazi regime and also raised the issue of Göring's news item. Bally did not disagree with Jung's stated desire to create order out of the reigning confusion concerning the fundamental bases of the human psyche; however, he wanted to know why Jung presumed in 1933 that the core of this burning issue was a hypothesized difference between a Jewish and Germanic psychology. Furthermore, if Jung really believed that the future of psychotherapy hung on this issue, why then did he neglect both to define the means by which he would determine the differences and to clarify how a psychotherapist's race might falsify his results and practice? Bally ended by emphasizing that any editor of a *gleichgeschaltete* journal who raised the "Jewish question" in 1933 would naturally be viewed as supporting a "psychotherapy of German descent" (Bally 1934).

Bally's assertion was borne out by the pronouncement of Dr. Walter Cimbal (1877–1964) in the very same issue of the *Zentralblatt* in which Göring's news item was published. Cimbal, the Society's manager, wrote that the seventh Psychotherapeutic Congress, to be held in Nauheim in April 1934, would address this very question. The following quote shows that Cimbal's conference announcement was the source for Bally's title. Along with discussing how the German and the supranational organizations would work together, the conference would also address the question of a Germanic-oriented psychotherapeutic practice:

> As the foreword from the editor [Jung] has announced, the Congress will also serve the purpose of formulating a psychology and psychiatric medicine of German (Germanic) descent.
>
> [Der Kongress wird ebenso, wie das Geleitwort des Herausgebers es für das Zentralblatt ankündigt, der Ausgestaltung einer deutschstämmigen (germanischen) Seelenkunde und Seelenheilkunst dienen.]
>
> (Cimbal 1933, 144)

Cimbal further announced that a special edition of the German Society for Psychotherapy would be published in February 1934, to be followed every two months with a special edition from one of the other national groups. The first article to be published was "The National-Socialist Idea in Psychotherapy" (*Die nationalsozialistische Idee in der Psychotherapie*) by Dr. Göring, followed by articles by other German psychotherapists (143). One assumes that all of these psychotherapists had sworn to use Hitler's *Mein Kampf* as their guiding principle in their psychotherapeutic work.

Jung wrote a rejoinder to Bally in the *Neue Zürcher Zeitung,* entitled "Contemporary Issues" (*Zeitgenössisches*). Jung claimed that he assumed the presidency for the sake of science, to ensure that psychotherapy would survive under the new regime in Germany. To have refused the presidency would have been an act of egoism, cowardice, and betrayal of friendship toward his German colleagues (Jung CW 10 (1934a):1016; Jung 1972, 1:280–281). Jung's claim that psychotherapy might have been discontinued in Germany hardly seems plausible in light of the fact that Göring was not only a psychotherapist, but the founder of a new – and competing – Society. Jung's assertion further suggests not only that Jung's friendships with non-Jewish Germans took precedence over his loyalty to his Jewish friends and colleagues, but also that Kretschmer was a disloyal coward.

Jung further defended his raising of the Jewish question by stating that it was a "complex, a festering wound" (Jung CW 10 (1934a):1024). Elsewhere Jung had defined complexes as an assemblage of associations of high psychic intensity, comprised not only of thoughts, but also of strong feelings, so that whenever a word related to the complex is mentioned, its associations are also activated. Because most complexes are unconscious, they reside in the psyche out of control of the conscious mind and therefore have a certain autonomy (Jung CW 3 (1907):79–82). Complexes may be either personal or collective, the latter arising when the collective psychological attitude no longer functions and a new one is needed. As this shift takes place, individuals may feel disoriented and the group as a whole may appear to be in a state of collective psychosis (Jung CW 8 1965 [1919]):594–595).

Given this view, Jung's naming anti-Semitism a complex was no doubt compelling, and it has been suggested Jung wanted to effect a change in Nazi policy towards the Jews by investigating this "wound" (Bair 2003, 452). Perhaps had he discussed this complex in this manner in his 1933 *Zentralblatt* editorial, Bally might not have objected. However, Jung did not propose that the collective German psyche should be psychotherapeutically treated to discover there the source of its complex; rather, both in his editorial and his reply to Bally, Jung claimed that there were inherent psychological differences between Jews and people of Germanic stock (see also Jung 1972, 1:193). In indignant tones, Jung wrote:

> May it not therefore be said that there is a Jewish psychology too, which admits the prejudice of its blood and its history? And may it not be asked wherein lie the peculiar differences between an essentially Jewish and an essentially Christian outlook? Can it really be maintained that I alone among psychologists have a special organ of knowledge with a subjective bias, whereas the Jew is apparently insulted to the core if one assumes him to be a Jew? Presumably he would not have one assume that his insights are the products of a mere cipher, or that his brain emerged only today from the featureless ocean of non-history.
>
> (Jung CW 10 (1934a):1027)

In these lines, Jung shifted slightly the terms of the debate: in his editorial, Jung had opposed the *Jewish* to the *Germanic*; in his reply to Bally, to the *Christian*. He explicitly racialized Jewishness by referring to Jewish "blood." Moreover, through the opposition to Christianity, he implied, if not a racialization of the religion, then a correspondence between the essence of the religion and the psychological characteristics of a different race. In sum, Jung's view of Jews echoes the claims he made about people of African descent: despite changes in geography, language, and culture, Jews had remained essentially the same – and fundamentally different from people of Germanic descent and Christian heritage.

Despite the controversy already sparked by his editorial, Jung again wrote about the alleged fundamental differences between Jewish and Germanic psychology in his article, "The State of Psychotherapy Today" (*Die gegenwärtige Lage der Psychotheraphie*) (1934) and published it in the very next edition of the *Zentralblatt*. At the same time (1934), Göring published *German Psychiatry* (*Deutsche Seelenheilkunde*). It included the following ten articles:

1 M. H. Göring, "Die nationalsozialistische Idee in der Psychotherapie"
2 G.R. Heyer, "Die Polarität, ein Grundproblem in Werden und Wesen der deutschen Psychotherapie"
3 W. M. Kranefeldt, "Freud und Jung"
4 C. Haeberlin, "Die Bedeutung von Ludwig Klages und Hans Prinzhorn für die deutsche Psychotherapie"
5 L. Seif, "Volksgemeinschaft und Neurose"
6 J. H. Schultz, "Der Yoga und die deutsche Seele"
7 F. Künkel, "Die dialektische Charakterkunde als Ergebnis der kulturellen Krise"
8 H. Schultz-Hencke, "Die Tüchtigkeit als psychotherapeutisches Ziel"
9 H. v. Hattingberg, "Neue Richtung, neue Bindung"
10 W. Cimbal, "Aufgaben und Wege zu einer deutschen Seelenheilkunde"

Eight of these same articles were printed in the general edition of the journal, *Zentralblatt für Psychotherapie* 7, no. 1 and 2 (1934). The only differences were that Cimbal's article was not published and Göring's was replaced with Jung's "The State of Psychotherapy Today." On the page facing the table of contents and headed "Current News" (*Aktuelles*), it was explained that the journal would focus regularly on the psychotherapeutic research in individual countries. Because the Society had just been reorganized along international lines, it was decided to begin with German contributions, allowing other countries more time to organize an overview. Given this explanation, why did an article by a Swiss head the collection of German articles? Not because Jung had no choice, as has been suggested (Lewin 2009, 38). Rather, the content of Jung's article provides the answer.

In "The State of Psychotherapy Today," Jung interwove his theory of psychological processes with an especially bitter critique of Freudian psychoanalysis. Although Freud one-sidedly reduced all things infantile to sexuality, wrote Jung, *infantile* has two meanings: that which is merely symptomatic of regression or lack of development (as Freud recognized), and that which is embryonic and emergent. The former demonstrates an infantile unwillingness; the latter, a will towards adaptation (Jung CW 10 (1934c):345, 359).

Jung further explained that neurotic symbolism is ambivalent, in that a neurosis has both negative and positive aspects, and points both towards the past and the future. The patient has within him "another" personality of a religious nature that lies hidden in the unconscious, consisting of a conflict of oppositions that creates the energy one needs to rejuvenate one's life. The cure for a neurosis is not to dispense with it, but to learn how to bear it by confronting that "other" aspect of the personality, thereby creating a state of psychic wholeness (para. 359). The religious "other" within the psyche should not be dismissed as nothing but an illusion, as Freud had claimed in *Future of an Illusion* (para. 368); after all, humanity has long sought the "propitiation of the gods" and recognized the "perils of the soul" (para. 367–368). Hence, the task of contemporary psychotherapy is to recognize and overcome the split between the human and the divine within the individual psyche (para. 367). Two years later, Jung restated these themes in more mythopoetic form in "Wotan" (see Chapter 6).

Jung then delved into what he believed to be the fundamental differences between Aryan or Germanic and Jewish psychology, without the quote marks around the racial term "Aryan" found in the English CW that imply Jung wished to problematize this term (para. 353, 354). Jung reiterated his earlier claims about the two-sided nature of the Germanic barbarian psyche in terms that indicate, once again, that Jung considered this psyche dangerous, yet also extremely capable of manifesting a new and positive collective psychic orientation. In contrast, Jung argued, Jewish psychology was overly civilized and lacked the creative, youthful qualities necessary to manifest this highly significant psychological phenomenon. Note that Jung interpreted Aryan essence through the lens of the discourse on the Germanic barbarian, as indicated in his description of its youthfulness. He thus equated the *Germanic* with the *Aryan*, even prioritizing the former. Jung wrote:

> The Jewish race as a whole – at least that is my experience – possesses an unconscious which can be compared with the "[*sic*]Aryan"[*sic*] only with reserve. Creative individuals apart, the average Jew is far too conscious and differentiated to go about pregnant with the tensions of unborn futures. The "[*sic*]Aryan"[*sic*] unconscious has a higher potential than the Jewish; that is both the advantage and the disadvantage of a youthfulness not yet fully weaned from barbarism. In my opinion it has been a grave error in medical psychology up till now to apply Jewish categories – which are not even binding on all Jews –indiscriminately to Germanic and Slavic Christiandom. Because of this the precious secret of the Germanic peoples – their creative and intuitive depth of soul – has been explained as a morass of banal infantilism, while my own warning voice has for decades been suspected of anti-Semitism.
>
> (Jung CW 10 (1934c):354)

Jung's descriptions of the *Germanic* or *Aryan* and *Jewish* align with the two very different concepts of the *infantile* that Jung discussed earlier in the paper. They also overlap with two different levels of concepts of *primitivity*: primordial, embryonic, and regenerative in the case of "Aryans," and infantile and instinct-bound in regard to Jews. Yet the Jew is not merely infantile, but also "far too conscious and differentiated." As previously discussed, Jung viewed scientific rationalism and materialism as signs that modern civilization had degenerated and reverted back to a primitive state (Chapter 4). Like modern society itself, Jews paradoxically represented to Jung a mixture of primitivity and over-civilization.

Jews had been influenced by antiquity, wrote Jung; however, the Jew was by nature a nomad. Hence, the Jewish unconscious "has never created a cultural form of its own and probably never will," because Jews have to rely on a rather civilized host-nation to develop their instincts and abilities (para. 353). As in his "The Role of the Unconscious," Jung used the word *Wirtsvolk* to describe the "host-nation." Although this translation is strictly speaking a correct translation, it effaces Jung's meaning. When people play host to guests, they are *Gastgeber*. Yet when a living organism hosts a parasite, it is a *Wirtsvolk*. In contrast, English uses the same word for these two very different meanings of "host." Jung used the biological term *Wirtsvolk*, implying that the German population constituted an organic being on which the Jews were parasitically feeding.

Furthermore, Jews were physically weak, like women (by which Jung apparently meant Jewish men and either "Aryan" or all women). By combining their feminine aspects with their much older, cultured consciousness, Jews (i.e. Jewish men) could observe the shadow side of the psyche especially well, pointing out other peoples' weak spots (para. 353). Jung might very well have defended his racial stereotypes by referring to the work of a Jew besides Freud. In *Sex and Character* (*Geschlecht und Charakter*, 1903), the Jewish author Otto Weininger (1880–1903) accused Jews of being like women, in that both allegedly lacked personalities, were collectively minded, and incapable of forming a state (Boyarin 1997, 284).

Jung then contrasted the allegedly effeminate, uncreative and parasitic Jews with the Germanic-"Aryan" Christian people, a group designation in which Jung included himself, when he argued that "we have been entrusted by fate with the task of creating culture" (para. 353). With the pronoun "we," Jung indicated clearly enough that he belonged to this destiny-laden collective. In these lines, Jung trotted out several clichés about Jews: first, that Jewish men represented a kind of gender hybrid or "third sex" (Gilman 1993, 9, 31–32, 38–39; Boyarin 1997, 272); second, that Jews fed parasitically on other peoples' cultures (Samuels 1993, 302; Arvidsson 2006, 103–104), and third, that they generally lacked the talent to create the arts of civilization by themselves (Boyarin 1997, 245; Gilman 1993, 26). In contrast, he presented the "Aryans" as masculine and creative.

In 1927, Freud had described as illusory the belief that only Indo-European races had the ability to create culture (Freud 1968, 31–32); Jung's lines from

1934 read like a refutation of this claim. Freud's naming both this myth and the disbelief in infantile sexuality as illusions received a sharp rebuke by Jung in the following lines:

> The "[*sic*]Aryan"[*sic*] unconscious, on the other hand, contains explosive forces and [creative] seeds of a future yet to be born, and these may not be devalued as nursery romanticism without psychic danger. The still youthful Germanic peoples are fully capable of creating new cultural forms that still lie dormant in the darkness of the unconscious of every individual – seeds bursting with energy and capable of mighty expansion.
>
> (Jung CW 10 (1934c):353)

Jung then called for psychotherapists to consider the "unparalleled tension and energy [force]" (*die unerhörte Spannung und Wucht*) of the Germanic unconscious that gave rise to National Socialism (para. 354; Jung 1934, 9).

One German psychotherapist, Gustav R. Heyer (1890–1967), heeded Jung's call in an article directly following Jung's entitled, "Polarity, a Foundational Problem in the Development and Essence of German Psychotherapy" (*Die Polarität, ein Grundproblem in Werden und Wesen der deutschen Psychotherapie*) (Heyer 1934, 17–23). Heyer was a member of Jung's school (Jung CW 10 (1935):1060); since his article also appeared in Göring's *German Psychiatry*, he must have also sworn to implement Nazi ideology in his psychotherapeutic practice. Heyer praised Jung for considering the polarity of life without falling into the trap of positively valuing one pole while judging the other negatively, as did Freud, Adler and the German vitalist philosopher Ludwig Klages. Such one-sidedness belonged not to the polytheistic German spirit, but rather to both the monotheistic "spirit of the Jewish Yahweh" (*jüdischen Jahwe-Geist*) and "the Christian mindset" (*der christlichen Einstellung*). Heyer agreed with Jung's assessment of the personal equation concerning Jewish and Germanic psychology (Heyer 1934, 20, fn. 1), stating that, while Freud was an important pioneer, that which was "Semitic" (*das Semitische*) was "essentially foreign to us" (*uns wesensfremd*) (22).

Jung's teaching, however, differed markedly from that of Freud, wrote Heyer, for the two poles of outer and inner orientation, as well as of sexuality and individuality, were equally balanced in his theory of psychological types. Jung had therefore best carried forward the work of the Romantics, for he understood that "it is, after all, German to be able to bear, understand and overcome tensions" (*ist es doch deutsch, Spannungen ertragen, verstehen und bewältigen zu können*). As if foreseeing Jung's essay on "Wotan the wanderer" two years later, Heyer argued that Jung's psychology demonstrated that "we" are "wanderers between two worlds" (*Wanderer zwischen zwei Welten*), between the conscious and the unconscious, the individual and the collective, and the mind and soul (*Geist und Seele*) (23). One needed to live out these tensions consciously, or else one would fall victim to the "menace to the German essence" (*Gefahr deutschen Wesens*):

not Jews, but rather, "*feeble* liberality" (*die* schwächliche *Liberalität*) (Heyer 1934, 17–18, emphasis in original).

Heyer then drew an analogy between the life of the individual and that of a people (*Volk*). Both could become habit-bound, formalized and routinized. However, that which is "new and yet primordial, creative, and unspoilt" (*noch Uralt-Neues, Schöpferisches und Unverbrauchtes*) could break through this routinization and shake it off with tremendous force. Sketching a motif that Jung would explore in "Wotan," Heyer wrote that "out of destruction and ruin" (*aus Zerstörung und Vernichtung*) could come new life, like a new springtime or a second childhood (19). But since the process of rebirth was difficult and even dangerous, Heyer insisted that a "psychological master" (*seelenkundiger Meister*) was necessary, and he recommended Jung as the proper guide for the difficult undertaking (the establishment of the Third Reich) currently in process (20, 23).

Jung's Jewish students responded differently to Jung's "The State of Psychotherapy Today" in a debate that ensued in the pages of the *Jewish Review: Journal of the Zionist Association for Germany (Jüdische Rundschau: Organ der Zionistischen Vereinigung für Deutschland)*. The discussion was dominated by Jung's students James Kirsch (1901–1989) and Erich Neumann (1905–1960), both of whom had fled to Palestine when Hitler came to power in Germany. Kirsch argued that Jung mistook Freud's negative, one-sided psychological outlook as representative of Jewish psychology as a whole, when it really represented late nineteenth-century *Galuth* (exile or diaspora) psychology. Neumann disagreed with Kirsch, claiming that negativity was part of the Jewish moral instinct. Both men, however, concurred with Jung that Jews had lost contact with their foundations and with their primordial creative source, which could be found again by returning to the original homeland (Kirsch 1934; Neumann 1934). In this regard, they agreed with Jung and a host of Jewish doctors that Jewish self-hatred and the rejection of Jewish religious identity had led to neurosis (Gilman 1993, 110). But they remained silent on Jung's stereotyping Jewish men as effeminate and parasitical, as well as his admiration of National Socialism, and they failed to challenge Jung's stark division between Jewish psychology and an "Aryan" unconscious.

In *völkisch* ideology, the national landscape was the vehicle through which each member of the *Volk* was connected to each other and to the cosmos (Mosse 1964, 15). Apparently, Jung and his Jewish students felt Jews would have a greater chance of individuation were they to return to their original homeland, Palestine, and Jung was interested in Neumann's experiences there. In a letter dated December 22, 1935, Jung wrote that Neumann's "very positive conviction that the Palestinian soil is vital for a Jewish individuation is dear to me" (Neumann 1991, 281). Furthermore, the debate in the *Jüdische Rundschau* suggests that Jung's main Jewish disciples had strong Zionist leanings, which emerged in part out of the same matrix of *völkisch* mysticism and ideology of race that produced anti-Semitic *völkisch* ideology. They thus shared with Jung the belief that Jewishness constituted, if not a separate race, then a distinct nation based on cultural unity and territorial possession (Mosse 1978, 123ff.).

The invention of a Germanic mythology

In "The State of Psychology Today," Jung based his argument on reigning stereotypes about Aryans and Jews. He did not try to support his views through recourse to mythology, which he did two years later in "Wotan." This neglect is surprising, especially since the Romantic idea of the organic unity of a people, its geography, and its cultural products had already made its way into the field of psychology by the early twentieth century. For example, myths were understood by psychoanalysts such as Karl Abraham (1877–1925) and Herbert Silberer (1882–1922) as the collective dreams of a given people (Shamdasani 2003, 139–140). Jung incorporated this idea of myth as a collective dream into his own psychological theory: like the personal unconscious, he wrote, the collective unconscious may also dream, but what it dreams is myth (Jung CW 8 (1950 [1928]):301, 325).

Given Jung's abiding interest in both dreams and myths, he must have been struck by the myth of a dream in the Eddic poem known as "Baldr's Dreams" (*Baldrs draumar)* (Larrington 1996, 243–245). Snorri's *Edda* describe in great detail the accidental slaying of Odin's son Baldr by his other son Hodr, who was tricked by the treacherous half-breed Loki (Snorri 1987, 48–49). The impossibility of adequately avenging this tragic death according to the rules of feud (see Lindow 1997, 134–135) sets off the events that lead to *Ragnarök*, the total war involving the Æsir, the Vanir, and the forces of nature. In "Baldr's Dreams," Odin rides to the realm of the dead to find a seeress who will reveal the prophetic meaning of Baldr's disturbing dreams that foretell his doom. In the Eddic poem "Vafthrudnir's Sayings" (*Vafþrúðnismál*), Odin, disguised as a wanderer, engages in a wisdom contest with the giant Vafthrudnir. The wanderer wins by asking the giant what Odin whispered into his dead son's ear as Baldr was placed on his funeral pyre (Larrington 1996, 48). What Odin says is unknown, but some scholars assume that Odin told Baldr he would be reborn (39), as is related in the Eddic poem, "The Seeress's Prophecy" (*Völuspá*).

These Germanic mythological themes were incorporated by Wagner into his operas. Wagner in turn inspired many members of the *völkisch* movement to use the Eddic poems to express in literary and dramatic fashion their longing for a national rebirth and a specifically Germanic messiah. Along with the Germanic hero Siegfried, the Icelandic figure Baldr was heralded as the Germanic god of light and a Christ-like redeemer, who would overcome the darkness reigning in modern society (Baumann 2005, 97; Zernack 1996, 498–499). For example, the choric tragedy *Mittsommer*, written in 1905 by dramatist Ernst Wachler (1871–1945), and Ludwig Fahrenkrog's *Baldur* (1908) combined motifs of natural times of change, such as the solstices, with the myth of Baldr's death and rebirth, to express their cultural pessimism and hope for a better future. After World War I, the theme of Baldr's death and resurrection continued to be popular, as the story offered the hope of a cultural rejuvenation after Germany's crushing defeat in World War I (Zernack 1996, 498–499, 502). Jung, too, interpreted certain Germanic mythological figures (Siegfried and Wotan) through the lens of nature mythology in his own "encounter with the unconscious" (Jung 2009, 242; ibid., fn. 122).

How might Jung have interpreted the myth of Baldr? According to Snorri's *Edda*, Baldr's mother futilely sought to protect her son from danger by winning promises from almost all creatures that they would not harm her son. After he dies, he does not go to Valhalla, the realm of warriors, but to the abode of the dead overseen by the goddess Hel. According to the psychological theory presented in *Transformations and Symbols of the Libido*, this could represent the dual mother and the possibility of rebirth. However, Jung did not discuss Baldr at all in the original version of this book. Nor did Jung mention Baldr in the "Wotan" essay, although he made other references to ancient Germanic mythology in this work. Instead, Jung named a non-Germanic legendary figure: Ahasverus, the Wandering Jew.

In "Wotan," Jung described Ahasverus as a "projection" to explain the rabid anti-Semitism of the Third Reich. Except for *archetype*, *projection* is the only other psychological term in the entire "Wotan" essay, a curious fact, considering that it purports to be a depth-psychological explanation of National Socialism. Jung claimed that the "motif of the wanderer who has not accepted Christ was projected onto the Jews, in the same way that one typically finds psychic contents that have become unconscious to oneself in another person." He called the coincidence between the rise in anti-Semitism and the "awakening of Wotan" "a psychological subtlety that may perhaps be worth mentioning [. . .]," leaving the reader to imagine what Jung meant by the pregnant ellipsis with which he originally ended his sentence (The ellipsis was replaced by a period in Jung CW 10 (1947 [1936]):374.)

Since Jung described what he believed to be the characteristics of Jewish psychology in other works as a collective *Volk*-psychology comprised of essential and unchanging psychological constants, one might expect that he would interpret the Wandering Jew as a product of Jewish psychology. He could have found just such interpretations in contemporaneous psychological works, such as that written by Dr. Henry Meige (1866–1940), a psychiatrist at the famous Salpêtrière Hospital in France. In "The Wandering Jew in the Clinic: A Study in Neurotic Pathology" (1893), Meige suggested that the legend of the Wandering Jew (*le Juif-errant* in French) was born from the allegedly inherent tendency of Jews towards vagabondage, a medical term denoting a kind of hysteria often connected with an inner restlessness that forced a person to rove aimlessly (Meige 1986, 191–194; Gilman 1993, 117).

Unlike his contemporaries in the field of medicine, however, Jung did not interpret Ahasverus as an aspect of Jewish psychology, but rather, he understood correctly that the legend was of Christian origin, and he described it as a projection. According to Jung, people project onto others those aspects of their psychic contents that they find embarrassing and incompatible with their persona. However, the contents that are projected are not only inferior characteristics; rather, they may also contain quite worthy and positive psychic items that a person has disowned due to low self-esteem (Jung 1921, 657). These contents often appear in archetypal form as gods or demons. When these contents are projected onto another person, the recipient of the projection is either idealized or despised. These contents can instead be introjected, a process which is similar to projection, except the object is one's own ego; hence, introjection leads either to megalomania or an inferiority complex (640). It is therefore necessary that a person become conscious of and assimilate these psychic contents in both their positive and negative aspects.

Although the recipient of the projection is not necessarily either as angelic or demonic as the projection makes him or her appear, Jung believed that there is something about the recipient that acts as a suitable "hook" for the projection (Jung CW 7 (1960 [1943]):152). It is not that the person him- or herself is a devil or a god, but that the relationship between the person projecting a psychic content and the object of projection contains some aspect that allows the projection to take place (ibid.). How then, do the Jews provide the right vehicle for the projection of what aspect of the Germanic psyche? And how does the Wandering Jew symbolize that projected psychic content? To answer these questions, it is necessary to examine the legend of the Wandering Jew, along with Jung's interpretations of it prior to 1936.

The figure of the Wandering Jew (known in German as *der ewige Jude,* the Eternal Jew) has several possible antecedents, including Jesus granting his beloved disciple John eternal life (John 21:22–23) and an officer of Pilates striking Jesus (John 18:22). These biblical references found their way into various medieval stories, but the most significant tale for the development of the story of Ahasverus is that related by Roger of Wendover (d. 1236) in his *Flores Historiarum* (1237) and retold by Matthew Paris (1220–1259) in his *Chronica Major* (1571). In this story, the Roman Cartaphilus, Pilate's doorkeeper, struck Jesus on his way out the door to hurry him on his way. Jesus replied that he would go, but the attacker would stay, which branded him with the curse of eternal, earthly life, a reversal of the gift of eternal salvation in heaven. Cartaphilus repented and received Christian baptism. Under the name of Joseph, he was now residing peacefully in Armenia (Edelmann 1986, 4–5; Schaffer 1986, 28).

The story of Jesus's heckler cursed with eternal life on earth was transformed in the seventeenth century from the pagan Cartaphilus who became settled once he converted to Christianity into a never-redeemed and hence ever-roaming Jew. This transformation took place in 1602 during the Reformation in Germany, in a pamphlet entitled *A Short Description and Tale of a Jew Named Ahasverus (Kurtze Beschreibung und Erzehlung von einem Juden mit Namen Ahasuerus)* (Schaffer 1986, 28). This pamphlet went through twenty editions that same year and quickly became a chapbook, spreading the story of Ahasverus first across Germany and then across Europe (Edelmann 1986, 5, 8). The eight-page work relates a story said to have been told by Paul von Eitzen (1521–1598), a bishop of Schlesvig and a church reformer, who had died four years before the first publication of the pamphlet. Von Eitzen had studied with

Germany's great educational reformer, the *Praeceptor germaniae* Philipp Melanchthon (1497–1560) in Wittenberg, as well as with Martin Luther (1483–1546) at the time when Luther was composing his viciously anti-Jewish work, *Concerning the Jews and their Lies* (*Von den Jüden und iren Lügen,* 1543). The name of Paul von Eitzen was probably invoked by the pamphlet's author to grant credibility to his story of the Wandering Jew (Schaffer 1986, 31).

According to the pamphlet, von Eitzen related that, while he was still a student, he had visited his parents in Hamburg in either 1547 or 1542 (ibid.). One day at church, he saw a penitent wanderer named Ahasverus, a Jewish shoemaker, who claimed to have been on the scene when Jesus was led to his crucifixion. When Jesus rested against his house, Ahasverus sought to drive him away, whereupon Jesus answered: "I will stay and rest, but you shall go." According to von Eitzen, Ahasverus has been wandering ever since (Edelmann 1986, 6).

In this tale of Christ's persecutor, the author reversed the earlier tradition in which the repentant heckler stays in the same place, while Jesus continues on his way. Jesus sends the unkind Jewish cobbler packing to roam the world, telling his tale in a state of heartfelt penitence until Christ returns at the end of time. Ahasverus claims to be a living witness to the passion of Christ; hence, he provided an eye-witness account of the Crucifixion and therefore of the truth of Christianity (Schaffer 1986, 31, 34). After relating this story, the pseudonymous author of the pamphlet drew its moral for his readership: Ahasverus should be a warning to atheists and unbelievers.

From a Jungian perspective, the legend of the Wandering Jew (like the morning ritual of the Kôôny) could be interpreted as evidence of the Western archetype of the self, Christ. Like the Kôôny, Ahasverus himself did not understand the significance of what he had witnessed; thus, he remained unredeemed. Yet despite his own ignorance, he transmitted evidence of the archetype of the self to those who were capable of understanding the symbol's meaning.

Jung first mentioned the Wandering Jew in *Transformations and Symbols of the Libido*, where Ahasverus symbolizes an aspect of the human psyche that is immortal. The first literary sources for the legend of the Wandering Jew go back to the thirteenth century, wrote Jung, but he assumed a much earlier oral tradition that had its source in the East. Jung quickly took up this new thread spun by his own speculation that led him the Islamic figure Al-Khadir (al Chidher) who, according to Sufi legend, was a divine guide to Moses. Jung then connected not Ahasverus but Al-Kadhir to solar heroes, such as Christ and Mithras (Jung 1925, 217). Given Jung's denouncement of Judaism in this book and his more favorable comparison of Mithras, Christ and Wotan, one wonders if Jung was familiar with the contemporaneous scholarly claim that the source of Sufism was not Muslim (i.e. Semitic), but Aryan (Masuzawa 2005, 203). Several pages of mythological analysis later, Jung argued that "the gods, 'a Chidher or a St. Germain,' are our immortal part, which, though incomprehensible, dwells among us somewhere" (Jung 1925, 227). Jung named this immortal part the libido, and imbued it with both solar and phallic symbolism (Jung 1925, 228ff). In light of Christian male anxiety over Jewish circumcision (Gilman 1993, 49ff), it is not surprising that the name of Ahasverus had long since been dropped from the discussion.

Nine years later in *Psychological Types* (1921), Jung described Ahasverus for the first time as a projection, while also connecting the Wandering Jew to the psychological state of barbarism. In his analysis of the poem *Prometheus und Epimetheus* (1881) by the Swiss poet Carl Spitteler (1845–1924), Jung interpreted Prometheus as representing the psychological type of introversion and Epimetheus, extraversion. He further interpreted the precious jewel of Pandora as the psychic birth of a new god. The jewel and symbol of redemption falls into the hands of a wandering Jew; Jung interpreted this scene as a theft and the Jew as Ahasverus. He then compared the theft of the jewel to the medieval Christian accusation that Jews regularly stole the Eucharist wafer, sticking pins into the symbolic body of Christ in an act of ritual murder. Jung then brought the various threads of his analysis together as a diagnosis of projection: Ahasverus represented that portion of the personality (presumably the European one) that was incompatible with a Christian orientation and was therefore repressed (*verdrängt*), forced out of consciousness, and then projected onto those people who never accepted Christ as their Messiah, the Jews. Jung described the projected aspect of the psyche as "this unredeemed, undomesticated, ill-behaved, or barbaric bit" (*dieses unerlöste, nicht domestizierte, unerzogene oder barbarische Stück*) (Jung 1921, 375), presumably that dark side of the Germanic psyche that Jung had discussed three years earlier in "The Role of the Unconscious" (1918) that had never been domesticated by Christianity. In this line, Jung brought together the ancient stereotype of the barbarian as an animal in need of domestication, with the Christian conceit that only this one religion promised true salvation.

In *Psychological Types*, Jung used the term *barbarian* as found in theories of unilinear evolution, in that it represented a higher level of development than the *primitive*. In Jung's psychologized version of this anthropological theory, the primitive lives in a collective unconscious state, in which the oppositions (good/evil, light/dark, spiritual/chthonic, etc.) have not yet been separated. This separation occurs through the process of psychological evolution to the stage of the barbarian, in which one half of all oppositions is made conscious and the other unconscious. Jung argued that the development of individual consciousness always presupposes a certain crippling of the instincts that comes with the evolution of humanity from primitive to barbarian, and this explains why the primitive is generally free from the one-sidedness of the barbarian. Jung believed that the barbarian was therefore prone to an arbitrary one-sidedness, which could move him with tremendous force, as evidenced by Berserker rage (described in Icelandic sagas) and the state of running amok. The one-sidedness could be overcome when the psyche produces a reconciling symbol as a dynamic and regulating function, which would correct the psyche's imbalance (Jung 1921, 293–295).

The legend of Ahasverus represented to Jung a mythological projection of the Christian psyche's undomesticated, unredeemed barbarian side, that aspect that thwarted the "effect of redemption" (*Erlösungswirkung*). Jung psychologized the religious concept of redemption as the state of being conscious, that is, that the primitive aspects of the psyche have been domesticated and thereby civilized. It was the uncivilized, still-barbaric and unredeemed portion of the psyche that caused the modern Westerner's characteristic restlessness, or in Jung's own words, "The restlessness is a concrete expression of the lack of redemption" (*Der Ruhelosigkeit ist ein concreter Ausdruck der Unerlostheit*) (375).

Fifteen years later, in 1936, Jung once again concerned himself with Ahasverus, describing the Wandering Jew as a projection of the Germanic archetype Wotan, the restless wanderer. The comparison between the Wandering Jew and Wotan was already a staple of folklore studies (Blind 1986, 174, 181; Hartwich 2000, 193); Jung gave it a depth-psychological twist. The analytical psychologist Siegmund Hurwitz (d. 1994) argued that the Wandering Jew represents "the latent heathen and Jewish side" in the Western Christian psyche (Hurwitz 1986, 224). Given that he was one of Jung's close associates, perhaps his interpretation reveals Jung's actual meaning. However, according to Jung's own genealogy of the legend in "Wotan," it appears that Jung would have only agreed with the religious designation "heathen." The correct ethnic term would not be Jewish, but Germanic. Following Jung's explanation of projection, the Jews acted as a suitable "hook" for this unredeemed portion of the Germanic psyche, both because of their historical homelessness and constant migrations, and because they rejected Jesus as their savior. Ahasverus was not Jewish at all, according to Jung; rather, the restless wanderer Wotan had been projected onto the unredeemed Jews once the Germanic peoples had converted to Christianity, making the Wandering Jew originally Germanic and heathen.

In "Wotan," Jung referred to the Germanic archetype as "a totality" (*eine Ganzheit*) (Jung CW 10 (1947 [1936]):394), meaning that it contains all the oppositions within itself. Jung had already explored this in "The Role of the Unconscious," in which he described the Germanic barbarian psyche as not only dangerous, but full of promising spiritual aspects waiting to be realized (CW 10 (1918):20). Hence, the unredeemed Wotanic aspect of the Germanic psyche would not only be symbolically dark, but light as well. Indeed, Ahasverus points beyond himself to a figure of light, to the preeminent symbol of psychological wholeness in Jungian psychology, Christ. As a projection, then, Ahasverus thus also gestures towards the other half of the Germanic heathen psyche and its own symbol of redemption: the Germanic figure of light, Baldr. This claim will be explored in greater detail in the next chapter.

Bibliography

Title

"Baldr returns home" (*Balder kehrt heim*): from the German translation of the Old Norse poem, *Völuspá* ("Prophecy of the Seeress"), "Die Kunde der Wala," in Hans von Wolzogen (trans.). 1875. *Die Edda: Götterlieder und Heldenlieder: Aus dem Altnordischen.* Leipzig: Philipp Reclam, p. 151. My translation.

Sources

Abraham, Hilda C. and Ernst L. Freud (eds). 1965. *A Psychoanalytic Dialogue: The Letters of Sigmund Freud and Karl Abraham, 1907–1926*, trans. by Bernard Marsh and Hilda C. Abraham. New York: Basic Books.

Arvidsson, Stefan. 2006. *Aryan Idols: Indo-European Mythology as Ideology and Science*. Chicago: University of Chicago Press.

Bair, Deirdre. 2003. *Jung. A Biography*. Boston: Little, Brown and Co.

Bally, Gustav. 1934. "Deutschstämmige Psychotherapie." *Neue Zürcher Zeitung* 343 (Feb. 27).

Baumann, Schaul. 2005. *Die Deutsche Glaubensbewegung und ihr Gründer Jakob Wilhelm Hauer (1821–1962)*. Religionswissenschaftliche Reihe 22. Marburg: Diagonal.

Benz, Wolfgang. 2004. *Was ist Antisemitismus?* Munich: C. H. Beck.

Bishop, Paul. 1995. *The Dionysian Self: C. G. Jung's Reception of Friedrich Nietzsche*. Monographien und Texte zur Nietzsche-Forschung 30. Berlin: de Gruyter.

Bogdan, Henrik. "The Influence of Aleister Crowley on Gerald Gardner and the Early Witchcraft Movement." In Murphy Pizza and James R. Lewis (eds), *Handbook of Contemporary Paganism*, Leiden: Brill, pp.81–107.

Blind, Karl. 1986. "Wodan, the Wild Huntsman, and the Wandering Jew." In Galit Hasan-Rokem and Alan Dundes (eds), *The Wandering Jew: Essays in the Interpretation of a Christian Legend*. Bloomington: Indiana University Press, pp.169–189.

Boyarin, Daniel. 1997. *Unheroic Conduct: The Rise of Heterosexuality and the Invention of the Jewish Man*. Berkeley: University of California Press.

Brickman, Celia. 2002. "Primitivity, Race, and Religion in Psychoanalysis." *Journal of Religion* 82(1):53–74.

——. 2003. *Aboriginal Populations in the Mind: Race and Primitivity in Psychoanalysis*. New York: Columbia University Press.

Cimbal, Walter. 1933. "Bericht des Geschäftsführers über die Weiterführung des Zentralblattes und der 'allgemeinen ärztlichen Gesellschaften für Psychotherapie.'" *Zentralblatt für Psychotherapie und ihre Grenzgebiete einschliesslich der medizinischen Psychologie und psychischen Hygiene* 6(3):141–144.

Cocks, Geoffrey. 1985. *Psychotherapy in the Third Reich*. New York: Oxford University Press.

Edelmann, R. 1986. "Ahasuerus, the Wandering Jew: Origin and Background." In Galit Hasan-Rokem and Alan Dundes (eds), *The Wandering Jew: Essays in the Interpretation of a Christian Legend*. Bloomington: Indiana University Press, pp.1–10.

Fanon, Frantz. 2008. *Black Skin, White Masks*, trans. by Richard Philcox. New York: Grove Press.

Freud, Sigmund. 1968. *Future of an Illusion*. Volume 21, The Standard Edition of the Complete Psychological Works of Sigmund Freud. London: Hogarth Press and the Institute of Psycho-analysis.

——. 2001. *Totem and Taboo*. Volume 13, The Standard Edition of the Complete Psychological Works of Sigmund Freud. London: Hogarth Press and the Institute of Psycho-analysis.

Gilman, Sander L. 1993. *Freud, Race, and Gender*. Princeton, NJ: Princeton University Press.

Göring, M. H. 1933. "Mitteilung des Reichsführers der 'Deutschen allgemeinen ärztlichen Gesellschaft für Psychotherapie.'" *Zentralblatt für Psychotherapie und ihre*

Grenzgebiete einschliesslich der medizinischen Psychologie und psychischen Hygiene 6(3):140–141.

——. 1934. *Deutsche Seelenheilkunde*. Leipzig: Hirzel.

Grimm, Jacob and Wilhelm. 1880. *Teutonic Mythology*, vol. I, trans. by James Steven Stallybrass. Cambridge: Cambridge University Press.

Hartwich, Wolf-Daniel. 2000. *"Deutsche Mythologie:" Die Erfindung einer nationalen Kunstreligion*. Berlin: Philo Verlag-Gesellschaft.

Heyer, G.R. 1934. "Die Polarität: Ein Grundproblem in Werden und Wesen der deutschen Psychotherapie." *Zentralblatt für Psychotherapie und ihre Grenzgebiete einschliesslich der medizinsichen Psychologie and psychischen Hygiene* 7, no. 1–2 (1934): 17–23.

Hurwitz, S. 1986. "Ahasver, the Eternal Wanderer: Psychological Aspects." In Galit Hasan-Rokem, and Alan Dundes, (eds), *The Wandering Jew: Essays in the Interpretation of a Christian Legend*. Bloomington: Indiana University Press, pp.211–226.

Jung, C. G. 1912. *Wandlungen und Symbole der Libido: Beiträge zur Entwicklungs-geschichte des Denkens*. Leipzig: Franz Deuticke.

——. 1921. *Psychologische Typen*. Zurich: Rascher & Cie.

——. 1925. *Psychology of the Unconscious: A Study of the Transformations and Symbolisms of the Libido; A Contribution to the History of the Evolution of Thought*, trans. by Beatrice M. Hinkle. New York: Dodd, Mead.

——. 1933. "Geleitwort." *Zentralblatt für Psychotherapie und ihre Grenzgebiete einschliesslich der medizinsichen Psychologie und psychischen Hygiene* 6(3):139–140.

——. 1934. "Zeitgenössisches." *Neue Zürcher Zeitung* 437 and 443 (Mar. 13/14).

——. 1953-1991. *Collected Works*, ed. by Sir Herbert Read, Michael Fordham, and Gerhard Adler. New York: Pantheon Books; Princeton, NJ: Princeton University Press.

——. 1965. *Memories, Dreams, Reflections*, rec. and ed. by Aniela Jaffé, trans. by Richard and Clara Winston. New York: Vintage.

——. 1972. *Briefe*, ed. by Aniela Jaffé with Gerhard Adler. Three Volumes. Olten: Walter.

——. 1989. *Analytical Psychology: Notes of the Seminar Given in 1925*, ed. by William McGuire. Princeton, NJ: Princeton University Press.

——. 2009. *The Red Book*, ed. by Sonu Shamdasani, trans. by Mark Kyburz, John Peck, and Sonu Shamdasani. New York: W.W. Norton & Co.

Kirsch, James. 1934. "Die Judenfrage in der Psychotherapie: Einige Bemerkungen zu einem Aufsatz von C. G. Jung. Leserzuschrift." *Jüdische Rundschau* 43:11.

Larrington, Carolyne. 1996. *The Poetic Edda*. Oxford: Oxford University Press.

Lewin, Nicholas Adam. 2009. *Jung on War, Politics and Nazi Germany: Exploring the Theory of Archetypes and the Collective Unconscious*. London: Karnac.

Lindow, John. 1997. *Murder and Vengeance among the Gods: Baldr in Scandinavian Mythology*. Helsinki: Suomalainen Tiedeakatemia.

Masuzawa, Tomoko. 2005. *The Invention of World Religions: Or, How European Universalism Was Preserved in the Language of Pluralism*. Chicago: University of Chicago Press.

McGuire, William (ed.). 1974. *The Freud/Jung Letters: The Correspondence between Sigmund Freud and C. G. Jung*. Princeton, NJ: Princeton University Press.

Meige, Henry. 1986. "The Wandering Jew in the Clinic: A Study of Neurotic Pathology." In Hasan-Rokem and Dundes (eds), *The Wandering Jew: Essays in the Interpretation of a Christian Legend*. Bloomington: Indiana University Press, pp.190–194.

Mosse, George L. 1964. *The Crisis of German Ideology: Intellectual Origins of the Third Reich.* New York: Grosset & Dunlap.

——. 1978. *Toward the Final Solution: A History of European Racism.* New York: Howard Fertig.

Myers, Steve. 2009. "The Cryptomnesic Origins of Jung's Dream of the Multi-Storeyed House." *Journal of Analytical Psychology* 54:513–531.

Neumann, Erich. 1934. "Die Judenfrage in der Psychotherapie." *Jüdische Rundschau* 48(5).

Neumann, Micha. 1991. "On the Relationship between Erich Neumann and C. G. Jung and the Question of Anti-Semitism." In Aryeh Maidenbaum and Stephen A. Martin (eds), *Lingering Shadows Jungians, Freudians, and anti-semitism*, Boston: Shambala, pp.273–289.

Nietzsche, Friedrich. 2002. *Beyond Good and Evil*, trans. by Rolf-Peter Horstmann and Judith Norman Cambridge: Cambridge University Press.

Samuels, Andrew. 1993. *The Political Psyche*. London: Routledge.

Schaffer, Aaron. 1986. "The Ahasverus Volksbuch of 1602." In Galit Hasan-Rokem and Alan Dundes (eds), *The Wandering Jew: Essays in the Interpretation of a Christian Legend,* Bloomington: Indiana University Press, pp.27–35.

Serrano, Miguel. 1966. *C. G. Jung and Hermann Hesse: A Record of Two Friendships,* trans. by Frank MacShane. London: Routledge & K. Paul.

Shamdasani, Sonu. 2003. *Jung and the Making of Modern Psychology: The Dream of a Science.* Cambridge, UK: Cambridge University Press.

Snorri Sturluson. 1987. *Edda*, trans. and ed. by Anthony Faulkes. London: Dent.

Zernack, Julia. 1996. "Anschauungen vom Norden im deutschen Kaiserreich." In Uwe Puschner, Walter Schmitz und Justus H. Ulbricht (eds), *Handbuch zur 'Völkischen Bewegung' 1871–1918*. Saur: Munich, pp.482–511.

6

WOTAN AND "THE ARCHETYPAL *ERGRIFFENHEIT*"

A tragedy in three parts

Wotan as diagnosis

Wotan, the ancient Germanic high god who, as Odin, wanders across the pages of Old Norse sagas, was once praised by medieval Scandinavian poets as both a god of war and a mighty conqueror (Snorri 1976). When the Germanic tribes converted to Christianity, Wotan was dethroned and packed off to the forested spaces of folk tales. There he became the leader of the frightful Wild Hunt, which took place on stormy, wind-filled nights. In legends he continued his peregrinations, wearing a long mantle and a broad-brimmed hat that shaded his one-eyed face, an outfit characteristic of the figures for which he was sometimes mistaken – a Christian pilgrim from Rome, or Ahasverus, the Jewish cobbler who had denied Jesus rest on his way to the crucifixion and was condemned to wander until the Second Coming (Blind 1986, 177, 181, 185).

In 1936, Wotan appeared in a new guise as an archetype in Jung's diagnosis of National Socialism. In his short but pregnant twelve-page essay "Wotan," published in March 1936 in the *Neue Schweizer Rundschau,* Jung played the doctor to his "patient," Germany, interpreting Wotan as a supra-individual psychological factor of the deepest significance, which he claimed was responsible for the upheaval taking place across the border. In contrast to his universalist portrayal of archetypes, Jung defined Wotan as a racial archetype, inborn in and characteristic of the Germanic peoples, especially the Germans (Jung CW 10 (1947 [1936]):389).

"Deeply embedded in the recesses of the German psyche", Jung wrote, this archetype had lain dormant like "a latent epilepsy" since the conversion to Christianity (para. 391). Yet now this collective psychic force had burst out of its constraints to grip (*ergreifen*) the German people. Through decades of treating both psychotic and neurotic patients, Jung concluded that the irruption of such archetypal powers could anticipate a breakdown of the personality and the advent of schizophrenia. Yet it could also signal a necessary first step towards psychological wholeness through individuation. The essay on Wotan and his restless wanderers is rife with the expectations, hopes, and fears of the attending physician, who is watching the patient in the throes of autonomous archetypal forces and who is unable to predict with certainty whether the outcome will be descent into collective madness or the spiritual rebirth of an entire people.

Yet Jung performed more than just the role of doctor in this essay. Like Nietzsche's satyrs in *The Birth of Tragedy,* Jung was also an entranced audience member, watching a tragedy as it unfolded. Likewise, Germany was not just a patient being overwhelmed by a neurotic conflict, but a heroic individual battling his fate even as he succumbed to it. Jung employed tragic motifs in numerous places in the "Wotan" essay, and it is a recurrent motif throughout his oeuvre. Jung's view of the tragic resounds with Hegelian and Nietzschean overtones concerning the conflict of oppositions and their reconciliation; indeed, this is a refrain that Jung constantly reiterated throughout his career, whether he was examining the functioning of the individual psyche, the transformation from one historical epoch to another, or the basic structure of a religious system. Furthermore, Jung's writings on Goethe's *Faust,* as well as Nietzsche's *Birth of Tragedy* and *Thus Spoke Zarathustra*, also indicate a deep-abiding interest in the tragic. This theme was embraced by many scholars of ancient Germanic religion, who described Germanic heroes as tragic figures stoically meeting their destiny. These various sources form the backdrop of "Wotan" as tragedy; reading them in conjunction with Jung's diagnosis of the German case helps illuminate the "secret of coming events in Germany" that Jung suggested in "Wotan" was soon to be revealed (para. 384).

This chapter considers the "Wotan" essay, not just as a medical diagnosis, but also as a description of a tragedy. It discusses the essay's chief concepts, wandering and *Ergriffenheit*, and the ideas of the men Jung viewed as exemplary case studies of the peculiar condition that had befallen the Germans. The analysis of Jung's selective reading of ancient Germanic myth illustrates how he developed both his image of the Germanic archetype and a psychological defense of the Nazi regime. Because Jung believed that archetypes are the psychological counterparts to the biological instincts, this chapter further illustrates what he regarded as the particular Germanic instinct corresponding to the Wotanic archetype, and therefore what constituted, for Jung, the very essence of Germanism. Furthermore, the prophetic utterances that run throughout the work reveal Jung performing the role of prophet and spiritual master, who read the signs of the times and pronounced the historical moment to be *kairos*.

The persona and the tragic flaw

Considering Jung's breadth of knowledge, his understanding of the tragic probably had many sources, including Aristotle, Hegel, and Nietzsche. Aristotle's *Poetics* defines tragedy as an art form that portrays a protagonist of renowned character in battle with a greater power, such as the gods, fortune or fate. Through this confrontation, the protagonist suffers a downfall, evoking fear and pity in those who witness it. The protagonist's misfortune stems not from evil but from error, or *hamartia,* a Greek archery term that means "missing the mark" and which is often translated as "tragic flaw." Only in the Middle Ages was the term imbued with moral connotations (Bushnell 2008, 86). The philosopher Georg Wilhelm Friedrich Hegel (1770–1831), in his *Lectures on Fine Art,* considered the heart of tragedy a conflict of two equal and opposing set of ethics. For Hegel, the tragic flaw is the protagonist's identification with a "single moral claim." His one-sidedness threatens the totality of a metaphysical moral system, which struggles to maintain its integrity. This struggle results in the hero's downfall, with the moral system reconciling opposing forces to maintain its unity (ibid. 75; Krieger 1965, 32–33). In *The Birth of Tragedy*, Friedrich Nietzsche described this art form as the unification of two opposite aesthetic principles, the Apollonian principle of order and the intoxicating, chaotic Dionysian principle. The Apollonian and Dionysian are fundamental forces of nature, the principle of individuation and the primal unity of all things respectively, which were united through the genius of the Hellenic will. Tragedy concerns a "crisis of knowledge," in that the Greeks espied the immutable essence of the world, which renders human action meaningless. Recognizing the overwhelming forces of nature and the absurdity of his own action in light of that knowledge, the Greek hero overcomes his pessimism through Apollonian illusion. Though life be but a dream, the Hellene wills to keep dreaming (Bushnell 2008, 68, 70–71; Nietzsche 1967, 33–36, 42). Although these three authors defined tragedy differently, what they bequeathed to Jung were the ideas of a protagonist's struggle with a force greater than himself, his singleness of purpose, the clash of opposing forces, and the need for their reconciliation, written so as to lend universal validity to the individual protagonist's struggle. These are themes that course their way through Jung's oeuvre and the "Wotan" essay in particular.

Jung described the basic structure of the psyche in tragic terms similar to those of Hegel. The psyche has both an inner and outer aspect that fluctuate around a center-point, which acts as a self-regulating system to maintain psychic equilibrium. Jung described this fluctuation as a "tragic counterplay between inside and outside," which "represents, at bottom, the energetics of the life process, the polar tension that is necessary for self-regulation." This movement of the psychic energy had been represented literarily by the struggles between Job and God, and the wager between God and Mephistopheles in *Faust* (Jung CW 7 (1963 [1928]):312).

The interplay between the outer and inner is central to the individuation process. Jung explained that the ego is usually identified with the persona, although the persona is in reality not individual, but both arbitrary and collective, being the title, the office, or the social role by which a person is recognized by others. Still, the dissolution of the persona is frightening and painful, leaving one feeling unstable and unsure of oneself. Jung believed that the path to psychological wholeness lay in bridging one's ego with the collective unconscious and archetypes. The path of individuation drives the psychic energy inward toward deeper levels of the psyche and past various archetypal forms where true individuality is to be found. Hence, the cure of a neurosis may often entail a necessary regression before the psychic energy can move forward in a progressive direction away from the inner subjective space and back out towards the objective world, integrating the power of the archetypal forms into consciousness and thereby expanding and enriching the personality (para. 245–247, 254).

The patient and simultaneously tragic protagonist about whom Jung was writing in "Wotan" was the Germanic psyche itself, which Jung characterized in other writings as restless, fragmented and full of tension (Jung 1934, 203), reflecting the general psychological condition of modern western society. As discussed in previous chapters, Jung claimed that this fragmentation was caused initially by the imposition of a foreign religion, Christianity, which had crippled the instincts of the Germanic barbarian while splitting its psyche in two, civilizing one half while repressing the other (Jung CW 10 (1918):17). This split was then exacerbated by the growth of natural science, which created a sharp division between faith and reason in the West (Jung 1936b, 172). It was as if the collective persona of the Germans as civilized, rational, and Christian (Jung CW 10 (1947 [1936]):373, 385, 397) was dissolving, allowing the repressed side of the Germanic barbarian psyche to irrupt once again; at the same time, the collective Germanic libido appeared to have "introverted," or moved inward to its own hidden depths, to seek a solution to the malaise of modern society from an earlier level of development. In tragic terms, the Germanic persona as Christian and rational was a tragic flaw. Its one-sidedness had repressed not only the problematic side but also the natural morality of the barbarian, and these two ethical forces, the Christian and the barbarian, were now coming into conflict (Jung CW 10 (1918):17–20).

At the very center of the psyche is what Jung called the self, or the "God within us" (Jung CW 7 (1963 [1928]): 399). In the German case, Jung named this god Wotan (Jung CW 10 (1947 [1936]):398); hence, Wotan must be the Germanic archetype of the self. Since the collective German persona had been shattered by the irruption of this archetypal force unleashed by National Socialism, then in Jungian terms one could say that the Germans were experiencing what Pietikäinen calls "individuation writ large, or *national* individuation" (Pietikäinen 2008, 597; emphasis in original). Jung himself made this claim both in private correspondence and in a seminar. On Aug. 12, 1934, Jung wrote to his Jewish disciple Erich Neumann that the biblical figure of Jacob was "the *quintessence* of the Jew", representing a "symbolic attempt at a collective individuation" [. . .] just as "historically, Hitler represents the same for the Germans" (Liebscher 2015, 54[7J]; emphasis in original). Furthermore, on May 10, 1933, Jung described in his *Visions* seminar the Nazi takeover of power as individuation:

> It is a regression and injustice, there is no doubt about that; but they [the Germans] cannot get together as a nation, they cannot celebrate their love feast, if strangers are in between. Of course, you can say that Jews are scapegoats; of course they are scapegoats, but other people, individuals, do the same thing. In the process of individuation, for instance, they

> exclude many things, they may desert their relations, which is unjust, cruel, or foolish perhaps, but it serves that one purpose of individuation, of coming together.
>
> (Jung 1984, 1:976; as quoted in Pietikäinen 2008, 600)

Not content to analyze the psychological underpinnings of historical events, Jung instead reduced them to developments within a psychological sphere. He did so by de-Germanizing Jewish Germans by calling them "strangers," while also exonerating the German people and its new government of persecuting the Jews. Jung admitted he knew this persecution was taking place, yet justified it as it served the presumably higher purpose of the psychological creation of the people's community (*Volksgemeinschaft*) through a national individuation process.

Wotan as wanderer and the changing meaning of wandering

Despite purporting to provide a diagnosis of the German situation, Jung used only two terms – *archetype* and *projection* – from his own lexicon of psychological concepts. The essay's reigning motifs, *wandering* and *Ergriffenheit,* are not, strictly speaking, psychological concepts at all. The first term, like Wotan himself, tends to peregrinate in Jung's work. While he was still at the Burghölzli Clinic, Jung wrote several case studies about people afflicted with *Wandertrieb*, or "wanderlust," a word that literally means "the drive to wander." As a medical term, it meant "vagabondage," a pathological mental state characterized by an inner restlessness leading someone so afflicted to rove aimlessly (Jung GW 1 (1902):18–20, 101–108; (1903):206, 212–219; (1903):323f.; and (1904):362–364).

Yet by 1936, Jung radically changed the meaning of this term. In his lecture on "Psychological Factors Determining Human Behavior," delivered at the Harvard Tercentenary Conference on Arts and Sciences, Jung proposed a new class of instincts, which he called the "*drive to activity*." These include the "urge to travel" (in German: *Wandertrieb*), the "love of change," "restlessness" (in German: *Unrast*), and the "play-instinct." These are drives that rouse a person to life when the other instincts of hunger and sexuality have been satisfied (Jung CW/GW 8 (1942 [1936]):240). Thus, in the same year that he referred to Wotan as *der rastlose Wanderer* (the one who wanders restlessly), and an *Unruhestifter* (one who causes unrest in others) (Jung GW 10 (1947 [1936]):373, 374), Jung redefined *Unrast* and *Wandertrieb* as positive instincts of vitality and expansion.

Indeed, the change in meaning of *wandering* can be traced back to Jung's 1912 *Transformations and Symbols of the Libido.* In this book, Jung redefined libido to mean not the sexual drive but psychic energy in general, or more specifically, "the never-restless desire," which is exemplified by the figure of the wanderer (Jung 1925, 231). Jung categorized several mythological characters as wandering figures, including Gilgamesh, Dionysus, Hercules, Christ and Mithras (524, fn. 76), all of whom Jung associated with the sun, symbol of the libido. The immortal sun symbolizes the libido, explained Jung, because it is the aspect of the individual that lives eternally through psychic connection with the whole of humanity (231). Jung supported this Romantic and pantheistic view with contemporary theories on the origin of religion as developed by Max Müller and Ernest Renan, both of whom believed that religion had its origins in solar worship. Jung even cited Renan as saying the sun was the most rational representation of God found in nature (127). Jung's image of the eternally restless, ever-questing libido has Faustian overtones: in his 1918 "The Role of the Unconscious," he defined libido as "'stormy longing'" (*stürmisches Verlangen*), a phrase cut from the English CW (compare Jung CW 10 (1918):7 with ibid. GW 10 (1918):7).

In *Transformations and Symbols of the Libido*, Jung explained that the libido itself is split (Jung 1925, 480). One half, remaining enthralled by the animal instincts, wants to return to the womb. The other half uses the incest taboo to channel psychic energy into analogous alternatives, thereby moving the individual out of unconscious identification with the collective. Another way of describing this process is that part of the psychic energy strives after the Apollonian principle of individuation, whereas the other half seeks regression to a Dionysian-like collective unconscious state. It can, however, be channeled via symbols of sacrifice and rebirth away from instinctual gratification and into a higher form of Dionysian connection with all of life (303, 479). Jung explained the significance of the symbolism of solar heroes as follows:

> [. . .] the heroes always resemble the wandering Sun, which seems to justify the fact that the myth of the hero is a sun myth. . . [It is] the myth of our own suffering unconscious, which has an unquenchable longing for all the deepest sources of our own being; for the body of the mother, and through it for communion with infinite life in the countless forms of existence.
>
> (Jung 1925, 231)

Here, wandering no longer signifies in Jung's thought a mental affliction or form of degeneration. Rather, it represents the introversion of the libido towards the center of the psyche. By progressing once more towards the outer world, the libido brings the numinous power of archetypal forms with it, thereby expanding consciousness. The effect is similar to mystics turning inward to discover a universal spiritual source at the core of their own being, which allows them to experience a spiritual oneness with all of creation; in Jung's theory, this mystical union takes place between the unconscious and individual consciousness.

To illustrate this process, Jung did not present a case study of a patient, but rather referred to "the Master," Goethe, whose Faust descended with Mephistopheles to a mysterious realm where "the Mothers" await (*Faust*, Part II, Act I, Scene 5). Goethe had based this scene on the ritual descent participants in the ancient Greek Eleusinian mysteries made to the goddesses Demeter and Persephone in order to be rejuvenated (Jung 1912, 198–199; Noll 1994, 173). Although this book was written well over two decades before the publication of "Wotan," this chapter will show that the descent and ascent of the wandering solar hero, as well as the tragic figure of Faust, stand behind the image of Wotan as wanderer. Their reflection in the Wotanic archetype indicates that when Jung called Wotan "the restless wanderer," what he had in mind was not a pathological condition, but the possibility of a spiritual rebirth on a national scale.

The meaning of *Ergriffenheit*

Along with wandering, Wotan's other chief characteristic was that of *Ergriffenheit*: Wotan was an *Ergreifer*, and the Germans were *ergriffen*. The original essay reads, "Vielleicht dürfen wir diese Allgemeinerscheinung als 'Ergriffenheit' bezeichnen. Mit diesem Ausdruck ist zunächst ein 'Ergriffener' gesetzt, sodann aber auch ein 'Ergreifer'" (Jung 1936a, 661–662). Jung originally provided no definition of *Ergriffenheit.* The definition of "the state of being seized or possessed" (Jung CW 10 (1947 [1936]):386) is a post-war interpolation in the text, and carries a negative connotation; in particular, the word "possessed," when used in a Christian cultural context, is typically followed by the expression, "by the devil." While *Ergriffenheit* can mean "a state of being seized," the translation of the term as "possession" is simply wrong, for this would be *Besessenheit* in German. This error appeared in a highly condensed English translation of "Wotan" that appeared in the *Saturday Review of Literature* in 1937; in this work, the term was defined as "being emotionally 'seized, moved, possessed'" with no explanation of who or what was being quoted (ETH Hs 1379:191).

The chief meaning of *Ergriffenheit* and the past participle *ergriffen* is a deep stirring in one's soul. It can indicate the personification of an impersonal force, such as the consuming or grasping nature of fire, sickness or the sword; or the state of being held captive, either by an abstract power, such as sleep or pain, or by a strong emotion. In a negative sense, one can be seized by melancholy (*Wehmut)*, rage (*Wut*), or despair (*Verzweiflung)*; more positively, *ergriffen* can be paired with terms suggesting an elevated religious state, such as reverence (*Andacht)* and heavenly delight (*himmlisches Behagen*) (Spalding 1964, 671–672).

The incorrect alignment of *Ergriffenheit* with "possession" strips out the "double attitude" with which Jung regularly wrote to reflect the paradoxical nature of the psyche (Bair 2003, 475), and more specifically, the ambiguous, ambivalent and even positive qualities of Jung's dual-natured Wotanic archetype. Furthermore, as discussed in Chapter 3, Jung regularly used the term to describe the effect of the archetypes on the psyche, translating *Ergriffenheit* into English as "seized," "gripped," or "caught" – the last two words being how he described his own "encounter with the unconscious" to his audience in his 1925 private seminar (Jung 1989, 80, 88, 97). Since *Ergriffenheit* is one of the chief concepts of the essay, the incorrect English translation has distorted the entire meaning of "Wotan" for scholars who have relied on the work's English-language edition (i.e., Bair 2003, 455; Bishop 1995, 308; Ellwood 1999, 60; Lewin 2009, 265–268;

Noll 1994, 134; Pietikäinen 2008, 597, 598), yet German scholars also overlook the word's multiple connotations and historical significance (Langwieler 2010, 37, where such a discussion should have taken place in his text and does not).

A glance at Jung's original German-language edition of his 1957 book *The Undiscovered Self* demonstrates the contrast between *Besessenheit* and *Ergriffenheit* in Jung's theory. Like "Wotan," this book concerns contemporary societies and mass movements. In this text, Jung denounced modern mass society and its ruling scientific rationalism. People are reduced to mindless masses which can be easily manipulated by slogans and propaganda that stir their emotions and override their reason. This results in a "collective possession" (*Besessenheitszustand*) (Jung CW/GW10 (1957):490). As an antidote to this spiritual sickness, Jung advocated what he considered to be a genuine religious experience, that is, a direct relationship between an individual and a higher power. The "subjectively overwhelming numinosity of the experience," by which one is "*seized*" (German: *ergriffen* [emphasis in original], para. 566), lends a person such a sense of inner security and self-awareness that he can resist being dissolved into the mass of modern society.

In 1921, Jung diagnosed an ancient case of *Ergriffenheit* in *Psychological Types* when discussing Nietzsche's *The Birth of Tragedy*. Jung interpreted the opposition of the Apollonian and the Dionysian as though it were a distant mirror reflecting similar psychic conflicts faced by modern Westerners, in that the conflict between these two primal forces corresponded to a split in the psyche of the ancient Greek. The civilized Greek man found himself gripped (*ergriffen*) by his own suppressed barbarian side, which stripped him of his individuality and threatened to dissolve him back into the Dionysian collective unconscious. The Greek psyche's civilized Apollonian side was horrified to be caught by its own instincts, and this generated the psychic conflict that resulted in the birth of tragedy. Jung argued that the essence of tragedy was therefore not aesthetic, as Nietzsche thought, but both religious and psychological, and that the miracle of the Hellenic will was a unification of oppositions on an unconscious level (Jung 1921, 198–200), illustrated in the reconciliation of the two gods at Delphi, (197). The conflict's resolution came not from outside, but from the collective unconscious of the group in question, which generated a religious symbol by which the psychological oppositions could be brought into a new synthesis on a higher level of consciousness. This, in turn, generated a greater capacity to create the arts of culture and civilization.

The meaning of *Ergriffenheit* in Jung's diagnosis of the ancient Greek origin of tragedy reflects the idea of "primal ontic seizure," which is how the religious studies scholar Steven Wasserstrom says the term was understood by intellectuals during the Weimar and Nazi eras. Both Jung and the philosopher Martin Heidegger (1889–1976) used the term in this sense in their respective seminars on Friedrich Nietzsche's *Thus Spoke Zarathustra*, as did the anthropologist Leo Frobenius (1873–1938). Furthermore, sociologist and philosopher Theodor W. Adorno (1903–1969) used the word *Ergriffenheit* to describe the renowned scholar of Judaism Gerschom Scholem (1897–1982), who Adorno said was "moved through and through" by his subject (Wasserstrom 1999, 31–32).

Ergriffenheit is also a chief concept of the Eranos conference, an annual meeting for the academic study of religion. Eranos was established in 1933 by Olga Froebe-Kapteyn (1881–1962) in Ascona, Switzerland, and Jung was considered the conference's *Spiritus Rector*. Froebe-Kapteyn insisted that the conference speakers be "stirred" *(ergriffen)* by their research, in that they should have an inner sympathy with their subject. As the Eranos website states, "The life of ERANOS arises from the inspired science of its speakers. As to their selection, Olga Froebe-Kapteyn followed a clear concept. A speaker at ERANOS is one who 'delves into the fullness of his inner visions and seeks to retain them in scientific form'" (Eranos, n.d.).

Similar to this understanding of *Ergriffenheit*, some scholars considered a disinterested, objective stance towards the object of study to be a mechanistic form of scholarship, which came under attack after the catastrophe of World War I (Krech 2002, 60). Following Otto's lead, scholars such as Hauer, Söderblom, Wach, Gerardus van der Leeuw (1890–1950) and Friedrich Heiler (1892–1967) developed what they called an "understanding study of religion" (*verstehende Religionswissenschaft)*, in which the religious experience or religious feeling was not only the object of research, but also a research method (61–62). As Otto argued in *The Idea of the Holy*, the religious studies scholar must already be deeply moved by his own subjective experience of religion in order to adequately investigate it (Otto 1958, 8).

The idea of "primal ontic seizure" was also foundational to Hauer's *The Religions: Their Becoming, Their Meaning, Their Truth* (*Die Religionen: Ihr Werden, Ihr Sinn, Ihre Wahrheit,* 1923). Hauer, who plays a leading role in Jung's "Wotan" essay, argued that the origin of genuine religion lay in the experience of "being or becoming stirred or deeply moved" (*Ergriffensein* or *Ergriffenwerden*) (Hauer 1923, 25, 45), which indicates an experiential knowledge of the divine based on an overpowering inner feeling of its presence. Like other religious studies scholars of his day, Hauer believed that a common experience forms the foundation of all religions everywhere – in his theory, *Ergriffensein* – but that individual religions have different developmental trajectories. However, Hauer reflected a post-World-War-I interest in prophets and personalities, and the hope for renewal following a downfall, when he argued that some religions degenerate; yet from a deteriorated state a religious genius may arise, who provides new revelations of the eternal truth (25).

Hauer derived his theory of "being moved" (*Ergriffensein*) from Otto's *The Idea of the Holy*. In this work, Otto claimed that the experience of the Holy, a transcendental power he called *the numinous*, is foundational to all religions. An encounter with the numinous engenders a feeling of "creature-consciousness," which suggests "a creature, submerged and overwhelmed by its own nothingness in contrast to that which is supreme above all creatures" (Otto 1958, 10). An encounter with the numinous produces states ranging from stupor to mystical transcendence, while the numinous also exercises an irresistible power of attraction. Its energy is vital and forceful, often experienced either as "the wrath of God" or mystical love (13–33, quote on 31). The concept of *Ergriffenheit* as "primal ontic seizure" was therefore central to Otto's work. After analyzing the main elements of the numinous, he quoted from Goethe's *Faust* lines that Otto believed epitomized an encounter with the Holy:

> Awe is the best of man: howe'er the world's / Misprizing of the feeling would prevent us, / Deeply we feel once gripped, the weird Portentous. [Das Schaudern ist der Menschheit bestes Teil / Wie auch die Welt ihm das Gefühl verteuere / Ergriffen fühlt er tief das Ungeheure.]
>
> (Goethe, *Faust,* Second Part, Act I, Scene V; in Otto 1958, 40, fn. 2)

Ergriffenheit as *Volksgeist*

As previously shown, Jung appropriated Otto's neologism *the numinous* to describe the power of the archetypes, which "grip" (*ergreifen*) a person and engender the unique feeling of numinosity. Hence, when Jung wrote in the "Wotan" essay that the Germans were in a state of *Ergriffenheit*, he implied not that they were "possessed," but rather that they were experiencing an original religious encounter with "the Holy," in Jung's psychological sense of an inner, yet collective force. The connection to Otto's definition of *Ergriffenheit* as a numinous experience is underscored by Jung's allusion to two figures that he believed shared an ancient kinship with Wotan: Christ and Dionysus (Jung CW 10 (1947 [1936]):373). Furthermore, Jung depicted Wotan as a wind that blows where it will, seizing everything it finds in its way, with no-one knowing either its origin or its destination (para. 391). This is a paraphrase of John 3:8, which describes those "born of the Spirit." Jung also compared the Germans to Christ's apostles, whose house "was filled with a 'mighty [rushing] wind'" (*von einem 'gewaltigen Winde erfüllt'*) by the Pentecostal Spirit (CW/GW 10:389). Jung even called the present situation *kairos*. The English CW interprets *kairos* as "the present moment in time" (para. 398), yet Jung knew Greek better: in ancient philosophy, *kairos* indicates an opportune moment; in tragedy, a "critical moment," both "a crisis and a test" (Bushnell 2008, 42); and in Mark 1:15, the time fulfilled by God.

Jung's portrayal of Wotan as wind evokes the ancient portrayal in Homer's Iliad of the wandering god of frenzy, Dionysus (Cancik and Schneider 1996, 652), who made his divine entrance (Parousia) in Jung's "Wotan" as "an elemental Dionysus breaking into the Apollonian order" (Jung CW 10 (1947 [1936]):391). In quieter times, Jung wrote, Wotan slumbered in the collective psyche of the Germans like "a latent epilepsy" (para. 391), a disease long thought to be caused by the visitation of a divine power and still known in Jung's day as the "holy sickness" (Höfler 1899, 114). When Jung stated that the Germans were in a state of *Wütens* or "fury" (Jung CW/GW 10 (1947 [1936]):388), he no doubt had the association with epilepsy in mind; furthermore, he knew that this word, etymologically related to the name Wotan and the German word for rage (*Wut*), could convey intense states of many kinds, from rage, to intoxication, to a Dionysian-like ecstasy (Grimm 1960, 2495).

Yet the "living god" of whom Jung wrote was neither Christian nor Greek, but Germanic, and he specifically named *kairos* Wotan (Jung CW 10 (1947 [1936]):398). Through this and other expressions, Jung created a portrait of an entire nation being moved by a primordial, racially determined, inner divine power comparable to the Pentecostal Spirit. Furthermore, he created an esoteric correspondence between Wotan and the blond-haired members of the German Youth Movement, whom he wrote were the first to be roused by Wotan, calling them "restless wanderers" (German: *rastlose Wanderer*, para. 373), the same term Jung applies to Wotan himself (*der rastlose Wanderer*), suggesting an experience of *unio mystica*. These youths, he wrote, had been wandering from "Sicily to the North Cape" in Norway (para. 375), implying the Germanic god had stirred the entire western Indo-Germanic realm, thereby echoing Hauer's racial-cultural focus in his *Deutsche Gottschau* (Hauer 1934, 3). Furthermore, the well-known Cosmic Circle members that Jung named – the poet Stefan George, vitalist philosopher Ludwig Klages, and esotericist Alfred Schuler (Jung CW 10 (1947 [1936]):375) – epitomized the kinds of people (artist, philosopher and mystic) in whom the creative fantasies issuing from the spiritual depths of the collective unconscious may best reveal themselves (Jung CW 10 (1918):13). Finally, Jung included the "simple folk" (Jung CW 10 (1947 [1936]):373), creating a vision of a *Volk* bound together in mystical union across the class divisions that had long threatened to rend modern society apart. Jung in effect theorized a collective racial libido that he called "Wotan." This amounted to a psychologization of the *Volksgeist*, a Romantic-turned-*völkisch* belief that one's innermost self was rooted in an essence shared with other members of one's people, the national landscape, and the cosmos (Mosse 1964, 15–16, 22). Jews were excluded.

Ergriffenheit, cosmogonic Eros, and culture-creating capacity

Due to what Jung called "a classical stamp" (Jung CW 10 (1947 [1936]):375) on the south of Germany, the three named members of the Cosmic Circle (excluding the Jewish member, Karl Wolfskehl, 1869–1948) mistook Wotan for the cosmogonic *Eros*. They described the cosmogonic *Eros* as a gripping or infusing divine power, that is, an *Ergreifer* in Otto's sense of mystical love. This force lent them a heightened perception of life and an extraordinary creative power. For example, in *Vom Kosmogonischen Eros* (1922), the vitalist philosopher Ludwig Klages depicted the ancient mystical experience of union with the suprahuman *Eros* in ways that parallel Jung's theory of the dissolution of the persona and the irruption of archetypal images. Klages wrote that the cosmogonic *Eros* is the force that liberates the soul from the deadly power of the *Geist*, the rational mind that hungrily seeks to draw everything within reach of its rationalizing power (Klages 1981, 61–62). As with the dissolution of the persona as described by Jung, this liberation engenders a necessary suffering, for the *Geist* undergoes a death, either through an inner *Sprengung*, the experience of being blown apart, or an inner *Schmelzung*, a dissolution (67). Once freed from the rational mind, however, the soul may unite with the cosmos through the act of mystical contemplation (*Schauung*) of the things of the world, recognizing their inner, living essence as primordial images (*Urbilder*) (100–102). The union of soul and archetype gives birth to the inner "dancing star" about which Nietzsche had rhapsodized in *Thus Spoke Zarathustra* (102; Nietzsche 1968a, 6/1:13).

Likewise, the mystic Alfred Schuler created his own theory of the cosmogonic *Eros* called *telesma* that he presented in a lecture series, "On the Essence of the Eternal City" *(Vom Wesen der ewigen Stadt)* in the winter of 1917–1918. Although these lectures were not published until 1940 (Schuler 1940), Jung was apparently aware of the general ideas of Schuler, possibly through their mutual associate Oskar A. H. Schmitz, who had encountered the Cosmic Circle during a stint in Schwabing (Schmitz 1926). Jung further assumed that his audience, too, was familiar with Schuler's ideas, since he named him in "Wotan" thirteen years after Schuler's death (Jung CW 10 (1947 [1936]):375). In his lectures, Schuler described *telesma* (from Greek *telein*, "to make perfect, complete") as a substance comprised of electrons consisting of two poles, one active, the other passive, which together continually beget and give birth to light. *Telesma* is a constantly flowing current of ethereal light, raining down out of the primordial cell of the cosmos like a cold shower, sending shivers through a person as it unites with its warm counterpart in the blood. This engenders what Schuler called "the essential life" (*esentielles Leben)*. This cosmic, holistic life-energy creates the capacity not only to feel deeply but to create the arts of culture (Schuler 1997, 220–221).

Two figures best embodied the telesmatic power, Schuler said, one mythological, the other historical. Before the dawn of time, an androgynous youth and his equally androgynous mother were the preeminent symbols of telesmatic power (264). She is a half-moon, which between her two end-points births and begets the shining star, the child (237). Since the dawn of history, the bisexually balanced spiritual power of *telesma* has been endangered by a one-sided masculine will, which unleashed a reign of terror on the feminine principle (229). In ancient Rome, however, one group was able to combine the masculine will with the bisexual telesmatic power to become figures of *Übermensch*-like stature: the Caesars (268). The emperors concentrated *telesma* in themselves by creating sites and games where telesmatic power could be generated. For example, Schuler described the chariot races of the *Circus Romana* as a telesma-producing event that resulted in a collective mystical experience (262–263).

Finally, Germany's would-be "spiritual savior" (Norton 2002, xi), the poet Stefan George, produced his own artistic vision of the cosmogonic *Eros* in his *Maximin Cycle,* published in 1907 in his book of poetry, *The Seventh Ring (Der siebente Ring)*. Maximin was based on Maximilian Kronberger, a young man worshipped by George, who died an early death (335ff.). George overcame his grief by transforming Maximilian into a majestic child-god named Maximin, whose image resonates with the archaic vision of the cosmos-creating divine love, the cosmogonic *Eros*. In Jungian terms, George had projected the archetype of the self onto the young man Maximilian. When Maximilian died, George overcame his suffering by withdrawing his libidinal energy from the outer object and introverting it, thereby discovering a god within. Now residing in the very blood of the poet, this god filled George with inspiration, a spiritual power by which the poet conceived and created new works of art (George 1982, vols 6–7, 89–111, especially 90, 99, and 109).

Ergriffenheit as initiation and deification

What Klages, Schuler and George described was the mystical experience of merging with a divine source – in a word, *Ergriffenheit.* This experience is an act both of initiation and of deification, a transfiguring experience that is accompanied by the deepest suffering and the greatest ecstasy. Bruno Goetz portrayed such a scene in his 1919 novel *The Kingdom without Space (Das Reich ohne Raum)*, a book Jung claimed contained "a very strange vision" (Jung CW 10 (1947 [1936]):384). Jung mentioned Goetz's book again in two other works (CW 9/1 1951 [1940]:269; ibid., 1948 [1945]:396, fn. 9), where his portrayal of the story is quite negative. Note the dates: 1940 and 1945 respectively. One can easily surmise that the course of events in Nazi Germany had a negative impact on Jung's reading of Goetz's book, but within the context of the 1936 "Wotan" essay, the evaluation appears on the whole positive.

Goetz's "strange vision" relates the story of Melchior's encounter with the small, brown-faced boy named Fo (Chinese for Buddha). Fo leads a band of wandering youths who, like Jung's solar heroes seeking the source of all being, renew themselves in the "kingdom without space" so that they may continue their ceaseless wanderings, transforming themselves from one form into another in their quest for endless experience (Goetz 1919, 61–62). To join Fo and his band, Melchior chooses to undergo a rite of initiation, which results in a bloody crucifixion scene: in the middle of a meadow, the youths nail Melchior to a cross that visually unites heaven and earth. The youths put a crown of thorns on his head, made of rays of moonlight that prick his forehead and make it bleed. As Melchior hangs on the cross, a shaft of sunlight pierces his chest and rips it open, causing his blood to gush out on and into the earth (58–60). He is thereby transformed into a living tree, while the youths become animals that lounge beneath his branches and birds that nest in his hair, residing again in the Garden of Eden (60). Heaven and earth, human and animal, blood and soil – what began as an agonizing death is transformed into a mystical initiation rite leading to a *coniunctio oppositorum* and new life.

Jung once experienced a similar ordeal, which he described as his "deification" in his 1925 private seminar on analytical psychology (see Chapter 3). The scene took place during the period of Jung's "confrontation with the unconscious"

(1913–1919) and may be the experience of *Ergriffenheit* to which Jung alluded in a letter to Hauer, dated March 10, 1936 (Jung 1972, 1:272). After telling his audience in 1925 about his archetypal vision, Jung then explained the necessity of avoiding both identification with the images and their dismissal; rather, it was essential to become conscious of the real meaning of them, thereby freeing oneself from their grip, yet able to access their creative power (Jung 1989, 99).

A highly creative if ultimately deadly case of *Ergriffenheit* was that of Friedrich Nietzsche, whose *Thus Spoke Zarathustra* became the focus of Jung's weekly seminar in Zurich from 1934 until the outbreak of World War II. According to Jung, Nietzsche's declaration that God was dead left a hole in the collective psyche that he himself tried to fill; he identified himself with God's would-be replacement, the Superman, which then overpowered him (Jung 1988, 2:903). Nietzsche had written about the Superman in an inspired state (Nietzsche 1968b, 6/3:337–338), which Jung interpreted to mean that his book's contents had arisen from the depths of the collective unconscious and were thus archetypal in nature (Liebscher 2001, 331).

Jung apparently believed that the power lying behind Nietzsche's revival of the Zoroastrian prophet was the Germanic archetype, for in "Wotan," Jung claimed that after Nietzsche had declared the death of the Christian god, a new god appeared to him (Jung CW 10 (1947 [1936]):376). Always interested in dreams, Jung related Zarathustra's nightmare of the mighty wind that rips open the gates of a graveyard he is overlooking, hurling a casket before him out of which tumble a thousand peals of laughter. Zarathustra's beloved disciple claims that the dreamer is both the powerful wind and the coffin full of laughter (para. 377–378). Jung then wrote, in a line deleted from the English edition, "In this image, Nietzsche's secret becomes powerfully apparent (*In diesem Bild tritt Nietzsches Geheimnis mächtig hervor*)" (Jung 1936a, 659). The secret, it seems, is that Nietzsche, who "had no knowledge of Germanic literature" (Jung CW 10 (1947 [1936]): 376), was seized by the god to whom he as German was kin and whose very spirit he embodied (para. 379). Jung insisted that underneath Nietzsche's syphilis was schizophrenia (Jung 1988, 2:797); not a venereal disease, but rather Wotan drove the philosopher mad, and Nietzsche became "the most complete victim of the Hunter-God" (*völligstes Opfer des Gott-Jägers*). This startling statement is followed by the assertion, deleted from the English edition, that, "in the last analysis, even Zarathustra's powerful self-liberation does not change anything" (*woran auch Zarathustras gewaltsame Selbstbefreiung im letzten Grunde nichts mehr ändert*) (Jung 1936a, 660).

While Jung believed Nietzsche to represent a highly significant if ultimately fatal case of *Ergriffenheit*, an exemplary case was Jung's friend, Jakob Wilhelm Hauer, whom he had first gotten to know at Keyserling's School of Wisdom (Pietikäinen 2008, 597). In "Wotan," Jung portrayed Hauer as a tragic hero and a "conscientious scholar," whose 1934 book *Deutsche Gottschau* could not be read "without emotion" (Jung CW 10 (1947 [1936]):398). Jung neglected to mention that the book detailed a pseudo-history of a millennia-long struggle between the

"Indo-Germanic" (*indogermanisch*) and the "Near Eastern-Semitic" (*vorderasiatisch-semitisch*) worlds of faith, the origin of which Hauer placed in the mythic time of prehistory. He also made no note of Hauer's devotion to National Socialism (in 1935, before "Wotan," Hauer had joined the National Socialist League of University Lecturers; Dierks 1986, 279). Instead, Jung wrote that the *Ergreifer* was driving Hauer to bridge through his scholarship the "dark forces of life" and the "shining world of historical ideas" (Jung CW 10 (1947 [1936]):398), as if the struggle of the Hellenic will to unite the Apollonian and Dionysian were being reenacted in Germany in the 1930s. Hauer's own restless spirit had led him to reject Christianity in favor of a deep, indwelling source of spirituality through scholarly study, thereby overcoming the divide between science and faith. Thus, Hauer pointed the way to prevail over the two main causes of the fragmented Germanic psyche, Christianity and materialistic science.

In "Wotan," Jung suggested that Hauer himself was a kind of *Ergreifer,* in that Jung diagnosed his German Faith Movement as a case of *Ergriffenheit*. Jung suggested to its members that they recognize and accept that they had fallen "into the hands of a living god," which was "no disgrace," but rather "a tragic experience" (para. 398), implying that the grip of the Wotanic archetype was one that no individual German could withstand, regardless of one's level of consciousness. Jung further recommended to the German Christians that they join Hauer's movement, since "German Christian" is a "contradiction in terms" (para. 397). If it was unclear which God Jung had in mind when he wrote to Schmitz in 1923 that the Germanic peoples needed a "new experience of God," by 1936 Jung clarified the confusion: the state of *Ergriffenheit* that was revealing itself in Germany demonstrated that "the 'German' god is the god of the Germans" (para. 397).

In his seminar on Nietzsche's *Thus Spoke Zarathustra* on February 5, 1936, Jung made a curious remark about Hauer, stating, "I must say that I am very grateful to the Germans for their paganistic movement, at the head of which is my friend Professor Hauer who taught us the Tantric Yoga, and who has now become a saviour of the fools" (Jung 1988, 2:813). This statement seems almost mocking, as if Hauer himself might be a fool. However, a year earlier, in his *Visions* seminar on March 7, 1934, Jung told his audience:

> I don't want to talk politics, but I can tell you one very interesting psychological item: when I was in Germany, I was consulted by some leading Nazis who wanted to keep me there [. . .] But why? I said, "I am no politician, I am a psychologist, what have I to do with your enterprise?" And he replied: "Exactly, you are a psychologist, you are outside of the whole thing, so you are the man who could tell us what we are doing." You see they don't know . . .
>
> (Jung 1984, 1:1342)

Jung then compared the man to God: "That man did exactly what the creator has done" (ibid.). Jung explained that God made all the beasts of the world in an unconscious state, then needed Adam, that is, humanity, to explain creation to the Divine by naming the animals (Gen. 2:20). God in this passage is similar to the East Africans who pray to the sun or to Mr. Müller who hides Easter eggs. Neither can explain why they do what they do (see Chapter 4). The Nazis – like the Godhead itself – create, but do so completely unconsciously. What Jung hoped for was the light of consciousness to break through into the storm of National Socialist state-building (Jung 1984, 1:1342). Jung concluded his point by putting himself in the position of Adam vis-à-vis God: "And what that fellow in Germany wanted was that I should name things" (ibid., 1343).

Jung had already declared himself in 1925 the person who knew how to name the images for what he believed they were: archetypes. He considered the Germans to be in a state of not knowing, the moment when consciousness is flooded with collective unconscious material. This was a dangerous moment which could lead to insanity, but if the force of the conscious mind were brought to bear on the images, they could be named and integrated and thereby expand consciousness beyond what had previously been achieved. In this passage, Jung in effect declared himself both a scientist and a spiritual master, able to see the "inner essence" of world events and to describe them in (his own) scientific terms.

The rebirth of a nation

Jung believed that the gap between "the dark forces of life" and the illuminated realm of ideas that Hauer was bridging should result in a spiritual rebirth. This process would be symbolized by a youthful divine figure, as Jung illustrated in his *Zarathustra* seminar. On November 21 and 28, 1934, the seminar participants discussed Nietzsche's chapter on "Of the Three Metamorphoses," in which the spirit transforms from the heroic, burden-bearing camel that confronts the dragon of "thou shalt," the latter being Nietzsche's inversion of the Judeo-Christian god of commandments. Thereafter, it turns into the lion, which creates the space necessary for the spirit's transformation into the creative and innocent child, who affirms its own power to create new values.

According to Jung, the dragon of "thou shalt" represented a religion codified into a lifeless system. Because people unreflectively obey a law external to themselves, they lack real morality, which requires the freedom to choose. Only by the free and conscious exercise of one's will can a person develop self-responsibility and a sense of what is truly moral. The lion represents the rejection of externally imposed laws and a rigid and universal moral code. Hence, the lion and its wildness naturally precede the final transformation of the spirit into the child – the sun, the mandala, and the self-creating, self-rolling wheel, all symbolizing the process of individuation (Jung 1988, 1:170–171; Nietzsche 1968a, 6/1:25–27).

On February 26, 1936, the seminar discussed a line from "The Child with the Mirror:" "Verily, like a storm cometh my happiness and my freedom! But mine enemies shall think *the evil one* roareth over their heads." Jung, who would have recently finished the "Wotan" essay, stated that this passage referred to Wotan, the god of wind and storm, who was transformed into the devil by Christianity. He explained that Wotan's sacrifice of his eye to the well of Mimir symbolized the necessity to look into the abyss of the unconscious. As Nietzsche had described in *The Birth of Tragedy,* this was a terrifying experience. Jung then referred to the dual nature of Wotan and said that "first the destruction is most visible; and since Wotan is a historical figure we cannot hope that it is a progression. I am convinced that behind it something else follows, but it won't be Wotan. It cannot be" (Jung 1988, 2:870).

What Jung meant was that the libido was not yet rising toward consciousness; instead, it was still following a regressive movement downwards towards the collective unconscious. This was the decisive moment that Jung had elucidated twenty-four years previously in *Transformations and Symbols of the Libido*, when a person's psychic energy regresses to the level of the primordial images. If the libido remains fixed there, the images would flood the psyche, and a person – or an entire nation – could go mad. This was the "archetypal *Ergriffenheit,*" which Jung referred to on June 3, 1936 (Jung 1988, 2:975). Although an editorial footnote misleadingly defines *Ergriffenheit* only as "emotion," Jung himself described in metaphorical terms the flooding of psychic boundaries by a sea of archetypal material, which would be recontained once a reconciling symbol appeared. The key was to reverse the flow of the libido in a progressive direction by making the Germans conscious of what was going on, something that Jung, as doctor and spiritual master, believed he could do.

If the Germans could come to consciousness of the real source driving the National Socialist movement, then what should follow symbolically was the child, which is what Jung himself predicted would happen once the storm of Wotan had passed. On May 6, 1936, during a seminar discussion of the pregnant lioness in "The Child with the Mirror," Jung once again referred to the chapter, "Of the Three Metamorphoses." Jung interpreted the load-bearing camel as the pregnant mind, filled with suppressed psychic material. The camel then gives birth to the lion; the suppressed state transforms into a spirit of freedom. Wotan is "the spirit of the lion, and out of the spirit the child is born – for the time being only a lion cub, something absolutely undefined which needs development and care" (897–898). It was as if the collective German psyche was rejecting the morality that had been imposed on it from without (by Christianity and rationalism), while its psychic energy was searching for the natural morality of its repressed barbarian side that Jung had mentioned eighteen years previously (Jung CW 10 (1918):20). If the two sides of the Germanic psyche could be fruitfully united, the result would be a higher level of consciousness than before – in short, a spiritual rebirth and the freedom to claim one's own values as symbolized by the child.

Jung gestured toward the coming of the child in "Wotan" when he briefly discussed Goetz's *The Kingdom without Space,* which Jung claimed foretold "the secret of coming events in Germany" (Jung CW 10 (1947 [1936]):384). Furthermore, wrote Jung, the story "anticipates the conflict between the realm of ideas and life, between Wotan's dual nature as a god of storm and a god of secret musings" (para. 384). In Goetz's book, these are symbolized by the evil Ulrich von Spät, a Nietzschean "last man" (Nietzsche 1968a, 6/1:13) who wants to turn people into automatons, and Fo and his adventurous band of wandering youths, who von Spät manages to capture. In the final chapter, Melchior enters a theater and sees the enchanted boys standing on stage, surrounding an image of Ulrich. From their midst, Melchior's double steps forward and shakes Fo awake. The youths then stab Ulrich and free themselves (Goetz 1919, 157–158). Melchior then wanders alone out into the snow-covered streets, and says to the air, as if speaking to Fo:

> The circles are closed; it is finished. My shadow freed your shadow. The enemy has been conquered [. . .] Where are you now lingering on the wide earth? [. . .] the earth will not remain mute: your word calls out from all of life, your breath resounds from each body, your love blooms in each heart. The cross is being erected. The awakened ones pour their blood into the veins of the earth and transform themselves from one form to another. The new game begins [. . .] Step out of the dense night of the woods to us in naked fire, young flame, singing flame, lord and child!
>
> [Die Kreise schließen sich [. . .] es ist vollendet. Mein Schatten hat deinen Schatten befreit. Der Feind ist zerrissen . . . Wo weilst du jetzt auf der weiten Erde? [. . .] Die Erde wird nicht mehr stumm sein: dein Wort ruft aus allem Leben, dein Atem klingt aus jedem Leibe, deine Liebe blüht aus jedem Herzen. Das Kreuz wird aufgerichtet. Die Erwachten ergießen ihr Blut in die Adern der Welt und wandeln sich von Gestalt zu Gestalt. Das neue Spiel hebt an [. . .] Tritt aus Laubnacht zu uns in nacktem Brande, junge Flamme, singende Flamme, Herr und Kind!]
>
> (Goetz 1919, 158–159)

Melchior then follows a trail of blood-drops in the snow, which turn out to be rose-petals that lead him up a fog-enshrouded hill. A figure precedes him, giving off a silver light that turns to gold. As Melchior reaches the top, a ray of sunlight pierces the fog, clearing it to reveal Fo, red roses entwined around his head and loins, flaming arms outstretched as if crucified. As Melchior gapes in rapturous wonder at the transfigured Fo, his heart explodes and the book ends. This vision of an illuminated child-redeemer *is* "the kingdom without space" (160), which Melchior gasps out as he sinks to the ground. Fo is the *Ergreifer* of the youths and of Melchior, who is carried away in the explosive form of rapture (*Sprengung*) not unlike that which Klages claimed was experienced by Germanic heroes who fell in battle (Klages 1981, 72–73). What Jung described in 1930 as Goetz's "primordial vision" (German: *Urvision*) (Jung CW/GW 15 (1930):142) was the mystic in ecstatic union with the Godhead, this time represented by Nietzsche's image of the highest metamorphosis of the spirit: the child.

Ancient Germanic myth, the seeress's prophecy, and resurrection

Because Jung claimed to find the fundamental characteristics of archetypes in mythology (Jung CW 10 (1947 [1936]):391), it remains to be seen whether ancient Germanic myths relate the experience of the "archetypal *Ergriffenheit,*" of the conflict of psychic oppositions followed by spiritual rebirth. In "The Role of the Unconscious," Jung explained that the inherited collective unconscious forms the basis for the similarity of mythical motifs and images from around the world. It produces images and myths not derived from an individual's personal life story, but rather, "the story of mankind: the unending myth of death and rebirth, and of the multitudinous figures who weave in and out of this mystery." Access to this deeper level of the unconscious is achieved only at the death of the ego and a rebirth into a spiritual realm. According to Jung, "[W]ithout the sacrifice of man as he is, man as he was – and always will be – cannot be attained" (Jung CW 10 (1918):12, 13). "Man" in this line has two meanings: the man of today refers to the ordinary, relatively collectivized and ego-driven individual, whereas the man of the past and the future is an archetypal figure: the *Anthropos*, the Christ, the self.

Despite this universalistic statement made in 1918, eighteen years later in "Wotan," Jung sought to define a race- or *Volk*-specific archetype. Racial differentiation on a psychological level is determined by the archetype specific to a given race, which informs its character and behavior:

> This [personification of archetypes] could be done the more readily on account of the firmly established primordial types or images which are innate in the unconscious of many races [*Völkerstämme*] and exercise a direct influence upon them. Because the behaviour of a race takes on its specific character from its underlying images we can speak of an archetype 'Wotan.' As an autonomous psychic factor, Wotan produces effects in the collective life of a people and thereby reveals his own nature.
>
> (Jung CW/GW 10 (1947 [1936]):391)

It follows therefore that the nature of this archetype is to be found in the mythology developed by the ancestors of modern-day people of Germanic heritage, and should reveal their fundamental, racially delimited nature. Considering Jung's view that myth encodes the essence of the human, past, present and future, he not surprisingly positioned his portrait of the Germanic people and their archetype within a prophetic frame. He opened the "Wotan" essay with a prediction from the French seer Nostradamus (1503–1566) that Paganism would someday return to Germany, and he concluded with a quote from an Old Norse poem known as "The Seeress's Prophecy" (*Völuspá),* recorded in the thirteenth-century *Poetic Edda.*

Jung mentioned "The Seeress's Prophecy" at the very beginning of the second (and last) essay on Germany that he wrote for the *Neue Schweizer Rundschau*, immediately after the end of World War II. In "After the Catastrophe" (1945), Jung wrote that the quote from this poem with which he had ended "Wotan" had gestured prophetically to the destruction that had since been wrought across Europe:

> The quotation from the *Voluspo* with which I ended ["Wotan"], about Wotan "murmuring with Mimir's head," pointed prophetically to the nature of the coming apocalyptic events. *The myth has been fulfilled*, and the greater part of Europe lies in ruins.
>
> (Jung CW 10 (1945):400; emphasis added)

Both "After the Catastrophe" and "Wotan" were republished in 1946, together with other essays Jung wrote on Germany during the war, in *Aufsätze zur Zeitgeschichte* (*Essays on Contemporary Events*). In the 1946 version of the "Wotan" essay, and in every version since then, the work concludes with several lines taken from "The Seeress's Prophecy" that foretell catastrophe and the death of the gods. These lines suggest that both the old Norse poet and Jung predicted – accurately – the catastrophic events of World War II. These lines have the effect of shading the entire essay for a post-World War II reader, in that they imply that Jung had condemned National Socialism in "Wotan." However, the original edition of "Wotan" ends only with these words: "Then at last we shall know what Wotan is saying when he 'murmurs with Mimir's head'" (Jung CW 10 (1947 [1936]):399). Although the reference to Wotan murmuring over the head of Mimir is indeed taken from the "Seeress's Prophecy" (Larrington 1996, 10, str. 46), there are no additional lines of poetry from the poem, these being a post-war interpolation in the text (Grossman 1999, 114).

What did Jung mean when he suggested that what Wotan pondered over the head of the wise Mimir would become known? During his *Zarathustra* seminar on June 24, 1936, Jung spoke of the power of an *Ergreifer* to act catastrophically on those it seizes, yet he added a telling point: what comes afterwards. Jung referred to a "catastrophic wind that breaks into social existence," which is "the manifestation of the spirit in its most original form:"

> So a savior is one who seizes, the *Ergreifer* who catches people like objects and whirls them into a form which lasts as long as the whirlwind lasts, and then the thing collapses and something new must come. That is the great wind described in the Pentecostal miracle, because there two worlds were clashing together, the world of the slaves and the world of the highly differentiated mind.
>
> (Jung 1988, 2:1030)

Although he did not clarify during this session of the seminar what the "something new" was, Jung knew from "The Seeress's Prophecy" what it should be: the rebirth of the world and the return of Baldr, son of Odin. In this poem, which dates to ca. 1000, an ancient Germanic sibyl tells of the beginning and the end of the age ruled by Odin (Wotan). The first war of the world takes place between two distinct groups of gods, the dominant Æsir and the less powerful Vanir. This is followed by the death of the fair Baldr, Odin's legitimate heir, whose blind brother Hodr is tricked into slaying him by the half-breed Loki. This killing sets in motion the course of events leading to total war and a final battle between the gods and the giants, the complete downfall of the Odinic age, and the death of all the gods associated with it. Yet a miracle occurs: the world is reborn and both Baldr and Hodr return to rule together a new, paradisiacal land called Idavoll, with Hoenir of the Vanir also in attendance (Larrington 1996, 4–13).

What did Jung think might be revealed after the National Socialist "Germanic time of storm and stress" (Jung CW 10 (1947 [1936]):390) passed? This is rendered more transparent by referring to the translation of the *Edda* Jung used in the "Wotan" essay printed in *Aufsätze zur Zeitgeschichte.* This was the 1875 translation by Hans von Wolzogen, who was also the editor of the *Bayreuther Blätter*, the main organ of the Wagnerian Bayreuth Circle. Wolzogen was convinced that the *Edda* represented a personified solar mythology along the lines sketched by Wagner in "The Wibelungen" (the spelling here is correct). Wolzogen followed Wagner's interpretive scheme in that he claimed that the Old Norse poems of gods and heroes represented a heroicized nature mythology. Wolzogen interpreted "The Seeress's Prophecy" to be the story of the seasonal change of winter to spring, Wotan representing the winter sun, and Baldr the sun of the new year. Seen through a mythic lens, wrote Wolzogen, the solar year thus becomes part of divine history, and the old god Wotan dies to be reborn as his own son, Baldr:

> What spring and summer were is an age; the winter is the downfall of the world and the twilight of the gods; the young spring is a new world and the rebirth of the gods. [. . .] That is the mystery of the mythology: the terrestrial is represented as transcendental, earthly life as the life of the gods.
>
> [Was Frühling und Sommer war, ist ein Weltalter; der Winter ist Weltuntergang und Götterdämmerung; der junge Frühling ist eine neue Welt und Wiedergebürt der Götter [. . .] Das ist das Geheimnis der Mythologie: das Irdische wird als ein Ueberirdisches vorgestellt, das Erdleben als ein Götterleben.]
>
> (Wolzogen 1875, 139)

More specific to Jung's explanation of the Third Reich is Wolzogen's interpretation of the final stanzas of "The Seeress's Prophecy," which predict that Baldr will return and live happily together with his brother and murderer Hodr. The god Hoenir, who played a role in the creation of humanity, will speak prophecies. The Eddic poet then also claims that "the sons of two brothers" will occupy the world together (Larrington 1996, 12). Wolzogen interpreted the two brothers as referring not to Baldr and Hodr, but rather to Wotan of the Æsir and Hoenir of the Vanir, whose union heals the rift between the two races of gods, from which "all evil arose" (*alles Unheil entsprang*) (Wolzogen, 151, fn. 1).

Since for Jung myth represented psychological events in symbolic form, Jung may have interpreted "The Seeress's Prophecy" in the following way: The original state of unconscious wholeness, in which the pairs of opposition were not yet separated, had been split apart, as symbolized in the war between the Æsir and the Vanir. One half of each pair had been made conscious, while the other was thrust into the unconscious. This unredeemed portion, now represented by the blind (i.e. dark) Hodr, then seized the civilized portion of the psyche, as signified by the fair Baldr. The ensuing neurotic conflict resulted in a catastrophe, the total war between the gods with their differentiated minds, and the giants, the forces of nature. This conflict was overcome through the reconciliation of Baldr/Wotan and Hodr/Hoenir. Following Wolzogen's interpretation, the dark archaic god Wotan was to be reborn on a higher level as a solar figure of light, Baldr, through the collective individuation process of the German(-ic) people, which would reestablish psychological wholeness on a higher level of consciousness than had been previously possible. Wotan himself was a "totality," wrote Jung (Jung CW 10 (1947 [1936]):394), who contained the opposing characteristics of stormy and mantic within himself, and thus embodied both the conflict of oppositions and their reconciliation that Jung believed to be foundational to psychic self-regulation. Wotan, the Germanic archetype of the self that had manifested itself in projected form as the Wandering Jew, was the reconciling symbol that had sprung directly from the Germanic psyche. This interpretation follows the one Jung himself made concerning the fair Apollo and the dark Dionysus. Since Jung believed that true healing comes from within one's own psyche, not from without (Jung 1934, 203), the reconciling symbol needed to heal the split in the Germanic psyche was not to be found at Delphi – nor in Galilee – but on the Germanic plain of Idavoll.

Ergriffenheit as state-building power

Jung had noted in the final years of World War I that the de-Christianization of Europe had led to a blossoming of new religious movements and a resurgence of Gnosticism, as if the collective psychic energy of the Germanic peoples was searching for a new path to God. Apparently, Jung thought that the German youth movement, Zarathustra's dream, the Cosmic Circle's writings on the cosmogonic *Eros,* and Bruno Goetz's vision of a kingdom without space were all signs of the spirit on the move, like a river in search of its old channel (Jung CW 10 (1947 [1936]):395). This river also seemed to be questing after a leader who could overcome the fragmentation of Weimar society and restore the presumed wholeness of the original empire. Houston Stewart Chamberlain, whom Jung mentioned in "Wotan," would have concurred. On the day after Hitler's Beer Hall Putsch on November 9, 1923, Chamberlain published an article in the newspaper *Völkischer Beobachter*, entitled "God Wills It!" In it, he wrote, "If [post-World War I Germans] find a man whose heart beats in harmony with theirs – a born leader – then I shall not be anxious about Germany's future. And is it not whispered everywhere that the man has appeared and waits among us for this hour?"

(as quoted in Field 1981, 439). Jung apparently agreed with this sentiment. In a lecture to the Cultural Association (*Kulturbund*) in Vienna in November 1932, entitled "The Development of the Personality," Jung contrasted in disparaging terms the "normal person" of modern mass democracy with the "personality" of the dictator:

> "Personality training" has become an educational ideal that turns its back upon the standardized, mass-produced, "normal" human being demanded by the machine age. It thus pays tribute to the historical fact that the great, liberating deeds of world history have sprung from leading personalities and never from the inert mass, which is at all times secondary and can only be prodded into activity by the demagogue. The huzzahs of the Italian nation go forth to the personality of the Duce, and the dirges of other nations lament the absence of strong leaders.
>
> (Jung CW 17 (1934 [1932]):284)

When he edited this work for publication in 1934, Jung added the footnote, "Since this sentence was written, Germany has also found its leader" (284) (*Seitdem dieser Satz geschrieben wurde, hat auch Deutschland seinen Führer gefunden*) (Jung, GW 17(1934 [1932]):284, fn. 2. The English translation erases the possessive "its leader.") Moreover, a year before on Radio Berlin, Jung had expressed a generally positive view of Hitler, citing him as saying that a leader must go his own way. Such a sentiment resonated with Jung's own interpretation of the *Imitatio Christi* and the individuation process (see Chapter 3).

In "Wotan," Jung suggested that other people viewed Hitler not merely as a great personality, but had gone so far as to deify him (Jung CW 10 (1947 [1936]):386). Jung offered instead to explain the Hitler phenomenon by way of his archetypal theory. Yet his own chain of associations also led to a deification of the German *Führer*. Jung wrote that Wotan's "cousin" Dionysus preferred to stir women, the Maenads, into action, and Jung called these women rather dangerous "female storm-troopers" (para. 386). Jung curiously failed to mention the Valkyries, female warrior figures in Germanic mythology, and instead contrasted Greek female mythological figures to the brown-shirted Storm Troopers, a National Socialist all-male paramilitary group. Jung continued by claiming that Wotan gripped men (*Männer*), making him a specifically masculine god, and his chief followers were the Berserkers, the "bodyguards of mythical kings" *(Leibgardisten mythischer Könige)* (GW para. 386). The English edition mistranslates the term *Leibgardisten* as "blackshirts." Although the *Schutzstaffel*, or S.S., wore black, and were the bodyguards for leading Nazi officials, the Blackshirts had nothing to do with National Socialism; rather, they were an Italian fascist paramilitary group active from immediately after World War I to the end of World War II (Payne 1995, 95–96). This inaccurate historical reference obscures the Germanic mythological connection Jung made between Hitler, Wotan and the Berserkers: Hitler stood in the same line as the kings of the ancient Germanic peoples, whose original ancestor was Wotan himself

(Byock 1990, 8). Hitler had been infused with the spirit of Wotan the *Ergreifer*, becoming an *Ergreifer* in his own right, thereby forming a mystical union with the German people as their *Führer*. In these allusions, Jung came dangerously close to affirming the Nazi slogan of "one people, one empire, one leader" (*Ein Volk, ein Reich, ein Führer*). Moreover, in line with the *Männerbund* theory of the Germanic studies scholar Otto Höfler, Jung limited this mystical union to the male half of the German *Volk*.

Furthermore, since the ascension of Hitler to power, wrote Jung, "Wotan the Wanderer had awakened" (*Wotan der Wanderer war erwacht*), mistranslated into English as "Wotan the Wanderer was on the move" (Jung CW/GW 10 (1947 [1936]):373). Germans had long told legends of heroes such as the Holy Roman Emperor Friedrich Barbarossa (1122–1190), who had never died but merely disappeared. They were said to be sleeping, but would awaken one day in a time of great need to rescue the empire and to lead it once more (See 2005, 140). When Jung wrote that Wotan had only been sleeping at Kyffhäuser (Jung CW 10 (1947 [1936]):389), Friedrich Barbarossa's abode, not only did Jung equate Wotan with Friedrich Barbarossa, but he aligned Hitler, filled with Wotan's spirit, with the myth of the once and future German redeemer.

Jung's allusion echoes that of Chamberlain, who had met Hitler on "German Day" in Bayreuth on September 30, 1923. After their meeting, the elderly Chamberlain wrote a letter to Hitler dated October 7, 1923, calling him Germany's future savior, "the true awakener [who] is at the same time the bestower of peace" (as quoted in Field 1981, 436). This was the first sign of support for the Nazi movement by a person renowned both nationally and internationally, and it influenced Hitler's decision to attempt his Beer Hall coup (438).

With the founding of the Third Reich, wrote Jung, the aimless wandering of the unemployed had been transformed into goal-directed marching masses, producing a "spectacle of a people's migration in place" (*das Schauspiel einer Völkerwanderung an Ort*) (Jung CW/GW 10 (1947 [1936]): 373). This line is mistranslated in the English edition as "the spectacle of a nation migrating from one place to another." Jung's choice of the term *Völkerwanderung* would certainly bring to a reader's mind the Germanic tribes' search for new territory 1600 years previously, known historically as the Migration Period (300–700 CE). These migrations are alluded to in the heroic lays of the *Poetic Edda*, when Germanic tribes overran the western half of the Roman Empire. Just as at the beginning of time, when, as the prologue of Snorri's *Edda* reports, Odin led his people from Troy into Northern Europe (Snorri 1987, 3), so Hitler was now reiterating the actions of his ancestral god by producing yet another movement of the *Volk*.

Yet Jung quite pointedly wrote that, rather than the Germans migrating elsewhere, the movement was taking place in the same location, implicitly inside the collective German psyche. Simultaneously, thousands of people were fleeing into exile. This is a chilling image, especially in light of the fact that German Jews had been stripped of many civil rights the year before (Benz 2006, 142), and thousands of Jews – including Jung's Jewish students James Kirsch and

Erich Neumann – had already fled their country. In resonance with the *völkisch* belief that a people was racially and mystically connected to its land – made official Nazi policy under the banner of "blood and soil" (Arvidsson 2006, 192; See 1994, 312) – Jung created a portrait of a people in mystical union with their god and their leader, retaking their land from a foreign people whose influence Jung deemed "corrosive" (Samuels 1993, 293), through a process he believed necessary if the Germans as a people were to individuate. Jung's 1936 evocation of the historical *Völkerwanderung* as a theatrical model for current events by no means indicates that he would have supported Hitler's "Final Solution" to exterminate the Jews, decided in 1942; rather, he seems to have shared the perspective of his friend Hauer, who argued that Jews did not have the right to their own religion within the territorial boundaries of their host-race (Baumann 2005, 89). Thus, the solution to the "Jewish question" was not extermination, but separation.

In Jung's *Zarathustra* seminar on May 22, 1935, Jung summed up the collective state of *Ergriffenheit* with a word that resonated well with the religious theory of Hauer and the political theory of Hitler: blood. This movement in the collective Germanic unconscious was located below in the blood, he argued, not coming from a light above. Hence, the comparison to the Pentecostal Miracle 2,000 years previously was partial at best, because what was currently taking place was unique in the "conscious history of man" and quite dangerous (Jung 1988, 500). Again on February 5, 1936, around the time Jung was probably writing "Wotan," he interpreted the unrest taking place across Europe as an upheaval not in the political, but in the religious and biological realms, arguing that "Germanic blood" was the driving force behind it all:

> As far as the German mentality reaches in Europe – and it reaches, as you know, from the Urals to Spain – we see religion upset; in the most Catholic of all countries, Spain, the church is completely overthrown. And that is old Wotan, you could not name it better, the wind came and blew the thing to bits. Fascism in Italy is old Wotan again; it is all Germanic blood down there, with no trace of the Romans; they are Langobards, and they all have the Germanic spirit.
>
> (Jung 1988, 814)

Many of the participants in this seminar were Americans, including Jung's patron Mary Conover Mellon. Perhaps due to the mixed nature of Jung's audience, he trotted out the well-worn cliché of Swiss neutrality. But the reality was quite different. "Few other countries have had such a great number of extreme right-wing associations per capita and size of the geographical territory as had Switzerland during the Hitlerian era," writes Alan Morris Schom, in his *Survey of Nazi and Pro-Nazi Groups in Switzerland, 1930–1945* (Schom 1998, 2). In fact, the national government of Switzerland actively discriminated against Jewish refugees as early as 1933, by denying them "political fugitive" status (76).

Germanic instincts: going under and overcoming

Because Wotan was, to Jung, an archetype, one question remains to be answered, which concerns its accompanying instincts. The archetypes are, according to Jung, the psychological counterparts to the biological instincts (Jung 1927, 106). If archetypes are tied to the instincts, and if Wotan is a specifically Germanic and especially a German archetype, what instincts are inherently and specifically Germanic? The answer to this question is rife with Nietzschean and tragic themes: the nature of the Germanic psyche was to undergo a downfall, so as to rise to higher levels of consciousness needed to create new forms of culture.

Because instincts are *a priori,* automatic behavioral responses to life situations, one could also say that this was Germany's *fate.* After its defeat in World War I, the nineteenth-century teleological and progress-based view of history was replaced by an idea first developed during the Thirty Years' War and which corresponded to the Germans' seeming destiny to experience cycles of catastrophe followed by regeneration. Known as the "flight forward" (*Flucht nach vorn*), this view of history suggested that each defeat would bring a resurgence of power and vitality in its wake. After World War I, many *völkisch* leaders combined the idea of a flight forward with the notion of fate to argue that it was Germany's destiny to suffer defeat again and again in order to rise to ever-higher spiritual heights (Baumann 2005, 20).

Wagner had already explored this idea in "Wieland the Smith" (1849–1850), based on the Old Norse Poem "The Lay of Volund" (*Völundarkviða*). Wieland, after having had his Achilles tendons severed by the treacherous King Neiding, fashions for himself a pair of wings by which he escapes his enslavement (Wagner 1966, 1:215248). In "Wotan," Jung, too, seemed to refer to this idea, when he called Germany a "land of spiritual catastrophes, where nature never makes more than a pretence of peace with world-ruling reason" (Jung CW 10 (1947 [1936]):391). Jung reiterated this theme at the end of his essay, when he assured his audience that the stormy side of Wotan as represented by National Socialism would not be the last word; rather, Wotan's ecstatic and mantic characteristics would also manifest themselves. He wrote that the reawakening of the ancient god is "ein Rückschritt und Rückgriff," translated into English with a French expression, "*reculer pour mieux sauter*" (GW/CW10:399). This phrase means "to step back in order to jump forward better." Coupled with the line from "The Seeress's Prophecy," Jung's readers would have understood that he believed National Socialism to be a necessary regression of the libido to the collective unconscious before it could once again flow in a progressive direction and create a state of psychological wholeness.

In "Wotan," Jung praised a book that resounds loudly with the theme of a destined downfall followed by rejuvenation: Martin Ninck's *Wotan and the Germanic Belief in Destiny* (*Wodan und germanischer Schicksalsglaube,* 1935). Ninck argued that the ancient Germanic religion revolved around the twin beliefs in Wodan (southern German for Wotan) and destiny (*Schicksal*) (Ninck 1935, 3). Wodan's chief characteristic of "inexhaustible wanderer" (*unermüdlicher Wanderer*) was intimately tied to his roles as war-god and god of storms (69, 72), as well as lord of ecstasy and the rapturous Berserker rage (86–87). Ninck further described war as fate that has been unleashed, as demonstrated in the great battle described in "The Seeress's Prophecy." Not even the gods could escape their destiny: they, too, were born and would die, only to be born again (190). In this great battle, which pitted the Æsir and the Vanir against natural and supernatural forces of chaos, the most beloved and highest gods perished, along with the world – yet a new and better world would emerge: "But out of the womb of fate a new world arises that is more beautiful than the old one, an era that is better than the one that has passed" (*[A]ber aus dem Schoße des Schicksals entsteigt eine neue Welt, schöner als die alte, ein Zeitalter, besser als das vergangene*) (191).

Ninck then created an image of a *unio mystica* between Odin and human warriors who die on the battlefield by comparing their self-sacrifice to Odin's ordeal on the World-Tree Yggdrasil. Willing to suffer the ultimate price – self-sacrifice – Odin was rewarded with wisdom, growth and creative power. Ninck considered the capacity to create culture an essential aspect of Odin's character, describing the god as if he had Faust in mind:

> Now the myth of Odin reveals to us its full significance [. . .] He bends down and, groaning, takes the tree's staves of runes, and falls to the ground. Then he becomes wise, grows and begins to thrive: word leads him to word and work to work.
>
> [Jetzt eröffnet sich uns der Odinsmythus in seiner vollen Bedeutung [. . .] Er neigt sich, nimmt stöhnend die Runenstäbe des Baumes auf und stürzt zur Erde. Da wird er weise, wächst und beginnt zu gedeihn, Wort führt ihn zu Wort und Werk zu Werk.]
>
> (Ninck 1935, 307)

Like Ninck, Jung found in Wotan his model for this culture-creating capacity, which he presented in his *Zarathustra* seminar on February 19, 1936. In discussing the chapter, "The Child with a Mirror," Jung interpreted Zarathustra's statement, "Wounded am I by my happiness," to signify the wound that the originally seamless unconscious suffered when individual consciousness emerged from it. In other words, said Jung, God deprives himself of a bit of divinity in order to bequeath it to humanity. To illustrate his point, Jung described Wotan's ordeal on Yggdrasil as a necessary self-sacrifice and descent to the collective unconscious to bring the runes, a sign of civilization, to the Germanic barbarians (Jung 1988, 2:854–855). Although previously Jung had interpreted Christianity as a civilizing agent, these mythological speculations echo the German humanists, who rejected the pope's claim that the Christian church was the power that civilized the once-barbaric *Germanen*.

Jung's theory suggested that a collapse due to the conflict of oppositions could be a positive sign of an incipient breakthrough to a higher level of psychic development than existed before. Applied on a mass scale, Jung suggested that a national going-under was necessary before a people could rise to higher heights of cultural creation and worldly power. Throughout his oeuvre and in "Wotan," Jung described these oppositions in many ways; in his 1936 essay, he added east and west. When Jung referred to Wotan as a force coming from a place of emergence, Asia, perhaps he had in mind Hauer's claim that the discovery of the self began in the eastern Indo-European realm of ancient India, but would be completed in western "Indo-Germanic" space. Mythically, Asia (Troy) was Wotan's original home; northwestern Europe, the site of his ascension to power (Snorri 1987, 3). As Indo-European scholars had long argued, the same was true of the "Aryan race." These various lines of thought may lie behind Jung's evocative image of Wotan as a gale wind blowing in from Asia to Western Europe, resulting in power – intellectual, artistic and political:

> [Wotan] is a wind that blows into Europe from Asia's vastness [and incipience (*Anfänglichkeit*)], sweeping in on a wide front from Thrace to the Baltic, scattering the nations before it like dry leaves, or inspiring thoughts that shake the world to its foundations.
>
> (Jung CW/GW 10 (1947 [1936]): 391)

In but a few highly evocative images, Jung wove together the dominant images of the Germans from the Romantic era, to Nietzsche, to leading scholars of Old Norse literature of Jung's day: the Germans were the ruling race (*die Herrenmenschen*), as well as a people of poets and philosophers (*das Volk der Dichter und Denker)* (See 1994, 82, 112, 223, 287–289).

Jung's references to the restless Wanderer and the storm and stress of National Socialism raise the specter of Goethe's Faust, whose shade stalks across the pages of the "Wotan" essay. This is no accident, for Faust represented to Jung a successful reconciliation of the oppositions, after having explored by turns both love and power. Unlike Jewish psychology, which remained stuck at the level of the primitive, the exemplar of the German man was able to plumb to the primordial depths of the soul. At the end of Goethe's play, Faust dies and is raised to Heaven, which Jung interpreted in psychological terms to mean that Faust had transcended his ego and his one-sidedness, and had reached the fullness and completion of the self (Jung 1921, 267–269). Jung implicitly compared himself to Faust in this regard when, in his attempt to demonstrate why his psychological system was an improvement over that created by Freud, he stated that Freudian theory represented sexuality and Adlerian psychology was focused on power (Jung 1960 [1943], 55). For Jung, both Freudian and Adlerian systems were one-sided and could not lead to completion (*Vollendung*), unlike (implicitly) Jung's own.

Conclusion

In the "Wotan" essay, Jung presented the Germanic archetype as a restless wanderer, like Fo and his youths, who tumble through the cosmos in search of ever more mysteries, more suffering and more bliss. This going-under and overcoming was a dangerous journey, as it meant descending to the collective unconscious and facing the power of the numinous archetypes. This undertaking could end disastrously, as Jung believed it had in the case of Nietzsche. Witnessing a regression on a mass scale in Nazi Germany, what Jung evidently believed was that the renewal prophesied in ancient Germanic myth would come to pass – if the collective Germanic libido could be turned in a positive direction. Yet the German case was no mere neurosis, according to Jung. His naming the German illness a case of *Ergriffenheit* signified an encounter with the Holy as an inborn divine power. Despite the ambivalence about National Socialism Jung espoused in his private seminars, this close reading of the "Wotan" text indicates that Jung's view of the Third Reich – at least up to the penning of the "Wotan" essay in 1936 – was largely favorable.

Near the conclusion of the "Wotan" essay, Jung suggested that outsiders judged the Germans too harshly, as if they were personally responsible for what was happening in their country – an unfair assessment, he believed, considering the autonomous and impersonal character of the archetypal force that had gripped them. Rather, he wrote, they should be seen as the *Erleidenden*, a word that is spaced for emphasis in the original essay, and which is inaccurately translated into English as "victims" (Jung CW 10 (1947 [1936]):398; cf. ibid. 1936a, 669). The verb *erleiden,* meaning "to suffer, to sustain," had been nominalized by Jung as a present participle; hence, *Erleidenden* means "the ones who suffer or sustain." Unlike the English "victim," the term in German carries the connotation of the noble bearing of great difficulties. In the context of Jung's analysis of the German case as one of *Ergriffenheit,* and against the background of the mystical musings of Klages, Goetz, Schuler, and George, the word has strong esoteric connotations of the most terrible suffering that is the necessary price of admission to the deepest mysteries, borne in imitation of one's god.

There is a final dimension to the idea of suffering within the "Wotan" essay that cannot be left unaddressed, which is the question of who exactly suffers, at the hands of whom and for what. Jung himself pointed to two bodies of sufferers: the Germans, who were suffering *for* their god, and the Jews, who suffered *from* him. He wrote in the penultimate paragraph of "Wotan" that it was terrible to fall into the hands of a living god – surely those outside the Yahweh experience had found it difficult; and the Allah experience had likewise been unpleasant for Christians (para. 398). Suffering could mean (according to Klages) the explosion of the ego in ecstatic embrace with the godhead; yet, it could also spell the destruction of those people unfortunate enough to be in the vicinity of this mystical experience and thus caught in its conflagration. Because the archetypal forces are autonomous, believed Jung (para. 395), the Germans were simply swept up in their power (para. 398). Yet in his analysis of Wotan as the Germanic archetype, Jung never suggested a side to the god that represents reason or rationality, unlike Dionysus's counterpart in Apollo. Rather, Wotan's other side is inspirational. Thus, Jung's theory leaves no room for personal responsibility, rational reflection, or empathy for those who do not belong to Wotan's entourage of the "blessed people" (Jung 1965, 230–231).

Jung seemed to have felt that, as a doctor, he was impelled to try to make the Germans conscious of what was happening to them, so that they could resolve their psychic conflict and initiate a higher state of psychological wholeness and reconciliation. Unfortunately, this apparently did not include shouldering a citizen's responsibility to defy the injustices committed by one's government against fellow citizens or neighboring states. Instead, as a spiritual master who believed he could read the signs of the times, Jung pronounced the Wotanic irruption of National Socialism not only a tragic, but also a *religious* moment of *kairos*, drawing lines of associations to the New Testament that indicated he believed this particular moment in time to be one fulfilled by the Spirit. Jung's naming the German case a state of *Ergriffenheit* signified nothing less than that the Third Reich was an encounter with the Holy. The parallels Jung created between Wotan and Hitler, between the Third Reich and ancient Germanic mythology, and between Faust and current events in Germany, created a picture of harmonious wholeness that belied the fact of hate-based exclusion that would soon unleash genocide. By interpreting the Third Reich via his own theory of individuation, through the lens of the allegedly timeless truth of myth, and as a tragedy being enacted on the world stage, Jung lent universal significance and an undeserved dignity to yet another disastrous chapter of German history.

Bibliography

Title

"the archetypal *Ergriffenheit*": C. G. Jung, 1988. *Nietzsche's Zarathustra: Notes of the Seminar Given in 1934–1939*, ed. by James L. Jarrett. Princeton, NJ: Princeton University Press, 2:975.

Sources

Arvidsson, Stefan. 2006. *Aryan Idols: Indo-European Mythology as Ideology and Science.* Chicago: University of Chicago Press.

Baumann, Schaul. 2005. *Die Deutsche Glaubensbewegung und ihr Gründer Jakob Wilhelm Hauer (1821–1962).* Religionswissenschaftliche Reihe 22. Marburg: Diagonal.

Benz, Wolfgang. 2006. *A Concise History of the Third Reich,* trans. by Thomas Dunlap. Berkeley and Los Angeles: University of California Press.

Bishop, Paul. 1995. *The Dionysian Self: C. G. Jung's Reception of Friedrich Nietzsche.* Monographien und Texte zur Nietzsche-Forschung 30. Berlin: de Gruyter.

Blind, Karl. 1986. "Wodan, the Wild Huntsman, and the Wandering Jew." In Galit Hasan-Rokem and Alan Dundes (eds), *The Wandering Jew: Essays in the Interpretation of a Christian Legend.* Bloomington: Indiana University Press, pp.169–189.

Bushnell, Rebecca. 2008. *Tragedy: A Short Introduction.* Malden, MA: Blackwell.

Byock, Jesse L. (trans.) 1990. *The Saga of the Volsungs: The Norse Epic of Sigurd the Dragon Slayer*. Berkeley and Los Angeles: University of California Press.

Cancik, Hubert and Helmuth Schneider (ed.). 1996. *Der Neue Pauly: Enzyklopädie der Antike*. Stuttgart; Weimar: J.B. Metzler.

Dierks, Margarete. 1986. *Jakob Wilhelm Hauer, 1881–1962: Leben, Werk, Wirkung; Mit einer Personalbibliographie*. Heidelberg: L. Schneider.

Ellwood, Robert. 1999. *The Politics of Myth: A Study of C. G. Jung, Mircea Eliade, and Joseph Campbell*. Albany: State University of New York Press.

Eranos: The Annual Event in Scholarship: An Introduction. (n.d) Available at: http://www.eranos.org/content/html/english/introduction.html (Accessed: July 25, 2015).

Field, Geoffrey G. 1981. *Evangelist of Race: The Germanic Vision of Houston Stewart Chamberlain*. New York: Columbia University Press.

George, Stefan. 1982. *Sämtliche Werke in 18 Bänden*. Stuttgart: Klett-Cotta.

Goetz, Bruno. 1919. *Das Reich ohne Raum*. Potsdam: Kiepenheuer.

Grimm, Jacob and Wilhelm. 1960. *Deutsches Wörterbuch*. Leipzig: S. Hirzel.

Grossman, Stanley. 1999. "C. G. Jung and National Socialism." In Paul Bishop (ed.), *Jung in Contexts: A Reader*. London: Routledge, pp.92–121.

Hauer, Jakob Wilhelm. 1923. *Die Religionen: Ihr Werden, Ihr Sinn, Ihre Wahrheit*. Berlin: W. Kohlhammer.

——. 1934. *Deutsche Gottschau*. Stuttgart: Gutbrod.

Höfler, Max. 1899. *Deutsches Krankheitsnamen-Buch*. Munich: Piloty & Loehle.

Höfler, Otto. 1934. *Kultische Geheimbünde der Germanen*. Frankfurt am Main: Diesterweg.

Jung, C. G. 1912. *Wandlungen und Symbole der Libido: Beiträge zur Entwicklungsgeschichte des Denkens*. Leipzig: Franz Deuticke.

——. 1921. *Psychologische Typen*. Zurich: Rascher & Cie.

——. 1925. *Psychology of the Unconscious: A Study of the Transformations and Symbolisms of the Libido; A Contribution to the History of the Evolution of Thought*, trans. by Beatrice M. Hinkle. New York: Dodd, Mead.

——. 1927. "Die Erdbedingtheit der Psyche." *Der Leuchter* 8:83–137.

——. 1934. "Zur Empirie des Individuationsprozesses." *Eranos Jahrbuch* 1: 201–214.

——. 1936a. "Wotan." *Neue Schweizer Rundschau: Wissen und Leben*, n.s., 3(11): 657–669.

——. 1936b. "Yoga and the West." In *Prabuddha. Bharata, or Awakened India*. Sri Ramakrishna Centenary Number, pp.170–177 (ETH-Bibliothek Zurich (Switzerland), ETH Zurich University Archives, Hs 1379:185).

——. 1937. "Wotan." In *Saturday Review of Literature* XVI(25):3–4, 18, 20 (ETH-Bibliothek Zurich (Switzerland), ETH Zurich University Archives, Hs 1379:191).

——. 1946. *Aufsätze zur Zeitgeschichte*. Zurich: Rascher & Cie.

——. 1953–1991. *Collected Works*, ed. by Sir Herbert Read, Michael Fordham, and Gerhard Adler. New York: Pantheon Books; Princeton, NJ: Princeton University Press.

——. 1965. *Memories, Dreams, Reflections*, rec. and ed. by Aniela Jaffé, trans. by Richard and Clara Winston. New York: Vintage.

——. 1972. *Briefe*, ed. by Aniela Jaffé with Gerhard Adler. Three Volumes. Olten: Walter.

——. 1984. *Visions: Notes of the Seminar Given in 1930–1934 by C. G. Jung*, ed. by William McGuire. Princeton, NJ: Princeton University.

——. 1988. *Nietzsche's Zarathustra: Notes of the Seminar Given in 1934–1939*, ed. by James L. Jarrett. Princeton, NJ: Princeton University Press.

——. 1989. *Analytical Psychology: Notes of the Seminar Given in 1925*, ed. by William McGuire. Princeton, NJ: Princeton University Press.

Klages, Ludwig. 1981. *Vom kosmogonischen Eros*. Bonn: Bouvier.

Krech, Volkhard. 2002. *Wissenschaft und Religion: Studien zur Geschichte der Religionsforschung in Deutschland 1871 bis 1933*. Tubingen: Mohr Siebeck.

Krieger, Murray. 1965. "Tragedy and the Tragic Vision." In Robert W. Corrigan (ed.), *Tragedy: Vision and Form*. San Francisco: Chandler, pp.30–41.

Langwieler, Günther. 2010. "'Wotan:' A Political Myth of the German Collective Unconscious: Three Debates of Shadow Aspects of the Collective Identities of Germans and Jews in the Germany of National-Socialism." In Murray Stein and Raya A. Jones (eds), *Cultures and Identities in Transition: Jungian Perspectives*, London: Routledge, pp.30–40.

Larrington, Carolyne. 1996. *The Poetic Edda*. Oxford: Oxford University Press.

Lewin, Nicholas Adam. 2009. *Jung on War, Politics and Nazi Germany: Exploring the Theory of Archetypes and the Collective Unconscious*. London: Karnac.

Liebscher, Martin (ed.). 2001. "'Wotan' und 'Puer Aeternus': Die Zeithistorische Verstrickung von C. G. Jungs Zarathustra-Interpretation." *Nietzsche-Studien: Internationales Jahrbuch für die Nietzsche-Forschung* 30: 329–350.

——. 2015. *Analytical Psychology in Exile: The Correspondence of C. G. Jung and Erich Neumann*, trans. by Heather Mccartney. Princeton: Princeton University Press.

Mosse, George L. 1964. *The Crisis of German Ideology: Intellectual Origins of the Third Reich*. New York: Grosset & Dunlap.

Nietzsche, Friedrich. 1967. *The Birth of Tragedy and the Case of Wagner*, ed, and trans. by Walter Kaufmann. New York: Vintage.

——. 1968a. *Also Sprach Zarathustra: Ein Buch für Alle und Keinen*. In Giorgio Colli and Mazzino Montinari (eds), *Nietzsche Werke: Kritische Gesamtausgabe,* 6/1. Berlin: Walter de Gruyter.

——. 1968b. *Ecce Homo*. In Giorgio Colli and Mazzino Montinari (eds), *Nietzsche Werke: Kritische Gesamtausgabe*, 6/3. Berlin: Walter de Gruyter.

Ninck, Martin. 1935. *Wodan und Germanischer Schicksalsglaube*. Jena: Eugen Diederichs.

Noll, Richard. 1994. *The Jung Cult: Origins of a Charismatic Movement*. Princeton, NJ: Princeton University Press.

Norton, Robert. 2002. *Secret Germany: Stefan George and His Circle*. Ithaca, NY: Cornell University Press.

Otto, Rudolph. 1958. *The Idea of the Holy: An Inquiry into the Non-Rational Factor in the Idea of the Divine and its Relation to the Rational*, trans. by John W. Harvey. London: Oxford University Press.

Payne, Stanley G. 1995. *A History of Fascism, 1914–1945*. Madison: University of Wisconsin.

Pietikäinen, Petteri. 2008. "Future's Past: C. G. Jung's Psychoutopia and the 'German Revolution' of 1933." In Horst Junginger (ed.), *The Study of Religion under the Impact of Fascism*. Leiden: Brill, pp.591–611.

Samuels, Andrew. 1993. *The Political Psyche*. London: Routledge.

Schmitz, Oscar A. H. 1926. *Dämon Welt: Jahre der Entwicklung*. München: Müller.

Schom, Alan Morris. June 1998. *Survey of Nazi and Pro-Nazi Groups in Switzerland, 1930–1945*. Los Angeles: Simon Wiesenthal Center.

Schuler, Alfred. 1940. *Fragmente und Vorträge aus dem Nachlass*, intro. by Ludwig Klages. Leipzig: Barth.

——. 1997. *Cosmogonische Augen: Gesammelte Schriften*, ed. with notes by Baal Müller. Paderborn: Igel.

See, Klaus von. 1994. *Barbar Germane Arier: Die Suche nach der Identität der Deutschen.* Heidelberg: C. Winter.

——. 2005. "Die politische Rezeption der Siegfriedfigur im 19. und 20. Jahrhundert." In Volker Gallé (ed.), *Siegfried – Schmied und Drachentöter*, Worms: Worms-Verlag, pp.138–155.

Spalding, Keith. 1964. *An Historical Dictionary of German Figurative Usage.* With the assistance of Kenneth Brooke. Oxford: Basil, Blackwell & Mott Ltd.

Snorri Sturluson. 1987. *Edda*, trans. and ed. by Anthony Faulkes. London: Dent.

——. 1976. *Egil's Saga*, trans. by Hermann Pálsson and Paul Edwards. Harmondsworth, NY: Penguin.

Wagner, Richard. 1966. *Prose Works*, trans. by William Ashton Ellis. Eight Volumes. New York: Broude Brothers.

Wasserstrom, Steven M. 1999. *Religion after Religion: Gerschom Scholem, Mircea Eliade, and Henry Corbin at Eranos*. Princeton, NJ: Princeton University Press.

Wolzogen, Hans von. 1875. *Die Edda: Götterlieder und Heldenlieder; Aus dem Altnordischen*. Leipzig: Philipp Reclam.

7

"AFTER THE CATASTROPHE"

Wandering diagnoses and changing relationships post-"Wotan"

Introduction

In the same month that "Wotan" was published, Hauer resigned as the president of the German Faith Movement. He believed that the rise of Nazism demonstrated the truth of his religious vision, and that he himself had been called to be a leader of a collective spiritual renewal (Baumann 2005, 78). Despite his faith, the lines of potential rupture between the disparate groups that comprised the big-top German Faith Movement finally cracked in 1936, forcing Hauer to give up his leading position. Still, he continued to believe that National Socialism was a spiritual movement emerging out of the depths of the collective Germanic soul, and in 1937, he joined the Nazi Party (Dierks 1986, 279).

Several months after publishing "Wotan," Jung traveled to Massachusetts to receive an honorary doctorate from Harvard University and to lecture at its 300th anniversary. His trip was marred by a storm of protest against him that broke out in the university's student newspaper, *The Harvard Crimson*. The prominent Harvard psychologist Dr. Henry Murray (1893–1988), who, on Jung's advice, had started an extramarital affair to avoid divorce (Noll 1997, 92), intervened in the debate on Jung's behalf and Jung participated as planned (Samuels 1993, 295).

These two events may suggest why Jung began as early as 1936 to change his diagnosis of Germany soon after publishing "Wotan." This chapter explores several post-"Wotan" works in which Jung attempted to distance himself from the Nazi reign of terror by emphatically denouncing Hitler and National Socialism. Jung never apologized in these works, nor clearly admitted that he had once looked favorably upon Hitler and the Third Reich. Rather, in order to extricate himself from the web of positive associations he had spun in his "Wotan" essay, Jung created a series of reversals in his images of Germany, Faust, Hitler, and Wotan. These reversals were probably driven more by a need to protect himself than by any heartfelt change of perspective about "Germanic" and "Jewish" psychology. Indeed, in an unpublished text Jung wrote after the war, he defended his belief in the differences between "Jewish" and "Aryan-Germanic-Christian-European" psychologies (Bair 2003, 514). Furthermore, his writings on both Wotan and Yahweh in the 1950s and 1960s bore similar ideas to earlier works on "Germanic" and "Jewish" psychology. Before examining Jung's wandering diagnosis, this chapter examines the ongoing relationship between Hauer and the Zurich School of analytical psychology that lasted until 1939, and suggests some possible reasons for its final break.

Race, religion and National Socialism: Hauer and Jung post-"Wotan"

Given Hauer's own belief in an inner divine power called the self, he was drawn to Jung's psychological theory. The two men first met at Keyserling's School of Wisdom in the 1920s (Bair 2003, 434); Jung then attended Hauer's lecture on yoga and psychotherapy at the General Medical Congress for Psychotherapy in Baden-Baden in 1930 (Dierks 1986, 283). In 1932, the two men held a joint lecture on Kundalini Yoga at the Psychological Club in Zurich in 1932 (Jung 1996). Hauer also dedicated his 1932 book, *Yoga as Salvation* (*Yoga als Heilweg*) to Jung (Hauer, dedication page, 1932). Jung then invited Hauer to collaborate on an intellectual journal which would unify the academic disciplines through a shared worldview (the plan was never realized) (Dierks 1986, 284).

In 1934, Hauer was invited to deliver a lecture at the Eranos Conference (Hauer 1935b), where Jung was the reigning *Spiritus Rector*. Hauer spoke on the ancient Indo-Aryan doctrine of the self, a theme he also wrote about for the *festschrift* commemorating Jung's sixtieth birthday (Hauer 1935a, 220–336). Hauer never lectured at Eranos again, but not because he was banned (as reported in Bair 2003, 434). Rather, he declined further invitations from Froebe-Kapteyn for two reasons: first, the German press had portrayed the Eranos participants as connected with the occult, which would reflect badly on Hauer; second, Hauer felt it more important to dedicate himself to articulating what he believed were the specificities of his own people's racially determined spirituality (Dierks 1986, 288).

In 1936, Hauer was prohibited from leaving Germany, which Jung regretted. Jung tried to arrange to meet in January 1937, when Jung would be in Königsfeld for a conference (Jung to Hauer, Dec. 21, 1936, Hs 1056:5001), probably the work week of the *Bund der Köngener* that Hauer had founded. Indicating the radical shift his religious beliefs had undergone over the years, Hauer refused to go because of the stong Christian presence; he would be an outsider there (Hauer to Jung, Dec. 12, 1936, Hs 1056:4447). Instead of the two men meeting, Jung lectured on analytical psychology at the *Köngener Kreis* (Daur 1937, 35–43).

Hauer had long been preoccupied with the role of the unconscious in religion, and wanted to explore more fully what he believed to the determining factors of race (*Artbestimmtheit*) in the development of religion. He therefore wrote to Jung on May 12, 1937, to propose a seminar on the significance of race in religious evolution (BA N1131/139, fol. 21). Jung replied on June 7, 1937, suggesting a different topic. Jung explained that the anthropological definition of race still awaited clarification; hence, it would prove too difficult to execute a seminar on race and religion properly. Jung did not deny that race was an important factor in the development of a given religion; indeed, he claimed to understand the deepest corners of Jewish psychology and could thus ascertain how the Jewish race conditions Jewish religion. However, Islam poses a real challenge, he wrote, because not only were different races Muslim, but also people previously non-Muslim had converted to the religion over the centuries. Although Jung had published his "Wotan" article just one year previously, he tellingly did not mention Germanic peoples and their conversion to Christianity. He concluded by suggesting a religious-historical topic instead (BA N1131/139, fol. 19–20).

If Jung had meant to change Hauer's mind about the relationship between race and religion, he failed: On June 12, 1937, Hauer replied that he understood Jung's reservations, assuming they had to do with the "special situation in Zurich" (*besondere Lage in Zürich*), a statement he did not elucidate. Moreover, he believed his topic fit the bill proposed by Jung; after all, he wrote, the topic of race and religion was a historical one. Furthermore, since Hauer was already working on a book with this theme, he understood the difficulties to which Jung alluded. He approached the theme from a historical angle; what he wanted from Jung and his group was a psychological perspective. Hauer insisted that foundational racial differences were essential to the evolution of religion, but acknowledged there were significant cases where the racial essence of a people and a religion diverged, such as Muslim Aryans in India and Christianity in the West. Hence, he also wanted to explore the adoption of foreign cultures by given racial groups. Hauer then proposed a seminar in which he would systematically examine the evolution of religious forms, providing examples especially from the Indo-European and the Near-Eastern-Semitic realms (BA N1131/139, fol. 18).

Plans were then laid to hold the seminar, and Toni Wolff made the arrangements. Hauer was to stay with the Jung family during his visit (Hauer to Wolff, Jan. 25, 1938; BA N1131/140, fol. 302), and was personally invited by Emma to do so (Dierks 1986, 282). Hauer was also asked to participate in the Club's Carnival party (Wolff to Hauer, Feb. 1, 1938, BA N1131/140, fol. 301). Regarding the seminar, Wolff suggested that the word *race* not appear in Hauer's title. Due to the concept's complexity, as well as the dilettantish treatment of the term, it left a bad taste in many people's mouths (Wolff to Hauer, July 21, 1937, BA N1131/140, fol. 309). Hauer agreed to this stipulation, but assured Wolff that he would deal with "the reality of race in the morphogenesis of religion" (*die Wirklichkeit Rasse in der religiösen Gestaltwerdung*) (Hauer to Wolff, July 29, 1937, BA N1131/140, fol. 308).

Early on in the seminar's planning, Wolff explained to Hauer in a letter dated February 1, 1938, that the new political situation in Europe might reduce participation, as international travel had become difficult. She further offered to reduce participation of a certain segment of the Club membership, should Hauer prefer it. Specifically, Wolff suggested excluding "non-Aryans" from the seminar, demonstrating the Club's willingness to accommodate the Nazi scholar of religion. She wrote:

> Among the club members, there are several non-Aryans. If their participation should pose any difficulties for you, then we would have to make it known that they are to be excluded. On the other hand, if that is not necessary, that would of course be more comfortable for us.
>
> [Unter den Clubangehörigen befinden sich einige Nichtarier. Sollte deren Teilnahme irgendwelche Schwierigkeiten für Sie bedeuten, so müssten wir natürlich bekannt machen, dass sie ausgeschlossen sind. Wenn es hingegen nicht darauf ankommt, ist uns das natürlich angenehmer.]
>
> (BA N1131/140, fol. 301)

Although Wolff did not specify that "non-Aryan" meant "Jewish," Hauer understood her to mean just that. In his reply dated February 3, 1938, Hauer reminded Wolff that Jews were still allowed to study at German universities (at least as of early 1938). His views on race were clear to everyone, he wrote, yet he insisted he treated the issue in a strictly scientific manner. Hence, Hauer rejected the suggestion that "non-Aryan" club members should be excluded from his seminar: "The difficulties you assume in relation to several club members do not exist for me," he wrote. "I see no reason why they should not participate" (*Die von Ihnen vermuteten Schwierigkeiten mit Beziehung auf einige Klubangehörige bestehen für mich nicht. Ich sehe keinen Grund ein, warum diese nicht teilnehmen sollten.*) (BA N1131/140, fol. 300).

This incident was by no means the first time the Psychological Club of Zurich showed a willingness to restrict Jewish involvement. An earlier incident arose in 1932, when Friedrich Spiegelberg, once Hauer's student, wrote his former professor, on May 20, to ask if he could participate in the upcoming seminar on the symbolism and psychology of kundalini yoga. Spiegelberg also expressed his enthusiasm for Jung's *Transformations and Symbols of the Libido* (BA N1131/170–424, fol. 425). In his reply to Spiegelberg on May 24, 1932, Hauer wrote that he would be happy to have his former student participate (BA N1131/170, fol. 423). Spiegelberg then apparently wrote the Psychological Club for permission, referring to his correspondence with Hauer, as evidenced by Jung's letter to Hauer, dated June 23, 1932. Jung felt differently than Hauer about Spiegelberg's attendance, and asked whether this was the same Spiegelberg who was "an intellectual Jew" (*ein intellectueller Jude*). If so, then he was "somewhat in doubt [about the invitation to participate] and fear[ed] for the quality of the atmosphere [of the seminar]" (*Ich muss gestehen, ich bin etwas im Zweifel und fürchte für die Qualität der Atmosphäre.*) (BA N1131/170, fol. 281). Based on Jung's statement to Dr. Wolfgang Kranefeldt (1892–1950) in a letter written in 1934, it may be assumed Jung feared that the "intellectual Jew" Spiegelberg would have a "corrosive" effect on the seminar (Samuels 1993, 293).

In his reply to Jung on July 2, 1932, Hauer wrote that he never realized that Spiegelberg was Jewish. Although he did admit that his former student tended towards "intellectualistic exaggeration" (*intellektualistische Überspitztheit*), he doubted that the young man would impose himself on the discussion. Ultimately, since Hauer posed no objection to Spiegelberg's attendance (BA N1131/170, fol. 277), the student received an invitation (Wolff to Hauer, July 19, 1932, BA N1131/170, fol. 273). This letter exchange shows that it was not Hauer, soon to become the leader of the German Faith movement, but rather Jung, the supposedly neutral Swiss, who encouraged a policy of exclusion against Jews.

The practice of excluding Jews became enshrined in the Psychological Club's by-laws in 1944, when the Club secretly added an appendix limiting the percentage of Jews among full members to 10 per cent and guest members to 25 per cent. One can reasonably speculate that Jung knew of the appendix, because his long-term mistress Wolff was the Club's president. The appendix was not removed until 1950 (Samuels 1993, 305). Although Jung often argued that psychological oppositions could and should be reconciled (Bishop 1999, 9), one binary opposition – Germanic-Aryan vs. Jewish-Semitic – proved to be irreconcilable in Jungian thought from at least 1912 onwards. This conflict had real consequences for many people in contact with Jung and the Psychological Club of Zurich throughout the 1930s and 1940s.

During the week of March 7–12, 1938, Hauer gave a series of lectures at the Psychological Club under the title, "The Essence of Religion: Law of Religious Development" (*Das Wesen der Religion. Gesetz der religiösen Entwicklung*) (Hauer, 1938, title page of ms.). The theme of the Zurich lectures reflected Hauer's central concerns in his 1923 book *The Religions: Their Becoming, Their Meaning, Their Truth* (Dierks 1986, 82). In this early work, Hauer had written about the presumed significance of race for religious evolution. That he continued to discuss this topic in 1938 should have surprised no one at all familiar with his work.

During his stay in Zurich, Hauer kept a diary, in which he noted early in the week that he was "too 'German'" (*zu "deutsch"*) for the Swiss and international audience. On Wednesday, he wrote that he and Jung slowly reached mutual understanding. By the end of the week, however, he wrote that his views on race, religion, and National Socialism had been met with "amazing openness" (*erstaunliche Aufgeschlossenheit*) by many participants, and the seminar concluded "with great success" (*mit einer vollen Erfolg*) (Dierks 1986, 297). He then sent a follow-up note to Wolff, expressing strong feelings of gratitude for the opportunity to hold the seminar. He further wrote "that Prof. Jung and I have come much closer this time than last time" (*dass Prof. Jung und ich uns diesmal noch viel näher gekommen sind als das letztemal*) (BA N1131/140, fol. 296).

Once back at the Karl Eberhard University in Tübingen, Hauer wrote to Jung on May 26, 1938, to tell him about his rector's response to Hauer's report on the seminar. According to Hauer, the rector Prof. Hoffman and the younger generation of German psychiatrists found Jung's theory very promising for Germany and hoped to see Jungian psychology implemented there. He also expressed his and Hoffman's dismay over photos Jung had apparently shown to Hauer, in which Jung was portrayed with an oversized nose and dark-rimmed glasses. According to Jung, some dastardly Jews had falsified the photo to discredit

Jung's theory as "Jewish psychology" (BA N1131/139, fol. 13). A more logical explanation is that an anti-Jewish group wanted to discredit Jung by making him look stereotypically Jewish. Still, Hauer and Hoffman were all too ready to agree with Jung's bizarre hypothesis.

Two days later on March 28, 1938, Hauer wrote an official report to Prof. Christian Julius Mergenthaler (1884–1980), the Minister President of Baden-Wuerttemberg. Hauer contrasted the more favorable reception of the 1932 Kundalini seminar to the one he had just held by explaining that the Swiss public was generally mistrustful about the "central meaning of the powers of race, the soil, the group [and] the people for religion" (*die zentrale Bedeutung der Kräfte der Rasse, des Bodens, der Gruppe, des Volkes für die Religion*). Hauer had faced difficulties making himself understood to his audience because they were "biased by an extraordinarily strong individualism" (*in einem ausserordentlich starken Individualismus befangen*). By engaging in personal conversations, however, he was able to win over several participants and thereby create a better atmosphere. Finally, after talks with leading figures of the Psychological Club, Hauer was able to explain the "religious and spiritual driving powers in current political events in Germany" (*die religiösen und gistrigen [sic] Triebkräfte im heutigen politischen Geschehen in Deutschland*), and he managed to awaken interest in the topic of how race influences the evolution of religion. Furthermore, both Carl and Emma Jung showed great sympathy for Hauer's topic. "Both are thoroughly open for the new Germany," Hauer declared (*beide [sind] für das neue Deutschland durchaus aufgeschlossen*). He therefore advocated that Jung's psychology be encouraged in Germany (BA N1131/139, fol. 211).

The correspondence between Wolff and Hauer lasted until 1939. On Feb. 8, Wolff wrote to congratulate Hauer on his new bride. Hauer had decided to divorce his first wife and leave a barren marriage to have children with a new wife (BA N1131/140, fol. 289). At some point after this date, but before 1941, the relationship between Hauer and the Zurich School came to an end. On February 10, 1941, Hauer responded to a letter from the writer Emma von Pelet, whom Hauer had once assisted in Tübingen when she was conducting research on the Indian mystic Ramakrishna (1836–1886). Von Pelet wrote to Hauer from Ascona to express her interest in the relationship between yoga and analytical psychology (Dierks 1986, 298). In his long and impassioned reply, Hauer expressed his belief that the National Socialist movement in Germany was a "new revelation of constructive powers of life" (*eine neue Offenbarung der schaffenden Lebensmächte*) related to blood and race. Hauer had tried his best to convince the members of the Psychological Club in Zurich of this supposed reality. He had hoped that Jung would follow in the footsteps of Philipp Melanchthon to become Germany's new *Praeceptor germaniae*. However, whatever interest Hauer had managed to awaken in Jung for Germany's cause did not last (BA N1131/136, fol. 58).

Several possible reasons may be given for the breach between Hauer and Jung. First, in 1938, the German psychiatrist Oswald Bumke published a book called *Psychoanalysis and Its Children: A Confrontation with Freud, Adler and Jung*

(*Die Psychoanalyse und ihre Kinder: eine Auseinandersetzung mit Freud, Adler und Jung*). Apparently, Jung felt this book falsely portrayed him and his theory. The promise of Hauer and Hoffman to defend Jung (Hauer to Jung, Mar. 26, 1938, BA N1131/139, fol. 13) satisfied neither him nor Jung's associate C.A. Meier (1905–1995), who assumed Bumke's devastating critique of both analytical psychologists represented official German opinion (Meier to Hauer, Oct. 12, 1938, BA N1131/139, fol. 191–192). Second, Hauer had already indicated in his report to Mergenthaler that the individualism in Jung's social circle hindered his full acceptance of Hauer's conviction that the racial collective held the most power and promise for a psycho-spiritual renewal. Finally, the invasion of Poland by Germany on September 1, 1939, had shown the world that the forces of National Socialism were not the creative powers of life, but the destructive powers of greed and aggression. World War II had broken out on Switzerland's borders, and Jung stepped away from the professor's robe Hauer had wanted to offer him.

The wandering diagnosis

On June 26, 1932, Jung was interviewed on Radio Berlin by his former student, Dr. Adolf von Weizäcker, neurologist, psychiatrist, member of the C. G. Jung Society in Berlin, and Hauer's close associate. Jung reiterated his disdain for mass society that he expressed in his Vienna *Kulturbund* talk and presented Hitler as a strong masculine leader of his people. Similar to that of Karl Vietor, who claimed Hitler led the German people to march towards new goals (Engster 1986, 77) (see Chapter 2), Jung praised Hitler as "the spearhead of the phalanx of the whole people in motion." While criticizing the "drone" of "aimless" parliamentary debates, Jung implied Hitler's rightful position at the top by stating that "every movement culminates organically in a leader" (McGuire and Hull 1980, 78). This view would change significantly during the 1930s and 1940s.

Jung began revising his view as early as October 1936, in an interview called "The Psychology of Dictatorship" published in the London *Observer*. Jung ascribed the problems facing modern societies to a more basic primitivity. Reactivated tribal instincts, he said, were causing the upheaval then taking place among nation-states both near and far. In this view, Hitler, Mussolini, Stalin, and Roosevelt were not the heads of modern nation-states, but rather "tribal leaders." To keep the stirred-up tribal instincts from getting out of control, Jung believed that the dictatorships in Germany, Russia and Italy were necessary. Yet Jung's preferred form of government was monarchical. Despite his own citizenry of a democracy of venerable age, Jung claimed that "a decent oligarchy – call it aristocracy if you like – is the most ideal form of government," and he praised the English gentleman for his ability to rule the world (McGuire and Hull 1980, 102–104).

Jung went on to describe Hitler as a medicine man and seer (103, 104). These terms, reminiscent of the mana personality, reflect Jung's psychologization of the anthropological model of evolution. According to Jung, the archetypal mana personality arose from the affective responses people had to extraordinary men who seemed endowed with some kind of supra-individual power. This affective response became inscribed onto the collective psyche and internalized in the unconscious of the modern Western individual. In Jung's diagnosis of Hitler, the German chancellor appeared as a primitive medicine man, which meant that the German nation was the equivalent of a primitive horde. At the same time, Jung described the violent *Schutzstaffel* (S.S.) as an elite caste of knights ruling sixty million natives (103). This statement echoes Jung's general view that only some people were of an aristocratic nature and that the "masses" were no more advanced than "primitives." Since Hitler stood at the head of the elite S.S. and all of Germany, he, like Wotan, appeared to embody stark oppositions.

The description of Hitler as a seer resonated to some degree with Jung's portrait of Wotan as a mantic in the "Wotan" essay (Jung CW 10 (1947 [1936]):399); however, in the *Observer* interview, Jung compared Hitler to the non-Germanic – and feminine – Delphic Sybil (McGuire and Hull 1980, 104). This indicates not only a racialized but also a gendered shift in Jung's diagnosis of Hitler and his people. Rather than an encounter with the Germanic archetype of the self, one involving primarily the male half of the German population (Jung CW/GW 10 (1947 [1936]): 386), Jung seemed to suggest an individuation process in reverse, from the mana personality to anima possession.

Jung again both primitivized and demasculinized Hitler in an interview three years later with the English pastor and psychologist Howard L. Philp. This interview was published in the London *Psychologist* in May 1939 under the title "Dr. Jung Diagnoses the Dictators." Here Jung compared Hitler to a medicine man and seer, then to "primitives," when he described Hitler as having "no real *personal* psychology" (141). According to Jung, Hitler was only obeying a voice issuing out of the collective German unconscious, one apparently feminine. He explained that the unconscious appeared in a man's mind as a female figure, the anima, and a man must come to terms with her. Hitler, said Jung, had failed in this endeavor and had therefore fallen under her spell. With this diagnosis, Jung completed the negation of his earlier view that Wotan had gripped or stirred (*ergriffen*) men, including Hitler; instead, Hitler was anima-possessed (McGuire and Hull 1980, 144).

Jung then compared Hitler unfavorably with Mussolini, a man who "fills his uniform," while Hitler appeared more like a little boy. According to Jung, "Hitler does not even fit into his clothes" (143). The puerile condition of Hitler's body mirrored the psychological condition of the nation of which Hitler was the mouthpiece. Eschewing Jung's own 1918 portrayal of the youthful Germanic barbarian's promise of spiritual rejuvenation, Jung instead described Germany in 1939 in political terms as a "young nation," plagued by an inferiority complex and jealous of the older nations France and Great Britain, which had "rich colonies and all that belongs to a fully matured nation" (142). Rather than being manly men like the English gentleman who ruled "savages," Hitler and his people were effeminate, puerile primitives.

Jung repeated his diagnosis of Germany's alleged degenerate, puerile masculinity after the war. On May 11, 1945, an interview with Jung appeared in the Zurich newspaper *The Week's World* (*Weltwoche*), entitled "Will the Souls Find Peace" (*Werden die Seelen Frieden finden*). Jung had long dropped his diagnosis of *Ergriffenheit*, instead arguing that Hitler had "infected" (*angesteckt*) the Germans and that the Nazi leaders were "possessed men" (*Besessene*). The demonic power that had possessed the Germans was a strong inferiority complex of a juvenile nation that had yet to wean itself from its mother. German adolescent psychology was related both to homosexuality and the missing anima figure in literature (Goethe being an exception) (Anon., 1945, n.p., ETH Hs 1058a:256).

In 1945, Jung published a follow-up article to "Wotan" in the *Neue Schweizer Rundschau* called "After the Catastrophe," in which he diagnosed the Germans as having an enormous inferiority complex, which had resulted in a mass psychosis. This led to the crimes of the Nazis and an ensuing sense of collective guilt. Jung charged Germany with betraying Christian values and European civilization, as well as basic human morality (Jung CW 10 (1945):402–407, 429). Furthermore, not only did all Germans suffer from guilt due to the crimes committed by the Nazis; this guilt had descended upon all of Europe.

Jung continued the new line of diagnosis he had begun in 1939, describing Hitler as an effeminate, adolescent, and cunning hysteric, whose neurosis reflected the collective hysteria of the Germans (para. 419). Jung portrayed Hitler and the Germans as Nietzsche's "pale criminal," who feels remorse and self-condemnation for a deed he committed (Bishop 1995, 316). The horrific act committed by Hitler was apparently to tell a massive lie, as shown by Jung's diagnosis of *pseudologia phantastica*. This illness is a form of hysteria characterized by the sufferer's tendency to believe his own lies. Medical doctors around the turn of the last century claimed this illness was especially characteristic of male homosexuals (Gilman 1993, 165). Thus, Jung not only again feminized Hitler, but also queerified him. Just as Jung had salvaged the concept of *civilization* by displacing the problems of modern society onto a presumed inner primitive, Jung recovered his era's heteronormative definition of *masculinity* by shifting the blame onto a psychological feminine or queer aspect.

A year earlier, in a radio talk entitled "The Fight with the Shadow," broadcast in Great Britain on November 7, 1946, Jung went a step further in his diagnosis of Hitler. Jung argued that the German *Führer* was the "foremost victim of disorder and unchecked greed," which led to his dream of a "new order." Indeed, Hitler was the "most prodigious personification of all human inferiorities [. . .] an utterly incapable, unadapted, irresponsible, psychopathic personality, full of empty, infantile fantasies, but cursed with the keen intuition of a rat or a guttersnipe." In this talk, Jung moved away from all previous diagnoses of Hitler as moved by the Germanic archetype Wotan, as a mana personality or as anima-possessed. Instead, by describing Hitler as a vagabond and social outcast, Jung portrayed him as the shadow (Jung CW 10 (1947 [1946]):454).

The drastic transformations in Jung's image of both Hitler and the Third Reich were extended to Faust and Wotan. Faust was no longer the restless wanderer who descended into the collective unconscious in his quest for power, wisdom, and rejuvenation, nor an artist's vision of the unification of oppositions to achieve a state of psychic wholeness. Instead, in "After the Catastrophe," Faust had become an unrepentant murderer, who projected his inner evil outwards in the phantasm of the devil, Mephistopheles (Jung CW 10 (1945):423). Furthermore, Wotan was not a Germanic archetype that had been transformed into the devil by medieval Christian theologians; instead, Jung himself demonized Wotan as the collective German shadow (para. 418).

Jung even changed the diagnoses of his German patients' dreams that he had made during and after World War I. In "The Fight with the Shadow," he claimed that as early as 1918, he had noticed images of "primitivity, violence, cruelty: in short, all the powers of darkness" in the unconscious contents of every one of his German patients (para. 449). Perhaps Jung was alluding to his 1918 reference to the "blond beast" in the depths of the Germanic psyche, prowling in its cage in the hope of finding a way out (Jung CW 10 (1918):17). Rather than assuming that these images had emerged in response to "a certain brutalization of conscience" (Mosse 1978, 174) that Germans suffered due to the trauma of World War I, Jung suggested that these contents had indicated a certain movement in the collective German unconscious. His patients' dreams revealed "terrific suffering and destruction," which was followed by symbols of "the forces of *order*" (Jung CW 10 (1947 [1946]):450; emphasis in the original). Jung interpreted this as a dangerous symptom that could lead – and indeed had led – to totalitarianism.

However, previous discussions in Chapters 2 and 3 show that Jung had made very different diagnoses of his German patients' dreams between the wars. For example, in his 1918 article, "The Role of the Unconscious," Jung had presented a female patient's dream of a bull leaping out of control and breaking its leg as it landed. Jung did not describe this dream in terms of chaos and order, but rather as a cry of compassion for the necessary crippling of one's animal instincts. Furthermore, in 1928, Jung had interpreted the emergence of the wind god Wotan in a female patient's dream as a symbol of healing that cured her father complex (Jung CW 7 (1963 [1928]):218–219).

Sympathizer, collaborator, suspect, or persecuted?

Was Jung a Nazi sympathizer, an agent for the United States secret service, a victim of Nazi persecution, or all of the above? As the previous analysis shows, Jung was initially supportive of National Socialism, but his enthusiasm faded over the course of the 1930s. Still, he never relinquished his belief in fundamental racial differences between "Germanic" and "Jewish" psychologies. He also remained president of the International Medical Society for Psychotherapy and, along with Mattias Göring, co-editor of its journal until 1940 (Samuels 1993, 300).

Jung denied that he collaborated in any way with the Nazis; rather, he insisted he was persecuted by them. For example, in 1940, an anonymous governmental official from Bern supposedly called to say that Jung was targeted for liquidation

(Bair 2003, 468). This assertion is regularly repeated by scholars and biographers (e.g. Post 1975, 194; Schoenl 1996, 53), but so far, Jung seems to be the only source for this claim (Jung CW 10 (1946):464). Furthermore, Jung asserted his books had been banned by the Nazis. Bair cites two letters from L. Fernau, which confirm that Jung's books were officially banned by the Nazis in Germany and France sometime after 1940. These letters were written in 1942 and 1943, and the author was the Leipzig distributor for Jung's publishing house Rascher (Bair 2003, 462, 800, n. 166). Fernau's claim needs to be questioned, however. The official website of the city of Berlin has published the Nazi Black List (list of banned books) on-line. All the works of Sigmund Freud and his daughter Anna appear on the list; the only Jung listed is the communist author Franz Jung (1888–1963) [INT1]. In other words, the works of Carl Gustav Jung were never banned by the Nazis.

Jung further claimed that yet another group persecuted him: the "Freudian Jews." In a letter dated September 24, 1945, Jung referred to the "absurd rumor" started by "Freudian Jews" that he was a "Nazi" in a resentful letter filled with anti-Jewish diatribe to Mary Conover Mellon (53–54). Mary Mellon was Jung's patient and the wife of Paul Mellon (1907–1999), who was the patron of the Eranos Conference and the Bollingen Foundation, which publishes Jung's *Collected Works*.

Paul Mellon was also the head of Gulf Oil and worked for U.S. intelligence services during the war. Allen Dulles (1893–1969), the station chief of the Office of Strategic Services in Zurich and founding director of the CIA, was instrumental in getting oil reserves for the war, which benefited Gulf Oil (Wasserstrom 1999, 153). In 1943, Jung began assisting Dulles, who referred to Jung as "agent 488" (Bair 2003, 492–493).

Despite Jung's assistance to Dulles, the United States Federal Bureau of Investigation (FBI) had begun investigating charges against Jung of being a Nazi collaborator. In 1944, FBI agents questioned the New York-based analytical psychologist Eleanor Bertine about him. She in turn warned Jung that he was under investigation (Schoenl 1996, 53). Eranos founder Froebe-Kapteyn had also been under investigation since 1941 after a trip to the United States to collect symbolic material (Bair 2003, 479). It was Dulles of the OSS who personally exonerated both Jung and Froebe-Kapteyn (Wasserstrom 1999, 153). Dulles himself was not above suspicion, however; he is considered a Nazi appeaser (ibid., 318, fn. 60).

After the war ended, Geoffrey Parsons of the *New York Herald Tribune* caught wind of these rumors and wrote a letter dated Dec. 21, 1945 to Dulles. Parsons described a "Jewish campaign" against Jung, while also stating that "the supporters of Dr. Jung asserted that he was on the black list of the Nazis." He was responding to Albert D. Parelhoff, who had sent a letter critical of Jung to the newspaper (Bair 2006, 511). In his reply dated Jun. 2, 1946, Dulles answered, "As far as I recall there was no German blacklist which was available to the public." He also wrote that there was a book for OSS agents in which were listed the names of people in foreign countries whom the agents should avoid, but Dulles was uncertain whether Jung's name was contained therein (Buresch-Talley 2002, 46, 47). It appears that Dulles neither substantiated nor refuted the assertions; he merely carefully avoided directly answering Parsons.

These facts indicate why Jung's immediate post-war diagnosis of Germany, Hitler, Wotan and even Faust diverge so strongly from his portrayals of these figures before and during World War II. Jung had not simply "fallen afoul of contemporary history," as he claimed (Bair 2003, 463). Rather, he actively participated in the politics of his day, even in his role as psychologist. By ultimately diagnosing all things German as pathological at the end of World War II, Jung saved his reputation and career.

Question to Jung's *Answer to Job*

In 1952, Jung wrote *Answer to Job*, in which he explored the history of consciousness in the Judeo-Christian godhead. According to Jung, the wrathful Yahweh of the *Book of Job* is completely unconscious and generally unaware of his feminine aspect. Jung depicted Yahweh in extremely negative terms: full of rage, paranoid, and narcissistic (CW 11 (1952):504). Yahweh acts like a natural calamity, wreaking havoc in the life of his loyal servant, Job, all the while demanding to be loved and revered (para. 604). Given His enslavement to His own emotions, Yahweh seems to be, in Jungian terms, "anima-possessed." Repeating what he had already said in his Visions seminar on March 7, 1934 (see Chapter 6), Jung argued that God needed humanity as a vehicle, so to speak, to become conscious; hence, he chose to incarnate in the form of Jesus Christ. The assumption of the Virgin Mary, declared official church doctrine in 1951, signaled to Jung a significant movement in God's process of individuation.

Bishop describes the book through the Haeckelian theory of "ontogeny recapitulates phylogeny," in that individual individuation recapitulates the individuation of the Godhead. Jung detailed in this book a move from an undifferentiated state to the unification of God and humanity in the symbol of Christ. Bishop describes the book as an interpretation of "the history of humanity, from its pre-history to the present day, in terms of an unfolding 'process of individuation'" (Bishop 2002, 81). The book thus reiterates some of the Christocentric themes Jung had first started to explore in his 1912 *Transformations and Symbols of the Libido*, where he presented Christian symbolism as the paradigm of human psychological maturation, with Judaism stuck at a pathological level (see Chapter 5).

Despite his omniscience, Yahweh is extremely limited in consciousness. Jung described Him as *unzurechnungsfähig*, using the same word that he first used for the Jewish god in his 1912 book. Although Bishop interprets this word as a state of disassociation (Bishop 2002, 129), Jung himself described the word as a "primitive awareness" (CW 11 (1952):638), meaning that Yahweh perceives the outer world just enough to act on it. His acting is blind, however, because Yahweh lacks conscious, rational thought. Thus, the Jewish god is an immature know-it-all, much like Freud's "primitives" and their childish belief in the omnipotence of their thoughts (Freud 2001), as well as those "intellectual" Jews whom Jung had wished to keep out of his seminar at the Psychological Club in Zurich.

The story of Job acted as a means for Jung to explore the dual nature of the Godhead. As Yahweh practically pummels his faithful servant into dust, Job seeks an advocate on his behalf – in Yahweh (Jung CW 11 (1952):167). Jung explored this dual nature in the theme of the hostile brothers, represented by Cain and Abel in Judaism and Christ and Anti-Christ in Christianity. This split in the mind of God echoes Jung's earlier preoccupations with the split libido he had first mentioned in his 1912 book, where he described the oppositions within the libido itself (Jung 1925, 480). The theme of the split nature of the divine also resonates with Jung's portrait of the dual-natured Wotan, as well as with the various "hostile brothers" and oppositions he explored in his 1936 essay on the Germanic god. This split nature is one that Jung had argued was characteristic of the Germanic barbarian psyche as well.

Despite Jung's penchant for comparison, however, Wotan makes no appearance in Jung's narration of the drama of Job and his god Yahweh. This absence is striking, because, as a god whose name signifies fury, Wotan was certainly as much driven by his emotions as Yahweh. Since both gods are full of wrath, why did Jung not compare them? Perhaps because of the difference in meaning between *Ergriffenheit* und *unzurechnungsfähig*, the former term which Jung applied to Wotan and the latter by which he described Yahweh. As previous chapters have shown, *Ergriffenheit* relates to the primordial religious experience of an encounter with the Holy as such; *unzurechnungsfähig* indicates a pathological state. One would have hoped that, post-Holocaust, Jung might have rethought his diagnoses of both Germanic and Jewish psychologies and their hypothesized archetypal images. If anyone could have been described as insane, it was Wotan and the Germans, not Yahweh and the Jews.

Wotan as Spirit: Germanic or universal?

Just as Jung's diagnosis of the Jewish god remained constant over the decades, so too did his overall assessment of Wotan as Spirit, notwithstanding his condemnation of the god immediately following World War II. Still, Jung's view of Wotan also contained some surprising twists. After having declared in 1936 that Wotan was the god of the Germans (Jung CW 10 (1947 [1936]):397), three years later, Jung expanded the Wotanic experience to Jews, people considered in his day to be thoroughly un-German(-ic). In a letter dated Nov. 15, 1939, Erich Neumann wrote from Tel Aviv to describe a dream of an old pilgrim. This pilgrim was first threatened by Nazis; then a father-prince and son appeared, and the father told the pilgrim to head off. The pilgrim grabbed a hat and staff and left, being denied the chance to say good-bye to the son (Liebscher 2015, 29N). Interestingly, Neumann interpreted the pilgrim as Wotan, not the Wandering Jew representing collectively the German Jews that the Nazis had driven from their homeland.

On Dec. 16, 1939, Jung replied, accepting Neumann's association of the pilgrim with Wotan. He explained that Neumann's dream was not due to the "Germanic regression" then taking place in Germany, but rather to a spiritual movement then gripping the "entire cultural world (Wotan as the wind God = Pneuma)." For this reason, Wotan could appear to a Jew – although only a German one. This Wotanic-Pneumatic wind was causing rapid changes around the world and hence transcended "racial differences" (30J).

In this letter, Jung went against his earlier tendency to separate "Jewish" and "Germanic" psychologies at a deep level, as exemplified in a letter to Neumann dated Aug. 12, 1934. Here Jung argued that the biblical story of Jacob wrestling with the angel (Gen. 32:22–32) symbolically represents a Jewish-specific attempt at collective individuation (Liebscher 2015, 7J). In this letter as elsewhere, Jung considered Jews a race apart from Germans. Yet in his 1939 letter, Jung followed a different model, in which both the "Semitic" and the "Aryan" races together occupied the top rung of the evolutionary ladder (Stocking 122). The rest of the world that did not count as "cultured" was excluded from Jung's 1939 fantasy of a collective spiritual rebirth.

In later works, Jung's view of the double-natured god demonstrated once again the ambivalence in Jung's image of the Germanic god that he expressed in the "Wotan" essay, although he emphasized Wotan's explosive nature. For example, in his letter to the Chilean diplomat Miguel Serrano dated September 14, 1960, Jung reiterated his claim that Wotan had never disappeared, but remained a latent force in the collective psyche. However, the archetype appeared in universal guise as the mover behind a coming "world-wide Wotanistic experiment" (Serrano 1966, 103). Moreover, in 1956, Jung wrote a short piece called "Wotan and the Rat-Catcher" (*Wotan und der Rattenfänger*), based on the German fairy-tale of the Pied Piper of Hameln. In this work, Jung compared Wotan to both the Berserkers and Dionysus, describing the Germanic god as the "unleasher of frenzy and passions" (*Entfeßler von Rausch und Leidenschaften*), whose "essence is ecstasy" (*Sein Wesen ist Ekstase*), as well as the force that sets things in motion (Jung 1956, 75). Jung left unclear in this work whether he considered Wotan to be a Germanic-specific or a universal psychological aspect.

Finally, in *Memories, Dreams, Reflections*, Wotan reappeared in his Germanic folkloric aspect. Jung described a dream he had once had of a large ghostly wolfhound on the hunt for a human soul. Jung interpreted the hound as his mother's psychopomp and the dream as prophetic, for he later discovered that she had just died. Jung believed that her soul had thereafter been reclaimed by the god of his Alemannic forebears (Jung 1965, 313). This was Wotan as the Wild Huntsman and head of the army of the dead, called the *sälig Lüt* (*selige Leute*) in the Alemannic dialect, a term that means "the blessed folk" (230–231).

Conclusion

Jung made in private his only admission of guilt over his previous enthusiasm for National Socialism, which is contained in a letter that the Jewish studies scholar

Gerschom Scholem wrote to Aniela Jaffé on May 7, 1963. In this letter, Scholem explained why he decided to continue to attend the Eranos conference after World War II. During the war, the rabbi Leo Baeck, Jung's co-lecturer at Keyserling's School of Wisdom in 1927, had been interned in the Austrian/Czech concentration camp Theresienstadt. After his release, he made his way to Switzerland in 1946, refusing to visit Jung due to Jung's anti-Semitic writings from the Nazi era. When Jung learned that Baeck was in town, he sought him out in his hotel. Baeck confronted Jung with what he had heard about Jung's activities during the Nazi reign of terror, to which Jung replied that "I slipped up" (*ich bin ausgerutscht*). This admission apparently had a profound effect on the rabbi, and he and Jung became reconciled. When Scholem asked Baeck how he should respond to an invitation he had just received to an upcoming Eranos conference, Baeck strongly encouraged him to accept (Jaffé 1989, 100). Jung never admitted in public that he had "slipped up," however, and one wonders if he could have without ruining his career. In any case, Jung's rather vague three-word statement owes its status as an apology and admission of guilt less to its wording than to Baeck's decision to interpret it this way.

Nearing the end of his life, in the summer of 1958, a student wrote to Jung, inquiring about the astonishing letter he had penned to Freud back on Feb. 11, 1910, in which he advocated turning psychoanalysis into an ecstatic religion celebrating Christ as the god of the vine (Jung 1973, 1:19, fn. 8). What is known of this letter appears only in a footnote attached to the 1910 text. One must wonder why the editors decided not to publish the letter itself, because they suppressed not only the name of the pupil, but also Jung's full reply. The German edition of the *Briefe* indicates that the student was female (*eine Schülerin*) (Jung 1972, 39, n. 8), and one may suspect the correspondent was Aniela Jaffé, Jung's secretary and co-editor of the *Letters*. Furthermore, one is left to speculate if the purpose of publishing the astonishing 1910 letter was to print Jung's retraction of it, that is, to demonstrate his post-World War II regret about his earlier views. Despite my misgivings about these editorial maneuvers, I still find the excerpt worth quoting. According to the editorial note, Jung replied on April 9, 1959, with the following words:

> Best thanks for the quotation from that accursed correspondence. For me it is an unfortunately inexpugnable reminder of the incredible folly that filled the days of my youth. The journey from cloud-cuckoo-land back to reality lasted a long time. In my case Pilgrim's Progress consisted in my having to climb down a thousand ladders until I could reach out my hand to the little clod of earth that I am.
>
> (Jung 1973,1:19, fn. 8)

Perhaps this statement may be Jung's greatest admission of error for having played the spiritual master who could read the signs of the times as an incipient spiritual renewal on a mass scale.

Bibliography

Title

"After the Catastrophe": C. G. Jung, *Collected Works* (CW) 10:400–443, ed. by Sir Herbert Read, Michael Fordham, and Gerhard Adler. New York: Pantheon Books; Princeton, NJ: Princeton University Press.

Sources

Bair, Deirdre. 2003. *Jung. A Biography.* Boston: Little, Brown and Co.

Baumann, Schaul. 2005. *Die Deutsche Glaubensbewegung und ihr Gründer Jakob Wilhelm Hauer (1821–1962).* Religionswissenschaftliche Reihe 22. Marburg: Diagonal.

Bishop, Paul. 1995. *The Dionysian Self: C. G. Jung's Reception of Friedrich Nietzsche.* Monographien und Texte zur Nietzsche-Forschung 30. Berlin: de Gruyter.

—— (ed.). 1999. *Jung in Contexts: A Reader.* London: Routledge.

——. 2002. *Jung's Answer to Job: A Commentary.* Hove and New York: Brunner-Routledge.

Buresch-Talley, Joan Dulles. 2002. "The C. G. Jung and Allen Dulles Correspondence." In Aryeh Maidenbaum (ed.), *Jung and the Shadow of Anti-Semitism*, Berwick, ME: Nicolas-Hays, pp.39–54.

Daur, Rudolf (ed.). 1937. "C. G. Jung auf unserer Arbeitswoche. " *An der Schwelle. Bericht über die Arbeitswoche des "Köngener Kreises" in Königsfeld, vom. 1. Bis 6. Januar 1937, über Grundfragen des Seelenkunde und Seelenführung.* Heilbronn: Eugen Salzer, pp. 35–43.

Dierks, Margarete. 1986. *Jakob Wilhelm Hauer, 1881–1962: Leben, Werk, Wirkung; Mit einer Personalbibliographie.* Heidelberg: L. Schneider.

Freud, Sigmund. 2001. *Totem and Taboo.* Volume 13. The Standard Edition of the Complete Psychological Works of Sigmund Freud. London: Hogarth Press and the Institute of Psycho-analysis.

Gilman, Sander L. 1993. *Freud, Race, and Gender.* Princeton, NJ: Princeton University Press.

Hauer, Jakob Wilhelm. 1932. *Yoga als Heilweg.* Stuttgart: Kohlhammer.

——. 1935a. "Die Indo-arische Lehre vom Selbste im Vergleich mit Kants Lehre vom Intelligiblen Subjekt." In *Die kulturelle Bedeutung der Komplexen Psychologie: Festschrift zum 60. Geburtstag von C. G. Jung*, ed. the Psychological Club of Zurich, Berlin: Julius Springer, pp. 220–336.

——. 1935b. "Symbole und Erfahrung des Selbst in der indo-arischen Mystik." *Eranos Jahrbuch* 2:35–96.

——. 1938. *Das Wesen der Religion. Gesetz der religiösen Entwicklung.* Partial copy (PDF document) of Hauer's seminar manuscript.

Jaffé, Aniela. 1989. *From the Life and Work of C. G. Jung,* trans. by R. F. C. Hull and Murray Stein. Am Klosterplatz, Einsiedeln, CH: Daimon.

Jung, C. G. 1925. *Psychology of the Unconscious: A Study of the Transformations and Symbolisms of the Libido; A Contribution to the History of the Evolution of Thought*, trans. by Beatrice M. Hinkle. New York: Dodd, Mead.

——. 1953–1991. *Collected Works*, ed. by Sir Herbert Read, Michael Fordham, and Gerhard Adler. New York: Pantheon Books; Princeton, NJ: Princeton University Press.

——. 1956. "Wotan und der Rattenfänger: Bemerkungen eines Tiefenpsychologen." *Der Monat: Eine internationale Zeitschrift* (Oct.):75-76.

——. 1965. *Memories, Dreams, Reflections,* rec. and ed. by Aniela Jaffé, trans. by Richard and Clara Winston. New York: Vintage.

——. 1996. *The Psychology of Kundalini Yoga: Notes of the Seminar Given in 1932 by C. G. Jung*, ed. by Sonu Shamdasani. Princeton, NJ: Princeton University Press.

——. 1972. *Briefe,* ed. by Aniela Jaffé with Gerhard Adler. Three Volumes. Olten: Walter.

——. 1973. *Letters,* sel. and ed. by Gerhard Adler, with Aniela Jaffé, trans. by R. F. C. Hull. Two Volumes. Princeton, NJ: Princeton University Press.

Liebscher, Martin (ed.). 2015. *Analytical Psychology in Exile: The Correspondence of C. G. Jung and Erich Neumann*, trans. by Heather McCartney. Princeton: Princeton University Press.

McGuire, William and R. F. C. Hull (eds). 1980. *C. G. Jung Speaking: Interviews and Encounters*. London: Picador.

Mosse, George L. 1978. *Toward the Final Solution: A History of European Racism.* New York: Howard Fertig.

Noll, Richard. 1997. *The Aryan Christ: The Secret Life of Carl Jung.* New York: Random House.

Post, Laurens van der. 1976. *Jung and the Story of our Time*. New York: Pantheon.

Samuels, Andrew. 1993. *The Political Psyche*. London: Routledge.

Schoenl, William. 1996. *Major Issues in the Life and Work of C. G. Jung.* Lanham, MD: University Press of America.

Serrano, Miguel. 1966. *C. G. Jung and Hermann Hesse: A Record of Two Friendships,* trans. by Frank MacShane. London: Routledge and K. Paul.

Stocking, George. 1968. *Race, Culture, and Evolution: Essays in the History of Anthropology*. New York: Free Press.

Wasserstrom, Steven M. 1999. *Religion after Religion: Gerschom Scholem, Mircea Eliade, and Henry Corbin at Eranos*. Princeton, NJ: Princeton University Press.

Websites

[INT1] Berlin.de. "Verbannte Bücher: Online-Veröffentlichung der Liste der von den Nationalsozialisten verbotenen Schriften." Available at: https://www.berlin.de/rubrik/hauptstadt/verbannte_buecher/ (accessed Sept. 5, 2015).

Archived Material

Letters from the Federal Archive of Germany (Bundesarchiv), Coblenz, Germany

Correspondence between Jakob Wilhelm Hauer and Friedrich Spiegelberg

Friedrich Spiegelberg to Jakob Wilhelm Hauer, May 20, 1932. BA N1131/170-424, fol. 425.
Jakob Wilhelm Hauer to Friedrich Spiegelberg, May 24, 1932. BA N1131/170, fol. 423.

Correspondence between Jakob Wilhelm Hauer and Carl Gustav Jung

Jakob Wilhelm Hauer to Carl Gustav Jung, March 26, 1938. BA N1131/139, fol. 13.
Jakob Wilhelm Hauer to Carl Gustav Jung, May 12, 1937. BA N1131/139, fol. 21.
Carl Gustav Jung to Jakob Wilhelm Hauer, June 7, 1937. BA N1131/139, fol. 19-20.
Jakob Wilhelm Hauer to Carl Gustav Jung, June 12, 1937. BA N1131/139, fol. 18.
Carl Gustav Jung to Jakob Wilhelm Hauer, June 23, 1932. BA N1131/170, fol. 281.
Jakob Wilhelm Hauer to Carl Gustav Jung, July 2, 1932. BA N1131/170, fol. 277.

Correspondence between Jakob Wilhelm Hauer and Toni Wolff

Toni Wolff to Jakob Wilhelm Hauer, July 19, 1932. BA N1131/170, fol. 273.
Toni Wolff to Jakob Wilhelm Hauer, February 8, 1939. BA N1131/140, fol. 289.
Toni Wolff to Jakob Wilhelm Hauer, July 21, 1937. BA N1131/140, fol. 309.
Jakob Wilhelm Hauer to Toni Wolff, July 29, 1937. BA N1131/140, fol. 308.
Jakob Wilhelm Hauer to Toni Wolff, January 25, 1938. BA N1131/140, fol. 302.
Toni Wolff to Jakob Wilhelm Hauer, February 1, 1938. BA N1131/140, fol. 301.
Jakob Wilhelm Hauer to Toni Wolff, February 3, 1938. BA N1131/140, fol. 300.
Jakob Wilhelm Hauer to Toni Wolff, July 29, 1938. BA N1131/140, fol. 296.

Correspondence between Jakob Wilhelm Hauer and Emma von Pelet

Jakob Wilhelm Hauer to Emma von Pelet, February 10, 1941. BA N1131/136, fol. 58.

Correspondence between Jakob Wilhelm Hauer and Carl Alfred Meier

Carl Alfred Meier to Jakob Wilhelm Hauer, October 12, 1938. BA N1131/139, fol. 191-192.

Correspondence between Jakob Wilhelm Hauer and Christian Julius Mergenthaler

Jakob Wilhelm Hauer to Christian Julius Mergenthaler, March 28, 1938. BA N1131/139-211, fol. 211.

Materials from the ETH-Bibliothek Zurich (Switzerland): ETH Zurich University Archives, C. G. Jung Papers Collection

Anon. 1945. *Werden die Seelen Frieden finden: Ein Interview mit Prof. Dr. C. G. Jung*. No page numbers. Hs 1058a:256.
Letter from J. W. Hauer to C. G. Jung, Dec. 12, 1936. Hs 1056:4447.
Letter from C. G. Jung to J. W. Hauer, Dec. 21, 1936. Hs 1056:5001.

8

THE "MOST COMPLICATED PSYCHOLOGY"

The reception of analytical psychology in contemporary Heathenism

From archetype to god

The worship of Wotan has once again been gaining adherents over the past several decades. Today, many Germanic-based belief systems known collectively as Ásatrú, Odinism, Norse Paganism or Heathenism, as well as explicitly white supremacist groups who use ancient Germanic myths and symbols, can be found primarily in the United States, Great Britain, Germany, and Western Europe [INT6]. To the chagrin of Jung's fans who wish to protect his image from any associations with racism, National Socialism or anti-Semitism, it is those very works in which Jung theorized a German unconscious and archetype that Germanic religion revivalists embrace. Coupled with Jung's status not as a spiritual master per se, but as a psychologist who detailed the mysterious depths of the human psyche, these works are used to validate the claim of many Heathens that religion is genetically inherited and racially determined. This chapter explores the issue of race in contemporary Heathenism or *Ásatrú* through the words of the historian George Mosse:

> The impact of racism in modern times derives from the fact that it became a secular religion based upon science and history: it laid claim to the best of two worlds, that of science, which provided new "truths" from the eighteenth century onward, and that of history, which forged a link to traditions which were fast dissolving in the modern world.
>
> (Mosse 1988, 85)

Using Mosse's quote as a guide, this chapter argues that ethnic and racist Heathens combine certain ideas about science, race and religion to construct a new, race-delimited religion, appropriating Jungian psychology to further this aim.

Self-designations of contemporary Germanic-based religions

Ásatrú, Heathenism, Norse Paganism, Odinism – what's in a name? These terms designate a loosely networked contemporary religious movement based on ancient

Germanic religious traditions. Although this religion is part of the wider Pagan revival taking place in the West, practitioners usually do not call themselves Pagans, a word derived from Latin. Instead they call themselves Heathens, from Germanic languages (e.g., German, *Heide*, pl. *Heiden*). Other terms include the Northern Tradition and *Ásatrú* (Anglicized as Asatru). *Ásatrú* is an Icelandic neologism that means "trust in the Æsir," the chief pantheon of the ancient Germanic gods. The name *Ásatrú* was coined by Sweinbjörn Beinteinsson (1924–1993) when he founded the group Ásatrúarfélagið in Iceland in 1973. Ásatrúarfélagið has been legally recognized as a religion by the Icelandic government. The term *Ásatrú* was picked up by American groups, such as the Asatru Folk Assembly and the Asatru Alliance (often written without accent marks). A member of these groups is known as an Asatruer (pluralized in English either with "s", or with the Icelandic vowel shift from -er to -ar). Practitioners on both sides of the Atlantic use the term Odinism, usually to emphasize the worship of Odin over other Germanic deities. Whereas Kaplan writes that American Odinists tend to belong to the white racist movement (Kaplan 1997, 69), Gardell argues that many of the self-described Odinists he met during his field research in the United States expressed a greater interest in occultism than some self-designated Asatruers, who were more concerned with racial issues (Gardell 2003, 152). Ásatrú is preferred in both Scandinavia and Germany (Asprem 2008; Maréchal-Haas 2012). The German *Heidentum*, cognate with English Heathenism, actually refers generally to Paganism; to delineate a Germanic-specific form of Paganism, the label *germanisch* must be appended. In what follows, I use "Heathenism" to describe the movement as a whole, because the term is used in both Great Britain and the United States and the analysis that follows is drawn largely from the Anglo-cultural realm. I use the anglicized "Asatru" to refer to specific American Asatru groups or Asatru more generally.

As indicated by the various designations, this new religious movement lacks a central authority and a fixed dogma (Blain & Wallis 2009, 415). Rather, Heathen groups tend be organized as federations of smaller groups called "kindreds." Despite its name, a kindred is not necessarily family based, but is rather a community of practitioners who meet face-to-face, although some exist only in "virtual space" on the Internet or through mail ministries (Gardell 2003, 157). Heathens often also form guilds, where members practice mead brewing, rune magic, hunting, or handicrafts. Kindreds, guilds and larger bodies may be overseen by priests known as *gothar* (from Icelandic *goði*, pl. *goðar*), who are considered the "first among equals," while councils of "elders" handle kindred administration (Flowers 1981, 285; Gardell 2003, 158).

Organization and emphasis differ from group to group. For example, Stephen McNallen, one of the most influential leaders of American Asatru, is the chief priest of the federation Asatru Folk Assembly; however, he wields no authority over member kindreds (Flowers 1981, 285). The Odinic Rite-UK also has *gothar* and grants warrants to those groups who wish to align themselves with its guiding principles (282). The Rune-Gild, established by Edred Thorsson (a.k.a. Stephen E. Flowers) in the United States and led by Freya Aswynn in Great Britain, is primarily interested in an esoteric interpretation of the ancient Germanic script known as the runes. The members of this group use Thorsson's *Nine Doors of Midgard* as curriculum, supplemented by Aswynn's *Leaves of Yggdrasil.* The Gild has a hierarchical structure comprised of apprentices, fellows, and masters, modeled partly on medieval guilds, and partly on the university system, with fellows required to write a scholarly, annotated work on Germanic religion before being accepted as masters (Thorsson 2004, 24–25, 201).

Beliefs and practices: an overview

Contemporary Heathenism is a reconstructionist religious movement, meaning that it is not part of a longstanding, living tradition; rather, the members use ancient and medieval writings and artifacts related to the Germanic realm to "reconstruct" what they claim is the religion of their ancestors and to follow their ancestral traditions within a modern context (Blain & Wallis 2009, 414–415; Harvey 2007, 283–286; Kaplan 1997, 73; Thorsson 1989). In the words of the Rune-Gild leader Freya Aswynn:

> So the task at hand is to delve into the original sources as far as is possible, and from there to extrapolate the trend and follow this line of imaginary development up until the present day, thereby to restore the old Northern religion, integrated and acceptable, in a twentieth-century environment, backed up and emphasized by twentieth-century occult techniques (without the questionable benefit of twentieth-century politics!).
>
> (Aswynn 1990, xxv–xxvi)

The Heathen image of the cosmos is drawn from mythic material contained primarily in the *Poetic Edda* and *Prose Edda,* described in Chapter 2, and to a lesser extent in the medieval Icelandic sagas. Along with these primary source materials, members also use secondary scholarly literature on ancient Germanic religions (Flowers 1981, 283–284; Kaplan 1997, 70), as well as personal experience and intuition, which one unnamed North American member referred to as UPG, or "unusual personal gnosis" (Blain & Wallis 2009, 414; Flowers 1981, 283–284; see also Aswynn 1990, 110; Thorsson 1989, 5). Some Heathens also use the writings of many of the Germanic Faith and German magical circles from before and after World War II (Thorsson 1990, 7–8). Others draw on practices in medieval Icelandic sagas, such as *seid* in the *Saga of Eirik the Red* (Magnusson & Pálsson 1965, 81–83) to recreate those elements of practice that have not been preserved, adjusting them to meet the needs, imagination, and structures of modern communities (Harvey 2007, 284–285).

Like other contemporary Pagans, Heathens hold that the divine is immanent in both humans and nature. However, Heathens relate to their gods in different ways. Some members see them as real and self-existing entities or forces of nature.

Others describe them in Jungian terms as archetypal forces, that is, as psychological counterparts of the biological instincts that guide human action (Flowers 1981, 289; Gardell 2003, 156–157; Thorsson 1989, 63–64). Some authors argue via Lamarck and Jung that these archetypes were formed in the challenging Migration Period and the harsh northern climate. These tough living conditions formed virtues such as family loyalty and courage that then became encoded in the Germanic soul (e.g., Gundarsson 1993, 2–3). The gods are also seen as expressions of the pervasive and diffuse power of the numinous. Possibly reading Otto's neologism through Jungian archetypal theory, some Heathen authors such as McNallen see the gods as "a numinous logic-defying reality, something apprehended only by means of symbols, something that speaks to us on deeper levels where words are inadequate" (as quoted in Adler 1986, 287). This power is then constellated into the images of the deities.

Rituals and practices among Heathens generally include *blots*, *symbels*, *seid, galdor*, and runic divination. A *blot* is an offering, usually of food or drink. It may be a simple and individual ritual, related to household deities or personal needs, or performed as a community practice. A *symbel* is a ritual toast, made to venerate the deities, commemorate the ancestors, praise deeds accomplished or reinforce a community member's commitment to fulfill a promised act (Blain & Wallis 2009, 416, 419–422; Gundarsson 1990, 221–222). *Seid* is a shamanic-like practice that involves ecstatic and mind-altering techniques. Although this practice was traditionally ascribed to women, today men practice it as well (Blain & Wallis 2009, 427–428). *Galdor* is a magical runic practice involving chanting, singing, or mentally "projecting" the runes, and may be used in divination, talismanic magic and sympathetic magic (Thorsson 2004, 35, 82). Some Heathens also combine runic magic with yogic-like postures in community rituals (Gardell 2003, 160; Gründer 2009, 137–140). Finally, a trip to any major American bookstore will demonstrate the widespread (and not just Heathen) interest in runes as a means of divination.

Holidays and regular celebrations may include the three major festivals of Winter Nights or New Year (*Vetrnaetra*), between mid-October and mid-November; the twelve Nights of Yule (*Jul*) and the Winter Solstice; and *Ostara*, the spring equinox. Some groups also celebrate Midsummer, as well as the full and new moons (Blain & Wallis 2009, 420; Flowers 1981, 290–291; Gundarsson 1990, 219–220). Many groups have a yearly festival cycle of six great celebrations, but some groups celebrate the eight festivals found among other Pagan groups (Blain & Wallis 2009, 420; Harvey 1996, 57). Additionally, kindred members commemorate rites of passage, such as births, marriages and deaths, and some people partake in *Utsittning,* a ritual similar to Native American vision quests (Gardell 2003, 161). American practitioners also often participate in an annual Althing, which is a large collective gathering of kindreds. During this multi-day festival, attendees perform rituals, play music, hold feasts, work out organizational policies, and discuss social and political issues (Kaplan 1997, 87). Finally, holidays may be historical and site-specific. For example, since 2000, when October 9 was declared a day to commemorate the legendary Icelandic explorer Leif Erikson, many American Asatruers celebrate the day to honor their presumed ancestor (Gardell 2003, 151). Likewise, the Odinic Rite-UK celebrates the White Horse Stone in Kent on October 12. This is believed to be the burial site of Horsa, who in the fifth century conquered ancient Brytta with his brother Hengist (Harvey 1996, 55–56).

Some Heathen groups also have codes of ethics. For example, the Troth emphasizes "Boldness, Truth, Honor, Troth, Self-Rule, Hospitality, Industry, Self-Reliance, Steadfastness, Equality, Strength, Wisdom, Generosity, and Family Responsibility" [INT 21]. The Odinic Rite-UK lists "nine noble virtues" as their guiding principles, including courage, truth, honor, fidelity, discipline, hospitality, industriousness, self-reliance, and perseverance (Blain & Wallis 2009, 424; Gardell 2003, 157). The original "Nine Virtues of Ásatrú" of the Asatru Folk Assembly differed from the ethical codes of the Odinic Rite and the Troth by emphasizing "ancestry." The Asatru Folk Assembly now focuses on the sustenance and defense of a folk community, its heritage and its ancestry. It also encourages joy in living and the acquisition of wealth, advocates law and justice within the community and "the warrior principle" against forces deemed hostile to it. Finally, it promotes strong families, the pursuit of knowledge and wealth, loyalty to oaths, and the development of leadership and other skills [INT3]. Some researchers and practitioners have noted that such values hardly differ from those of the Protestant-based, capitalist-oriented societies that have given rise to these reconstructed religious paths (Blain and Wallis 2009, 424; Gardell 2003, 157). Moreover, the rejection of salvation from an outside source, and the emphasis on the individual's decision to live life with "courage and honor" ([INT8]), place Asatru in the spectrum of the modern bourgeois spirituality of self-redemption, explored in Chapter 3.

Race and religion

What is striking about the literature on Heathenism is the central role that "race" and "ancestry" play in the religion's theology and politics. Religious studies scholars Mattias Gardell and René Gründer use a tripartite model organized around this issue to examine American and German Heathenism respectively: on one extreme are anti-racist, inclusive groups, and at the other extreme are explicitly "Aryan" supremacist, *völkisch* or racist groups. Straddling the two are ethno-cultural groups (Gardell 2003, 162–164, 165–257, 258–283; ibid., 2009, 611; Gründer 2009, 141–142). Graham Harvey (2007, 286–287) obfuscates these distinctions by categorizing "ethnic paganisms" solely as non-Heathen East European *völkisch* Paganisms. This masks the fact that many Heathens describe their religion in ethnic terms or espouse a racist *völkisch* ideology. Indeed, the issue of race seems to affect the movement more broadly, because even non-racist groups must often explicitly distance themselves from racial exclusivism on their websites (e.g., Asprem 2008, 62).

Although the movement as a whole has shared beliefs and practices, Heathenism (like all other religions) has adapted itself to each country's cultural and political circumstances (e.g., Asprem 2008; Blain and Wallis 2009, 101; Schnurbein 1992, 87–89; Strmiska 2000). For example, American Heathenism has its roots in the more virulently racist end of the Heathen spectrum, specifically the Odinist Fellowship of Else Christensen (1913–2005). An adherent of Danish national-bolshevist Nazism, Christensen immigrated to North America after World War II. Inspired by American Nazism and the ideas of the Australian Church of Odin founder Rud Mills, Christensen founded the Odinist Fellowship in 1969 (Gardell 2009, 614) and a prison outreach ministry in the early 1980s (617). Christensen saw in Jungian theory support for her belief in an Aryan "folk soul," which she interpreted as a genetically inherited, racially specific collective unconscious. The origin of Odinism, she claimed, "is in our race, its principles encoded in our genes" (as quoted in ibid., 615). A statement in her group's magazine *The Odinist* vividly illustrates Mosse's contention that the modern construction of race has become a secular religion. According to the unnamed Odinist author:

> The most distinguishable feature of Odinism is that for the first time a religion has declared itself founded upon the concept of race, with its correlation to culture and civilization. Without race there is nothing; therefore our first duty is a study of race and the significance of Aryan people to world history.
>
> (As quoted in Adler 1986, 289; [INT2])

Another racist group is Wotansvolk, founded in 1995 by David and Katja Lane and Ron McVan (Gardell 2009, 618). David Lane (1938–2007) was a member of the violent white supremacist group the Order, once identified "as the most serious domestic terrorist threat in the country" (Michael 2009, 47). Lane participated in bank heists and robberies of armored cars, as well as the murder of the Denver radio talk show host Alan Berg in 1984 (Gardell 2003, 195; Michael 2009, 45–46). After going to prison, Lane wrote racist tracts that first expressed the views of the white supremacist Christian Identity movement, but later advocated Odinism as a warrior's path for white racists (Michael 2009, 50). Lane also originated the fourteen-word statement popular with white racists, "We must secure the existence of our people and a future for White children" (Gardell 2009, 618; Kaplan 1997, 94).

Wotansvolk enjoys legal status as a religion under the name of the Temple of Wotan, which has a high priest and a board of Trustees called the Guardians of the Faith (Michael 2009, 53). The organization spreads its message through the Internet, white power music (Gardell 2009, 618), and an ever-expanding prison outreach of over 300 prison "kindreds," officially recognized by the United States Federal Bureau of Prisons (623). Wotansvolk has also published *Temple of Wotan: Holy Book of the Aryan Tribes*, a work that contains Jung's "Wotan" essay, Germanic rituals and oaths, information on the runes, and excerpts from the *Poetic Edda*. According to Gardell, "Wotansvolk combines an Aryan call to arms with an esoteric teaching, based in part on Jungian psychology, völkisch philosophy, and occult national socialism" (618). Like Christensen, Lane and McVan draw on Jung's Germanic writings to argue that each race has a "racial soul," which they define through a Jungian lens as a racially delimited and genetically transmitted collective unconscious (620; [INT7]; see also Michael 2009, 52).

The *Temple of Wotan* contains a foreword written by the Chilean diplomat and "esoteric Hitlerist" Miguel Serrano (1917–2009) (McVan 2000, xv). Born in Santiago, Chile, Serrano held various diplomatic posts in different countries: India (1953–1962), Yugoslavia (1962–1964), Romania and Bulgaria (1964–1970). He was also an emissary to the International Atomic Energy Agency in Vienna and the United Nations Industrial Development Organization (UNIDO). As a young man, Serrano joined the primarily anti-communist Nazi party in Chile (est. 1932) in 1938, and began publishing his own pro-Nazi journal, *The New Age (La Nueva Edad)* in 1941. A year later, he was inducted into a Chilean esoteric order, which linked fascist ideology to Kundalini yogic theory and a Nietzschean will to power (Goodrick-Clarke 2002, 174–176).

During a trip to Europe in the 1950s, Serrano met and befriended both the novelist Hermann Hesse (1877–1962) and Jung. Jung wrote a letter to Serrano, dated January 14, 1960, which Serrano used as the foreword to his mystical novel, *The Visits of the Queen of Sheba* (*Las visitas de la Reina de Saba,* 1960) (Serrano 1966, 68). Serrano wrote several other books in which he incorporated Jungian themes, such as *El/Ella: Book of Magic Love* (*Elella, el libro del amor mágico*, 1973) and *Nos: Book of Resurrection* (*Nos: libro de la Resurección*, 1980). He also published *C.G. Jung and Hermann Hesse: A Record of Two Friendships (El círculo hermético, de Hesse a Jung,* 1965), in which he described his meetings with the two famous men. There is no sign of Serrano's National Socialist leanings in this book, and he portrayed in positive terms Jung's claim that Christ is the symbol of the self in the West. His dismissal by President Allende and his rejection by General Pinochet may have pushed him back towards rightwing extremism. Serrano later became disenchanted with Jung, seeing him as opportunistic, in that he aligned himself with Nazism during its reign in Germany, but after the war, tried to erase the evidence of his former support.

Disappointment in Jung did not mean disavowal of his theory, however. Relatively late in life, Serrano wrote a trilogy he called "esoteric Hitlerism": *The Golden Band: Esoteric Hitlerism* (*El Cordón Dorado: Hitlerismo Esotérico*, 1978); *Adolf Hitler, the Ultimate Avatar* (*Adolf Hitler, el Último Avatãra*, 1984); and *Manu: For the Man Who Will Come* (*Manú: Por el hombre que vendra*, 1991). In these works, Serrano argued that the Third Reich was an activated archetypal force that would destroy the old world order and usher in a new age (Goodrick-Clarke 2002, 174–176). He incorporated Jung's theory of diverging Germanic and Jewish collective psyches into his dualistic, racialized gnostic worldview, in which the Aryans, spiritual beings of light, battle against a dark lord, the Hebrew god Jehovah understood as the Demi-Urge of base matter (Serrano 1987, 152). For Serrano, the alleged fundamental differences in psychologies also indicate completely different gods and demons for each group of people. He further claimed that blood was the most mysterious of all substances, with origins in another universe; the collective unconscious is the "memory that lies in the blood." In three interviews from the 1930s, Jung had stated that Hitler listened to the voice of the Germanic collective unconscious (McGuire and Hull 1980, 103–104, 125–128, 143–144); Serrano interpreted that voice as the voice of this extraterrestrial blood ([INT20], 96).

The worldviews of the Odinist Fellowship, Wotansvolk and Serrano represent the extreme racist rightwing of contemporary "Aryan" religiosity, not the mainstream of contemporary Heathenism, which is comprised of ethnic and inclusive groups. At the same time, the boundary between racist and ethnic Asatru is often a porous one. Gardell notes the difficulty of dividing racist and ethnic Heathenism, when he asserts that the "organic relation between ethnicity and religion" presumed by ethnic Heathens implies that their religion, including its worldview and code of ethics, has a genetic component to it. Hence, the line dividing racist and ethnic groups often gets blurred.

Even the borders of the categories Gardell has established are not always clear. For example, Gardell classifies folkish Asatru as racist. This is somewhat confusing, given the fact that he lists the Asatru Folk Assembly under the category of "ethnic" Norse Paganism, despite the group's own embrace of the term *folkish*. The term *folkish* calls up associations to other words in English, such as *folk*, *folksy*, and *folklore*, words that convey that which is familiar and "down-home." An uncommon English word, *folkish* also brings to mind the German word *völkisch*, the racist connotations of which are now recognized in contemporary German culture.

The main ethnic Asatru groups in the United States are the Asatru Folk Assembly and the Asatru Alliance. The former was founded in 1972 as the Viking Brotherhood in Wichita Falls, Texas, by Stephen McNallen, who was influenced by Christensen (Gardell 2003, 260). In 1976, the Viking Brotherhood became the Asatru Free Assembly, which then splintered in 1986 into two groups, the "folkish"-ethnic Asatru Alliance and the inclusive Troth. After working as a military journalist, McNallen returned to the Heathen scene and was dismayed by the presence of "liberals, affirmative-action Asatrúars, black gođar, and New Agers" there (as quoted in ibid., 261). He subsequently established the Asatru Folk Assembly in Grass Valley, California, as an ethnic form of Asatru in 1994, which stresses "warrior values" and "ancestry." The Asatru Folk Assembly publishes the magazines *Runestone* and the warrior-oriented *Wolf Age* (ibid.). Together with Thorsson, McNallen developed a theory called metagenetics, which links ancestry and spirituality through Jung's racial writings (discussed below).

The Asatru Alliance is closely related to the Asatru Folk Assembly and is headed by Valgard Murray. He was introduced to Odinism through Elton Hall, the head of the American Nazi Party in Arizona, and like McNallen, also had contact with Christensen early in the 1970s. Murray became vice-president of the Odinist Fellowship; his Arizona Kindred was its first recognized kindred. The Asatru Alliance is today an association of autonomous kindreds (Gardell 2003, 261).

Both the Asatru Folk Assembly and the Asatru Alliance are home-grown American groups. Still, the members see themselves as intimately connected to Europeans of Germanic descent through common ancestry. For example, the Asatru Alliance uses the same list of answers to "Frequently Asked Questions" as the Asatru Folk Assembly, in which one may read that Asatru is the native religion of Europeans and their descendants, wherever they may now be located on the globe [INT9].

A group in Great Britain that could be classified as ethnic is the Odinic Rite (established in 1973), which claims to represent "the organic spiritual beliefs and way of life of the indigenous peoples of Northern Europe" and emphasizes "Faith, Folk, Family" (Harvey 1996, 56; [INT16]). The group further argues that each "race" has its own traditions that it should honor, and that racial and cultural plurality lead to social stress and confusion (Harvey 1996, 60). Like the Odinic Rite, the group Hammarens Ordens Sällskap ("In the Company of the Hammer") is also ethnic, with a membership based on Swedish descent. Members venerate the Vanir, the gods that rule production and reproduction. This religious orientation reflects the interest this group has in independent organic farms and folk-based crafts. Members reject the worship of Odin, insisting that this god embodies war (59).

The Rune-Gild appears more "ethnic" than not, while eschewing race or ancestry in favor of language as the criterion of inclusion. In earlier works, the Rune-Gild founder Edred Thorsson suggested that religion is a matter of racial or ethnic ancestry (Thorsson 1989, 61, 65). Today, the Rune-Gild rejects racism "without detracting from pride in one's own traditions" and is open to anyone who demonstrates "'contact'" with the "'Northern Folk-soul'" (Harvey 1996, 58). This contact seems to have more to do with one's mother tongue than one's racial or ancestral heritage, because the website of the Rune-Gild refers to people "interested in the heritage of the Germanic or Gothic peoples" as "all those who live in countries where a Germanic language (for example English) predominates" [INT19]. It is unclear whether the Rune-Gild has in mind only countries like the United States, Canada, Great Britain, New Zealand and Australia, or if its members realize that English is an official language of India and many African countries.

What differentiates ethnic from racist Heathenism, writes Gardell, is that racist Heathens hold rituals to preserve and strengthen the "Aryan" race, lay plans for a future racial war and actively participate in an underground armed resistance against the government. In contrast, ethnic Heathens focus on the gods and the seasons in their rites (Gardell 2003, 275). Furthermore, despite connections to racist groups in the formative years of the Asatru Alliance and Asatru Folk Assembly, their leaders now exclude avowed neo-Nazis and fascists, and they actively eschew the (overt) mixing of politics and religion. Indeed, racist pagans regularly denounce McNallen and Murray for failing to defend the "Aryan race."

Moreover, unlike white supremacist groups, ethnic Asatruar express a kind of "separate but equal" philosophy. Just as they believe their own religion is genetically encoded in their collective "folk soul," so too, they assert, is that of other peoples. While they claim that no one culture is superior to another, they also tend to reify and essentialize culture, imagining discrete racial groups with discrete cultures that have existed since the dawn of humanity. For example, one Asatru member explained to the Pagan journalist Margot Adler that it would puzzle her if African-Americans applied to her group for membership, because she would want to know why they were not interested in "their own religious roots" (Adler 1986, 288). Similarly, the members of the Odinic Rite-UK believe that the mixing of cultures leads to "confusion," arguing instead that each "race" should develop its own traditions. McNallen adamantly rejects membership from non-whites in Asatru. He argues that each "folk" has its own collective soul connected to a long line of ancestors, which one cannot arbitrarily adopt (Gardell 2003, 273). As Gardell points out, "[A]lthough most take exception to racism, adherents of the ethnic position share certain presuppositions with racist paganism" (Gardell 2009, 611). Furthermore, both the Southern Poverty Law Center and the Coalition for Human Dignity categorize these American ethnic Asatru groups as part of the white racist movement (274), and at least one ethnic Asatru leader, Max Hyatt of Wodan's Kindred, has intentionally aligned himself with ethnic Asatru in order to make the religion more acceptable in today's society, while opining that Asatru is the true "religion for the white race" (276–277).

Groups at the "inclusive" end of the spectrum not only welcome any person regardless of race or ethnicity who feels "called" to this religion, but often extend their welcome beyond ethnic boundaries to embrace people of other religious paths or diverse gender and sexual orientations. For example, the American Vinland Association in San Francisco rejects all forms of discrimination, accepting as members "those who say that they are Tru," without reference to race or ancestry [INT1]. Also located in the San Francisco Bay Area is the group Hrafnar, spiritual home of the Pagan author Diana Paxson, who collaborated with Marion Zimmer Bradley on the popular *Avalon* series. Hrafnar is open to all people "whom the gods have called to this path" [. . .] "regardless of gender, ethnic origin or sexual orientation" [INT5]. The Norwegian group Bifrost distances itself from racist groups such as Vigrid, led by the neo-Nazi Holocaust revisionist Tore Wilhelm Tvedt, and explicitly warns Neo-Nazis to seek membership elsewhere (Asprem 2008, 60–62). Furthermore, the Odinshof in Great Britain openly embraces multiculturalism, multiple faiths, and lesbigay people (Harvey 1996, 57; [INT17]; [INT18]). Finally, the Ring of Troth understands religion to be a matter not of race or ancestry, but of "heart and soul." This group is ethnically pluralistic, gender egalitarian, environmentalist, and open to other forms of Paganism (Gardell 2003, 163). Its mission statement welcomes "all people, whatever their religious, cultural, or ancestral background, gender or sexual orientation, who have developed or wish to develop a relationship with our Gods and Goddesses, and would like to know more about Asatru" [INT21].

Jenny Blain and Robert Wallis, both of whom are Pagan practitioners and social scientists, claim that Heathens who are either ethnic or inclusive keep their distance from the extreme right; however, they do not indicate what percentage of the entire Heathen population belongs to which general category (Blain and Wallis 2009, 422). Thorsson suggests that the ratio of racist to nonracist Astaruar is 40:60, whereas Valgard Murray thinks there is an even 50:50 split between the two wings. Both Thorsson and Murray believe the racist members to be more committed to their views than those in the non-racist groups, who are more likely to explore other paths beside that of Asatru. Where ethnic Asatru fits into the divisions proposed by Thorsson and Murray remains unclear (Gardell 2003, 153).

The role of Jungian theory in contemporary Heathenism

As the previous discussion suggests, Jungian theory provides another source of religious reconstruction, especially for those Heathens who consider their religion to have a racial or ethnic basis. Generally speaking, several contemporary Heathens have developed the following points drawn from Jung's writings in their own works: the inheritability of archetypes; a Germanic archetype of the self; a racially delimited unconscious; and the exoneration of Germans for Nazi-era atrocities by describing historical events in archetypal terms.

Like racist Heathens, ethnic Asatruar utilize Jung's theory that archetypes are built into the structure of the brain to justify their claim that cultural and religious heritage is inherited biologically [INT11]. Ethnic Heathens argue that, despite the conversion of the Germanic tribes to Christianity in the Middle Ages and the misuse of ancient Indo-European religious symbols by the Nazis, Heathenism is experiencing a revival because it belongs to the genetic inheritance of people of Northern European descent. As evidence of this claim, several Heathen authors quote Jung's "Wotan" essay, which neatly combines the two strands of racial theory that Mosse had designated as racial mysticism and the science of race.

Along with Jung's more general archetypal theory, certain Heathen authors use his hypothesis of a Germanic-specific archetype. For example, Jung's implicit claim that Wotan is the Germanic archetype of the self forms the basis of Thorsson's curriculum for the Rune-Gild. In *The Nine Doors of Midgard,* Thorsson describes Wotan as the Heathen Self, which is cultivated through the Rune-Gild's spiritual exercises (Thorsson 2004, 17, 23, 48). Thorsson differentiates this path from other Odin-oriented forms of Heathenism by asserting that, while Odinists pray to their god, members of the Rune-Gild are actually transformed into the divine, in the sense that the true self of the practitioner is also that of Wotan (17). This amounts to a sacralization of the person of Germanic descent through the development of a magical persona (26, 167). Ultimately, Thorsson sees the members of the Rune-Gild as the secret guardians of the Folk and as Wotan's "chosen people" (18).

Furthermore, certain authors use the theory of the racially delimited collective unconscious to argue for a biologically given cultural continuity. In the foreword to Aswynn's book, *Leaves of Yggdrasil*, the magician Lionel Snell (a.k.a. Ramsey Dukes) argues from a Lamarckian, or rather, Jungian standpoint that primordial humans made repeated experiences with language that seemed magical to them, and these early associations became "embedded in the group mind, or 'collective unconscious'" (as quoted in Aswynn 1990, xiii). Aswynn herself repeats this idea when she says that the repeated use of magic symbols engraved on rocks and stones in the Bronze Age in Europe over generations "invested the runes with special powers; consequently a large-storage memory bank was built up in the collective Northern unconscious" (Aswynn 1990, 109).

Finally, some authors reiterate Jung's exoneration of National Socialism in "Wotan" by recourse to archetypal theory. For example, Snell interprets the change of religion in Northern Europe as a kind of group psychic repression when he writes that the Germanic gods had been "driven down into the collective unconscious and abandoned." As in Jung's theory, Snell implies that archaic deities do not disappear when economic, political or cultural conditions change, since such conditions are not their true source; rather, gods represent whole religious systems that spring from a given population's shared psycho-biology. Having been shoved back into the archaic collective unconscious, the ancient gods became feral, Snell writes, like house pets released into the woods. When they were brought back into consciousness in the early twentieth century, their feral condition led to catastrophic results (Snell 1990, xiv).

Likewise, Thorsson claims that the Germanic deities, embodied in people of Germanic stock, have been experiencing a "reawakening." He alludes to the catastrophe of the Nazi-led World War II and Holocaust in terms that minimize the enormity of the massive crimes committed, while exonerating the people who actually carried them out: "That they [the deities] have been stirred has already been shown by some unfortunate events of this century," he writes. "As unpleasant and ineffective as these events proved to be, they are still signs of a fully living divine power. No other 'revivalist' movement can claim anything close to these signs of vitality" (Thorsson 1989, 68).

Snell and Thorsson exonerate early twentieth-century Germanic religious revivalists for their participation in and creation of doctrines and practices often laced with Germanic-supremacist and anti-Jewish sentiments. Instead, they displace blame for the murderous political movement of National Socialism onto Christianity for having suppressed Germanic religiosity in the first place. These kinds of esoteric explanations for historical events are par for the course in New Age and magical circles. They are also standard fare in other prophetic movements, including Jewish and Christian ones, in which political events may be interpreted as "God's wrath" or signs of the Second Coming of Christ. What they all have in common is that they mask the fact that the driving force behind historical events is not divine will but the activity of human actors.

Metagenetics

Today's biological sciences are dominated by genetic research. Not surprisingly, some Heathens seek to ground their claim of a race-based religiosity in genetics. One attempt is via Jungian psychology in a theory called "metagenetics," which has found widespread resonance among ethnic Asatruar (Gardell 2003, 270, 387, fn. 17; cf. Kaplan 1997, 80). McNallen first published the concept in an article of the same name, printed in 1980 in *Runestone*, calling metagenetics "a science for the next century" [INT13]. This article was republished in *Selections from Runestone: An Odinist Anthology* and tagged as the most important article published in the journal (Kaplan 1997, 197, fn.35). McNallen then revisited the argument in "Genetics and Beyond: Metagenetics – an Update" (1999), also published in *Runestone* and online on the Asatru Folk Assembly website [INT11].

This article illustrates how some contemporary Heathens such as McNallen weave together science, religion and race to support their claim that Asatru is genetically inherited. To do so, however, McNallen makes several leaps in his logic. He begins the first article with the ethnic Asatru tenet that "ancestry matters," by which he means "there are spiritual and metaphysical implications to heredity, and that we are thus a religion not for all of humanity, but rather one that calls only its own." The idea that there is a genetic link between religion and ancestry is not racist, argues McNallen, but a scientific fact. Drawing on research conducted by the Danish scientist Dr. N. Jule-Nielson showing that twins raised apart "have similar aptitudes and personalities," and a statement by the ESP researcher Dr. J. B. Rhine that identical twins seem to share an "exceptional telepathic rapport," McNallen concludes that non-twin kin must also share psychological and spiritual characteristics, not from living together, but rather from having common genetic compositions. He then extends this line of argument to all people of the same race [INT11]. McNallen also briefly mentions the work of Dr. Daniel G. Freedman, which indicated the possibility of inborn behavioral differences among newborns of different ethnic groups. McNallen points out that, in Norse and other cultures, people believed reincarnation took place only within families. He uses this ancient belief as evidence to support his claim that religion is genetically inherited, and once again extends the notion of family to cover an entire racial group.

Race, however, is a modern concept and was unknown in pre-Christian Norse culture (Gardell 2003, 161–162; Hannaford 1996, 8). Furthermore, McNallen seems unaware that Norse society lacked a static definition of family and kin relations. Because Iceland was a country founded by individual immigrants, not corporate family groups, the significance of different kinds of kin underwent certain changes. Unlike elsewhere in Norse society, where patrilineage and agnatic groups were chief social organizing principles, Icelanders formed alliances with cognatic kin members, in-laws, and even non-kin-based political associations to protect their property and conduct feuds (Byock 1988, 128). Furthermore, medieval Icelanders practiced many forms of "fictive kinship," such as foster brothers (*fóstbræðr*), sworn brothers (*svaribræðr*), and oath brothers (*eiðbræðr*) (Byock 1988, 127; Miller 1990, 172–173). None of these fictive kin relations was necessarily based on genetic affiliation, and the bonds of loyalty formed through them could predominate over those between blood relations. For instance, the *Edda* author Snorri Sturluson had been fostered to Jón Loftsson (d. 1197) as a child, and later remained more loyal to the powerful Oddaverjar clan at Oddi than to his own blood kin (Miller 1990, 173). Indeed, destitute kin members worked as servants to richer relatives (121–122). Even in Norway, extremely significant bonds were formed that were not kin-related, such as those related to marriages and assemblies. Although McNallen claims that "there are metaphysical implications to the bond of genetic kinship" [INT13], it would be more accurate to say that metaphysical implications are *imputed* to these phenomena, in the same way that metaphysical implications are imputed to kingship, temples, reliquaries, and so on, by historically conditioned human beings in specific social settings. And like those settings and beings, the presumed metaphysical implications are wont to change as the given society does.

McNallen then turns to Jung's claim that archetypes have a biological basis, quoting the footnote from Jung's *The Relations between the Ego and the Unconscious* (reprinted in CW 7) that was discussed in Chapter 5 ("Differing Primitivities of the 'Germanic Barbarian' and 'Jewish Psychology'"). In this quote, Jung maintained that there is a universal basis to the collective unconscious, but that because the racial and religious differences within the collective psyche are so fundamental, following the precepts of another group's psychology would harm one's own psychological health (Jung CW 7 (1963 [1928]):240, fn.8 in [INT13]). Jung racialized religion in this passage, lending the desired scientific justification to McNallen's claim that religion is genetically inherited. McNallen writes, "Thus the link between religion, which expresses itself in terms of archetypes in the collective unconscious, and biology – and hence race – is complete" [INT13].

That McNallen understands Asatru as a racial religion becomes even clearer in the penultimate paragraph of his "Metagenetics" article. He argues that religion is neither invented nor culturally transmitted. Rather, it arises from the biological makeup of a given people, "people" here defined not as a cultural entity but as a racial group. McNallen concludes, "We are intimately tied up with the fate of our whole people, for Asatru is an expression of the soul of our race" (ibid.).

In "Genetics and Beyond: Metagenetics – An Update" (1999), McNallen again defines metagenetics as having spiritual aspects. He suggests that the "mechanics" for this spiritual-genetic aspect may lie outside the DNA molecule itself. Hence, McNallen's theory remains inaccessible to scientific testing, despite his desire to wed science and religion in support of his racial claims.

McNallen divides his new definition of metagenetics into the categories of *relatedness*, *similarity*, *hierarchy*, *holism* and *spirituality*. *Relatedness* indicates "a connection, independent of time and space, which links human beings." *Similarity* narrows the application of the concept of relatedness to "people who are genetically related to each other" and who therefore "share a non-physical bond that is not dependent on location or time" (ibid.). McNallen possibly draws on Jung's theory of the "'geology' of the personality" to argue that *hierarchy* emphasizes degrees of relatedness and similarity of "Folksouls" from the least related (humanity in general) to the most related (family), with clans and tribes falling in between.

Holism indicates the mind-body-spirit connection, especially the body's presumed biological relationship to religion. Finally, *spirituality* is influenced by relatedness and similarity. In effect, McNallen asserts that people of the same race have a soul-substance in common that connects them psycho-spiritually with each other, wherever they may be in the world, despite differences in cultural background, religious upbringing, and language. In other words, McNallen hypothesizes a closer connection between himself and presumed religiously and racially pure ancestors living thousands of years ago, than between himself and other members of the multicultural and poly-ethnic society in which he actually lives.

McNallen then seeks to explain more clearly the implications of the terms summarized above. He begins by once again asserting that "[a]ncestry matters," emphasizing that a person is one with his or her ancestors, since they are reborn in later generations within the same family line. Although all people are related to each other, and to all of life, writes McNallen, the bond between those connected by the principle of genetic "similarity" is necessarily much more significant than any other form of similarity. The acts and rituals of Asatru therefore reinforce this similarity, since they strengthen the psycho-spiritual bonds between genetically related individuals "in a fairly immediate way" [INT11]. This statement of "European" siblinghood effectively excludes all those non-Germanic European populations whose ancestral religious beliefs and practices lie outside of the Germanic circle of deities and their human devotees, in particular the Hungarians, the Sami (Finns), and the Basque (see also [INT8]). Finally, McNallen states, "Our religion is a function of who we are, not just what we believe," because "our ancestors are encoded into our very beings." Ultimately, religion is not a matter of conscious choice or upbringing for McNallen; rather, all people should feel naturally drawn to their ancestral religion (ibid).

Gardell argues that the metagenetics theory is racist, because its claims extend beyond physical features to values and mores. According to metagenetics, cultural values are not taught, but genetically transmitted. White skin is correlated with a certain set of values –specifically, the Asatru Folk Assembly's "nine noble virtues" or its more current code of ethics – and in turn, these values are considered more properly white. The introduction of racially different genetic matter into a lineage allegedly dilutes the bloodline; thus, the values, culture and religion correlated with a given race are thereby also presumably diluted. One might assume that a so-called mixed-raced person would be able to worship two sets of deities equally, rather than neither. But according to the adherents of metagenetics, continues Gardell, a person of mixed racial heritage born and raised in the same cultural milieu as members of Asatru is inherently different, not just in superficial physical aspects, but in fundamental spiritual ones as well. Such a person would therefore be viewed as torn in his or her religious loyalties, and would be told by believers of the metagenetics theory to opt for only one religious tradition – as long as that one was not Asatru. Conversely, a person of northern European descent growing up in a non-Europeanized part of the world and speaking a non-European language would instantly qualify for membership (Gardell 2003, 271–273).

Not all Asatruar agree with McNallen's theory, and their reasons for disagreement are drawn from myth, history, and different national heritages. For example, the anti-racist Asatruer Gamlinginn claims that Asatru is a "multi-ethnic religion," based on the various lines of descent of the gods themselves: the sons of Thor, Magni and Modi, are the children of Jarnsaxa, a giantess, and the matrilineage of Odin is also of giant stock (Gardell 2003, 273–274). Furthermore, the former Lore Warden of the Troth Kveldulf Gundarsson dismisses the metagenetics theory by arguing that, because Viking men impregnated their Irish female slaves, contemporary Icelanders are therefore of mixed ancestry (Kaplan 1997, 77). In addition, Jón Ingvar Jonsson, the former Lawspeaker of Ásatrúarfélagið, believes that each national Asatru group should have more in common with indigenous religions within the same national boundaries, with whom they share culture, history and tradition, and less with Asatru groups elsewhere in the world, which have developed in different cultural and historical contexts (Strmiska 2000, 117–118). Moreover, the film director Mo Asumang celebrates her mixed cultural heritage (Ghana and Germany) in her documentary *Roots Germania*. After receiving death threats from a Neo-Nazi, she sets off on a quest to explore her roots in both cultures. This leads her into talks with both parents, conversations with hard-core racists, and celebrations with inclusivist, Goddess-oriented Pagans. The film concludes with her confronting her would-be assassin and asserting her kinship with her ancient Germanic forebears (Asumang 2007).

Finally, Irminsul Ættir member Garadyn McOisdealbhaigh published an online response paper, entitled "Metagenetics: The Fear of Penetration and the Penetration of Fear." He describes McNallen's theory as a "totalizing narrative that attempts to seal the borders and protect itself from contamination from the Other." He refutes McNallen's extension of the possibly genetically induced psychic bond between twins to other family members by arguing that the psychological connection demonstrated by kin members probably has more to do with "heightened intersubjectivity" due to social and cultural factors, not racial makeup, and he denounces McNallen's confinement of the concept of reincarnation to rebirth in family lines as "[a]n obvious apology for separatist ideology." Finally, he asserts that McNallen "almost hysterically" ignores the influence of culture to explain shared psychological dispositions, instead theorizing an eternal racial essence passed genetically from one generation to another largely without mutation. He argues that race is an unstable category, in that ethnically defined groups such as the Celts have for generations intermarried with people from other communities, thereby blurring their boundaries and transforming into new groups. The Asatruar themselves stem from a mix of multiple cultures from the time before and after the Neolithic revolution. These assertions lead McOisdealbhaigh to conclude, "Whose racial memory ends up on top?" While McOisdealbhaigh does not deny the "generative capacity for archetypal representation," he asserts that it is "not racially stable or fixed" [INT15].

McOisdealbhaigh's article points to the crux of the problem with McNallen's theory: it relies on the idea of race, a highly unstable and scientifically unsound concept that remains unanalyzed throughout his writings. The theory of metagenetics assumes racial purity, which in the United States is historically based on a legal fiction created to uphold the institution of slavery and Jim Crow segregation. Legally, a child who had only one black great-grandparent was deemed to be of black blood, regardless of the racial classification of the other grandparents. This "one-drop" theory still forms the basis of racial classification in the American legal system (Stoler 1995, 51), and has become part of the general American view of race, such that a person with any amount of African heritage and even with relatively lightly pigmented skin color is still considered "black."

In the colonial era, race came to serve the needs of the landed gentry, who used it to forge a wedge between white and black indentured servants and slaves, solidifying the status of blacks as the slave class, while penalizing whites who revolted with blacks against their common exploitation or who bonded with blacks through intimate relationships. Lower-class whites were thereby led to identify more with their upper-class white masters. At the same time, another legal maneuver encouraged a particularly brutal mixing of blacks and whites: under British common law, a child received his status from his father; colonial law reversed this rule when the mother was a slave. This legal switch tacitly justified the rape of black enslaved women by their white male masters, who exploited them to breed the next generation of slaves (Roediger 2008, 28–29). Today, the genetic makeup of a not insignificant percentage of contemporary Americans classified as black demonstrates evidence of white ancestry (Cavalli-Sforza 2001, 74).

Despite our tendency to sort people into discrete racial categories, the notion of racial purity is a fiction, and a particularly bad one at that. As the geneticist Luigi Luca Cavalli-Sforza explains, "[T]he careful genetic study of hidden variation, unrelated to climate, has confirmed that homogenous races do not exist. It is not only true that racial purity does not exist in nature; it is entirely unachievable, and would not be desirable" (Cavalli-Sforza 2001, 13). To produce a pure race would require the practice of strict inbreeding between very close relatives for well over twenty generations. This would not lead to the once dreamt-of "super-race," "Aryan" or otherwise, but physically weak and crippled human beings, prone to sickness and disabilities (13, 47). Furthermore, human populations are not discrete units; rather, there is a "genetic continuum" between them (40). Despite obvious physical differences between populations from very different parts of the globe, there is usually more genetic variation within groups than between them (Thomas 2000, 112).

The visible physical differences that usually indicate the geographical origin of a person's ancestors may have developed primarily due to environmental factors, and probably only after the emergence of modern humans in Africa 100,000 years ago, who then expanded into new climates. Skin color was probably originally dark, to protect humans against exposure to intensive ultraviolet radiation near the equator. Since the skin needs ultraviolet radiation to produce vitamin D from certain precursor molecules found in cereal grains (Cavalli-Sforza 2001, 10), white skin may have developed as human populations moved north, in order to allow more absorption of the less intense ultraviolent radiation in the Northern hemisphere. Other visible physical differences – nostril and eye shape, body build and hair type – also appear to be largely influenced by climate. However, how genes actually produce such changes in response to environmental conditions is unknown, because physical characteristics are genetically quite complex (11). In sum, the research of modern genetics does not support the notion of fixed racial groups; rather, this research indicates that the ideas of racial purity and an unchanging racial essence should be put in the same file of false scientific theories such as aether and phlogiston.

Race and religion, revisited

As the previous discussion shows, the ethnic Asatru notion of race or ancestry has strong religious connotations. The appellation "ancestors" is regularly applied only to those forebears who lived in the very remote past, excluding more recent ancestors who lived after the beginning of the Christian era in Northern Europe. For example, the Asatru Folk Assembly website poses the question "Why is 'the religion of our ancestors' the best one for us?" and answers it as follows:

> The religion which best expressed their innermost nature – Asatru – is better suited to us than is some other creed which started in the Middle East among people who are essentially different from us. Judaism, Islam, and Christianity are alien religions that do not truly speak to our souls. [INT17]

The reader is left with the impression that ancestors of the past millennium somehow just do not count as such. Perhaps they were too "conditioned" by the allegedly foreign religion of Christianity, just like McNallen's contemporaries, who are "genetically related" but reject such racialized metaphysics because they have "not yet shaken off the conditioning of modern culture" [INT12]. McNallen articulates the ethnic Asatru view that distinct racial groups with specific, racially determined religious orientations formed way back in a mist-shrouded prehistory [INT17]. This line of reasoning simply overlooks the ten or more centuries (depending on tribe and land) that the Germanic peoples have been Christian.

In contrast, Jung drew numerous affinities between the Christian and Germanic myths, as the discussion in previous chapters has shown. Even though he wrote in his 1923 letter to Schmitz that Christianity was a foreign religion, the parallels he drew between Christ and Wotan imply that he believed the presumed essence of Christianity corresponded to what in his eyes was inherently Germanic. Although many ethnic and racist Asatruar embrace certain tenets of Jungian theory, this is one aspect they would adamantly reject. Unlike Jung, they deny absolutely that Christianity could share affinities with the racial-religious makeup of Heathens.

Both Heathens and Pagans often portray Christianity as an interloper religion, a foreign product forced onto an ancient native community. For example, several Heathens declare Christianity to be an "alien religion imported from the Middle East" (Aswynn 1990, 57) or a "Middle Eastern cult" (Thorsson 1989, 11; [INT10]). In the cultural wars of the late twentieth century, the word "cult" was a pejorative applied to many new religious movements. Against this historical background, the word "cult" appears as a strategic rhetorical move by Heathens to trivialize the very religion whose members often condemned the new religions that developed during that time. The use of the phrase "Middle Eastern cult," however, calls to mind the term "Near Eastern spirit" (*vorderasiatischer Geist*) used by Hauer and other anti-Jewish German(ic) Faith adherents in the broader German cultural realm around the turn of the last century. Indeed, some white separatist Norse Pagans reject Christianity as a "Middle Eastern religion," arguing that it is essentially Jewish (Dobratz 2011, 294). Implicit in this claim is the view that Jews constitute a separate race. As the child of Judaism, Christianity must therefore spring from a different racial soul, one that also gave birth to Islam.

Race, religion and territorial rights

The claim that there is an inherent biological connection between race and religion contains ramifications for contemporary struggles over immigration, belonging, and group sovereignty. An article by McNallen, entitled "Wotan vs. Tezcatlipoca: The Spiritual War for California and the Southwest" (ca. 2007, [INT14]) shows how Jungian thought in tandem with racial mysticism may be marshaled in service of contemporary nativist and anti-immigration agitation. McNallen extends his racial-religious essentializing to an incredibly racially diverse group of people – Mexicans – for the rather invidious purpose of creating panic in whites against Latino immigrants to the United States.

He begins his piece by suggesting that the ancestral gods of the Aztecs and Mayans are beginning to stir again, which, according to hearsay, he says, happens before a political revolution. His evidence for his claim is the preponderance of new sightings of the Virgin of Guadeloupe in Mexico. He interprets these sightings of the Catholic Mother of God as cloaked images of Tonatzin, a term from Aztec mythology for female deities. Echoing Jung on the emergence of new spiritualities across Europe's early twentieth-century cultural landscape, McNallen speculates that these sightings indicate an upsurge of movement within the Mexican collective unconscious.

He increases his sense of urgency by discussing evidence of syncretism between the ancient indigenous religions and Catholicism – a phenomenon that is hardly new – under a title designed to invoke contemporary images from Eastern Europe of emaciated prisoners and mass graves: "Aztlan, Ancient Deities, and Ethnic Cleansing." He warns that the ancient deities of the warring Aztecs are awakening in the unconscious of Latinos everywhere, threatening an outbreak on par with what Jung detailed in his 1936 "Wotan" essay. McNallen takes Jung's seat to theorize Mexican racial archetypes, Tonatzin and Tezcatlipoca, whom he says are driving their people to war against whites. As in Nazi Germany, Mexicans are being seized by their folk-specific archetype, and like the catastrophe of the Holocaust and World War II, a disaster appears imminent. McNallen then asks rhetorically, "Can we expect any less from the bloodthirsty deities of the Aztecs, renowned for their warlike ways and human sacrifice on a mass scale?" [INT14]. The implication is that white people should fear for their lives when they witness Aztec dances being performed on Catholic feast days or observe the foot traffic in and out of the local *botanica*. Only late in the article does McNallen reveal what is really causing him concern: "being overwhelmed with illegal immigrants" [INT14]. McNallen makes no distinction between legal and illegal immigrants from Mexico, nor does he acknowledge that many "Mexicans" are actually American citizens.

Even works from what is considered the more inclusive branch of Asatru contain exclusionary statements that may be appropriated in contemporary struggles over territory, nationality, and citizenship. For example, in *Leaves of Yggdrasil*, Aswynn underscores the presumed connection between the primordial environment and genetic inheritance in her discussion of *othila*, the o-rune (ᛟ). The traditional meaning ascribed to this rune is "inherited land," and *othila* is etymologically related to Anglo-Saxon *atheling*, German *Adel*, and Dutch *edel*, all words meaning "prince, nobleman." Aswynn, however, interprets the rune so as to sanctify the initial conquest of the British Isles by the Angles and the Saxons. She writes:

> The mystery of blood and soil are also a part of this runic complex. Unfortunately, this mystery has been misrepresented by twentieth-century German politicians who had little knowledge of its real meaning. For the Anglo-Saxons, as for other nations in earlier times, the consecration of the soil by shedding blood in battle to conquer that territory ensured their willingness to defend it against subsequent would-be invaders.
>
> (Aswynn 1990, 100)

Kveldulf Gundarsson, the former Lore Warden and Master of the Elder Training Program of the Ring of Troth, acknowledges the racist implications of such runic interpretations. In *Teutonic Magic,* he writes that this rune "may also create a sense of racial or cultural prejudice;" therefore, one must take care not to be swayed by its negative influences. However, he also states that this rune "shows the mysteries of the ancestors and the blood-and-soil of the homeland as the truth held in all the beliefs about 'native earth'" (Gundarsson 1990, 158).

The phrase "blood and soil" arose in the *völkisch*-Romantic milieu of late nineteenth-century Germany, and was embraced by Richard Walther Darré (1895–1953), the Agricultural Minister (*Reichbauernführer*) of the Nazi government, who in works such as *A New Aristocracy Based On Blood And Soil (Neuadel aus Blut und Boden*, 1930) created a portrait of the Germans as originally aristocratic farmers wed to their land. Walther Wüst (1901–1993), a Nazi intellectual, Orientalist, and the Rector of the University of Munich (1941–1945), embraced

Darré's ideas and formulated the notion of "blood and soil" in the esoteric ways that some contemporary Asatruar seem to prefer, such as, for example, "Man – Blood Inheritance – Faith Power" (Arvidsson 2006, 192; See 1994, 312). "Blood and soil" was also the slogan according to which the S.S. judged the racial purity of people living in Eastern territories occupied by the Nazis, a life-or-death decision for those so judged.

Gundarsson's uncritical embrace of an official Nazi slogan seems puzzling, given that this "PC Pagan" has been a strong voice against racism in contemporary Heathenism, using both sociological and mythological studies of Old Norse culture to highlight kin formations that contradict the racial claims of ethnic and racist Asatruar (Gardell 2003, 163; Kaplan 1997, 77). His use of the "blood-and-soil" slogan is also deeply troubling because, along with Thorsson, Gundarsson is one of the early leaders of contemporary Heathenism who earned a Ph.D. Gundarsson wrote his doctoral thesis, *The Cult of Óðinn: God of Death?,* under the name of Stephan Grundy at the University of Cambridge in 1994. His perspective on historical sources therefore carries the weight of scholarly authority, lending support to interpretations such as Aswynn's, that the mystery of "blood and soil" was an ancient Germanic idea distorted by the Nazis, rather than one formulated by nineteenth-century nativist and racist movements that helped pave the way for National Socialism. Furthermore, the aforementioned books were published in the United States as part of Llewellyn Publications' Teutonic Magick Series; hence, ideas developed in pre-World War II and National Socialist Germany have been transmitted to a post-war American audience and presented as authentic ancient Germanic belief. Those Heathens who are serious about forming a non-racist religious practice will need to grapple with the reality of the modern Germanic religious revival's history, one which is fraught with the racism and nationalism that were prevalent in early twentieth-century German and European society.

The Kennewick Man and the "complications of American psychology"

Due to their views that each "race" has its own ancestral heritage and religion, some American ethnic Asatruar have been very supportive of Native American efforts to retain their own religious traditions against encroachments by cultural outsiders. Both Murray and McNallen have met with Native American leaders, and they argue that non-Native Americans should respect and leave alone the religious traditions of Native Americans. Murray proudly notes that certain tribal leaders consider him to be a healer of his people. Both he and McNallen have asked their Native American allies to send any white people looking for a new spiritual path to them (Gardell 2003, 281–282).

Despite this inter-religious cooperation, ethnic Asatruar and certain Native groups came into sharp conflict over an ancient skeleton known as the Kennewick Man. In 1996, this skeleton was discovered on the bank of the Columbia River in Kennewick, Washington. The bones were sent for analysis to the forensic anthropologist Jim

Chatters who, in reconstructing the skull's facial features, believed the head to have "Caucasoid" features. Indeed, Chatters' reconstruction bore an uncanny resemblance to the English actor Patrick Stewart, renowned as Captain Jean-Luc Picard of the television show, *Star Trek: The Next Generation*.

Based on his reconstruction, Chatters reports that he first believed the skeleton was that of a nineteenth-century trapper of European descent. However, according to subsequent radiocarbon tests, the skeleton turned out to be about 9,200 years old, one of the oldest skeletons discovered in the United States. An alliance of five Northwest Indian tribes – the Nez Perce, Umatilla, Yakima, Wanapum, and Colville – subsequently demanded the bones be handed over to them under the Native American Graves Protection and Repatriation Act (NAGPRA), while scientists clamored for access to the skeleton (Gardell 2003, 149; Thomas 2000, xxii).

Chatters' declaration that the man was Caucasoid caused a media sensation. His word choice implied that Europeans counted among the earliest human inhabitants of the Americas. Some journalists subsequently wrote headlines challenging the Native American claim to First Nation status (Thomas 2000, 114). The Caucasoid-like features modeled by Chatters also caught the attention of members of both Asatru and the white supremacist group Aryan Nations, who suggested that the Indian tribes involved wanted to hide evidence of a white presence in North America as old as that of Native Americans (Gardell 2003, 150).

In October 1996, McNallen and William Fox filed a lawsuit against the Army Corps of Engineers to prevent the Corps from turning the Kennewick Man skeleton over to the Northwestern Indian tribes. The complainants used current debates in American archaeology concerning the peopling of the Americas to argue that not only proto-Indians but also possibly proto-Caucasians trekked across the Bering Strait over 11,000 years ago (for two views on the debates, see Fiedel 2004 and Thomas 2000). Furthermore, according to the complaint, the Asatru Folk Assembly had the right to sue for the bones under NAGPRA, claiming that Asatru was the indigenous religion of ancient Germanic "tribal nations." The lawsuit further stated that "there is very convincing evidence that [the Kennewick] Man is a kinsman to plaintiffs rather than kinsman to the Umatilla tribes" [INT10].

On April 6, 1998, the Army Corps of Engineers defied an order of Congress to leave the Kennewick site alone, covering it with boulders, gravel, dirt, and densely planted trees. This move cost taxpayers $160,000 and made further research impossible (Thomas 2000, xxiv; Morell 1998, 25–26). McNallen responded by claiming that the Army Corps of Engineers wanted to hide the evidence of a mass murder – not one against Native Americans, but one against Europeans. He argued that it was whites who were the victims of genocide at the hands of Native Americans some 9,000 years ago, as if to negate the known history of a genocide perpetuated against Native Americans by Europeans since the landing of Columbus on Hispaniola. McNallen reportedly said, "[The Army Corps of Engineers] literally want to bury the evidence. I mean, this is a political hot potato. The idea of Caucasians that might have walked across the Bering land bridge along with the Native Americans is awesome. It changes the whole question of who was here first! Who genocided who?" (as quoted in Gardell 2003, 150).

After a three-year legal battle, the Asatru Folk Assembly gave up its bid for the bones due to lack of funds. McNallen responded to the failed bid with an anachronistic yet emotional and evocative statement: "In a world where the bones of Leif Erikson's men would be labeled 'Native American' there is no hope for a reasonable, logical, fair solution" (as quoted in Gardell 2003, 282). Assuming that the land Leif Erikson reached as reported in *The Saga of Eirik the Red* and *The Saga of the Greenlanders* was North America, then he landed on the northeast coast, not the northwest one. Furthermore, according to the sagas themselves, he and those following him never ventured farther than the coast (Magnusson and Pálsson 1965, 54ff., 64ff., 84ff., 91ff., 122). More importantly, Leif Erikson lived only 1,000 years ago, while the Kennewick Man is over 8,000 years older. Although McNallen's claim of ancestral connection to Leif Erikson is hardly plausible, the Kennewick Man controversy seems to have hit a nerve in the American Asatru scene. It has been discussed across the spectrum of American Heathenism, from the online Yahoo "Asatru Heathen" discussion group [INT22], to the response paper by Susan Granquist and Daniel J. O'Halloran, "Kennewick Man and Asatru," posted on the Irminsul Ættir website [INT4]. Hence, although McNallen's claim about Leif Erikson's men has little factual worth, it has a strong emotional appeal for those European Americans wishing to legitimate their claim to American soil. Indeed, the attempt on the part of the Asatru Folk Assembly to de-Indianize the Kennewick Man may be placed within a longer history of whites' attempts to deterritorialize Indians discursively by naming as the first Americans the Lost Tribes of Israel, mythical Welsh sailors, and ancient, non-Indian mound builders, who were then decimated by Indian invaders (Thomas 2000, xxix).

The archeologist David Hurst Thomas implicitly refutes the racial assumptions behind the Asatru legal claim when he explains the problems with Chatters' forensic reconstruction of the Kennewick Man's face. According to Thomas, forensic speculation may often (but not always) prove to be accurate when determining the racial classification of a contemporary bone (Thomas 2000, 113); however, it does not work historically, because physical features – even skull size and shape – can change under the influence of a host of factors. The Kennewick Man skeleton is over 9,000 years old. Just a few of the most salient factors that might have had a bearing on Kennewick Man's skull shape and those of his descendants include the relative lack of genetic diversity among the first immigrant groups to the Americas, with genetic diversity increasing with new arrivals; dramatic changes in climate in the past 10,000 years; new environments filled with different flora and fauna; the invention of agriculture; the introduction of new diseases from Europe; and the shifts in diet from pre-Neolithic to modern grocery-store fare (Thomas 2000, 115–116).

The mutability of human skulls was in fact demonstrated by the German-born American anthropologist Franz Boas (1858–1942) about 100 years ago. At the turn of the last century, craniometry was the scientific method of choice used to calculate racially determined intelligence differences (102). The cephalic index (the ratio of maximum skull breadth to maximum skull length) was considered a reliable determinant of a skull's racial classification. For example, whites were considered long-headed (dolichocephalic) and Mongolians round-headed (brachycephalic). In 1908, Boas decided to test the theory of discrete racial types through a study of New York City's immigrant population. He measured the head shapes of Russian Jewish boys and compared those measurements to data collected in Europe. To his surprise, he found striking differences in the cephalic index. A year later, he and his assistants measured the heads of immigrants who had just arrived at Ellis Island, and followed up with a door-to-door survey of various New York neighborhoods, measuring the heads of foreign-born parents and American-born children. All in all, the heads of 18,000 people were measured, including East European Jews, Bohemians, Sicilians, Poles, Hungarians and Scots. When he presented his findings in 1911, his conclusion read in part:

> Head form which has always been considered one of the most stable and permanent characteristics of human races, undergoes far-reaching changes coincident with the transfer of the people from European to American soil . . . These results are so definite that while heretofore we had the right to assume that human types are stable, all the evidence now is in favour of a great plasticity of human types, and the permanence of types in new surroundings appears rather as the exception than as the rule
> (as quoted in Thomas 2000, 104)

In effect, Boas demonstrated that environmental factors have a significant impact on skull size, thereby disproving the claim that race is a stable biological characteristic (Thomas 2000, 103–105).

Boas had already reached some of these conclusions by the time he lectured at the 1909 Clark University conference that both Freud and Jung attended (Shamdasani 2003, 277). This was Jung's first visit to the United States, and he incorporated the opinions he formed then about American race and culture into an essay on American psychology first published in 1930. Entitled "Complications of American Psychology," the essay may be found in the same tenth volume of Jung's *Collected Works* that houses many of his other writings on race cited by Asatruar. Despite the many references to Jung that one comes across when reading works by contemporary Heathens, this essay is conspicuously absent. A perusal of the essay quickly reveals why: the racial views Jung expressed in this work differ significantly from those of ethnic Asatruar.

In "Complications of American Psychology," Jung argued that white Americans –specifically, those of Germanic descent – were noticeably different from their ancestors and relatives in Europe. As discussed in Chapter 4 ("Going 'shenzi': Blackness as Mental Illness"), Jung claimed in this work that white Americans' mannerisms shared similarities with those of African-Americans due to racial "infection." The essay begins with a different quandary, however. Jung related that he was walking with an American colleague one day in Buffalo, New York at closing time. Hundreds of factory workers suddenly filled the street, and to his great surprise, Jung saw that the appearance of these (apparently) white workers showed signs of racial admixture with Native Americans. His American colleague scoffed at the idea; these workers were of Scottish, Irish and German descent, and there was probably not a drop of Indian blood among them. But Jung insisted: "[D]on't you see their faces? They are more Indian than European" (Jung CW 10 (1930):948). Jung then mentioned Boas' research as support for his personal observation, explaining that Boas had demonstrated measurable anatomical differences between European immigrants to the United States and the following, American-born generation (ibid.). He further reinforced Boas' conclusion by describing the children in a family of German immigrants that he visited in New York; according to Jung, the three children born abroad looked and behaved in significantly different ways from those born in the United States (para. 949).

Jung therefore concluded that "there is a marked difference" between white Americans and Northern Europeans, "within as well as without" (para. 967). Jung argued that every land has what he called a "genius" or "spiritus loci," which helps determine the atmosphere, the way people look, their language and behavior, their interests and ideals, and their politics and religion (para. 972). According to Jung, not just the cranium, but also the psyche of European-Americans seemed to have been affected by Native Americans, giving rise to what he called the reigning characteristic of American culture: the heroic ideal (para. 976). Beyond Americans' obsession with money, wrote Jung, Americans strive to be the best in everything they do, and loudly commend others for their achievements. They drill into their children the need to achieve, and happily watch heroes performing great deeds on the screen at the local cinema (ibid.). As further evidence for Indian spiritual influence in European-American culture, Jung mentioned the gladiatorial style of American sports; Christian Science, which Jung considered a form of shamanism; and secret societies such as the white racist terrorist organization Ku Klux Klan, which Jung shockingly and incorrectly compared to primitive mystery religions. Jung even espied the influence of "the red man" in the skyline of New York City, which, in his eyes, was similar to the outline of Taos Pueblo (para. 978).

As with his explanation of the influence of blacks on whites in America, Jung did not believe that the influence of Native Americans on European-Americans was due to cultural transmission or intermarriage; rather, Jung argued that European-Americans had been assimilated to the land of America on a deep psychic level. He wrote, "The foreign country somehow gets under the skin of those born in it" (Jung CW 10 (1930):968–969, quote in para. 969). Although he referred to Boas' research to support his theory, Jung's interpretation of Boas' conclusions was at odds with Boas' own understanding of race. Boas sought to de-stabilize the concept of race altogether by arguing that an ethnic group's physical characteristics could be altered by environmental changes. Jung, in contrast, spiritualized the notion of race in similar fashion to *völkisch* thinkers at the turn of the last century by arguing for an inherent connection between a racial group and the climate and geography in which it originally formed. For Jung, race was not just an aspect of human biology, but extended to the soul and soil as well.

Unlike American ethnic Asatruar, who theorize similarity between Europeans and European-Americans, Jung theorized difference, one that is both physical and psycho-spiritual. In Jung's eyes, European-Americans are decidedly not like Europeans; rather, they bear marked similarities to Native Americans. Jung referred to the environmental theory of Boas, but distorted Boas' conclusions in a *völkisch*, racial-mystical direction, assuming that a racially distinct spiritual essence comprised of a mixture between "blood and soil" had profoundly altered the racial-spiritual aspect of Americans of European descent. According to Jung, therefore, contemporary white Americans are not purely European, but are part Indian.

Jung's racial theory differs from the Asatru claim regarding the allegedly time-transcending nature of the metagenetic bond by making a German *völkisch* argument regarding the power of the soil to shape a people. Following Jung's logic, a Native American Kennewick Man could therefore very well be the ancestor of contemporary American Asatruar, because they are spiritually just as much the descendants of an *Indian* Kennewick man as a *European* one. Moreover, if Jung were right in his theory, a white American could justify an interest in Native American religious traditions as his or her ancestral religion, rather than the religion of contemporary Asatru.

Despite ethnic Heathens' reliance on Jungian psychology to defend their claim that "ancestry matters," their fundamental racial theory diverges sharply from that of Jung. The racial theory underlying the idea of metagenetics is the product of insidious racial politics in American culture and history, by which European settlers created a sharp cleavage between themselves and those whose lands and labor they expropriated. Jung's racial theory, no less insidious, was instead forged in the different cultural and historical context of German Romanticism and *völkisch* ideology, the latter articulating the desire to exclude all "foreign elements" by spiritualizing the relationship between a people and its territory.

Conclusion

Jung's psychology is only one of many forms of scientific discourse employed by those contemporary Heathens who seek to root their new religion in the credo of race. Whether their concepts are drawn from the science of religion, the reconstructions of proto-Germanic and Indo-European religious ideas, archaeological discoveries, genetics or analytical psychology, these scholarly discourses are marshaled by ethnic and racist Heathens, often in rather general and imprecise ways, to defend their religion as an expression of the race of its practitioners. However, scientific research demonstrates that race as a scientific category is spurious. Furthermore, detailed attention to the various claims made about race demonstrates that the concept itself is unstable and conditioned by differing cultural and historical contexts. Finally, the ethnic and racist Heathens mentioned here combine racial science and racial mysticism to justify often invidious claims about who rightfully belongs in a given territory – and who does not. Recognizing that many Heathens consider themselves to be non-racist and even racially inclusive, they should be encouraged to interrogate more thoroughly the ideology embedded in terms such as *ancestry*, *nation*, and *blood and soil*, as well as in the scholarly and Germanic Faith literature they often use as doctrine and inspiration for their religion today.

Bibliography

Title

The "most complicated psychology": C. G. Jung, "The Complications of American Psychology" (1930), *Collected Works* 10:980, ed. by Sir Herbert Read, Michael Fordham, and Gerhard Adler. New York: Pantheon Books; Princeton, NJ: Princeton University Press.

Sources

Adler, Margot. 1986. *Drawing Down the Moon: Witches, Druids, Goddess-Worshippers, and Other Pagans in America Today.* Revised Edition. New York: Penguin/Arkana.

Arvidsson, Stefan. 2006. *Aryan Idols: Indo-European Mythology as Ideology and Science.* Chicago: University of Chicago Press.

Asprem, Egil. 2008. "Heathens Up North: Politics, Polemics, and Contemporary Norse Paganism in Norway." *The Pomegranate* 10(1):41–69.

Asumang, Mo. 2007. *Roots Germania.* Written and directed by Mo Asumang. Potsdam, DE: MA Motion Filmproduktion / Mo Asumang.

Aswynn, Freya. 1990. *Leaves of Yggdrasil: Runes, Gods, and Feminine Powers.* St. Paul, MN: Llewellyn.

Blain, Jenny and Brian J. Wallis. 2009. "Heathenry." In Murphy Pizza and James R. Lewis (eds), *Handbook of Contemporary Paganism,* Leiden: Brill, pp.413–431.

Byock, Jesse L. 1988. *Medieval Iceland: Society, Sagas, and Power.* Berkeley: University of California Press.

Cavalli-Sforza, Luigi Luca. 2001. *Genes, Peoples and Languages*, trans. by Mark Seielstad. London: Penguin.

Dobratz, Betty A. June 2011. "The Role of Religion in the Collective Identity of the White Racialist Movement." *Journal for the Scientific Study of Religion* 40(2):287–301.

Fiedel, Stuart J. 2004. "The Kennewick Follies: 'New' Theories about the Peopling of the Americas." *Journal of Anthropological Research* 60(1):75–110.

Flowers, Stephen E. 1981. "Revival of Germanic Religion in Contemporary Anglo-American Culture." *The Mankind Quarterly* 21(3):279–294.

Gardell, M. 2003. *Gods of the Blood: The Pagan Revival and White Separatism.* Durham: Duke University Press.

——. 2009. "Wolf Age Pagans." In Murphy Pizza, and James Lewis (eds), *Handbook of Contemporary Paganism.* Leiden: Brill, pp.611–626.

Goodrick-Clarke, Nicholas. 2002. *Black Sun: Aryan Cults, Esoteric Nazism, and the Politics of Identity.* New York: New York University Press.

Gründer, René. 2009. "Runengeheimnisse: Zur Rezeption esoterischen Runen-Wissens im germanischen Neuheidentum Deutschlands." *Aries* 9(2):137–174.

Gundarsson, Kveldulf. 1990. *Teutonic Magic: The Magical and Spiritual Practices of the Germanic People*. St. Paul: Llewellyn.

Hannaford, Ivan. 1996. *Race: The History of an Idea in the West.* Washington, D.C.: Woodrow Wilson Center Press.

Harvey, G. 1996. "Heathenism: A North European Pagan Tradition." In G. Harvey and C. Hardman (eds), *Paganism Today: Wiccans, Druids, the Goddess and Ancient Earth Traditions for the Twenty-First Century*. London: Thorsons, pp.49–64.

——. 2007. "Inventing Paganisms: Making Nature." In J. Lewis, O. and Hammer (eds), *The Invention of Sacred Tradition*. Cambridge, UK: Cambridge University Press, pp.277–290.

Jung, C. 1953–1991. *Collected Works*, ed. by Sir Herbert Read, Michael Fordham, and Gerhard Adler. New York: Pantheon Books; Princeton, NJ: Princeton University Press.

Kaplan, Jeffrey. 1997. *Radical Religion in America: Millenarian Movements from the Far Right to the Children of Noah*. Syracuse, NY: Syracuse University Press.

Magnusson, Magnus and Hermann Pálsson (eds). 1965. *The Vinland Sagas: The Norse Discovery of America.* Harmondsworth, Middlesex, UK: Penguin Books.

Maréchal-Haas, Ann-Laurence. 2012. Lecture on contemporary Asatru in Germany in Carrie Dohe's seminar on "Germanic Myth and Ideology in Theory, Scholarship and Religion". Philipps University Marburg.

McGuire, William and R. F. C. Hull (eds). 1980. *C. G. Jung Speaking; Interviews and Encounters*. London: Picador.

McVan, Ron (ed.). 2000. *Temple of Wotan: Holy Book of the Aryan Tribes*. St. Maries, ID: 14 Word Press.

Michael, George. 2009. "David Lane and the Fourteen Words." *Totalitarian Movements and Political Religions* 10(1):43–61.

Miller, William Ian. 1990. *Bloodtaking and Peace-Making: Feud, Law and Society in Saga Iceland*. Chicago: University of Chicago Press.

Morell, Virginia. 1998. "Kennewick Man: More Bones to Pick." *Science* 279:25–26.

Mosse, George L. 1988. *The Culture of Western Europe: The Nineteenth and Twentieth Centuries.* Third Edition. Chicago: Rand McNally.

Roediger, David R. 2008. *How Race Survived U.S. History: From Settlement and Slavery to the Obama Phenomenon*. London: Verso.

Schnurbein, Stefanie von. 1992. *Religion als Kulturkritik: Neugermanisches Heidentum im 20. Jahrhundert*. Heidelberg: Winter.

See, Klaus von. 1994. *Barbar Germane Arier: Die Suche nach der Identität der Deutschen*. Heidelberg: C. Winter.

Serrano, Miguel. 1966. *C. G. Jung and Hermann Hesse: A Record of Two Friendships*, trans. by Frank MacShane. London: Routledge & K. Paul.

——. 1987. *Das goldene Band: Esoterischer Hitlerismus,* trans. by F. Urtho. Wetter, Teut-Verlag, R. Schepmann.

Shamdasani, Sonu. 2003. *Jung and the Making of Modern Psychology: The Dream of a Science.* Cambridge, UK: Cambridge University Press.

Snell, Lionell. 1990. Foreword to Freya Aswynn, *Leaves of Yggdrasil: Runes, Gods, and Feminine Powers*. St. Paul, Minn.: Llewellyn, pp.xi–xvi.

Stoler, Ann Laura. 1995. *Race and the Education of Desire: Foucault's History of Sexuality and the Colonial Order of Things*. Durham: Duke University Press.

Strmiska, Michael. 2000. "Ásatrú in Iceland: The Rebirth of Nordic Paganism?" In *Nova religio* 4(1):106–132.

Thomas, David Hurst. 2000. *Skull Wars: Kennewick Man, Archaeology, and the Battle for Native American Identity*. New York: Basic Books.

Thorsson, Edred. 1989. *A Book of Troth*. St. Paul: Llewellyn.

——. 1990. *At the Well of Wyrd: A Runecaster's Handbook*. New York: Samuel Weiser.

——. 2004. *Die Neun Tore von Midgard: Ein magischer Lehrplan der Runen-Gilde*. Uhlstädt-Kirchhasel, DE: Arun-Verlag.

Web pages and online sources

[INT1] American Vinland Association. (n.d.) *Our Charter*. This page no longer exists, but was previously available at: http://www.freyasfolk.org/charter.html (Accessed: April 5, 2011).

[INT2] Christensen, Else. 1985. *Odinism – Religion of the New Age*. This page no longer exists, but was previously available at: http://www.newnation.tv/forums/showthread.php?p=406819 (Accessed: April 10, 2011).

[INT3] Asatru Folk Assembly. (n.d.). This page no longer exists, but was previously available at: http://www.runestone.org/vrts.html (Accessed: April 21, 1998).

[INT4] Granquist, Susan. (n.d.) *The Kennewick Man Story*. Available at: http://www.irminsul.org/arc/199704a.html (Accessed: August 27, 2011).

[INT5] *Hrafnar*. (n.d.). Available at: http://www.hrafnar.org/ (Accessed: August 16, 2011).

[INT6] Irminsul Ættir. 2004. *Ásatrú Worldwide*. Available at: http://www.irminsul.org/aw/aw.html (Accessed: August 18, 2011).

[INT7] Lane, David. *Wotanism (Odinism)*. Available at: http://www.mourningtheancient.com/dl-2.htm (Accessed: May 24, 2015).

[INT8] McNallen, Stephen. 2008. "Asatru – A Native European Religion." YouTube video, 5:45. Available at: http://www.youtube.com/user/smcnallen#p/a/f/0/cDvPdW-BeEFc (Accessed: Nov. 11, 2011).

[INT9] —. *Asatru Q&A*. Asatru Alliance. Available at: http://www.asatru.org/aboutasatru.php (Accessed: May 24, 2015).

[INT10] —. *FAQ*. Asatru Folk Assembly. Available at: http://www.runestone.org/about-asatru/faq.html (Accessed: April 5, 2011).

[INT11] —. *Genetics and Beyond: Metagenetics – An Update*. Asatru Folk Assembly. Available at: http://www.runestone.org/articles/metagenet2.htm (Accessed: April 5, 2011).

[INT12] —. *In Defense of the Folkish View*. Asatru Folk Assembly. Available at: http://www.runestone.org/about-asatru/articles-a-essays/138-in-defense-of-the-folkish-view.html (Accessed: May 1, 2011).

[INT13] —. *Metagenetics*. Asatru Folk Assembly, 1985, updated and copyrighted 2007-2008. Available at: http://www.runestone.org/articles/metagenet1.htm (Accessed: December 21, 2008).

[INT14] —. *Wotan vs. Tezcatlipoca: The Spiritual War for California and the Southwest*. Asatru Folk Assembly, 2011. Available at: http://www.runestone.org/about-asatru/articles-a-essays/150-wotan-vs-tezcatlipoca-the-spiritual-war-for-california-and-the-southwest.html (Accessed: May 1, 2011).

[INT15] McOisdealbhaigh, Garadyn. *Metagenetics: The Fear of Penetration and the Penetration of Fear*. Irminsul Ættir. Available at: http://www.irminsul.org/arc/008gm.html (Accessed: May 24, 2015).

[INT16] Odinic Rite UK. *The Odinic Rite Q&A*. Available at: http://www.odinic-rite.org/main/faq/ (Accessed: April 5, 2011).

[INT17] Odinshof UK. 2011. *Buddhist community through the Dharmahof - Northern Buddhist Kindred.* Available at: http://www.gippeswic.demon.co.uk/odinshof.html (Accessed: April 5, 2011).

[INT18] Odinshof UK.2011. *Constitution of the Odinshof.* This page no longer exists, but was previously available at: http://www.gippeswic.demon.co.uk/ohconst.html (Accessed: April 5, 2011).

[INT19] Rune-Gild.2011. *Welcome to the Rune-Gild / Rune-Gild: Introductory Information*. This page no longer exists, but was previously available at: http://www.runegild.org/?page_id=19 (Accessed: April 5, 2011).

[INT20] Serrano, Miguel. 1984. *Adolph Hitler, der letzte Avatar*. Internet Archive. http://*www.archive.org* (Accessed: April 5, 2011).

[INT21] The Troth. 2011. *The Troth Mission Statement.* Available at: http://www.thetroth.org/index.php?page=mission&title=About%20Us%20|%20The%20Troth&css=style2&pagestyle=mid (Accessed: April 5, 2011).

[INT22] Yahoo Groups. "Asatru Heathen." Available at: https://groups.yahoo.com/neo/groups/Asatru/conversations/messages?messageStartId=1064&archiveSearch=true (Accessed: April 5, 2011).

9

CONCLUSION: "MAN AS HE WAS – AND WILL ALWAYS BE"?

Racial essentialism, scientific discourse, and new spiritualities

Race and religion in contemporary politics

In 2010, Thilo Sarrazin published *Germany Abolishes Itself: How We Are Putting Our Country at Risk (Deutschland schafft sich ab: Wie wir unser Land aufs Spiel setzen)*. A Social Democrat and former executive board member of the German Central Bank, Sarrazin accused the Muslim citizens of Germany of undermining German society. He made sweeping claims about Muslims' inability to integrate, their high birth rates and their lack of intelligence. To support his views, he filled his book with references to scientific studies, but the fact-finding investigations conducted by journalists and scholars alike easily showed how careless Sarrazin had been with the supposedly factual evidence he trotted out to bolster his inflammatory remarks. Still, his book became a bestseller and sparked a fiery debate, as people across Germany both praised and denounced him (Pollack 2013, 89). Sarrazin crossed a line on August 28, 2010, however, in an interview with the newspaper *Welt am Sonntag*. During the talk, he racialized Judaism by claiming that all Jews share the same gene, one that gives them a higher than average intelligence quota. Despite being an apparent compliment, the claim caused an uproar in a country that still wrestles with its National Socialist past. Furthermore, this assertion about Jewish genetics was embedded in a scathing attack on Germany's Muslim residents; that is, Sarrazin paid a compliment toward one minority group, Jews, in order to highlight the alleged failings of another minority, Muslims, whom Sarrazin tacitly racialized and homogenized as a single foreign group (Bode et al. 2010).

A year earlier, on January 20, 2009, Barack Hussein Obama was sworn in as the forty-fourth president of the United States of America; he is considered the first non-white man to occupy that office. While Obama was still running for president, clips from sermons given by Jeremiah Wright, Obama's former pastor at the Trinity Church of Christ in Chicago, were aired by ABC News in March 2008. These clips showed Wright denouncing racial and economic inequality in the United States, yet in terms and tones that led viewers to charge him with racism. Wright's ire raised the specter of the "angry black man," a ghost that began to haunt Obama as well. Although Obama's mother, Stanley Ann

Dunham (1942–1995), was a white American from Kansas and of English and Irish descent, some people questioned whether Obama could fairly and impartially serve all Americans as their president. In response, Obama gave a speech on March 18, 2008, at the National Constitution Center in Philadelphia, entitled, "A More Perfect Union." He distanced himself from Wright's statements, while addressing the fears and anger different racial groups in the United States have towards each other. He ended by calling on the nation to fulfill its historic mission by creating a better and more harmonious society (Obama 2008).

During this time, the rumor had been circulating that Obama was not born in the United States, but in Kenya, the home of his father, Barack Obama Sr. (1936–1982), or that he had become a citizen of Indonesia as a child and had therefore lost his U.S. citizenship. Although Obama had already given the press a copy of his Hawaiian birth certificate in 2008, doubts about his American birth continued to circulate. The ashes of this hysteria kept being fanned back into flames by Fox News, Republican politicians, and Donald Trump, a business magnate and Republican presidential candidate. Finally, Obama released the long form of his birth certificate and "roasted" Trump at the 2011 Annual White House Correspondents Dinner on April 30 (Obama 2011), thereby temporarily stilling the "birther" controversy and ending Trump's 2012 bid for the White House.

Yet another controversy was brewing over Obama's religious orientation. He faced a "smear" campaign online, in e-mail, and on Fox News, in which it was alleged that Obama was a Muslim, rather than the practicing Christian that he is. Despite repeated statements by the White House and a lack of evidence on the part of the conspiracy theorists, a survey conducted by the Pew Research Center showed that the number of Americans who believe that Obama is Muslim increased from 11 per cent in 2009 to 18 per cent in 2010 (Pew Research Center 2010).

As the authors of the 2011 multi-country European survey, "The Abasement of Others" (*Die Abwertung der Anderen*) demonstrate, people who express prejudice toward one social group are likely to discriminate against other groups as well. Furthermore, xenophobia and Islamophobia are strongly correlated (Zick, Küpper and Hövermann 2011, 79). Although one may not generalize from Europe to the United States, these survey results may shed light on the ongoing, myriad challenges to Obama's presidency due to his purported national, racial, and religious identities, which indicates that the categories of race and religion are blurred in many Americans' minds. Obama's White House victory signaled that his attempt to cast himself as a hard-working, well-educated, and racially unmarked middle-class man succeeded with a majority of voters, most of whom are white. Yet another politically influential part of the American population still clings to the myth that the United States is a white, Christian nation, and its leader should therefore reflect that state in his own being.

At the end of 2014, Germany convulsed when a movement to halt the alleged Islamification of Europe burst onto the streets of several cities. Calling itself Patriotic Europeans against the Islamification of the West (*Patriotische*

Europäer gegen die Islamisierung des Abendlandes, or PEGIDA), the movement quickly spread from its birthplace in Dresden, spawning other demonstrations from Cologne to Berlin to Leipzig. In response, masses of Germans counter-demonstrated for an open, tolerant society. As an American ex-pat living in Germany, I watched with interest and alarm as Germans contended with Germans over their changing national identity. PEGIDA since has dwindled in numbers, with small demonstrations still occurring like clockwork every Monday. Still, the fears and resentments the movement gave voice to are only increasing as more individual terrorist attacks occur and more refugees from Africa, the Near East and elsewhere risk their lives crossing the Mediterranean to reach Europe's shores. Ironically, a majority of Germany's immigrants through 2014 were probably European and Christian, not Muslim (Denkler 2015).

These contemporary controversies involving both high-ranking politicians and average citizens in two powerful western democracies demonstrate that the themes discussed in the previous pages are neither merely a historical problem, nor a marginal issue today. Indeed, the debates surrounding Sarrazin, Obama and PEGIDA connect to a central issue running through this work, which concerns the racialization of religion and the spiritualization of race. The present book illustrated these themes by first examining Jung's theory of a Germanic archetype and "Aryan" unconscious, then the reception of this theory in the ethnic and racist branches of contemporary Heathenism.

In our modern age, scientific discourse is one of the highest forms of authoritative speech, competing with and even superseding religious discourse. To use a term coined by Otto and psychologized by Jung, one could say that scientific discourse has itself become a kind of *numinosum*. Hence, founders of new religious movements often seek to incorporate scientific-sounding discourses into their religious doctrines to legitimize the social and political ideologies contained in their new spiritualities. Jung combined religious and scientific discourses in a particularly seductive way, because he masterfully wove together the objective language of science with the eternal language of myth. This pattern is repeated by the host of new religious movements that use Jungian theory to legitimate their new religiosities, from racialist and ethnic Asatru to the mythopoetic men's movement, from New Age to goddess spirituality.

A review of the book

The overview of the first chapter points to a major correction of the reigning view that Jung's "Wotan" was critical of National Socialism. I argued that this essay is not simply a depth-psychological perspective on National Socialism, nor are the themes time-bound to the Nazi era. Rather, they reflect ideas present in Jung's work since its inception. In "Wotan," Jung painted a portrait of what he believed to be the essence of the Germanic peoples. Jung interpreted Wotan as an archaic image of Spirit, comparable to the Spirit of God that hovered over the void before the first biblical act of Creation and the Pentecostal

Spirit that initiated the missionizing of Christ's apostles, which resulted in a new collective psychological orientation in the West. Jung's view of Wotan as Spirit was informed by contemporaneous theories of religion, especially those that presented the primordial religious experience as a soul-shaking encounter with the Holy as such. These theories was stimulated in part by the social malaise of modern society, the crisis of faith in Christianity, and the catastrophe of World War I. Jung, too, was concerned with these widespread social ills, and believed that modern society needed a new collective orientation on par with that from 2,000 years previously. He interpreted the god Wotan as a Germanic archetype and National Socialism as an individuation process *en masse*, indicating that he believed this new orientation could be born in the collective Germanic soul. Hence, Jung's theory might be seen as part of the "Germanization of Christianity" prevalent in his day.

To break out of the intellectual constraints of previous literature that limits discussion of Jung's "Wotan" essay to the Nazi era, the second chapter provided the background necessary to understand Jung's profile of a collective Germanic psyche, its presumed bases in "primitive" psychology, and its counter-image in "Jewish" psychology. In theorizing a collective Germanic psyche, Jung tapped into a 2,000-year-old discourse on the Germanic barbarian that developed during the Roman Empire's era of northern expansion. The image of the "barbarian" developed in this discourse was appropriated 1,500 years later by the German humanists, who created an interpretive framework that allowed Germans to imagine an illustrative past for themselves equal to that of the ancient Greeks and Romans. They argued that certain virtues were essential to the German people, including freedom, honor, loyalty, and youthfulness, and contrasted this hypothesized German essence to an external force, imagined both as its opposite and as a menace to Germanic authenticity.

By the late nineteenth century, this framework had been revised in several respects by a wide spectrum of German intellectuals and artists. First, they shifted the negative characteristics ascribed to the ancient Germanic tribes onto the many peoples Europeans sought to colonize, while they embraced the positive traits in the ancient cliché of the barbarian. Second, they claimed for themselves some of the characteristics ascribed originally to the Romans as part of the presumed Germanic essence, especially the power of state-building. Finally, after philologists united Rome and Germany in a larger linguistic and racial Indo-European or "Aryan" family, the image of the oppositional external force became transferred to "Semites." These lines of discourse appear throughout Jung's works on so-called primitive peoples, Jews, and people of Germanic descent.

The third chapter used the master-disciple typology provided by the historian of religions Joachim Wach to examine whether Jung should be viewed as a scientist or prophet. This served two purposes: first, to illuminate the ways in which the image cultivated by Jung and his followers fit the model, not of prophet, but of master; and second, to shift the focus away from Jung and onto his "disciples," that is, to his patients, secretary, and early biographers, and then to his historical context. This shift enabled a broader examination of the cultural, social, and intellectual conditions that nurtured the development of Jung's theory, which in turn made it both understandable and attractive to many of his contemporaries. The confusion over Jung's status was traced back to Jung himself, who intentionally sought to position his work between and inclusive of science and spirituality as a way to help his contemporaries out of the crisis of meaning then reigning in Europe, especially in the broader German-cultural and Protestant realms. To form a bridge between faith and reason, Jung incorporated into his theory several key concepts from the science of religion, including evolutionism, *mana* and *Ergriffenheit,* relying especially on works by scholars whose scientifically informed religiosity matched Jung's own. In addition, Jung placed his work within the field of holistic science, which was opposed to the competing mechanistic viewpoint. Moreover, his individuation process mirrors the contemporaneous Nietzschean-inspired spirituality of self-redemption. Many artists and intellectuals of Jung's day considered self-redemption as the way to complete the Reformation and hence a spirituality best suited to people of Germanic descent. It was within this nexus of ideas and these particular ways of understanding science and spirituality that Jung formulated his psychological perspective.

The fourth chapter explored Jung's theory of the phylogenetic unconscious and the archaic level of mind. Jung employed stock images of the "dark-skinned" and "noble savages" that he found in scholarly works on "primitive religion" to argue that so-called primitive peoples were the evidence for the archetypes and the collective unconscious. Jung's view of this archaic level of mind was ambivalent: as the repository of the instincts and collective forces, it could overwhelm an individual, leading to psychosis or to a dangerous collective phenomenon. At the same time, the collective unconscious was the source of all creativity, originality and rejuvenation, and the archetypes gave birth to revolutions in science, religion, art and philosophy. Jung often racially coded the negative or dangerous aspects of the collective unconscious as black, while portraying all people of black African descent as still stuck at a "primitive" level of mental development. The positive aspects of the collective unconscious are themselves not racially coded in Jung's theory, for the pre-eminent, non-figural symbol of the self, the sun, transcends the human realm. However, as Jung's model of the psyche as a house shows, Jung did racially code psychological evolution as white and even Germanic, as well as coding it religiously as Christian, and more specifically as Protestant. Jung believed that this particular collective psyche was especially problematic, due to the presumed separation between the unconscious and consciousness; yet it was precisely the extreme tension between these two poles in the Germanic psyche that could give rise to the new collective orientation Jung believed society needed after the breakdown of faith in traditional Christianity. The exploration of Jung's theory of the racially and religiously differentiated phylogenetic unconscious helped set the stage for the analysis of the "Wotan" essay in Chapter 6 as an expression of Jung's conviction that the National Socialist takeover represented an individuation process *en masse*.

Chapter 5 continued the investigation of Jung's concept of *primitivity* as applied to "Germanic" and "Jewish" psychology. It compared Jung's theory of a phylogenetic unconscious with that of his one-time associate turned rival, Sigmund Freud. The discussion showed how Freud displaced onto the image of the dark-skinned European "other" external to Europe stereotypes about Europe's religious and racialized internal "other," the Jew, who he then attempted to align with the "Aryan" under the rubric of *civilized*. Jung, on the other hand, split all three groups apart, in order to reserve the term *civilized* for the Germanic-Christian psyche. In several works written over the course of many decades, Jung portrayed the Jewish psyche as primitive in the sense of infantile and underdeveloped, employing stock stereotypes about Jewish religion, family relations, and racial traits. This analysis was followed by an examination of the legend of the Wandering Jew, which Jung surprisingly did not consider evidence of Jewish mental illness, as did many of his colleagues. Instead, he interpreted the Wandering Jew as the projection of an aspect of Christianized Germanic psychology. Recourse to the legend itself suggests that what Jung was alluding to was the western archetype of the self, Christ, understood through Germanic myth as Baldr.

Chapter 6 presented an in-depth analysis of the "Wotan" essay. Jung portrayed himself in this work not just as a psychologist diagnosing his patient, Germany, but as a master, who could see the reality behind historical and political events, thus declaring the Nazi takeover *kairos,* a divinely ordained moment in which a new collective orientation might emerge. The chapter analyzed one of the reigning motifs of the essay, *Ergriffenheit,* within the context of Jung's reception of the comparative study of religions, specifically the works of Rudolf Otto and Jakob Wilhelm Hauer, who used it to describe what they claimed to be the original religious experience, a state of being deeply stirred or gripped by the Holy as such. The chapter then examined earlier cases in Jung's theory of *Ergriffenheit*, in which two halves of the psyche come into conflict, the resolution of which leads to an increased capacity to create the arts of culture. The analysis continued to the "Wotan" essay itself, where Jung used the term *Ergriffenheit* to suggest that, under National Socialism, the Germans were in the midst of a collective individuation process. Through his portrait of the Germanic archetype Wotan, Jung psychologized and thereby essentialized the Romantic image of the Germans as "a people of poets and philosophers" as well as that of a Nietzschean "master-race."

Chapter 7 showed that Jung ultimately rejected Hitler as Germany's leader and mouthpiece in the hoped-for collective spiritual rebirth, yet by changing his diagnosis of Hitler as the *Führer* of a masculine movement to an effeminate hysteric. This and other reversals were probably driven more by the need to protect himself from allegations Jung faced after the war that he had sympathized with the Nazis. The chapter further looked at Jung's writings on Wotan and Yahweh in the 1950s and 1960s to indicate that the views he created of "Germanic" and "Jewish" psychology and their psychological contents was relatively stable over the decades. Finally, the chapter examined the relationship between Hauer and the Zurich School through the 1930s, which finally dissolved only after early 1939.

Jung's works as he originally published them provide the primary evidence for the claims made here. The pattern of mistranslations, deletions, and misleading editorial remarks found throughout the *Collected Works* and Jung's *Letters* cannot simply be dismissed as innocent mistakes made by Jung's translators and editors. Instead, they point to an attempt to suppress the evidence of Jung's particular interest in and hope for a hypothesized collective Germanic psyche. Nor can his utilization of colonialist and anti-Semitic discourse be shrugged off as Jung being merely a child of his times, or as the failure of an egalitarian-minded individual to find the right vocabulary to articulate his humanism. Rather, Jung was deeply, personally invested in these discourses of hierarchy and inequality, due to his belief in the superiority of a presumed Germanic-Christian psyche.

Chapter 8 explored the ongoing resonance of Jung's Germanic writings in contemporary Heathenism or Ásatrú, especially in the United States. Jung's status as a scientist proves attractive to founders of certain new religious movements, who rely (often quite casually and unsystematically) on scientific discourses to justify their new spiritualities. Jung's racialist writings appeal more to the ethnic and racist branches of Heathenism, the members of which often claim that the current revival of Germanic religion is due to a genetically inherited "folk-soul," born in the biological makeup of descendants of Northern Europe.

Situating the discussion of the reception of Jungian psychology in contemporary Heathenism against an examination of Jung's theory as developed within the context of his own day demonstrated that contemporary Heathenism is in some ways the heir to the same discourses of self-redemption and *völkisch* ideology developed in early twentieth-century pan-German culture that influenced Jung. However, contemporary Heathen authors diverge from Jung's original premises in significant ways, even while drawing on Jung's status as a scientifically trained psychologist and student of religions to legitimize their own religious and social claims. First, contemporary Heathenism continues the trajectory of the Germanic revival movement begun a century earlier that was strongly opposed to Christianity, whereas Jung's own view bore similarities to the Germanized Christianity of the Wagnerian circle. Indeed, just as Jung and his contemporaries appropriated the ancient Roman discourse on the Germanic barbarian and projected it onto so-called primitive peoples outside of Europe, today ethnic and racist Heathens appropriate the racialized anti-Jewish discourse of Jung and his contemporaries and project it onto Christianity, implying that this religion was birthed by a completely different racial "folk-soul." Second, certain contemporary Heathen authors disengage Jung's theory of the inheritability of archetypes from geography and climate, arguing for a transhistorical and fully deterritorialized racial essence that they presume directly dictates their religious choice. As the discussion of Jung's writings on Germanic peoples past and present demonstrates, however, he believed climate and geography to be a determining influence in the formation of a racialized *Volksgeist*.

Further research

Although the lines of inquiry pursued in the present work could be extended in various directions, I will limit my discussion to two. First, although Jung's work suggests that he considered himself to be a "psychologist of nations" (Samuels 1993, 274, 277–279), there is, as of yet, no book-length study of Jung's national typologies from a historical and critical perspective (but see Pietikäinen 1998). Such a study is warranted, given the fact that Jung essentialized the psychologies of not only Jews, Germanic peoples, and peoples of African descent, as explored in the present work, but also Arabs, the Chinese, Indians, and Native Americans, as well as Catholics, the European peasantry, the working class and women. A work on Jung as a "psychologist of nations" should analyze Jung's images of his many "others" not just from the perspectives of post-colonial theory and "Aryan" ideology, but Orientalism, gender studies and class theory, as well.

Another line of inquiry that the present work suggests would involve the reception of Jung's works by other new forms of religiosity besides Heathenism, including New Age Spirituality, the mythopoetic men's movement, neo-shamanism, and Wicca. Given the presence of both universalist and exclusivist claims in Jung's view of the development of human psychology, it is not surprising to see that some new religious movements utilizing Jungian theory rely on his exclusivist assertions (race in Heathenism and gender in the male-separatist mythopoetic men's movement), while other movements appear to be more universalistic in scope (i.e. New Age, neo-shamanism and Wicca). Close attention to how which aspects of Jungian theory are used might reveal limits to the universalism of some of these movements; as the case of Theosophy demonstrates, it is not uncommon to find in many avowedly inclusive spiritualities calls for a universal siblinghood cheek-by-jowl with a hierarchical ranking of humanity.

Race as a social construction that defines and maintains boundaries between groups of people continues to play a determining role in society, controlling access to jobs, education, civil rights, and natural resources. Rather than becoming either tolerant towards multi-culturalism or "color-blind," western democracies have witnessed an alarming upswing in racism and intolerance towards immigrants from non-European countries. To wit, there are currently over 1,000 hate groups in the United States (Southern Poverty Law Center 2011), and one-third of all Europeans believe that a natural hierarchy exists between whites and blacks (Zick, Küpper and Hövermann 2011, 67). This intolerance extends to religion, as demonstrated by widespread discrimination against both Jews and Muslims in Europe: Jews have faced harassment in 76 per cent of all European countries; Muslims, in 71 per cent of them (Pew Research Center 2015).

Despite the present rejection of the concepts of racial purity and stability by geneticists, anthropologists and other biological and social scientists (Cavalli-Sforza

2001, 13; Thomas 2000, 112), it is my firm conviction that "race" will become a much more significant social and political factor as globalization expands and the worldwide ecological crisis deepens, leading to increased immigration and a more intensive struggle over territories and their natural resources. The rising tension between populations will inevitably impact the theologies of many religions, both those advocating a universalist position (e.g. Francis 2015) and those arguing for ethnic and nationalist separatism (e.g. Ivakhiv 2005). As the present study demonstrates, exclusivist claims are often intertwined with universalistic ones, creating an insidious undercurrent of ideological justification of hierarchy, privilege, and domination that calls for rigorous scholarly investigation and disclosure.

Bibliography

Title

"man as he was – and will always be": C. G. Jung, "The Role of the Unconscious" (1918), *Collected Works* 10:13, ed. by Sir Herbert Read, Michael Fordham, and Gerhard Adler. New York: Pantheon Books; Princeton, NJ: Princeton University Press.

Sources

Bode, Kim et al. 2010. "Volksheld Sarrazin: Warum so viele Deutsche einem Provokateur verfallen." *Der Spiegel* 36:22–30.

Cavalli-Sforza, Luigi Luca. 2001. *Genes, Peoples and Languages*, trans. by Mark Seielstad. London: Penguin.

Denkler, Thorston. 2015. "Migrationsbericht: der Bundesregierung Einwanderung ist katholisch." *Süddeutsche Zeitung*, January 21. Available at: http://www.sueddeutsche.de/politik/migrationsbericht-der-bundesregierung-einwanderung-ist-katholisch-1.2314099 (Accessed: July 20, 2015).

Francis. 2015. *Laudato Si'. Encyclical Letter of the Holy Father Francis on Care for Our Common Home*. Available at: http://w2.vatican.va/content/francesco/en/encyclicals/documents/papa-francesco_20150524_enciclica-laudato-si.html (Accessed: July 9, 2015).

Ivakhiv, Adrian. 2005. "Nature and Ethnicity in East European Paganism: An Environmental Ethic of the Religious Right?" *Pomegranate* 7(2):194–225.

Pew Research Center. 2015. "Sidebar: Religious Hostilities and Religious Minorities in Europe" Latest Trends in Religious Restrictions and Hostilities, February 26. Available at: http://www.pewforum.org/2015/02/26/sidebar-religious-hostilities-and-religious-minorities-in-europe/ (Accessed: July 14, 2015).

Pew Research Center. 2010. "Growing Number of Americans Say Obama is a Muslim: Religion, Politics and the President." Updated October 13, 2011. Available at: http://pewresearch.org/pubs/1701/poll-obama-muslim-christian-church-out-of-politics-political-leaders-religious (Accessed: Oct. 13, 2011).

Pietikäinen, Petteri. 1998. "National Typologies, Races, and Mentalities in C. G. Jung's Psychology." *History of European Ideas* 24(6):359–373.

Pollack, Detlef. 2013. "Öffentliche Wahrnehmung des Islam in Deutschland." In *Islam und die deutsche Gesellschaft*, ed. Dirk Halm and Hendrick Meyer. Wiesbaden: Springer, pp. 89–118.

Obama, Barack. 2008. "A More Perfect Union." Speech held at the Constitution Center, Philadelphia, PA. Filmed March 18, 2008. YouTube video, 37:10. Available at: http://www.youtube.com/watch?v=zrp-v2tHaDo (Accessed: Jan. 15, 2012).

Obama, Barack. 2011. The 2011 Annual White House Correspondents Dinner at the Washington Hilton Hotel, Washington, DC. Filmed April 30, 2011. YouTube video, 18:54. Posted by CSPAN. Available at: http://www.youtube.com/watch?v=n9mzJhvC-8E (Accessed: Jan. 15, 2012).

Samuels, Andrew. 1993. *The Political Psyche*. London: Routledge.

Sarrazin, Thilo. 2010. *Deutschland schafft sich ab: Wie wir unser Land aufs Spiel setzen*. Munich: Deutsche Verlags-Anstalt.

Southern Poverty Law Center. 2011. "The Year in Hate and Extremism: Hate Groups Top 1000." *Intelligence Report* 141. Available at: http://www.splcenter.org/get-informed/intelligence-report/2011/spring (Accessed: May 1, 2011).

Thomas, David Hurst. 2000. *Skull Wars: Kennewick Man, Archaeology, and the Battle for Native American Identity*. New York: Basic Books.

Zick, Andreas, Beate Küpper, and Andreas Hövermann (eds). 2011. *Die Abwertung der Anderen: Eine europäische Zustandsbeschreibung zu Intoleranz, Vorurteilen und Diskriminierung*. Berlin: Friedrich-Ebert-Stiftung. Available at: http://www.fes-gegen-rechtsextremismus.de/pdf_11/FES-Studie%2BDie%2BAbwertung%2Bder%2BAnderen.pdf (Accessed: April 5, 2011).

INDEX

Note: Page numbers for figures appear in bold.

Made in the USA
Monee, IL
13 September 2026

62976829R00155